Native American Bibliography Series

The Pawnee Nation

An Annotated Research Bibliography

Judith A. Boughter

Native American Bibliography Series,
No. 28

The Scarecrow Press, Inc.
Lanham, Maryland • Toronto • Oxford
2004

SCARECROW PRESS, INC.

Published in the United States of America
by Scarecrow Press, Inc.
A wholly owned subsidiary of
The Rowman & Littlefield Publishing Group, Inc.
4501 Forbes Boulevard, Suite 200, Lanham, Maryland 20706
www.scarecrowpress.com

PO Box 317
Oxford
OX2 9RU, UK

British Library Cataloguing in Publication Information Available

Library of Congress Cataloging-in-Publication Data

Boughter, Judith A., 1940–
    The Pawnee nation: an annotated research bibliography / Judith
A. Boughter.
        p. cm. — (Native American bibliography series ; no. 28)
    Includes bibliographical references and indexes.
    ISBN 0-8108-4990-9 (alk. paper)
    1. Pawnee Indians—Bibliography. I. Title. II. Series.
Z1210 .P38 B68 2004
[E99 .P3]
016.978004'97933—dc22

                                                                2003025415

∞™ The paper used in this publication meets the minimum requirements of
American National Standard for Information Sciences—Permanence of
Paper for Printed Library Materials, ANSI/NISO Z39.48-1992.
Manufactured in the United States of America.

Contents

Editor's Foreword

The Pawnees remain among the most frequently mentioned Great Plains tribes within nineteenth-century primary documents. Explorers' accounts, military records, overland diaries, agents' reports, and frontier newspapers abound with eyewitness and secondhand descriptions of Pawnee life at a time when all members of the tribe were undergoing phenomenal changes due to increased pressure from the westward migration. Precisely because they were located within the Platte River Valley of Nebraska, along one of the most heavily traveled arteries of American migration, they became the subjects of endless public discussion. Many overlanders and government officials praised them for their noble qualities and martial restraint amid so many injustices directed toward them. Other migrants, bureaucrats, and opinion makers, however, stereotyped them as "savages," who stood in the way of white advance to the Pacific coast. After fifty years of buffeting by outside forces, the Pawnees were compelled to leave the sacred lands of their fathers and resettle on a reservation in Indian Territory—now Pawnee County, Oklahoma.

Judith Boughter has compiled the first exhaustive bibliography of the Pawnees and has provided useful annotations assessing the strengths and weaknesses of many of those sources. By arranging these publications into twenty-seven subject categories, she has given greater utility to the volume, and her thorough index alerts readers to sources that have relevance in multiple categories. Furthermore, her helpful Introduction navigates researchers through some of the most important depositories of Pawnee ethnographic and historic materials. These range from the well-established archival collections at the State Historical Societies of Nebraska, Kansas, and Oklahoma, to less obvious depositories such as various county historical societies, the Field Museum of Natural History in Chicago, and Swarthmore and Haverford Colleges. Her research within so many far-flung institutions testifies to the completeness of this bibliography, as well as Ms. Boughter's incisive understanding of the peoples' history.

It is hoped that this up-to-date research tool will prompt further research among historians, archaeologists, anthropologists, linguists, and literary analysts. It is especially important that these scholars and today's tribal members join hands to produce more systematic studies of twentieth-century Pawnee concerns. Indeed, part of the key to preserving tribal sovereignty and cultural vitality lies within these future endeavors.

Michael L. Tate
Professor of History and Native American Studies
University of Nebraska at Omaha

Preface

Because they ranged so widely over the Plains, particularly in the areas that are now Kansas and Nebraska, and because they interacted with both the Spaniards and the French during the international struggle to control the Great Plains, the Pawnees appear in many historical documents, from Spanish accounts to the journals of later American explorers and adventurers. In the nineteenth century, Hicksite Quaker agents and superintendents generated numerous reports regarding their Pawnee charges, and Presbyterian missionaries wrote wonderful accounts about the daily lives of these fascinating people. Modern writers, too, have followed the Pawnees from Nebraska to Indian Territory (later, Oklahoma), and have recorded tribal customs, ceremonies and culture. In recent years, Pawnee activists have taken the lead in the repatriation struggle and have fought for respectful burials of their ancestors' skeletal remains. Therefore, written sources on the Pawnees are as wide-ranging as the people themselves. It is the purpose of this bibliography to identify a large number of these varied sources within one volume and to provide a substantial basis for future research.

One of the greatest challenges in compiling this bibliography was deciding how to categorize the entries. Some sources, especially those on cultural topics, archaeology, and anthropology, do not fit into a strictly historical format, so the beginning chapters are thematic, concerned with subjects such as archaeology, material culture, sacred sites, language, and music. The chapters on early white contact, the Nebraska reservation period, missionaries, Quaker impact, treaties, and the Pawnees in Oklahoma, are more or less chronological. The North Brothers and the Pawnee Scouts have their own chapter, as do the annual reports of the Commissioners of Indian Affairs, repatriation and reburial, the Yellow Sun murder case, Nebraska's important repatriation legislation, and the extensive archival sources. I have made every effort to place each source in its most appropriate category. For sources containing material that might fall into several categories, please consult the subject index, which lists all mentions of each topic. Throughout the bibliography, references containing similar material are indicated within the annotations with the entry number in brackets. With the exception of a few that were unavailable for inspection, each source is annotated, and many are evaluated. The University of Nebraska Press and a few other publishers have reprinted a number of Pawnee sources, and these reprints are clearly noted where appropriate.

The National Archives in Washington, D. C., houses a great deal of Pawnee material, and many of the Bureau of Indian Affairs records are available on microfilm. But repositories in the Great Plains and around the United States also provide a wealth of information on the Pawnee Nation. The Nebraska State Historical Society in Lincoln possesses a number of manuscript collections that pertain to the Pawnees, as well as photographs that can be examined by computer. The collections at the library/archives are well-catalogued and easily accessible. Although newspapers articles appear throughout this bibliography, I have made no attempt to systematically cite small town papers from the Loup River region or other areas in Nebraska where events important to the Pawnees occurred. Fortunately for researchers, one of the strengths of the Nebraska State Historical Society is its extensive microfilmed collection of state newspapers dating back to the mid-1800s and available through interlibrary loan departments. Among these newspapers are those from Trenton, Guide Rock, Red Cloud, Fremont, and Columbus, all of which contain published news on the Pawnees. A number of small towns near the former Nebraska reservation host newspapers, but most began publishing after the Pawnees' removal to Oklahoma.

In Omaha, Nebraska, the Douglas County Historical Society, located on the grounds of historic Fort Omaha, has one large folder of Pawnee materials—mostly newspaper clippings and pamphlets. The Hitchcock County Museum in Trenton is a good source of information on the Massacre Canyon tragedy, and Genoa's United States Indian School Museum can provide materials on the Pawnee Industrial School established during the Nebraska reservation period.

A few manuscripts and a large number of nicely organized newspaper clippings are available at the Kansas State Historical Society in Topeka, and most of the writings of missionaries John Dunbar and Samuel Allis have been published in the Society's *Collections*. The high point of any research trip to Kansas would be a visit to the Pawnee Village Historic Site near Republic, which is the only intact, *in situ* Pawnee earth lodge in existence. The museum curator, Richard Gould, will happily answer any questions.

A trip to the Oklahoma Historical Society in Oklahoma City is a must for Pawnee researchers, especially those interested in the post-1875 period. Most of their Pawnee materials have been microfilmed, but a few are still in document form. Over the years, dozens of newspapers have come and gone in Pawnee County and in the vicinity of the modern tribal reserve, but according to the list available at the Oklahoma Historical Society, only the *Pawnee Chief* is still published.

I would caution researchers to allow adequate time for their Oklahoma Historical Society searches, since the Society has very few microfilm copiers, and the retrieval system for materials is cumbersome. In the microfilm room are drawers of annotated newspaper articles pertaining to the Pawnees, all on index cards—a treasure trove of information, but it is time-consuming to utilize. Fortunately, Oklahoma is currently building a new history center about a block from the state capital, which will house a modernized library and archives.

The Western History Collections at the University of Oklahoma in Norman, just a short drive from Oklahoma City, contains a number of important manuscripts, research notes, photographic collections, and audio tapes, along with excellent finding aids to help researchers access these sources. Guides to these collections have recently been published. (See entries 363a and 363b.)

Farther afield, Pawnee materials are also housed at the Southwest Regional Archives in Fort Worth, Texas, and the Field Museum of Natural History in Chicago has one of the finest collections of Pawnee artifacts in the United States, along with George A. Dorsey and James R. Murie's unpublished research notes. The very best primary sources regarding Pawnee-Quaker relations are located at the Friends Historical Library at Swarthmore College in Swarthmore, Pennsylvania, and the Quaker Collections of Haverford College in Haverford, Pennsylvania.

Although compiling a bibliography is a mostly solitary pursuit, I have been aided along the way by many generous people from Oklahoma to Pennsylvania who have shared their time and expertise. As always, the staff of the Nebraska State Historical Society was very professional, promptly retrieving manuscript materials from the archives, providing access to photographs, and making a huge number of photocopies in a short period of time.

Aware of my time constraints, Teresa Coboe and her student assistant at the Kansas State Historical Society quickly and cheerfully filled my many requests for library materials, then just as quickly photocopied hundreds of pages so that I could take them with me the same day. William Grace, reference librarian at the Kansas State Historical Society, provided me with a draft copy of the "Treaty of Smoky Hill."

Additional thanks go to Oklahoma Historical Society staff members Brian Basore, Nancy Laub, and Sandy Smith, who answered my many questions with unfailing good humor, and to archivists Chad Williams, who shared information with me by phone prior to my research trip, and William Welge, who discussed the Society's holdings with me after my arrival. Kristina Southwell, manuscripts librarian for the Western History Collections at the University of Oklahoma, provided extensive finding aids for the library's Pawnee collections, saving much valuable research time.

David Selden of the National Indian Law Library in Boulder, Colorado, located several articles and reports on repatriation that had been written for the Native American Rights Fund, and Pawnee scholar Roger Echo-Hawk provided me with a list of his published and unpublished writings, most of which appear in the bibliography.

I owe a special thanks to Richard Gould, curator of the Pawnee Village Museum Historic Site, who shared his knowledge of that intact Pawnee earth lodge with my husband and me, and has continued to keep in touch. Through interlibrary loan, Bill Chada, area archaeologist for the United States Bureau of Reclamation in Grand Island, Nebraska, provided a number of original archaeological reports on Pawnee villages and burial grounds threatened by the construction of the Fullerton Canal.

The staffs of the Morton-James Public Library in Nebraska City, Nebraska, the *Daily Camera* in Boulder, Colorado, and the *Wichita* (Kansas) *Eagle* kindly sent me copies of newspaper articles and editorials, and I am very grateful to the knowledgeable staff of the Friends Historical Library at Swarthmore College, who cheerfully guided me through their Pawnee materials and later loaned me microfilm of journals that I did not have time to examine during my research trip.

I am fortunate to have a former student and friend who provided me with wonderful articles on the Pawnees from the *Lincoln Journal-Star* and an occasional rare book found at a used book store. It was always a pleasure to find a surprise from Chuck Vestal in my department mailbox.

I could never have completed this project without the excellent Interlibrary Loan Department at my own institution, the University of Nebraska at Omaha, and I would especially like to thank John Schniederman and

Matt Rohde, who never complained about my barrage of loan requests, and who kept trying until they found dozens of obscure articles and documents. I truly appreciate their efforts on my behalf.

Financial assistance for out-of-state travel expenses was provided by a generous grant from the Charles and Mary Caldwell Martin Fund of the University of Nebraska at Omaha Department of History. My thanks to the Martin Fund Committee for helping to fund my research.

No one has been more instrumental in the writing of this work than Dr. Michael Tate, general editor of Scarecrow Press's Native American Bibliography Series, who encouraged me to write the bibliography of the Pawnees. Dr. Tate has been deeply involved with this project from inception to editing, and he has my sincere thanks.

But most of all, I would like to thank my husband, Chris, for his patience and support, not only for this project, but through the years.

Judith A. Boughter
Department of History
University of Nebraska at Omaha

Historical Introduction

Although they were relocated to Indian Territory (present-day Oklahoma) over 125 years ago, the Pawnee Tribe left a lasting imprint on northern Kansas and much of Nebraska. The remains of many of their sacred animal lodges are in Nebraska, and Pawnee historical sites abound along the Republican, Platte, and Loup rivers, where archaeologists have unearthed battle remnants, village sites, and burial grounds of this once numerous and powerful people. Unlike many Plains tribes who were sun worshipers, the Pawnees worshipped the stars, and in a practice probably unique among Plains Indians, they sacrificed humans to a powerful celestial being—the Morning Star.

Oral tradition says that the ancestors of modern Pawnees came to Nebraska and Kansas either from the Southwest or from the Southern Plains. The Pawnee Nation includes four distinct bands. According to most accounts, the first band to emigrate north was the Skidi (Skiri)—Wolf or Loup Pawnees—who either followed the buffalo or were driven north by drought or by enemies. By 1700, the Skidis were living along the Loup River in what is now East-Central Nebraska. The three so-called South Bands—the Chaui (Grand Pawnees), the Pitahawiratas (or Toppage), and the Kitkahahki (Republican Pawnees)—followed the Skidis north and settled on the Platte and Republican rivers. As the people moved north, they acquired horses and began shifting from a mostly agrarian lifestyle to an economy more dependent on hunting. Like many Plains tribes, the Pawnees followed an annual cycle of hunting and harvesting crops, with hunting becoming more important as time passed.

In the late seventeenth century, the Pawnees found themselves caught between the Spaniards and the French, who fought for control of the central Plains. As Spanish horses spread north on the Plains, guns came from the French who were located in the Mississippi River Valley. Both nations hoped for an alliance with the powerful Pawnees, but the tribe gravitated toward the French, who supplied them with small numbers of firearms.

France and Spain continued to jockey for position in the Great Plains, and each nation sent a fact-finding expedition into the field to try to gain information on its rival's activities. The Spaniards had learned that Frenchmen may have been living with the Pawnees on the Platte River, and in 1720, the Spanish government in New Mexico sent a military expedition under Don Pedro de Villasur north to investigate. At the junction of the Platte and Loup rivers, near modern-day Columbus, Nebraska, Pawnees and their Otoe allies attacked the Spanish force, killing Villasur and over thirty of his troops.[1] A bison skin painting of the battle shows French troops fighting alongside the Pawnees, but it is possible that these figures were added later.[2] In 1800, Spain turned Louisiana, which included the Pawnee homeland, over to France, who in turn sold the territory to the United States in 1803. Now Americans would control the fate of the Pawnees.

Throughout the 1820s, the four Pawnee bands had remained powerful, but this changed in the winter of 1831–1832, when a smallpox epidemic killed approximately half of the population—about 6,000 people. Because they lived in densely populated villages, the Pawnees were especially vulnerable to contagious diseases. In the mid-1830s, influenza and whooping cough spread through the villages, and in 1837–1838, smallpox returned. Diseases and incessant Sioux attacks further reduced the Pawnee population by almost 2,000 between 1835 and 1840.[3]

Because of their star worship and human sacrifices, whites considered the Pawnees one of the most "pagan" Plains tribes. In 1834, Presbyterian missionaries John Dunbar and Samuel Allis came to live among the Grand and Skidi Pawnees, hoping to end the Morning Star ceremony and turn these "superstitious" Indians into God-fearing Christians. The Pawnees treated Dunbar and Allis with respect, but the Skidis in particular resisted Christianity. Eventually the missionaries left the Pawnees as Sioux attacks became bolder and more frequent.

Between 1833 and 1857, the Pawnees signed three major treaties that drastically reduced their land base. In 1833, to make room for the Delaware Indians being relocated from Ohio and to settle native land disputes, government representatives persuaded the sick and hungry Pawnees to give up all rights to their lands south of the Platte River in return for a small annuity. In a council that lasted only six hours, the desperate Pawnees gave up 13,000,000 acres of land.[4]

In 1848, the Pawnees met with representatives of the United States Army and ceded another parcel of their territory—this time a sixty-mile-long strip of land along the Platte River that would be used to supply grass, timber, and game for Fort Childs, which was later renamed Fort Kearny. Once again, the Pawnees had surrendered land because they were in dire need of food and supplies.[5]

The passage of the Kansas-Nebraska Act in May 1854 established the territory of Nebraska, and settlers were impatient to move onto land that had once been described as the "Great American Desert." During the fall before the act became law, Commissioner of Indian Affairs George Manypenny came west to persuade most of the Nebraska tribes to sell their homelands to the government. On September 24, 1857, by the Treaty of Table Creek, sixteen Pawnee chiefs, four from each band, reluctantly agreed to sell all their remaining territory north of the Platte, keeping only a 288,000-acre reservation on the Loup River.[6]

The move to their new Nebraska reservation did not go smoothly. From the treaty signing until the summer of 1859, when they finally moved to the Loup, the Pawnees continued to live in three villages on the south bank of the Platte. This was now government land, and settlers were moving in. For all of 1858 and part of 1859, the Pawnees were caught between American settlers on the south and the Sioux on the north as they waited for their treaty to be ratified and for their annuities to arrive.

When the Pawnees did move north to their reservation, they found it already occupied by a group of Mormons who had settled there in 1857 and founded the town of Genoa at the extreme eastern end of the land set aside for their reserve. The Mormons asked the Indian Office to move the reservation boundary slightly west so that they could stay, but the government refused. The Mormons were paid for their buildings and then forced to leave. So the Pawnees inherited a reservation with a few buildings and some land ready to farm.[7]

This was good land, but the reservation had a major problem which became apparent right away. The Pawnee villages were constantly attacked by the Sioux, and the women were afraid to work in the fields. The Sioux also ruined Pawnee hunts by setting fire to the prairie grass and driving the buffalo away. In 1860, drought killed all the crops that the women had managed to plant.

Throughout the 1860s, good hunts alternated with poor ones, good growing seasons were followed by bad weather and plagues of grasshoppers, and the Sioux continued to attack the Pawnees. Both men and women resisted changes to their traditional way of life and schools set up to "civilize" Pawnee children were for the most part failures. By 1870, little had changed in Pawnee life: the people still hunted the dwindling supply of buffalo; the annual cycle remained intact; and important men continued to take multiple wives. No one was living in a frame house, no one dressed like the whites, and few Pawnees had become Christians.

During these troubled years, the Pawnees' main problem continued to be the Sioux, especially the Brulé bands, and the lack of protection from their constant raids. Why the continual warfare between the Pawnees and the Sioux? First, the Pawnees had many horses, which the Sioux wanted. Second, after the completion of the Union Pacific Railroad in 1869, the buffalo herds split into smaller groups that were fought over by the Sioux, Pawnees, and other tribes.

The third reason for the deep animosity between the Pawnees and the Sioux was the Pawnee Scouts, Indian soldiers under the command of Major Frank North and led by white army officers. Armed and paid by the government, the first group of seventy-seven Pawnee Scouts joined the army in 1864 to fight against the Sioux and Cheyennes. A larger group enlisted in 1865. The Pawnees served as advance scouts for white troops, but also fought as a unit in their own Indian style. In 1867, the Pawnee Scout unit was increased to 200 and given the job of guarding the Union Pacific Railroad.

While they were a great help to the army and to the railroad, the absence of so many Pawnee warriors left their villages more vulnerable to enemy attacks. The United States never really honored its treaty commitment to provide protection, and the government refused to arm the Indians so that they could protect themselves. The Pawnees were forced to provide their own security by building walls around their villages and hunting with other tribes.

Between 1869 and 1873, Pawnees continued to die, either at the hands of the Brulés directly or because the Sioux disrupted their farming and hunts and left them to starve. More than seventy deaths occurred in one day—August 5, 1873—when nearly 1,000 Oglala and Brulé warriors attacked Pawnee buffalo hunters in a ravine near the modern-day town of Trenton, in southwestern Nebraska, a place known ever since as Massacre Canyon. The Pawnees—men, women, and children—were slowed down by the weight of the meat and skins of hundreds of buffalo, and they could not escape.[8]

Massacre Canyon was the worst in a series of misfortunes that befell the Pawnees in these disastrous years, and many became convinced that there was no future for them in Nebraska. In October 1873, a Grand Pawnee leader, Big Spotted Horse, left Nebraska with 485 of his people, bound for the Wichita Agency in Indian Territory. A year later, at a council on the Nebraska reservation, the chiefs and leading men from each Pawnee band agreed to sell their land and follow the first group to a new home in what is now Oklahoma. This was a sad time for the Pawnees—they were leaving behind the land they loved, their sacred sites, and the graves of their ancestors.

The Pawnees immediately began to leave Nebraska. According to the 1875 superintendent's report, 1800 Pawnees, most of the tribe, spent that winter with the Wichitas on their reservation.[9] The Pawnee agent went south also, to choose a new reservation for his charges. Their new home was just south of the Osage Reservation, and was purchased with money that would come from the sale of their Nebraska lands. In June 1875, the Pawnees who were already in Oklahoma were led from the Wichita Agency to their new reservation, 150 miles away. That autumn, the last 350 Skidi Pawnees left their Nebraska homeland in government wagons. They took with them their sacred corn seeds to plant in their new home.[10]

Gradually, and often against their will, Pawnee families were settled on individual farms, and allotment in severalty was finally imposed in 1893. After lands were allotted to these Indians, about 171,000 acres of "surplus" land was sold to whites, most of whom were land speculators. The Pawnees received payment in advance for part of their land; the rest of the money was not paid until 1920, when the tribe took its case to court.

Like many tribes, the Pawnees filed a petition with the Indian Claims Commission when it began meeting in the late 1940s. Arguing that they had been paid only a fraction of what their land was worth, their attorneys asked for more than $30,000,000 for lands ceded to the United States in the nineteenth century. Finally, in June 1962, after all the claims, counterclaims, and adjustments were made, the Pawnees were awarded $7,316,096.55 for the more than 23,000,000 acres of land that had been bought from their ancestors for an average of ten cents an acre. From this figure was deducted nearly $900,000 in attorneys' fees, leaving the tribe with about $6,400,000.[11]

The Pawnees could not decide how to distribute the Claims Commission money. The House of Representatives and some tribal leaders wanted the money used for schools and job training in Oklahoma, but at the time only 453 Pawnees still lived on the "old lands." The rest (1,430) were scattered across twenty-eight states. So in March 1964, the tribal council voted for distributions to individual Indians, causing three council members to resign. In October 1964, each member of the Pawnee tribe received about $3,530. No land was ever returned to the tribe.[12]

Removal from their homeland was traumatic, and the failure of the government to adequately compensate them for their land was unfair, but perhaps the most shameful chapter in the history of white interaction with the Pawnees was the desecration and looting of ancestral graves by artifact hunters and both amateur and professional archaeologists. In 1923, Asa T. Hill, an amateur archaeologist, began opening Pawnee graves on a farm near Red Cloud, Nebraska. Hill believed that this farm was the site of the village where explorer Zebulon Pike allegedly met with the Pawnees in 1806, took down the Spanish flag and raised the flag of the United States. Altogether, about sixty-five bodies have been removed from this burial site. In 1942, Hill sold his collection of Pawnee skeletons to the Nebraska State Historical Society for $1.00. The Society would later loan the collection to the Smithsonian Institution.

In the summer of 1936, the bones of over 100 Indians, many of them Pawnees, were excavated on a farm near Salina, Kansas, and soon became a tourist attraction. The family that owned the farm created an Indian "burial pit" in a white tin shed, where tourists could view a circle of skeletons from a concrete walkway surrounding the burial ground. In 1989, the Kansas Legislature passed a law closing down this sorry roadside attraction. The state paid the farmer's family for the quarter-acre site and banned possession of human skeletal remains.[13]

Disturbances of Pawnee cemeteries in Nebraska by non-Indians prompted an outcry from the Indians of Nebraska and the Pawnees in Oklahoma. The Indians, led by attorneys of the Native American Rights Fund, began a campaign to force the Nebraska Legislature to pass a law to stop the desecration of Indian graves in the state. Finally, in 1989, The Nebraska Unicameral passed Legislative Bill (LB) 340, which provides: (1) that dead bodies and grave offerings must be returned to the tribes to which they belong; and (2) that unmarked burials throughout Nebraska will be protected in the future. This law passed only after bitter fighting between the Board of Directors of the State Historical Society and supporters of the law (see chapter 25).

On September 10, 1990, the Pawnee people reclaimed the remains of more than 400 of their ancestors and thousands of artifacts from the Nebraska State Historical Society in Lincoln. Members of the Pawnee tribe and representatives of the Historical Society met at the State Historical Museum to sign the papers. Later that day, 435 small wooden coffins were loaded into vehicles for the drive to Genoa, Nebraska, for reburial. Genoa was chosen for the reburial since it had been the site of the Nebraska Pawnee Reservation before the people were relocated to Oklahoma.[14]

The days of the Pawnee presence in Kansas and Nebraska are gone, and the trails west are now major highways. But along country roads and near small towns, historical markers constantly remind us that not so long ago, these intensely spiritual "People of the Stars" hunted buffalo in the Sand Hills and along the rivers, built earth lodges oriented toward the cosmos, conducted elaborate ceremonies, fought battles, and carefully buried their dead on land they believed would always be theirs. Red Cloud, Guide Rock, and Trenton, Nebraska, near Massacre Canyon are important sites associated with the Pawnees, but nowhere is the Pawnee spirit stronger than in Republic, Kansas, where a sacred bundle occupies a place of honor in a beautifully preserved earth lodge, and in Genoa, Nebraska, where the remains of hundreds of Pawnees were finally brought home to stay.

NOTES

1. John B. Dunbar, "Massacre of the Villazur Expedition by the Pawnees on the Platte in 1720," *Collections of the Kansas State Historical Society*, Vol. 11 (1909–1910), 397–423; Fred Thomas, "Art Depicts Spanish-Indian Conflict," *Omaha World-Herald* (13 July 1998), 31.

2. Thomas, "Art Depicts Spanish-Indian Conflict," 31.

3. David J. Wishart, *An Unspeakable Sadness: The Dispossession of the Nebraska Indians* (Lincoln: University of Nebraska Press, 1994), 81.

4. "Treaty with the Pawnee, 1833," 7 *Statutes at Large* 448.

5. "Treaty with the Pawnee—Grand, Loups, Republicans, etc., 1848," 9 *Statutes at Large* 949.

6. "Treaty with the Pawnee, 1857," 11 *Statutes at Large* 729.

7. Marguerette R. Burke, "Henry James Hudson and the Genoa Settlement," *Nebraska History* 41 (September 1960): 231–34; Jim McKee, "The Mormons, the Pawnees, and the History of Genoa," *Lincoln Journal-Star* (14 July 2002), 2K.

8. Paul D. Riley, "The Battle of Massacre Canyon," *Nebraska History* 54 (Summer 1973): 221–249; Garland James Blaine and Martha Royce Blaine, "Pa-Re-Su A-Ri-Ra-Ke: The Hunters that Were Massacred," *Nebraska History* 58 (Fall 1977): 342–58; John W. Williamson, "The Battle of Massacre Canyon: The Unfortunate Ending of the Last Buffalo Hunt of the Pawnees" (Trenton, Nebraska: *Republican Leader*, 1922), 1–23.

9. "Report of Superintendent Barclay White," in *Annual Report of the Commissioner of Indian Affairs (ARCIA)*, 1875, 311.

10. "Report of Agent William Burgess," in *ARCIA*, 1875, 321.

11. David J. Wishart, "The Pawnee Claims Case, 1947–64," in Imre Sutton, ed., *Irredeemable America: The Indians' Estate and Land Claims* (Albuquerque: University of New Mexico Press, 1985), 157.

12. Wishart, "The Pawnee Claims Case," 183–84.

13. "Treaty of Smoky Hill of February, 1989," Kansas State Historical Society, Topeka, Kansas.

14. David Swartzlander, "Remains and Artifacts of Pawnee Put on Truck for Burial at Genoa," *Lincoln Journal* (10 September 1990), 4; Bob Reeves, "Pawnee Remains Going 'Home' after Long Wait," *Lincoln Star* (11 September 1990), 1, 5.

1
Bibliographies, Indexes, and Guides

1. *American Indians: A Select Catalog of National Archives Microfilm Publications*. Washington, D.C.: National Archives Trust Fund Board, National Archives and Records Administration, 1998. 139 pp. An invaluable guide for researchers who wish to purchase microfilm reels from the National Archives. Ordering instructions are included, but before ordering microfilm, researchers should check current pricing and availability.

2. Beidler, Peter G., and Marion F. Egge. *The American Indian in Short Fiction: An Annotated Bibliography*. Metuchen, New Jersey: Scarecrow Press, 1979. 203 pp. A tribal index directs the reader to eleven Pawnee sources from journals and collections of short stories. The annotations are excellent.

3. Blaine, Martha Royce. *The Pawnees: A Critical Bibliography*. Bloomington: Indiana University Press, 1980. 109 pp. Lists 274 sources on the Pawnees. The citations are excellent, and these are all reliable and important sources. A real strength of this volume is the fifty-four-page bibliographical essay, which describes each entry.

4. Burgess, Larry E. *The Lake Mohonk Conference of Friends of the Indian: Guide to the Annual Reports*. New York: Clearwater Publishing Co., 1975. 149 pp. Introduction to this source explains the goals of this reform group that began meeting at Lake Mohonk, New York, in 1883 to discuss important Native American issues. Annual meetings were held until 1916. After a hiatus, one last conference took place in 1929. The entry for each annual meeting lists speakers and writers in attendance and subjects

discussed, but the thorough index lists no references to the Pawnees. These microfiche records are in the collections of some major libraries.

5. *A Chronological List of Treaties and Agreements Made by Indian Tribes with the United States.* Washington, D.C.: Institute for the Development of Indian Law, 1973. 34 pp. This brief reference work includes no treaty texts, but does provide the date of each treaty along with a citation of another source containing the complete text. Nearly all the citations are to *Statutes at Large.* Unlike many references, which are limited to treaties, this source also includes citations for executive agreements. An introduction by Vine Deloria, Jr., briefly explains the history and meaning of Indian treaties and agreements.

6. Clements, William M., and Frances M. Malpezzi. *Native American Folklore, 1879–1979: An Annotated Bibliography.* Athens, Ohio: Swallow Press, 1984. 247 pp. An outstanding, easy-to-use reference work that begins with a selection of general works, then divides North America into regions. Listed first in each region are general works for that area, followed by regional Indian tribes in alphabetical order. References at the end of each tribal list guide users to references to that tribe at other places in the bibliography. All of the entries have brief annotations, and a handy list of abbreviations at the beginning of the book identifies journals and other sources. Includes both an author and a subject index. Pages 99 through 101 contain fifty-five references to Pawnee folklore.

7. Cohen, Felix. *Felix S. Cohen's Handbook of Federal Indian Law.* Revised edition. Charlottesville, Virginia: Michie, Bobbs-Merrill, Law Publishers, 1982. 912 pp. One of the most useful of all studies about the evolution of Native American legal status. First published in 1942, then reprinted in 1971 by the University of New Mexico Press, it continues to be frequently consulted and quoted. This new edition includes post–World War II changes in Indian law.

8. Davis, Mary B., ed. *Native America in the Twentieth Century: An Encyclopedia.* New York: Garland Press, 1994. 787 pp. Martha Royce Blaine's entry on the Pawnees explains the modern tribal government, social programs, employment, and both successful and unsuccessful twentieth century attempts to preserve Pawnee language and culture. A fascinating essay on the powwow traces its beginnings to the Pawnee *Irushka* ceremony in the nineteenth century. The Pawnee ceremony and costume are described in detail, as is the oral tradition from which the *Irushka* dance originated.

9. Dawdy, Doris Ostrander. *Annotated Bibliography of American Indian Painting.* Contributions from the Museum of the American Indian, Heye Foundation, Vol. 21, Part 2. New York: Museum of the American Indian, Heye Foundation, 1968. 27 pp. Lists books and journal articles by and about Native American artists and exhibitions displaying their works. References to Pawnee artists, especially Acee Blue Eagle, appear throughout this dated, but still useful source.

10. Deloria, Vine, Jr., and Raymond J. DeMallie. *Documents of American Indian Diplomacy: Treaties, Agreements, and Conventions, 1775–1979.* 2 vols. Norman: University of Oklahoma Press, 1999. 1540 pp. In his introduction to this monumental work, Vine Deloria, Jr., points out the shortcomings of Charles J. Kappler's venerable second volume of *Indian Laws and Treaties.* Beginning with the pre-Revolutionary War period, this volume lists or reprints documents in sixteen categories, including many that Kappler neglected to include, such as unratified treaties, treaties between Indian tribes and states, and treaties rejected either by Indians or by the government. This is an excellent modern source that all researchers should consult. The index in volume two lists eleven treaties, agreements, and federal acts relating to the Pawnees.

11. DeWitt, Donald L., ed. *American Indian Resource Materials in the Western History Collections, University of Oklahoma.* Norman: University of Oklahoma Press, 1990. 272 pp. An invaluable, easy-to-use guide to these important Indian collections. Among the holdings pertinent to the Pawnees are a dozen photographic collections, including photos of Pawnee Bill's Wild West Show, the research notes of Pawnee historian Gene Weltfish and two microfilm reels of Weltfish's study of a Pawnee yearly cycle, twenty-four reel-to-reel tapes of songs, dance music, and Pawnee kinship terms, two microfilm reels of Karl and Iva Schmitt's research journeys, and one reel on G. C. Sibley's journey to the Pawnees. Also included are 695 audio tapes of Indian oral history interviews and sixty-nine audio tapes of "The Indians for Indians Hour," a radio show broadcast from Norman, Oklahoma, between 1943 and 1964. Government documents include photocopies of Southern Plains Indian agency records dating from 1804 to 1899 and a microfilmed Pawnee Agency letterbook from the agency in Nebraska, dated 1860–1874. The Western History Collections also include over 500 Indian newspapers and periodicals, in either hard copy or microform. No serious researcher can afford to overlook this unique collection.

12. Dockstader, Frederick J., comp. *The American Indian in Graduate Studies: A Bibliography of Theses and Dissertations.* 2d ed. New York: Museum of the American Indian, Heye Foundation, 1973. 362 pp. An extremely useful listing of theses and dissertations written between 1890 and 1955 at universities in the United States, Canada, and Mexico. Many of the 3,659 entries are accompanied by very brief annotations that often identify the tribe or tribes discussed. Annotations also indicate whether the source has been published or is available on microfilm.

13. Dockstader, Frederick J., and Alice W. Dockstader, comp. *The American Indian in Graduate Studies: A Bibliography of Theses and Dissertations.* New York: Museum of the American Indian, Heye Foundation, 1974. 426 pp. An update of the 1973 Dockstader bibliography that briefly annotates many of the theses and dissertations completed in universities in the United States, Canada, and Mexico between 1955 and 1970. Contains the index for both volumes. The index should be used with caution; under tribal headings, it only lists works with the tribal name in the title.

14. Evans, G. Edward, and Jeffrey Clark. *North American Indian Language Materials, 1890–1965: An Annotated Bibliography of Monographic Works.* Los Angeles: American Indian Studies Center, University of California, 1980. 154 pp. This is a valuable, carefully annotated bibliography, but it is very selective, and reveals no sources for the study of the Pawnee or other Caddoan dialects.

15. Fay, George E., comp. and ed. *Charters, Constitutions and By-Laws of the Indian Tribes of North America, Vol. 6; The Indian Tribes of Oklahoma, cont'd.* Greeley, Colorado: Occasional Publications in Anthropology. Ethnology Series, No. 7, Museum of Anthropology, Colorado State College, 1968. 129 pp. The Oklahoma Indian Welfare Act of 1936 provided that Indians could establish tribal governments. In January 1938, the Pawnee constitution and by-laws were ratified by tribal leaders, representatives of the Office of Indian Affairs, and the Department of the Interior. The Pawnee Corporate Charter was approved in June 1938. This volume reprints the full text of each document.

16. Freeman, John F., comp. *A Guide to Manuscripts Relating to the American Indian in the Library of the American Philosophical Society.* Philadelphia: American Philosophical Society, 1966. 491 pp. An extremely useful guide to the collections housed at the American Philosophical Society Library. The citations explain the content of each collection, its extent, and its format.

17. Gill, Sam D., and Irene F. Sullivan. *Dictionary of Native American Mythology.* New York: Oxford University Press, 1992. 425 pp. This well-arranged and very useful reference source lists dozens of Pawnee legends, cosmic phenomena, mythological creatures, and items of material culture. Each entry lists tribe, region, cross-references, and sources. The handy index lists terms by tribe. A forty-seven-page bibliography adds to the book's value.

18. Green, Rayna, and Nancy Marie Mitchell. *American Indian Sacred Objects, Skeletal Remains, Repatriation, and Reburial: A Resource Guide.* Washington, D.C.: National Museum of American History, Smithsonian Institution, 1990. 34 pp. This very brief specialized resource guide complied by Native Americans lists twenty-two pages of recent and older general works on repatriation and reburial and eight pages of federal, tribal, and state legislation on those topics, along with a few court decisions. Though not complete, this bibliography is a good starting point for research on repatriation. Unfortunately, none of the sources is annotated, making it difficult to determine which ones may refer to the Pawnees.

19. *A Guide to Newspapers Available on Microfilm.* Lincoln: Nebraska State Historical Society, 1994. This useful guide was prepared on microfiche by the Nebraska State Historical Society to provide researchers with the names and publication spans of all Nebraska newspapers available on microfilm through the Society. These microfilm reels are available for purchase or through interlibrary loan departments. Not all Nebraska newspapers are on microfilm, but most of the papers for smaller towns have been filmed. The guide is arranged in three sections: (1) newspaper listings under town of origin; (2) county listing of towns with newspapers; and (3) preferred titles. For information on the Pawnees, perhaps the best newspaper source is the *Platte Valley (Nebraska) Journal (Columbus Journal).* Other, smaller towns near the Pawnee reservation, such as Genoa, Fullerton, and Silver Creek, published newspapers, but most began publication after the Pawnees were moved to Indian Territory. Researchers wishing to utilize these newspaper reels should contact the Nebraska State Historical Society Library/Archives for availability and prices.

20. Haywood, Charles. *A Bibliography of North American Folklore and Folksong.* 2 vols. New York: Greenberg Publishers, 1951. Reprint. New York: Dover Publications, Inc., 1961. 1292 pp. Originally

published in one volume, the 1961 edition devotes volume two to sources on the American Indians north of Mexico, grouped by geographical area. This is a very ambitious project, but the bibliographic entries on each Indian tribe are far from complete. Pages 954–957 list Pawnee sources.

21. Hickerson, Joseph C. "Annotated Bibliography of North American Indian Music North of Mexico." Master's thesis, Indiana University, 1961. 464 pp. Very thorough bibliographic source with good annotations. Entries are indexed by both area and tribe, and a handy code to journal abbreviations is included. Lists thirty sources for Pawnee music.

22. Hill, Edward E. *Guide to Records in the National Archives of the United States Relating to American Indians*. National Archives and Records Service, General Services Administration. Washington, D.C.: Government Printing Office, 1981. 467 pp. This important reference holds the key to many Native American manuscript sources in the National Archives. The introduction explains the organization of the collections, and a history and description of each collection appears in the text. A very useful resource.

23. ———. *The Office of Indian Affairs, 1824–1880: Historical Sketches*. New York: Clearwater Publishing Company, Inc., 1974. 246 pp. This unique and useful resource presents short profiles of the Council Bluffs Agency, the Otoe Agency, and the Pawnee Agency, all of which served the Pawnees for a time during the nineteenth century. Histories of the Central and Northern Superintendencies, which had oversight of these agencies, are included as well. But the most valuable asset of this work is its "jurisdictional index," which guides researchers to the proper microfilm reels in the National Archives' microcopy 234 of Record Group 75, records of the Bureau of Indian Affairs. These microfilmed records for specific agencies are essential to thorough research.

24. ———. *Preliminary Inventories, No. 163: Records of the Bureau of Indian Affairs*. 2 vols. Washington, D.C.: National Archives and Records Administration, 1965. 459 pp. A detailed inventory of all materials in the National Archives' Record Group 75. Each citation is annotated and includes the size of a particular collection. A complete table of contents and index make this important reference source especially easy to use.

25. Hirschfelder, Arlene, and Paulette Molin. *Encyclopedia of Native Amer-*

ican Religions. Foreword by Walter R. Echo-Hawk. New York: Facts on File, Inc., 2000. 390 pp. Includes, along with the thought-provoking foreword, excellent descriptions of the Pawnee ghost dance hand game, the Hako, or calumet ceremony, the Iruska Society of medicine men, and the Young Dog's Dance, the Pawnee version of the Sun Dance.

26. *Historical Preservation in Nebraska.* Nebraska State Historical Society Preservation Series, Report No. 1. Lincoln: Nebraska State Historical Society, 1971. 158 pp. A unique source listing and describing sites within Nebraska that have been or will be preserved in compliance with the National Historic Preservation Act. Sites are listed by county and by subject. The Aboriginal, Prehistoric and Aboriginal, and Historic sections include well over thirty sites associated with the Pawnees and their possible ancestors. Exact locations are given for each site.

27. Hodge, William. *A Bibliography of Contemporary North American Indians, Selected and Partially Annotated with Study Guide.* New York: Interland Publishing, Inc., 1976. 296 pp. With 2,594 well-organized entries covering all aspects of modern Native American life and even listing newspapers, magazines, newsletters, and museums, this is a useful resource for research on most tribes. But inexplicably, the index lists no sources for the Pawnees.

28. Hoxie, Frederick E. *Encyclopedia of North American Indians.* Boston: Houghton Mifflin Company, 1996. 756 pp. Written by leading scholars, both Indian and white, this is an excellent collection of essays on Indian tribes, famous Indians, and topics such as treaties, reservations, and battles. Of particular interest are the sections on the Pawnee tribe and scouts. Also included is a lengthy biography of Pawnee intellectual James R. Murie. Unfortunately, no other Pawnees are profiled, but two essays, one on Geronimo and one on reservations, were written by Pawnee historian James Riding In.

29. Hunt, N. Jane, ed. *Brevet's Nebraska Historical Markers & Sites.* Sioux Falls, South Dakota: Brevet Press, 1974. 220 pp. Sixteen Pawnee sites are featured in this unique guide that reproduces historical markers throughout Nebraska and locates each marker on a map. The guide is conveniently divided into three geographical regions, and includes an essay on Fort Hartsuff, which was built on the North Loup River partly to protect the friendly Pawnees from Sioux raids.

30. Imholtz, August, ed. *A Guide to the Microfilm Edition of the Native*

American Reference Collection. Documents Collected by the Office of Indian Affairs. Part 1: 1840–1900; Part 2: 1901–1948. Bethesda, Maryland: University Publications of America, 1995, 2000. 459 pp. A guide to the 138 volumes of Indian Office documents available on microfilm. The excellent introductions to each part help direct researchers to particular topics, court cases, allotment, and Commissioners of Indian Affairs reports. Documents are indexed by tribe, reel number, and by frame number. Part 1 lists eighteen Pawnee sources, while Part 2 lists ten. This is an easy-to-use guide to an invaluable collection of government documents.

31. *Indian Rights Association Papers: A Guide to the Microfilm Edition, 1864–1973.* Glen Rock, New Jersey: Microfilming Corporation of America, 1975. 233 pp. An essential source for anyone researching the huge files of the Indian Rights Association (IRA). Each of the 136 microfilm reels is broken down by content. Also includes a brief history of the IRA, a summary of activities by year, and an index to the major people appearing in the correspondence.

32. *Inventory of Archives of Pawnee Indian Agency in Custody of Indian Archives Division, Oklahoma Historical Society,* Oklahoma City. 17 pp. A typed list of Pawnee sources identified by location in the Society archives, by topic, and by date. Also includes the number of pages of material on each subject. This guide does not designate which of the sources have been microfilmed, but this can be determined by cross-referencing this list with the Historical Society microfilm catalog [50], available to researchers for a small fee. Most of the materials at the Oklahoma Historical Society are post-1880 to about 1930.

33. Johansen, Bruce E., ed. *The Encyclopedia of Native American Economic History.* Westport, Connecticut: Greenwood Press, 1999. 301 pp. This reference work lists all aspects of the Native American economy and features essays on the economy of each tribe. The essay on the Pawnees, written by editor Johansen and Michael Tate, traces the economic history of the tribe as they accumulated wealth in the form of horses, then saw their fortunes decline as disease, Sioux attacks, and white settlement reduced their numbers and restricted their hunting range. Today, on their reserve in Oklahoma, they are a much smaller, less wealthy group, employed mainly as farmers and craftsmen.

34. ——. *The Encyclopedia of Native American Legal Tradition.* Westport, Connecticut: Greenwood Press, 1998. 410 pp. Contains brief bi-

ographical sketches of John Echo-Hawk, attorney and executive director of the Native American Rights Fund (NARF), his brother Larry
Echo-Hawk, the first Native American state attorney general in the
United States, and their cousin Walter Echo-Hawk, who, as senior staff
attorney for the NARF, was instrumental in the effort to have the remains of Native American people returned from museums and historical societies.

35. Johansen, Bruce E., and Donald A. Grinde, Jr. *The Encyclopedia of Native American Biography*. New York: Henry Holt and Company, 1997.
463 pp. An excellent index directs the reader to profiles of eight prominent Pawnees, some well-known and others more obscure. Included are
Curly Chief from the 1840s; George Drouillard, a mixed-blood Pawnee
who traveled with Lewis and Clark; John and Larry Echo-Hawk;
Petalesharo; Sharitarish; Sky Chief, who died at Massacre Canyon in
1873; and Big Hawk Chief, a Pawnee Scout who reportedly ran the mile
in under four minutes, seventy-five years before it would be done again.

36. Johnson, Steven L. *Guide to American Indian Documents in the Congressional Serial Set, 1817–1899*. New York: Clearwater Publishing
Co., 1977. 503 pp. An exhaustive search of Indian documents in the
Congressional Serial Set resulted in this invaluable guide, which lists
documents in the Serial Set to 1899. The thoughtfully arranged guide
lists documents by year, and the excellent index directs the researcher
to each mention of a particular tribe. Each entry is briefly annotated
and includes a complete citation, including the Serial Set volume. All
researchers should take advantage of this time- and labor-saving guide.

37. Jones, J. A. "Key to the Annual Reports of the United States Commissioner of Indian Affairs." *Ethnohistory* 2 (Winter 1955): 58–64. A
handy guide to these all-important Bureau of Indian Affairs documents.
Lists the Serial Set volume, document number, and page of each report
from 1825 through 1920.

38. Judd, Neil M. *The Bureau of American Ethnology: A Partial History*.
Norman: University of Oklahoma Press, 1967. 139 pp. Beginning with
John Wesley Powell, Judd traces the history of the Bureau of American
Ethnology through its leaders and through the many authors who contributed articles and essays over the years. The section dealing with authors is especially effective, as it presents a brief biography of each
writer and matches him or her with the publications to which he or she
contributed. To researchers, the book's greatest asset is the complete

list of annual reports, BAE bulletins, anthropological papers, River Basin surveys, contributions to North American ethnology, introductions to ethnographic studies, and miscellaneous publications. A very useful source.

39. Kappler, Charles J., comp. and ed. *Indian Affairs: Laws and Treaties.* 5 vols. Washington, D.C.: Government Printing Office, 1904–1941. Reprint New York: AMS Press, 1971. An absolutely essential reference source for researchers of the last two centuries of Indian-white relations. Despite being out-of-date, it remains a premier source of information on treaties and statutes concerning Native Americans. The volumes are easy to use, even for a researcher lacking legal training. Each volume updates the previous one, and each has its own detailed index. The five volumes contain numerous references to the Pawnees. Volume 2 of Kappler's work has been improved upon by Vine Deloria's 1999 *Documents of American Indian Diplomacy* [10].

40. Keenan, Jerry. *Encyclopedia of American Indian Wars, 1492–1890.* Santa Barbara, California: ABC-CLIO, Inc., 1997. 278 pp. Wars, individual battles, Indian tribes, and influential people are all listed in this ambitious work. A lengthy entry on the Powder River Expedition explains the role of the Pawnee Scouts. A shorter essay on the North brothers, an account of the important Battle of Summit Springs, and a brief biography of General Eugene Carr are also included.

41. Kelsay, Laura E., comp. *Cartographic Records of the Bureau of Indian Affairs.* Special List 13. Washington, D.C.: National Archives and Records Service, 1977. 187 pp. A guide to the Bureau of Indian Affairs maps in the Central Map Files, the Land Division, and Roads Division. Maps pertaining to the Pawnees range from their 1833 land cession to roads and water pipelines for Pawnee, Oklahoma, in the 1930s. Each set of maps is thoroughly described and dated.

42. Kendall, Daythal, comp. *A Supplement to A Guide to Manuscripts Relating to the American Indian in the Library of the American Philosophical Society.* Philadelphia: American Philosophical Society, 1982. 168 pp. An updating of John F. Freeman's guide published in 1966. It uses the same format to identify the American Philosophical Society's collections.

43. Lee, Dorothy Sara. *Native North American Music and Oral Data: A Catalogue of Sound Recordings, 1893–1976.* Bloomington: Indiana University Press, 1979. 463 pp. Lists songs and oral traditions recorded

over a period of eighty-three years. Each entry includes the performer, the collector, the repository, the culture group and area, subject, medium of recording, condition of recording, date, and accession number. The index lists thirteen Pawnee sources.

44. Littlefield, Daniel F., Jr., and James W. Parins. *A Biobibliography of Native American Writers, 1772–1924*. Native American Bibliography Series, No. 2. Metuchen, New Jersey: Scarecrow Press, 1981. 343 pp. Lists articles by Native Americans, published mostly in Indian journals. Indexed by subject and tribal affiliation, and each author is listed with a page reference. Twelve Pawnee writers are included. Most of the citations are complete, but there are no annotations.

45. ———. *A Biobibliography of Native American Writers, 1772–1924: A Supplement*. Native American Bibliography Series, No. 5. Metuchen, New Jersey: Scarecrow Press, 1985. 339 pp. Identical in format to the original volume. The supplement lists ten Pawnee authors, and unlike in the original, these entries have very brief annotations.

46. Loudon, Betty L., comp. *Index-Guide to Nebraska History Magazine, 1959–1979 (Volumes 40–60)*. Publications of the Nebraska State Historical Society, vol. 29. Lincoln: Nebraska State Historical Society, 1984. 274 pp. A more complete index than its predecessor [72], this guide contains every reference to each topic through twenty years of *Nebraska History*, the quarterly journal of the Nebraska State Historical Society, arranged in chronological order.

47. McDermott, John D. *A Guide to the Indian Wars of the West*. Lincoln: University of Nebraska Press, 1998. 205 pp. Roughly two-thirds of this book is devoted to the Indian wars themselves—the Indian view versus the white view—and the way the wars were portrayed in literature and on film. The rest of the volume divides the West into geographic regions and lists historic sites, battlefields, and museums relating to the Indian wars. In Nebraska, Forts Hartsuff, Kearny, and Robinson and the Massacre Canyon site are profiled, while the Summit Springs battlefield is included among the Colorado historic sites.

48. Matchette, Teresa F., comp. *National Archives Microfilm Publications in the Regional Archives System*. Washington, D.C.: National Archives and Records Administration, Special List 45, 1990. 284 pp. This is a handy guide to help researchers locate specific microfilm collections held by archives outside of Washington, D.C. Part I lists record groups

held by all eleven regional archives. Part II lists microfilm publications unique to individual regional archives, then provides descriptive lists of these holdings. A detailed subject index facilitates the search for particular people and topics. These lists are updated periodically as records are added, deleted, or transferred.

49. Mattes, Merrill J. *Platte River Road Narratives: A Descriptive Bibliography of Travel Over the Great Central Overland Route to Oregon, California, Utah, Colorado, Montana, and Other Western States and Territories, 1812–1866.* Foreword by James A. Michener. Urbana: University of Illinois Press, 1988. 632 pp. This superb bibliography is a must for researchers interested in emigrant diaries and journals. Many travelers along the Platte River Road had contact with the Pawnees. A large number of the 2,082 entries in this bibliography are rare manuscripts found in only one repository. The annotations are excellent and complete.

50. *Microfilm Catalog, 1976–1998.* Oklahoma City: Oklahoma Historical Society Archives/Manuscripts Division, 1998. 150 pp. This catalog may be purchased from the Oklahoma Historical Society, and lists Indian records held by the Society that have been filmed. A large amount of Pawnee material is included, but some of the Pawnee records remain in boxes and bound letterbooks. More records are in the process of being filmed. A printed overview of all the Society's Pawnee holdings is also available.

51. Murdock, George Peter. *Ethnographic Bibliography of North America.* New Haven, Connecticut: Human Relations Area Files, Inc., 1960. 393 pp. A valuable and easy-to-use bibliography of primary and secondary sources. Entries are divided into geographic areas by language groups, then by tribe. Contains over 100 entries on the Pawnees, plus the titles of dozens of general works pertaining to Plains Indians. Unfortunately, none of the entries is annotated.

52. Nichols, Frances S., comp. *Index to Schoolcraft's Indian Tribes of the United States.* Bureau of American Ethnology Bulletin 152. Washington, D. C.: Government Printing Office, 1954. 257 pp. This useful index provides citations and page numbers for Henry Rowe Schoolcraft's six-volume *Historical and Statistical Information Respecting the History, Condition, and Prospects of the Indian Tribes of the United States, Collected and Prepared under the Direction of the Bureau of Indian Affairs.* The index lists over four dozen references to the Pawnee bands.

53. Paterek, Josephine. *Encyclopedia of American Indian Costume*. New York: W. W. Norton, 1991. 516 pp. Thoughtfully arranged and beautifully illustrated with black and white photographs and line drawings, this is a wonderful resource. The encyclopedia is divided first by geographic areas, then by tribe, and finally by categories of dress and hair style. The easy-to-use index directs the reader to both tribes and types of costume, and illustrations are indicated in bold type. Pages 128–131 describe Pawnee costumes and include two excellent photographs. An invaluable resource for the researcher interested in Native American material culture.

54. Pritzker, Barry M. *A Native American Encyclopedia: History, Culture, and Peoples*. New York: Oxford University Press, 2000. 591 pp. Contains a generally good essay on Pawnee history and culture, but there are a few errors, especially concerning the treaty that created the Pawnee Reservation at Genoa, Nebraska. The index lists a total of twenty-six entries on the Pawnees, many of these referring to their relations with other tribes.

55. Prucha, Francis Paul. *A Bibliographical Guide to the History of Indian-White Relations in the United States*. Chicago: University of Chicago Press, 1977. 454 pp. An important bibliography containing citations for all types of published works. The extensive index adds to the value of this essential resource. Unfortunately, entries have no annotations as to quality and content.

56. ———. *Indian-White Relations in the United States: A Bibliography of Works Published 1975–1980*. Lincoln: University of Nebraska Press, 1982. 179 pp. An update to Prucha's bibliographical guide published by the University of Chicago Press. The format of this volume is the same, and like the original, it has no annotations.

57. Rajtar, Steve. *Indian War Sites: A Guidebook to Battlefields, Monuments, and Memorials*. Jefferson, North Carolina: McFarland Company, Inc., 1999. 330 pp. An easy-to-use guide to battle sites in the United States, Canada, and Mexico. Battles are arranged by state, then listed chronologically. Each entry includes a brief description of the event, along with its location and date. Entries pertaining to the Pawnees include the Villasur Expedition, several attacks on Pawnees by enemy tribes, including Massacre Canyon, and the Summit Springs battle and the role of the North brothers and the Pawnee Scouts. No new information here, but a nicely organized guide.

58. Reddy, Marlita A., ed. *Statistical Record of Native North Americans*. Detroit: Gale Research, 1993. 1661 pp. This huge volume presents Pawnee statistics in the form of tables. Beginning in about 1910 and including the early 1960s, it covers population, language, blood quantum, family sizes, education, literacy, and land holdings.

59. Rittenhouse, Jack D. *The Santa Fe Trail: A Historical Bibliography*. Albuquerque: University of New Mexico Press, 1971. 271 pp. A nicely done specialized bibliography with excellent annotations. Works listed include memoirs and general trail studies, as well as pertinent documents from the Congressional Serial Set. A supplemental index lists all congressional documents along with their entry numbers. The general index cites fifteen works dealing directly with the Pawnees, but a close look at other entries would also yield information on the Pawnees and their contacts with travelers and traders.

60. Ross, Norman A., ed. *Index to the Decisions of the Indian Claims Commission, 1948–1972*. New York: Clearwater Publishing Co., 1973. 158 pp. The foreword to this index explains the purpose and workings of the Indian Claims Commission, which began holding hearings on tribal claims in 1946. Tribal docket numbers are listed in order. The Pawnee docket number is 10, and decisions concerning the Pawnees from July 1950 to July 1963 are cited in the index, which does not include page numbers. The decisions are available on microfiche at major libraries.

61. ———. *Index to the Expert Testimony before the Indian Claims Commission: The Written Reports*. New York: Clearwater Publishing Co., 1973. 102 pp. Available at major libraries on microfiche, these records include written evidence presented to the Indian Claims Commission. The index contains tribal listings, author lists, and a main entry section, which identifies testimonies and their authors. Docket 10 lists 135 pages of anthropology notes on the Pawnees in Oklahoma, written by John L. Champe and Franklin Fenenga [84], and William G. Murray's 480-page, 2-volume appraisal of Pawnee tracts in Nebraska at the times of their four major treaties [677].

62. Snodgrass, Jeanne O., comp. *American Indian Painters: A Biographical Directory*. Contributions from the Museum of the American Indian Heye Foundation, Vol. 21, Part 1. New York: Museum of the American Indian Heye Foundation, 1968. 267 pp. The index lists seven Pawnees, and profiles of varying lengths provide both personal and professional data on each artist. Most of the sketches are brief, but a few, such as that of Acee Blue Eagle (Creek-Pawnee), are detailed.

63. Socolofsky, Homer E., and Virgil W. Dean. *Kansas History: An Annotated Bibliography*. Westport, Connecticut: Greenwood Press, 1992. 587 pp. The first in a series of bibliographies of the states, this volume contains about twenty references to the Pawnees in Kansas, many of them from the Kansas State Historical Society Collections.

63a. Southwell, Kristina L., comp. *Guide to the Manuscripts in the Western History Collections of the University of Oklahoma*. Norman: University of Oklahoma Press, 2002.

63b. ———. *Guide to the Photographs in the Western History Collections of the University of Oklahoma*. Norman: University of Oklahoma Press, 2002.

64. Svoboda, Joseph G., comp. *Guide to American Indian Resource Materials in Great Plains Repositories*. Lincoln: University of Nebraska—Center for Great Plains Studies, 1983. 401 pp. A valuable guide to manuscript materials in major collections, as well as in smaller, lesser-known repositories. Material on the Pawnees and people associated with them is identified and thoroughly described.

65. Tate, Michael L. *Nebraska History: An Annotated Bibliography*. Westport, Connecticut: Greenwood Press, 1995. 549 pp. Number 6 in the Bibliographies of the States of the United States. The chapters on native archaeology, historical Native Americans, and the frontier period include nearly 200 sources pertaining either directly or indirectly to the Pawnees. All have excellent, brief annotations.

66. Tiller, Veronica E. Velarde, ed. and comp. *Tiller's Guide to Indian Country: Economic Profiles of American Indian Reservations*. Albuquerque: BowArrow Publishing, 1994. 698 pp. This source lists Indian tribes in alphabetical order and includes tribal addresses, phone and fax numbers along with education and unemployment figures. The profile of the Pawnees traces their land cessions, current land holdings, and explains the organization of their tribal government. Also discussed are the modern Pawnee economy, gaming, reserve infrastructure, and community services.

67. Ullom, Judith C., comp. *Folklore of the North American Indians: An Annotated Bibliography*. Washington, D.C.: Government Printing Office, 1969. 126 pp. Directed mainly toward literature for children, this selected bibliography includes only seventeen citations on Plains Indians, two of which are classic works on the Pawnees. The entire book lists only 152 items, but the annotations are superb.

68. *U. S. Statutes at Large*. Washington, D.C.: Government Printing Office, 1789–Present. The full text of all ratified Indian treaties appears in this important source. Nearly all treaties approved between 1778 and 1845 are included in volume 7. Volumes 8 through 16 contain later treaties indexed by tribe and in chronological order, but random treaties do appear in later volumes. Along with the treaty text, *Statutes at Large* includes further congressional actions fulfilling treaty obligations.

69. *User's Guide to the American Indian Correspondence: The Presbyterian Historical Society Collection of Missionaries' Letters, 1833–1893*. Westport, Connecticut: Greenwood Press, n.d. 100 pp. A guide published in conjunction with the distribution of all the microfilmed missionaries' letters in the Presbyterian Historical Society's collection. An easy-to-use guide, it provides an index to the correspondence of each individual and lists the reel for those letters. A guide to the letter writers begins on page 15. Although the missionaries to the Omahas and other eastern Nebraska tribes are well represented, there is no mention of the Pawnees or the influential missionaries John Dunbar and Samuel Allis. Fortunately, many of their letters have been preserved in other sources, especially the *Collections of the Kansas State Historical Society*.

70. Waldman, Carl. *Bibliographical Dictionary of American Indian History to 1900*. New York: Facts on File, 2001. 506 pp. The six Pawnees profiled are Big Hawk Chief, a Pawnee Scout who ran an under-four-minute mile; George Drouillard, a mixed-blood guide for Lewis and Clark; Petalesharo of Morning Star Ceremony fame; Sharitarish, who visited Washington, D.C., in 1821; Sky Chief, who died at Massacre Canyon; and Turk, the semi-legendary Pawnee slave who may have described the province of Quivira to Coronado.

71. Weist, Katherine M., and Susan R. Sharrock. *An Annotated Bibliography of Northern Plains Ethnohistory*. Missoula, Montana: Department of Anthropology, University of Montana, Contributions to Anthropology No. 8, 1985. 299 pp. A well-organized and easy-to-use bibliography concentrating on the area of the Great Plains north of Pawnee country. However, it does list about two dozen references to the Pawnees, and these are thoroughly annotated. A very useful reference source, especially for Northern Plains tribes.

72. White, John Browning. *Index-Guide to Publications, 1885–1956, and Nebraska History Magazine, 1918–1958*. Publications of the Nebraska

State Historical Society, Vol. 24. Lincoln: Nebraska State Historical Society, 1958. Revised second printing, 1983. 141 pp. A handy index to all issues of the Transactions and Collections of the Nebraska State Historical Society and all issues of *Nebraska History* through 1958. Not all mentions of each topic are included, but each entry has a brief annotation.

73. ———. "Published Sources on Territorial Nebraska: An Essay and Bibliography." Ph.D. diss., University of Nebraska, 1953. 300 pp. Also appears as *Publications of the Nebraska State Historical Society*, vol. 23. Lincoln: Nebraska State Historical Society, 1956. A unique source written by a former librarian at the Nebraska State Historical Society, covering the years between 1854, when Nebraska became a territory, and statehood in 1867. Contains about twenty references to the Pawnee Indians, the North Brothers, and the 1859 "Pawnee War." Most are nicely annotated.

74. Wood, W. Raymond, comp. *An Atlas of Early Maps of the American Midwest*. Illinois State Museum Scientific Papers, Vol. 18, 1983. Ten oversize text pages and twenty-two plates. An excellent collection of maps dating from c. 1714 to 1856. For students of Pawnee history, the most important map is Plate 21, John Dunbar's drawing of the Loup Fork area that locates and names streams and Pawnee villages. The accompanying text by Michael K. Trimble compares the map to letters written by Dunbar. The original Dunbar map has been microfilmed by the National Archives, and can be found in the Bureau of Indian Affairs, *Letters Received from the Upper Missouri Agencies, 1824–1881*, Record Group 75, M234, Reel 5.

75. Wright, Muriel H. *A Guide to the Indian Tribes of Oklahoma*. Norman: University of Oklahoma Press, 1951. 300 pp. Although written over fifty years ago, this is still a useful source, since it limits itself just to native and transplanted Oklahoma tribes. The twenty-seven-page introduction is an overview of Oklahoma Indian history. Sketches of the tribes are listed in alphabetical order. Wright divides the Pawnees into two groups, listing the Skidi separately from the other three bands.

2
General Studies

76. *America's Fascinating Indian Heritage*. Pleasantville, New York: Reader's Digest Association, Inc., 1978. 416 pp. This beautifully illustrated book is designed for the general reader, and the Pawnees are mentioned numerous times in the chapter on the Great Plains.

77. Anderson, David. "The Early Settlements of the Platte Valley." Lincoln: *Collections of the Nebraska State Historical Society*, vol. 26, 1911, 193–204. In 1859, Anderson and a group of companions traveled the Platte River Road from Denver to Omaha. He describes many homesteads and ranches along the way, and there are mentions of the Pawnees when the travelers reached Fremont, Nebraska. Shopkeepers in Fremont kept up a lively trade with thousands of Pawnees camped on the bluffs just east of the town. Anderson and his friends crossed Rawhide Creek east of Fremont, and he retells the legend of the white man allegedly skinned alive by Pawnees after he murdered a Pawnee woman. The Pawnees themselves told him a far different version of the tale.

78. Blaine, Martha Royce. *Pawnee Passage, 1870–1875*. Norman: University of Oklahoma Press, 1990. 345 pp. The first part of this fine book is a cultural study of the Pawnees. The second section discusses the Pawnees shortly before, during, and shortly after their move from Nebraska to Indian Territory. An excellent account of a most difficult time in Pawnee history. Much of the material comes from Pawnee Agency records from the National Archives, Pawnee Agency letterbooks and council volumes at the Oklahoma State Historical Society, and the

journal of Barclay White, Quaker superintendent in charge of the Pawnees [1270].

79. ——. "To the Reservation." *NEBRASKAland* 62 (January–February 1984): 92–97, 100–1. Explains the rationale behind removing Nebraska Indians to reservations and discusses the problems the Indians faced once removed. Although not specifically about the Pawnees, many of the conditions described applied to them.

80. Brown, Dee. *Pawnee, Blackfoot, and Cheyenne. History and Folklore of the Plains from the Writings of George Bird Grinnell.* New York: Scribners, 1961. Gathers in one source selected works of Grinnell about the Indian tribes he knew best. Nearly all of the selections on the Pawnees are from *Pawnee Hero Stories and Folk Tales*, a more complete collection of Grinnell's writings.

81. Buecker, Thomas R., and R. Eli Paul, eds. "Go South and Be Free: John W. Williamson's Account of the Pawnee Removal." *Chronicles of Oklahoma* 65 (Summer 1987): 132–57; and (Fall 1987): 294–318. At the age of twenty-three, agency employee Williamson was put in charge of the Pawnee relocation from Nebraska to Indian Territory, and he delivered the people safely to their destination, the Wichita Agency. The story continues with the establishment of a new Pawnee Agency. The editors have wisely not changed Williamson's colorful prose, and so this remains a sometimes witty, always down-to-earth account of a traumatic event in Pawnee history. This is a rare source—the only known firsthand written account of the Pawnee removal. The original handwritten document remains with Williamson's family, but a microfilmed copy is housed in the Nebraska State Historical Society Archives.

82. Carlson, Paul H. *The Plains Indians*. College Station: Texas A&M University Press, 1998. 254 pp. Designed primarily as a textbook, and divided into thematic chapters. The index lists about two dozen references to the Pawnees, none of great length.

83. Catlin, George. *Letters and Notes on the Manners, Customs, and Conditions of North American Indians*. 2 vols. London: 1844. Reprint. New York: Dover Publications, Inc., 1973. 530 pp. Catlin's letters and notes, written during two tours in the West, are excellent and sometimes unique among accounts of Indian life. The newer edition of his work includes photographs of 257 of Catlin's original oil paintings. Some tribes, such as the Mandans, are described at length, but Catlin

devotes only a few paragraphs to the Pawnees—an account of the council with the tribe during which Colonel Richard Dodge arranged a prisoner exchange.

84. Champe, John L., and Franklin Fenenga. "Notes on the Pawnee." In *Pawnee and Kansa (Kaw) Indians*. New York: Garland Publishing, Inc., 1974, 23–169. This study was written for the Justice Department to provide information for the Indian Claims Commission. The ethnographic, historical, and cartographic data was used to determine Pawnee hunting grounds and village locations, and to provide proof of tribal identity. This is an excellent brief study of the Pawnees, utilizing reliable sources.

85. Clark, Jerry E. *The Indians of Eastern Nebraska at the Time of White Settlement: Ethnography of the Pawnee and Omaha*. Omaha: Douglas County Historical Society—Lamplighter Press, 1989. 17 pp. Compares and contrasts the lifeways of the Omahas and Pawnees. Among the subjects addressed are technology, subsistence, social organization, and religion.

86. Collister, R. Paul. "An Early Stage in Decline: The Pawnees as Seen Through Indian Office Correspondence, 1824–1835." Master's thesis, University of Nebraska, 1985. 185 pp. Using primarily Indian Office sources, the author suggests that the eleven-year period covered by this thesis was a time of transition for the Pawnees. Their traditional economy became stressed, their relations with the government became strained, but then they improved. By the 1830s, the Pawnees were considering changes to their subsistence system, but not to the same degree as the Otoes and Omahas, their neighbors to the east.

87. Connelley, William E. *A Standard History of Kansas and Kansans*, Vol. 1. Chicago: Lewis Publishing Company, 1918. 594 pp. Dated both in writing style and content, but contains a short history of the Pawnees in Kansas, accounts of wars and treaties between the Pawnees and other Kansas tribes, plus a lengthy discussion of the Pike-Pawnee Village site and the events that occurred there.

88. Critcher, Marge, Carolyn Boyum, Patti Huff, and Paul Olson, eds. *The Book of the Pawnees: Pawnee Stories for Study and Enjoyment*. Lincoln: Nebraska Curriculum Development Center, 1979. 60 pp. This slim volume of Pawnee history, folk stories, and trickster and coyote tales was designed for classroom use. All of the material is taken from works by George A. Dorsey, George Bird Grinnell, and Gene Weltfish.

89. Curry, Margaret. *The History of Platte County, Nebraska*. Culver City, California: Murray & Gee, 1950. 1011 pp. Huge volume contains several references to the Pawnees. Most important is an overview of the history and role of the Pawnee Scouts. Also mentions a Pawnee encounter with westbound Mormons on the Loup Fork in 1847.

90. Dawson, Charles. "The Pawnee Indians." In *Pioneer Tales of the Oregon Trail and of Jefferson County*. Topeka, Kansas: Crane & Company, 1912, 133–52. This chapter describes several phases of Pawnee life, such as burial customs, courtship, ceremonial dances, and buffalo hunts. The information is undocumented, and the overall tone is ethnocentric.

91. Dodge, Richard Irving. *The Plains of North America and Their Inhabitants*, edited by Wayne R. Kime. Newark: University of Delaware Press, 1989. 477 pp. This is the most recent edition of this important work, which has been published at least three times in the United States, and first appeared in 1877 in Great Britain under the title *The Hunting Grounds of the Great West: A Description of the Plains, Game, and Indians of the Great North American Desert*. Lt. Col. Dodge, a twenty-year veteran of western army service, was urged by a friend to write about his experiences. The result was one of the first comprehensive accounts of the Great Plains. The section on Indians is divided into categories such as tribal government, social life, religion, and warfare. The index lists fourteen brief references to the Pawnees.

92. Dorsey, George A., and James R. Murie. "Pawnee Notes and Manuscripts." Chicago: Field Museum of Natural History, Boxes A-1, A-2, Anthropological Archives, Department of Anthropology, 1902.

93. Dunbar, John B. "The Pawnee Indians: Their Habits and Customs." *Magazine of American History* 5 (November 1880): 321–42. Describes Pawnee trade, food sources, feasts, hunting methods, warfare, and traditional medicine and doctor societies.

94. ———. "The Pawnee Indians: Their Habits and Customs." *Magazine of American History* 8 (November 1882): 734–54. A continuation of Dunbar's 1880 article, this essay provides first-hand accounts of Pawnee religious rituals, including the Morning Star Ceremony, games, dances, astronomy, and character traits. Also briefly touches on Pawnee beliefs regarding death.

95. ———. "The Pawnee Indians: Their History and Ethnology." *Magazine of American History* 4 (April 1880): 241–81. Although this lengthy article

does contain some errors, it is still a valuable resource, since it is based upon Dunbar's first-hand observations while living with the Pawnees and answers to questions he asked members of the tribe. Dunbar touches on every aspect of Pawnee life, but his physical descriptions of the Pawnees themselves and his explanations of important customs and ceremonies may be the most useful.

96. Echo-Hawk, Brummett. "Brummett Echo-Hawk Tells the Pawnee Story." *Chicago Westerners Brand Book*, vol. 14, May 1957, 17–19, 22–23. This is a familiar Pawnee history made more colorful because it was told by a Pawnee in a conversational style. Echo-Hawk relates the story of his people and also shares his own experiences at the Pawnee Indian School in Oklahoma.

97. Ewers, John C. *The Horse in Blackfoot Indian Culture: With Comparative Material from Other Western Tribes*. Bureau of American Ethnology Bulletin 159. Washington, D.C.: Government Printing Office, 1955. 375 pp. References to the Pawnees are found primarily in the footnotes, and mention Pawnee hunting and raiding methods, care and treatment of horses, and uses of medicinal plants. A table also lists details on the Pawnee horse population at various times in the nineteenth century.

98. Fletcher, Alice C. *Indian Education and Civilization*. 48th Cong., 2d sess., 1888. S. Exec. Doc. 95. [Ser. 2264]. Reprint. New York: Kraus Reprint Co., 1971. 693 pp. Though primarily concerned with the history of Indian education, this is a much broader study of Indian policy. Because it includes nearly all tribes, coverage of the Pawnees is limited to data on their reservation in Oklahoma and synopses of treaties and congressional acts affecting the tribe. But overall, this is an excellent source of information on government policy and its impact on individual Indian tribes.

99. Foreman, Grant. *The Last Trek of the Indians*. Chicago: University of Chicago Press, 1946. 382 pp. This is a study of the removal of Indian tribes to Indian Territory (later, Oklahoma). Each tribe's experience is discussed separately. Pages 237–47 are devoted to Pawnee history in Nebraska and the tribe's relocation in 1874–1875. Besides this section, the book contains numerous mentions of the Pawnees.

100. Friesen, John W. *First Nations of the Plains: Creative, Adaptable and Enduring*. Calgary, Alberta: Detselig Enterprises, Ltd., 1999. 310 pp.

The two pages on the Pawnees do not give the author the opportunity to discuss Pawnee spirituality in any depth, although it is mentioned. Missionary efforts among the Pawnees in Oklahoma appear, but the earlier influence of Presbyterian missionaries Dunbar and Allis is ignored.

101. *Genoa, Nebraska Historical Stars.* Genoa, Nebraska: Genoa U.S. Indian School Foundation, 1996. 18 pp. This booklet, published in the town that was the center for the Pawnee Reservation in Nebraska, features three important historical aspects: the Pawnees; the Mormons who founded Genoa; and the U.S. Indian School, which was the Pawnee Industrial School until the Pawnees were relocated to Indian Territory. There is no new or unusual information included on the Pawnees, but the text incorporates wonderful photos and maps from several historical societies and museum collections.

102. Gilmore, Melvin R. "Aboriginal Geography of the Nebraska Country." *Proceedings, Missouri Valley Historical Association*, vol. 6 (1915): 1–15. Gilmore approximates what the area that became Nebraska was like before the coming of the white man, when only Siouan, Caddoan, and Algonquian peoples occupied the country. There is a brief discussion of the lifestyles of the different tribes, plus a list of rivers and their Indian names.

103. Griffiths, Thomas M. "Historic and Economic Geography of the Pawnee Lands." In *Pawnee and Kansa (Kaw) Indians.* New York: Garland Publishing, Inc., 1974, 171–278. Prepared for the Indian Claims Commission, this detailed study describes the geographic location and the economic condition of the Pawnees at the time of their land cessions in 1833, 1848, 1857, and 1875.

104. Gunnerson, Dolores, and Ken Bouc. "A Time of Change." *NE-BRASKAland* 62 (January–February 1984): 52–71. Traces the ebb and flow of power among Plains tribes and their relations with European powers. The Pawnees receive considerable mention, including a theory that female Pawnee captives introduced the formerly nomadic Apaches to corn growing and earth lodge construction.

105. Hamilton, Raphael N. "The Early Cartography of the Missouri Valley." *American Historical Review* 39 (July 1934): 645–62. Beginning with maps drawn by cartographers accompanying French explorers in the late 1600s, this collection traces the changes in maps of the Missouri Valley up to the 1860s. Several of these early maps are reproduced in

the text, and the Pawnees are located on all of them. Each map has notations explaining the changing spellings of tribal names.

106. Hansen, Margaret E. "Removal of the Indians from Nebraska." Master's thesis, Colorado State College of Education, 1949. 136 pp. The author attempts to cover too much material and covers none of it thoroughly. Pawnee history, culture, treaties, their reservation, and their removal to Indian Territory are all addressed, but the thesis is very disorganized.

107. Hazen, R. W. "History of the Pawnee Indians." Fremont, Nebraska: *Fremont Tribune*, 1893. 80 pp. This is not a true "history" of the Pawnees. Rather, it is mostly excerpts from the journals of Lewis and Clark, John C. Fremont, and Stephen Long, plus short essays by other writers. The sections apparently written by Hazen contain numerous errors. Overall, not a dependable source.

108. Heape, Roger Kent. "Pawnee–United States Relations from 1803 to 1875." Ph.D. diss., Saint Louis University, 1982. 368 pp. Utilizing Indian Office records, government documents, and the records of the American Fur Company, this superb study traces the decline in Pawnee power over a period of seventy-two years and explores the factors contributing to that decline. Ultimately, the Pawnees became victims of their own inability to adapt to changes and the United States government's failure to help them survive in their traditional homeland.

109. Hodge, Frederick Webb, ed. *Handbook of American Indians North of Mexico*. 2 vols. Bureau of American Ethnology Bulletin 30. Washington, D.C.: Government Printing Office, 1907–1910. Reprint. St. Cloud Shores, Michigan: Scholarly Press, Inc., 1968. 1,221 pp. Long a standard reference source, the handbook includes essays on specific tribes, material culture, and Indian personalities. It is currently being replaced by a twenty-volume series published by the Smithsonian Institution [144]. Alice C. Fletcher's generalized article on the Pawnees is in Part 2, pages 213–16.

110. Holder, Preston. *The Hoe and the Horse on the Plains: A Study of Cultural Development among North American Indians*. Lincoln: University of Nebraska Press, 1970. 176 pp. The Pawnees receive considerable mention is this study of village farming and nomadic hunting from horseback—the two major ways of life among the Plains Indians.

111. ———. "The Role of the Caddoan Horticulturists in Culture History of the Great Plains." Ph.D. diss., Columbia University, 1951. 135 pp. The Pawnees figure prominently in this excellent study of the history of Caddoan farmers and their reaction to both nomadic tribes and newcomers from Europe.

112. Hutchinson, Stephen K., comp. *Frontier Nebraska: Boone County Stories of Hardship and Triumph in the 1870s.* Lincoln: Foundation Books, 1998. 499 pp. Part diary, part memoir, but mostly excerpts from other sources regarding the settlement of Boone County in north-central Nebraska. The author does include a chapter entitled "Indians," and most of these entries relate to the Pawnees. All of the material relating to Indians is excerpted from other sources, and it is in no particular order. The sources are well documented, but the serious researcher should use this book only as a starting point and should refer to the original sources.

113. Hyde, George E. *The Pawnee Indians.* Denver: University of Denver Press, 1951. Reprint. Norman: University of Oklahoma Press, 1974. 372 pp. This pioneering work has been criticized by anthropologists, and many historians take issue with Hyde's strong opinions and his use of primary and secondary sources without benefit of footnotes. Yet this book is well written and remains a classic Plains Indian study.

114. Kallen, Stuart A. *The Pawnee.* San Diego: Lucent Books, Inc., 2001. 96 pp. This volume in the Indigenous Peoples of North America series is intended for young readers, and it is very well done. The six chapters of this slim volume follow the Pawnees from their early migrations to present-day life in Oklahoma. The book is well illustrated, and special interest boxes feature excerpts from works on the Pawnees by respected writers. A list of internet sources in the bibliography makes this work more attractive to young people. A highly recommended introductory source on Pawnee history.

115. Lacey, Theresa Jensen. *The Pawnees.* New York: Chelsea House Publishers, 1996. 103 pp. A volume in a series geared toward young adult readers. Contains no new or unique material and would not be particularly helpful to serious researchers, but it is a useful overview of Pawnee history and culture for general readers. Divided into chapters on Pawnee origins, tribal life, white contact, and modern Pawnees. Nicely illustrated, but there are no footnotes, and the tiny bibliography is entirely secondary sources.

116. Lewis, Malcomb. "Indian Maps: Their Place in the History of Plains Cartography." *Great Plains Quarterly* 4 (Spring 1984): 91–108. Discusses the cultural and geographic importance of maps drawn by proto-historic and historic Indian groups and cartographers. Because of its importance to Plains tribes, many Indian maps depict the Great Plains waterway system. The Skidi Pawnee celestial chart at Chicago's Field Museum is pictured and briefly explained.

117. Lowie, Robert H. *Indians of the Plains.* New York: McGraw Hill, 1954. Reprint. Lincoln: University of Nebraska Press, 1982. 222 pp. Originally commissioned as the first in a series of anthropological handbooks for the American Museum of Natural History, this study remains useful after nearly a half century in print. There are nearly three dozen references to the Pawnees, with the most extensive entries focusing on their religion and rituals.

118. McHugh, Tom. *The Time of the Buffalo.* New York: Alfred A. Knopf, Inc., 1972. Reprint. Lincoln: University of Nebraska Press, 1979. 339 pp. Discusses the preparation of sacred Pawnee "buffalo staffs," the hoop-and-javelin game as a way to attract buffalo, and relates the Pawnee myth of a robot-like buffalo skull that ate people, and the traditional tale "The Man Who Married a Buffalo," as told to George Dorsey by a Pawnee storyteller.

119. McKenney, Thomas, and James Hall. *History of the Indian Tribes of North America, with Biographical Sketches and Anecdotes of the Principal Chiefs.* 3 vols. Philadelphia: Edward C. Biddle, Publisher, 1836, Frederick W. Greenough, 1838, Daniel Rice and James G. Clark, 1844; Reprint in 2 vols. Kent, Ohio: Volair Limited Publishing Co., 1978. This beautiful work, guided through its publication by Commissioner of Indian Affairs McKenney, features only one Pawnee leader—Peskelechaco—a war chief whose portrait was painted by Charles Bird King in Washington, D.C.

120. Mails, Thomas E. *The Mystic Warriors of the Plains.* Garden City, New York: Doubleday & Company, Inc., 1972. 618 pp. A huge volume containing numerous cursory references to Pawnee dwellings, customs, clothing, medicine bundles, war paint, and religion, including a brief, somewhat inaccurate account of the Morning Star Ceremony. This source should be used with caution, since the references are so brief and general that they are practically useless.

121. Moore, Guy Rowley. "Pawnee Traditions and Customs." *Chronicles of Oklahoma* 17 (June 1939): 151–69. Adapted from the author's 1925 University of Oklahoma master's thesis, this article is mostly taken from the writings of missionaries and prominent ethnologists. No new material, but it is a quick, easy-to-read overview of Pawnee history and culture. Includes still another version of the Skidi Morning Star Ceremony.

122. Morgan, Lewis Henry. *The Indian Journals, 1859–62*. Ann Arbor: University of Michigan Press, 1959. Reprint. New York: Dover Publications, Inc., 1993. 276 pp. Although he failed in his attempts to visit the Pawnee villages in his sojourn in Nebraska, anthropologist Morgan did spend considerable time with Samuel Allis and his family in Bellevue, and Allis shared his knowledge of the culture and kinship organizations of the Pawnee bands.

123. Morse, Jedediah. *Report to the Secretary of War of the United States on Indian Affairs*. New Haven: S. Converse, 1822. Reprint. New York: Augustus M. Kelley Publishers, 1970. 400 pp. Included in the appendix to this report are brief sketches of three Pawnee bands, rather than the actual four, as they appeared in 1822. Also includes a speech given in Washington, D.C., by Chief Sharitarish and an account of Petalesharo's rescue of an Indian girl targeted to be sacrificed to the Morning Star. Especially useful for Morse's descriptions of Pawnee women.

124. Morton, J. Sterling, and Albert Watkins, eds. *Illustrated History of Nebraska*. 3 vols. Lincoln: Jacob North and Co., 1906–1913. Eastern Nebraska Indian tribes are covered briefly in volume 1, and the Plains tribes appear in volume 2. A chapter entitled "Territorial Military History" is useful, but it does contain significant errors and is written in an ethnocentric fashion.

125. Moulton, Candy. *Roadside History of Nebraska*. Missoula, Montana: Mountain Press Publishing Company, 1997. 391 pp. Part history and part travelogue, this is a unique source on Pawnee-related topics in Nebraska. Among the featured towns are Fremont, Columbus, Genoa, and Trenton, all with strong ties to the Pawnees or the North Brothers, leaders of the Pawnee Scouts. Includes excellent essays on the Grand Pawnee villages, the role of the Scouts, and the Indian School in Genoa, along with Massacre Canyon and the efforts to place a monument at that site.

126. Nabokov, Peter. *Native American Testimony: A Chronicle of Indian-White Relations from Prophecy to the Present, 1492–2000.* Foreword by Vine Deloria, Jr. New York: Penguin-Putnam, 1999. 506 pp. A collection of speeches, opinions, and accounts by Native Americans throughout their history of interaction with whites. The one Pawnee entry, called "Keep Your Presents," is Curly Chief's recollection of a fellow Pawnee's rejection of white men's goods at an unidentified treaty council.

127. Noble, Glenn. *Frontier Steamboat Town: First Fort Kearny—Nebraska City—Westward Impact.* Lincoln, Nebraska: Midgard Press, 1989. 257 pp. Incorporated into this book that is primarily a history of the Nebraska City, Nebraska, area is a chapter (27–39) containing considerable information on the Pawnees. Among the events discussed are attacks on travelers by Pawnee raiders, details of the 1857 Treaty of Table Creek, and a brief section on the "Pawnee War" of 1859.

128. Olson, James C., and Ronald C. Naugle. *History of Nebraska.* 3d ed. Lincoln: University of Nebraska Press, 1997. 502 pp. The Pawnees played an important role in the early history of Nebraska, and this history of the state presents a brief sketch of the Pawnee people, an account of their rout of the Villasur Expedition, and references to the treaties by which they surrendered most of their Nebraska Lands.

129. Oswalt, Wendell H. *This Land Was Theirs: A Study of North American Indians.* 3d ed. New York: John Wiley and Sons, 1978. 569 pp. Pages 219–53 of this survey contain an excellent introductory overview of the Pawnees from prehistoric times to about 1887. The essay touches on all aspects of Pawnee life, and includes a brief bibliography of standard books and articles on the tribe, whom the author considers typical of Plains Indians who lived in semi-permanent communities.

130. *The Pawnee.* Lincoln: Nebraska State Historical Society, Educational Leaflet no.1. 6 pp. A typescript printed by the Historical Society to familiarize non-specialists with Pawnee history, village life, religion, and other aspects of their culture.

130a. "Emergence of History Tribes: The Pawnee." *www.nebraskastudies. org.* Overview article on the historic Pawnees describes the tribal divisions, villages, earth lodges, farming and hunting methods, and mentions their religion. Illustrations are courtesy of the Nebraska Game and Parks Commission.

131. Carlisle, Jeffrey D. "Pawnee Indians." *The Handbook of Texas Online.* www.tsha.utexas.edu/handbook/online/articles/view/PP/bmp52.html. This online history of the Pawnees is a joint effort of the University of Texas at Austin libraries and the Texas State Historical Association.

132. *The Pawnee Nation Web Site.* www.pawneenation.org/history. This is the official web site of the Pawnee Nation of Oklahoma and contains, among other items, the general history of the Pawnee people, Pawnee oral traditions, and a tribal newsletter. This is a good place to begin an internet search of Pawnee information, but it does not replace more in-depth research.

133. Riding In, James T. "Keepers of Tirawahut's Covenant: The Development and Destruction of Pawnee Culture." Ph.D. diss., University of California, Los Angeles, 1991. 369 pp. This monumental study of his people by a major Pawnee scholar traces Pawnee culture and history up to the tribe's removal from Nebraska beginning in 1874. Every aspect of tribal life is explored in this excellent dissertation. The extensive bibliography leads researchers to many of the best sources for Pawnee history and culture.

134. ———. "Pawnee Removal: A Study of Pawnee-White Relations in Nebraska." Master's thesis, University of California, Los Angeles, 1985. 127 pp. Most historians argue that Sioux raids were the primary reason for the Pawnees choosing to leave Nebraska to relocate in Indian Territory. In this provocative thesis, Pawnee historian Riding In refutes this popular theory, stating that the Pawnees considered the Sioux merely an annoyance, and argues instead that it was pressure from whites—hostile settlers, buffalo hunters, timber thieves, even the Nebraska state government—that made removal inevitable. This is an excellent account of Pawnee removal from an Indian standpoint.

135. Rogers, Melvin P. "A History of the Pawnee Indians." Master's thesis, Oklahoma A&M University, 1940. 58 pp.

136. Sheldon, Addison E. *Nebraska: The Land and the People.* 3 vols. Chicago: Lewis Publishing Co., 1931. The chapter in Volume 1 on Nebraska Indians during the period of white contact contains a lengthy essay on Pawnee history and culture. Other chapters in this volume discuss Asa T. Hill and his connection to the Pike-Pawnee village and the work of Samuel Allis and John Dunbar, missionaries to the Pawnees. Volumes 2 and 3 are primarily biographical sketches of prominent white Nebraskans.

137. Shine, Michael A. "The Nebraska Aborigines as They Appeared in the Eighteenth Century." Lincoln: Nebraska Academy of Science, Nebraska History and Ethnology Series, Vol. IX, No. 1, 1914. 22 pp. Divided into twenty-five year periods, the paper is basically a list of facts taken from historical society collections, a few manuscripts, and several secondary sources. There is no new or unusual information here, but this printed version does include the 1812 Perrin du Lac map of the Nebraska region and a short opening essay on early Nebraska maps and map makers.

138. Shirley, Glenn. *Pawnee Bill: A Biography of Gordon W. Lillie*. Albuquerque: University of New Mexico Press, 1958. Reprint. Lincoln: University of Nebraska Press, 1969. 256 pp. The life story of Buffalo Bill Cody's sometime rival and sometime partner. Although this is a biography of the white entrepreneur whose wild west show featured Pawnee Indians, it is also a good portrait of the Pawnees themselves in the latter part of the 19th century. Also focuses on Major Frank North, leader of the Pawnee Scouts.

139. Smith, David Z. "Description of the Manners and Customs of the Pawnee Indians." *Moravian Church Miscellany* 3 (March 1852): 86–94. Brother Smith visited the Pawnees at a time when they were nearly destitute, and he expresses pity for the Indians, especially the women. This is an excellent description of Pawnee villages, lodges, farms, and methods of storing food. Smith was delighted to see that the Pawnees did not allow liquor into their villages.

140. "Special Edition, Souvenir Issue." *Genoa (Nebraska) Leader-Times*, 23 April 1997. 26 pp. This special edition was published to commemorate the 140th anniversary of the founding of the town of Genoa and the 150th anniversary of the Mormon Trail. The village of Genoa was founded by Mormons, but when it was discovered that the settlement was within the boundaries of the new Pawnee Reservation, the government asked the Mormons to move on, and Genoa became the site of the Pawnee Agency. Much of this issue is devoted to the United States Indian Industrial School, which evolved from the Pawnee Indian School of the reservation period. Includes photos of historical markers and the memorial to the 403 Pawnees reburied in Genoa in 1990.

141. Stearn, E. Wagner, and Allen E. Stearn. *The Effect of Smallpox on the Destiny of the Amerindian*. Boston: Bruce Humphries, Inc., 1945. 153 pp. The Pawnees receive only brief mentions in this classic study of

disease among American Indians, but conditions described among other tribes would pertain to the Pawnees as well.

142. Steinauer, Gerry. "The Loups: Lifeblood of Central Nebraska." *NE-BRASKAland* 76 (June 1998): 24–33. Although an environmental article and not specifically about the Pawnees, this piece does include a brief section on the Skidi settlements along the Loup River, which the Pawnees called *Its Kari Kitsu*, or "Plenty Potatoes River."

143. Stirling, Matthew W. "Indians of Our Western Plains." *National Geographic* 86 (July 1944): 73–108. Generalized coverage of Plains Indians that includes a version of the Morning Star Ceremony and Petalesharo's daring rescue and a photo of the Pawnee star chart. This article does contain errors.

144. Sturtevant, William C., general ed. *Handbook of North American Indians.* 20 vols. Washington, D.C.: Government Printing Office, 2001. This long-awaited replacement for Hodge's original handbook, published over 90 years ago, is expanded and updated, with essays by leading scholars on every aspect of North American Indian history and culture. Volume 13, Part 1 (Plains) contains an excellent 32-page chapter on the Pawnees by Douglas R. Parks, who includes a bibliographical essay directing readers to many of the most important Pawnee sources. Altogether, the index to the Plains volume has one-half page of references to the Pawnees. Researchers will also want to consult Volume 17, which is devoted entirely to Indian languages. References to the Caddoan language group and the Skidi and South Band dialects abound. For a longer summary of this volume, see Terry L. Steinacher's review in *Nebraska History* 83 (Summer 2002): 103.

145. Swanton, John R. *The Indian Tribes of North America.* Bureau of American Ethnology Bulletin No. 145. Washington, D.C.: Government Printing Office, 1952. 726 pp. Gives a two-page portrait of the Pawnees—their bands, their history and treaties, their population at different times, and places named for the tribe. Also lists names by which the Pawnees were known to other tribes.

146. "Toward Plains Caddoan Origins: A Symposium." *Nebraska History* 60 (Summer 1979): 131–293. A special issue of *Nebraska History* devoted to Plains Caddoan peoples. Along with an introduction by noted Plains archaeologist Waldo R. Wedel, this volume contains the following articles: "An Archaeological View of Pawnee Origins," by

Roger T. Grange, Jr.; "The Southwestern Periphery of the Plains Caddoan Area," by Christopher Lintz; "The Ethnohistorical Approach to Plains Caddoan Origins," by Mildred M. Wedel; "The Northern Caddoan Languages: Their Subgrouping and Time Depths," by Douglas R. Parks; "Bands and Villages of the Arikara and Pawnee," also by Parks; "Mythology and Folklore: Their Possible Use in the Study of Plains Caddoan Origins," by Martha R. Blaine; "Plains Caddoan Relationships: The View from Craniometry and Mortuary Analysis," by Douglas H. Ubelaker and Richard L. Jantz; "Caddoan Kinship Systems," by Alexander Lesser; and "Some Reflections on Plains Caddoan Origins," by Waldo R. Wedel. All researchers on the Pawnees should consult this important publication and its articles by noted Plains scholars.

147. Turner, Katherine C. *Red Men Calling on the Great White Father.* Norman: University of Oklahoma Press, 1951. 235 pp. This is not so much a history of entire Indian delegations to Washington as a series of profiles of individual Indians from each group who came to visit the presidents. The featured Pawnee delegation is the group who visited the nation's capital in 1821–1822, and which had among its delegates the young warrior Petalesharo of Morning Star Ceremony fame. The chapter on Petalesharo includes a romantic retelling of the daring 1817 rescue and the presentation of a medal by students from Miss White's Female Seminary. Despite its ethnocentricity and florid style, this is an entertaining account of the 1821 Pawnee visit to President Monroe. For a more authoritative account, see Herman J. Viola's *Diplomats in Buckskins* [149].

148. Tyson, Carl N. *The Pawnee People.* Phoenix: Indian Tribal Series, 1976. 105 pp. A volume in a series intended for a general audience, this Pawnee history offers no new information, but it does include a short section on the modern Pawnees. There are no footnotes and no bibliography—major shortcomings.

149. Viola, Herman J. *Diplomats in Buckskins: A History of Indian Delegations in Washington City.* Washington, D.C.: Smithsonian Institution Press, 1981. 233 pp. This is the definitive account of the many Indian delegations that visited Washington, primarily in the nineteenth century. Not merely a record of the "who" and "when" of delegations, it includes chapters on Indian social life in Washington, health problems of Indian ambassadors, and the impact of these Indian visitors on American arts and science, with emphasis on paint-

ings and photographs. An epilogue covering twentieth-century delegations brings the story up to the late 1970s. The Pawnees are mentioned numerous times, and the 1821 delegation led by Benjamin O'Fallon receives considerable coverage. Beautifully written and meticulously researched, this is an invaluable resource on Indian relations with the United States government.

150. ———. "Invitation to Washington—A Bid for Peace." *American West* 9 (January 1972): 18–31. A delightful account of the 1821 Indian delegation brought to the nation's capital by agent Benjamin O'Fallon. The Pawnee representatives dominated this large delegation. Artist Charles Bird King immortalized some of the members of this group on canvas, and seven of his paintings are reproduced in color in this essay. This material, minus the color reproductions, is included in Viola's excellent *Diplomats in Buckskins* [149].

151. Walters, Anna Lee. *Talking Indian*. Ithaca, New York: Firebrand Books, 1992. 222 pp. This gracefully written volume—part memoir, part oral history, and part folklore—reveals nothing new for the serious researcher, but it does give the reader a feel for the Pawnee heritage. The author, who is of Pawnee and Otoe descent, talks about her ancestors and how important her mixed Indian heritage has always been to her. Highlights of the book are an interesting and somewhat amusing rare glimpse of aging Pawnee scouts and a moving short chapter about a modern Indian couple searching for an ancient buffalo jump. When they find it, they also rediscover their roots.

152. Watkins, Albert. "Notes on the Early History of the Nebraska Country." Lincoln: *Publications of the Nebraska State Historical Society*, Vol. 20, 1922. 400 pp. These excerpts from accounts in early Missouri newspapers, presented in chronological order, deal mostly with the fur trade, the Oregon Trail, and Indian-white hostilities between 1808 and 1861. The Pawnees receive considerable attention: their population in 1809, a description of their villages along the Loup Fork, and an account of a deadly Pawnee-Sioux skirmish in the 1840s are reported. Also included is an account of Pawnee migrations due to the Sioux threat, and a brief description of the work of missionaries Allis and Dunbar.

153. Wedel, Waldo R. "Environment and Native Subsistence Economies in the Central Great Plains." *Smithsonian Miscellaneous Collections*, vol. 101, no. 3, 1942. 29 pp. Article concludes that early native peoples in Nebraska and Kansas, including the Pawnees, faced the same

types of climate extremes endured by later white farmers and reacted to them in much the same way, abandoning their farms when droughts became too severe or when insects, especially grasshoppers, destroyed their crops.

154. Weltfish, Gene. *The Lost Universe: Pawnee Life and Culture*. New York: Basic Books, 1965. Reprint. Lincoln: University of Nebraska Press, 1977. 506 pp. Although somewhat fictionalized, this is one of the most important accounts of Pawnee life in the mid-nineteenth century. Thoroughly researched, with much information taken from the Pawnees themselves, the book follows the Pawnee people during one year of their Nebraska reservation period. Hunting, planting, earth lodge construction, cultural events, including the Morning Star sacrifice, are all parts of this study. This book receives a generally favorable review in *Chronicles of Oklahoma* 43 (Autumn 1965): 352–53.

155. ———. "The Plains Indians: Their Continuity in History and Their Indian Identity." In *North American Indians in Historical Perspective*, edited by Eleanor Burke Leacock and Nancy Oestreich Lurie, 200–227. Prospect Heights, Illinois: Waveland Press, Inc., 1971. Weltfish briefly describes the Pawnee pipe ceremony and devotes four pages to the Skidi Morning Star Ceremony and the conflict surrounding human sacrifice.

156. Wheat, Carl I. *Mapping the Transmississippi West, 1540–1861*. 6 vols. San Francisco: The Institute of Historical Geography, 1957. This marvelous map collection actually covers the period to 1884, and later volumes include railroad maps, military charts, and routes to the gold fields. But for students of the Pawnees, the earlier maps, which mention the Pawnees by various names, are the most valuable. Both French and Spanish maps are reproduced, and the charts made by nearly all major exploring parties from 1717 to 1844 are included. Of special interest would be plates 98, 101, 129, 243, 255, 259, 315, 316, 353, 398, 401, 405, 417, 421, 438, and 482, all of which locate Pawnee villages or hunting grounds.

157. White, Richard. *The Roots of Dependency: Subsistence, Environment, and Social Change among the Choctaws, Pawnees, and Navajos*. Lincoln: University of Nebraska Press, 1983. 433 pp. Beautifully written and well researched, the third of this work devoted to the Pawnees approaches their culture from several disciplines—anthropology, ecology, and history. The author explains in lively prose how these re-

markable people survived for so long. But he also argues that the combined loss of all that made the Pawnees strong—the buffalo, their agriculture, their independence, and their ability to overcome adversity—led to their decline. A very useful source.

158. Wishart, David J. "The Old Villagers: The Pawnee." *NEBRASKAland* 62 (January–February 1984): 10–13, 15. Beautifully written account of Pawnee history from the 1820s to the 1857 treaty providing for their relocation to their reservation in modern-day Nance County, Nebraska. Includes descriptions of five Pawnee sacred sites.

159. ———. *An Unspeakable Sadness: The Dispossession of the Nebraska Indians.* Lincoln: University of Nebraska Press, 1994. 309 pp. This award-winning study of the fates of Nebraska Indians by an historical geographer is superbly done. The entire history of the Pawnees in Nebraska is interwoven with the histories of the Omahas, Poncas, and Otoe-Missourias. Excellent maps keep all the events in geographical context. An outstanding source that no student of the Pawnees should overlook.

160. Wissler, Clark. *Indians of the United States: Four Centuries of Their History and Culture.* Garden City, New York: Doubleday, 1949. 383 pp. In this dated survey, the entire brief chapter on the Caddoan family is devoted to the Pawnees and superficial coverage of their religion and village life. Does clear up the confusion regarding two Pawnee chiefs named Petalesharo, and explains each man's importance.

161. ———. "The Influence of the Horse in the Development of Plains Culture." *American Anthropologist,* n.s. 16 (January–March 1914): 1–25. Fine article explaining the distribution of horses to Indians throughout the Plains. Though not specifically concerned with the Pawnees, Wissler does mention them on several occasions. He states that horses were first mentioned in connection with the Pawnees in 1704, but they must have been mounted before then, since there is evidence of horse raiding by Pawnees in the early 1600s.

162. Zeller, Gertrude Nothstine. "History of the Pawnee Indians." Master's Thesis, Ohio State University, 1932. 98 pp. Neither well-written nor original, this thesis is at times judgmental and ethnocentric. Zeller attempts to cover a huge span of time in a few pages. There are more recent and much better studies of Pawnee history available to researchers.

3
Archaeology and Anthropology

163. "Archaeologists Examine Site of Indian Village in Reservoir Area." *Junction City (Kansas) Union*, 16 September 1967. Archaeology Department Clippings File, vol. 1, 1966–1981, 7–9. Kansas State Historical Society. Interest in this overlooked Indian village near Junction City, Kansas, revived with the building of the Milford Reservoir. State archaeologists believed it was a Pawnee village, and it would be the southernmost Pawnee site ever discovered.

164. Batie, Steve. "We Dig Herby." *NEBRASKAland* 48 (December 1970): 52–53. Tasteless, disrespectful article about two young men's discovery of a Pawnee skeleton at the Palmer archaeological site, known locally as "Indian Hill." The young men nicknamed the deceased Pawnee "Herby," wrote a school paper about their find, and took the skeleton to the University of Nebraska. A letter to the editor of *NEBRASKAland* was extremely critical of this "archaeological dig" and the tone of the article. See "Hip History." *NEBRASKAland* 49 (March 1971): 3,12.

165. Bengston, B. E. "An Ancient Village of the Grand Pawnee." *Nebraska History* 14 (April–June 1933): 124–29. Highly speculative article describing what is likely the site of a Pawnee village near the eastern boundary of Hamilton County, Nebraska, near present-day Hordville. A map of the site is included. This article and map are also part of MS 0710 at the Nebraska State Historical Society, where they appear with the title "A Small Historic Spot in Hamilton County."

166. Blackman, Elmer E. "Exploration of Aboriginal Remains in the Loup Valley." *Nebraska History* 7 (1924): 1–8. Based on the preliminary investigation of the Burkett Site in Nance County, Blackman determined that this was the site of the first permanent Skidi Pawnee village in Nebraska. He also asserts that this Loup River village was the legendary "Harahey" of Coronado fame.

167. Blakeslee, Donald J. "Toward a Cultural Understanding of Human Microevolution on the Great Plains." *Plains Anthropologist* 26 (November 1981): 93–106. Explains gene flow among Plains tribes by using as models trade systems, warfare, language, and material culture.

168. Blakeslee, Donald J., and Robert K. Blasing. "Indian Trails in the Central Plains." *Plains Anthropologist* 33 (February 1988): 17–25. Discusses the sites and landmarks associated with the Flint Hills and Pawnee trails in Kansas and Nebraska. Among the sites are permanent villages, campsites, cairns, burials, petroglyphs, and sacred Pawnee animal lodges. Includes a map showing many of the sites located in Kansas.

169. Blasing, Robert K. "Consultation Between the Bureau of Reclamation and the Pawnee Tribe." *Plains Anthropologist* 44, Memoir 31 (1999): 13–24. Thoughtful article regarding the Fullerton Canal and its impact on Pawnee historic sites and burials in Nance County, Nebraska. Every step of the way, the Bureau of Reclamation consulted with the Pawnee tribe. This is a case study in cooperation between a government entity and Native Americans. The bibliography includes a number of reports on the project available only through the Bureau of Reclamation.

170. ———. "Finding of Adverse Affect for the Fullerton Canal and Cultural Resource Protection Plan for the Palmer Site National Historic Landmark," 1991.17 pp. Report on file at the Bureau of Reclamation, Grand Island, Nebraska. This fascinating report explains that the Fullerton Canal, as planned, would flow across the Palmer Site in Nance County, Nebraska, an historic Pawnee village site that is on the National Register of Historic Places. The report presents four alternate canal routes and explains the impact of each one. Also included is the procedure that would be followed should Indian remains be disturbed. As in all Bureau of Reclamation documents containing sensitive site data, all maps are removed before photocopies are made.

171. Carlson, Gayle F., and Richard E. Jensen. *Archaeological Salvage and Survey in Nebraska: Highway Archaeological and Historical Salvage*

Investigations in Nebraska, 1965 to 1968. Nebraska State Historical Society Publications in Anthropology, No. 5. Lincoln: Nebraska State Historical Society, 1973. 240 pp. This report, a combined effort of the Nebraska State Historical Society and the Nebraska Department of Roads, was the result of a four-year survey of historic sites that may have been in the path of highway construction. Among the many findings are the results of investigations at Site 25NC20 (the Genoa Site), which revealed a number of Pawnee burials that had been disturbed by earthmoving equipment. The report also lists artifacts, both Indian and European, found at the site. Also thoroughly explained are excavations at the Linwood Site (25BU1), a former large Pawnee village on the south side of Skull Creek, in northeastern Butler County. The methods of excavation are explained, and drawings indicate where bones and artifacts were located. Although these are technical reports, they are clearly written and easy to understand.

172. Champe, John L. *Ash Hollow Cave: A Study of Stratographic Sequence in the Central Great Plains.* University of Nebraska Studies, n.s., no. 1. Lincoln: University of Nebraska Press, 1946. Reprint Lincoln, Nebraska: J&L Reprint Company, 1976. 130 pp. Includes a section on Pawnee village sites along Skull Creek in modern Butler County, and a brief description of the Bellwood Site north of David City, where a Pawnee village stood in about 1800. The western part of the Bellwood Site appears to be an earlier village related to the Loup River focus.

173. ———. "The Sweetwater Culture Complex." In *Chapters in Nebraska Archaeology,* vol. 1, no. 3. Lincoln: University of Nebraska, 1936, 253–99. After a careful excavation and examination of three houses and eight cache pits, archaeologist Champe tentatively identified this complex near Sweetwater, in southern Sherman County, Nebraska, as part of the Loup River focus of the Upper Republican culture.

174. Connelley, William E. "Notes on the Early Indian Occupancy of the Great Plains." *Collections of the Kansas State Historical Society,* vol. 14 (1915–1918), 438–70. Topeka: Kansas State Historical Society, 1918. Contains a rather fanciful account of Pawnee migrations onto the Plains and exaggerates the boundaries of their territory.

175. ———. "Origin of the Name of Topeka." *Collections of the Kansas State Historical Society,* vol. 17 (1926–1928). Topeka: Kansas State Historical Society, 1928, 589–93. Locates the four Pawnee bands in

the early 1800s, and argues that the name "Topeka" is an anglicized version of "Toppage," the southernmost of the Pawnee bands.

176. "Digging to Know Why Pawnees Left." *Kansas City Star*, 22 August 1965. Archaeology in Kansas Clippings, vol. 3, 209–212. Kansas State Historical Society. Interesting article about the archaeological crew composed of high school and college students who excavated the earth lodges at the Republic, Kansas Pawnee Indian village, under the supervision of State Archaeologist Thomas Witty. Includes a lovely description of the land around the old Indian village.

177. Duncan, Kunigunde. "Burial Pit, Village Remains Support Legend that Traces Customs to Ancient Israel." *Wichita (Kansas) Eagle Magazine*, 30 March 1958. Archaeology in Kansas Clippings, vol. 3, 153–54. Kansas State Historical Society. A highly speculative article tying the skeletons and burial practices at the Salina, Kansas, "burial pit" to ancient Druids and ultimately, back to biblical times. Cites Mark E. Zimmerman's theory that there is a link between the Pawnees and ancient Israelites [244], [245].

178. Dunlevy, Marion L. "Comparison of Cultural Manifestations of the Burkett and the Gray-Wolfe Sites." In *Chapters in Nebraska Archaeology*, vol. 1, no. 2. Lincoln: University of Nebraska, 1936, 151–247. In 1931, Dunlevy investigated the Burkett site in Nance County near Genoa, and the Gray-Wolfe sites in Colfax County, near present-day Schuyler, and by studying the cultural remains of the sites found that they are nearly identical. Two houses and five mounds were excavated at the Burkett site and two widely separated houses were studied at the Gray-Wolfe location. After extensive comparisons and analysis, especially of pottery remains, Dunlevy reached the conclusion that the two sites are more likely upper Mississippian than protohistoric Pawnee. Others disagree.

179. Echo-Hawk, Roger C. "Ancient Pawnee History: A Brief Survey of Caddoan Traditional Evidence Regarding Pawnee Ancestry in the Central Plains." Report submitted to the Native American Rights Fund, Boulder, Colorado, 1990.

180. ———. "At The Edge of the Desert of Multicolored Turtles." In *The Stobaco Site: A Mid-Eighteenth Century Skidi Pawnee Town on the Loup River*, edited by Steven R. Holen and John K. Peterson, 14–49. Nebraska Archaeological Survey Technical Report 95-01.

Lincoln: University of Nebraska State Museum, 1995. In his meticulously researched essay, Echo-Hawk traces the migrations of the Pawnee bands from c. 1000 A. D. to the nineteenth century. Calling on the works of a host of scholars, he explains the locations of the Skidi and the South Bands through history. Any researcher delving into the relationships among the Pawnee bands and their village sites should consult this work, which is available only through the Bureau of Reclamation as part of the larger study on the Stobaco Site [195].

181. ———. "Working Together—Exploring Ancient Worlds." *Society for American Archaeology Bulletin* 11 (September–October 1993): 5–6. Not about the Pawnees, but written by a Pawnee scholar, this essay calls for greater cooperation between the archaeological community and Native Americans in order to properly present ancient Indian history. Reprints a short essay designed to accompany a Denver art project honoring Native Americans of Colorado. The essay was criticized by both Indians and archaeologists—for different reasons.

182. Garret, John W. "The Birdwood Culture of the West-Central Plains." *American Antiquity* 31 (July 1965): 74–80. A study based on scattered literary references and investigations of about four decades ago. The Birdwood culture of the west-central Plains, especially west-central Nebraska, is dated about 1600 A. D., and was located along river banks. A later study [222] identifies one site previously associated with Birdwood culture as a Pawnee hunting camp of the Lower Loup phase.

183. Gilmore, Melvin R. "Some Place Names in Nebraska." *Publications of the Nebraska State Historical Society*, vol. 19. Lincoln: Nebraska State Historical Society, 1919, 130–39. Gilmore points out numerous rivers, streams, and villages whose names were derived from Indian words. Among the locations with connections to the Pawnees are the town of Leshara in Saunders County, the Loup and Republican rivers, and the Niobrara River, whose Pawnee name means, appropriately, "rapid river."

184. Grange, Roger T., Jr. "Ceramic Relationships in the Central Plains." Ph.D. diss., University of Arizona, 1962. 399 pp. This lengthy, technical, and meticulously researched dissertation describes and identifies all of the known Lower Loup focus and historic Pawnee sites and compares the pottery remains found at these sites to explore six hypotheses: (1) sites of the Lower Loup focus represent the protohistoric

Pawnees; (2) Lower Loup and Pawnee pottery changed over time; (3) it is possible to date the sequence of sites by using ceramic evidence; (4) it may be possible to detect variations in pottery made by different Pawnee bands; (5) Lower Loup focus sites may be closely related to only one Pawnee band—the Skidi; and (6) the Lower Loup focus may be related to other groups as well as the historic Pawnees. Maps locate all of the sites mentioned, and tables identify each site, and in the case of historic sites, include band affiliation.

185. ———. "Dating Pawnee Sites by the Ceramic Formula Method." *World Archaeology* 15 (1984): 274–93. Highly technical study explaining how Pawnee sites can be dated by examining pottery remains and matching them to established usage periods for that particular type of pottery. Includes a large number of charts and tables with data from various Pawnee sites.

186. ———. *Pawnee and Lower Loup Pottery*. Nebraska State Historical Society Publications in Anthropology, no. 3. Lincoln: Nebraska State Historical Society, 1968. 235 pp. This is a revised version of Grange's doctoral dissertation at the University of Arizona [184].

187. Grier, Bob. "Ash Hollow State Historical Park." *NEBRASKAland* 58 (June 1980): 24–35. Primarily a travel article, this essay also discusses John L. Champe's archaeological work at Ash Hollow [172] and includes a section on the battle between the Pawnees and the Sioux that took place there in 1835.

188. Gunnerson, James H. "The Ancient Ones." *NEBRASKAland* 62 (January–February 1984): 45–51. Traces the periods of Indian occupation of Nebraska from c. 1000 B. C. to 1800 A. D., including Pawnees. Chart shows house floor types from the different periods.

189. Hartley, R. J. "Ethnohistorical Background: The Calamus and Davis Creek Projects, Nebraska, Appendix A, Section 5." In *Cultural and Paleontological Resource Investigations within the Calamus and Davis Creek Reservoir Areas, Nebraska*. Lincoln: University of Nebraska Department of Anthropology, Division of Archaeological Research, Technical Report no. 80-04, 1981.

190. Holen, Steven R. "Anthropology: The Native American Occupation of the Sand Hills." In *An Atlas of the Sand Hills*, edited by Ann Bleed and Charles Flowerday, 201–17. Resource Atlas 5, Conservation and Survey Division. Lincoln: University of Nebraska, 1998. Drawing on early

French and Spanish accounts, as well as later American descriptions, this highly technical essay shows that the Pawnees occupied the eastern half of the Sand Hills of Nebraska as early as the late 1600s. Also points out the intense inter-tribal warfare over control of this buffalo-rich area. Missionary accounts state that the Pawnees hunted in the Sand Hills in the summer, but usually restricted their winter hunts to the area around the forks of the Platte River. Nicely illustrated, including a French map of Pawnee villages, dated 1718.

191. ———. "Bison Hunting Territories and Lithic Acquisition Among the Pawnee: An Ethnohistoric and Archaeological Study." In *Raw Material Economics Among Prehistoric Hunter-Gatherers*, edited by Anta Montet-White and Steven Holen, 399–411. Lawrence: University of Kansas Publications in Anthropology 19, 1991. Analysis of the Gray Site (probably a Grand Pawnee village) and the Burkett Site (likely a Skidi village) shows that the stone used for tools and weapons was acquired at considerable distance from the established Pawnee villages. Tracing the bison-hunting ranges of each group, Holen theorizes that the Pawnees gathered enough stone while on their bison hunts to meet their needs until the next hunting season. Stone gathering patterns changed as metal tools replaced stone ones, and as rival tribes disturbed Pawnee hunting patterns. Excellent maps illustrate the author's arguments.

192. ———. "Chipped   Stone   Tools."   *NEBRASKAland*   72 (January–February 1994): 124. This essay also appears in *Nebraska History* 75 (Spring 1994) with the same pagination. The early eighteenth-century Pawnees lived in an area with very little stone for tools. Investigations reveal that the Pawnees acquired most of their stone from the Flint Hills in east-central Kansas or along the Republican River in south-central Nebraska. These areas were popular Pawnee hunting grounds, and the bands gathered their stone for tools while in their semi-annual hunts, thus saving trips.

193. ———. "Lower Loup Lithic Procurement Strategy at the Gray Site, 25CX1." Master's thesis, University of Nebraska, 1983. 126 pp. Stone tools were an integral part of subsistence for the protohistoric Pawnees. This well-researched thesis discusses the ways in which the people of the Gray Site in east-central Nebraska obtained stone for tools. Holen tested four hypotheses, three of which he rejected. First, the quality of the stone did not determine where it was gathered. Sec-

ond, the Pawnees did not acquire their stone from the closest source; and third, very little lithic material was acquired through trade. The fourth scenario, and the most likely one, is that the Pawnees combined lithic procurement with bison hunting. For instance, the proto-Skidis used a lot of Republican River jasper, stone that was available in the southern part of their bison-hunting range.

194. Holen, Steven R., and Danial R. Watson. "Skidi-French Interaction: Evidence from the Stobaco Site." In *The Stobaco Site: A Mid-Eighteenth Century Skidi Pawnee Town on the Loup River,* edited by Steven R. Holen and John K. Peterson, 211–217. Nebraska Archaeological Survey Technical Report 95-01. Lincoln: University of Nebraska State Museum, 1995. French traders probably arrived in Skidi settlements like the Stobaco Site between 1680 and 1700 A. D. This essay surveys the literature on Franco-Skidi contact and assesses the impact on the Pawnees of this economic interaction. Archaeological evidence from this site indicates that the Pawnees traded with the French for brass pots, copper bracelets, mirrors, glass beads, gunflints, and even pipestone pipes of French manufacture.

195. Holen, Steven R., and John K. Peterson, eds. *The Stobaco Site: A Mid-Eighteenth Century Pawnee Town on the Loup River.* Nebraska Archaeological Survey Technical Report 95-01. Lincoln: University of Nebraska State Museum, 1995. 219 pp. This report, submitted to the U. S. Bureau of Reclamation, represents investigations done in connection with the Fullerton Canal irrigation Project to determine the site's eligibility for inclusion in the National Register of Historic Places and analyzes every aspect of this Skidi village site in present Howard County, Nebraska—ceramic and lithic finds, faunal remains, Euroamerican trade items, and the topography of the site. Experts believe the Stobaco Site may be the "missing link" between the Lower Loup (protohistoric Pawnee) focus and historic Pawnee villages. Maps and charts of a sensitive nature have been removed from this report.

196. Hudson, LuAnn. "Changes in Pawnee Lithic Economy in the Eighteenth and Nineteenth Centuries." Master's thesis, University of Iowa, 1982. 91 pp. Analysis of stone tools found at the Schuyler, Barcal, and Linwood sites in central Nebraska indicates that stone tool quality, quantity, and functions changed with the introduction of metal tools. There were now fewer stone implements, and it appeared

that the Pawnees were learning to manufacture and even repair metal tools. As it became more dangerous for the Pawnees to hunt bison in the Republican River valley, they lost access to the jasper that they had harvested there for many years. But with more Euro-American cutting tools available, high lithic quality was not as important.

197. ———. "Protohistoric Pawnee Lithic Economy." *Plains Anthropologist* 38 (November 1993): 265–77. Illustrates changes in early Pawnee material culture as European trade goods began to replace native stone tools. Stone tools took on a more symbolic function, and there was a change in the types of stone used in tool manufacturing.

198. Hughes, David T. "Three Sites on the Fullerton Canal: Archaeological Investigations in Central Nebraska by the Wichita State University, 1991." Report on file at the U.S. Bureau of Reclamation, Grand Island, Nebraska, 1992. In 1991, a team from Wichita State University investigated three sites lying in the path of construction of the Fullerton Canal to see if there were important Indian artifacts or burials there. Reports such as this are of a very sensitive nature, and often are missing maps and charts or have words blacked out.

199. Hughes, Jack Thomas. *Prehistory of the Caddoan-Speaking Tribes (Caddoan Indians III)*. New York: Garland Publishing, Inc., 1974. 411 pp. The last of three reports on the Pawnee and related tribes presented to the Indian Claims Commission. The report includes historical, traditional, linguistic, physical, ethnological, and archaeological evidence for Pawnee occupation of their claim area. This very useful source has an extensive bibliography, a time line for each group, plus an easily understood section comparing all aspects of the Caddoan tribes.

200. Jantz, Richard. L., D. W. Owsley, and P. Willey. "Craniometric Variation in the Northern and Central Plains." *Plains Anthropologist* 26 (November 1981): 19–29. A highly technical study of skulls from one prehistoric group and five historic Plains tribes, including the Pawnees. By comparing crania from a number of archaeological sites, the authors attempt to classify the skulls as to type. The article points out that many crania have been misclassified. Contains numerous charts and tables showing the results of this investigation.

201. "Kansan Finds Lost Indian Village—Fort." *Wichita (Kansas) Eagle & Beacon*, 15 January 1967. Archaeology Clippings File, vol. 1,

1966–1981, 5–6. Kansas State Historical Society. Reports the discovery of a second Pawnee earth lodge village in Kansas, this one near Junction City. The other, better-known village is near Republic. Preliminary reports date the village to the 1860s.

201a. "Emergence of Historic Tribes: Lower Loup Culture." *nebraskastudies. org.* Brief article explains the Lower Loup Culture connection to historic Pawnees and describes the Lower Loup lifestyle. Also included are an excellent image of a decorated artifact and a link to a map of protohistoric Pawnee cultures in Nebraska.

202. Ludwickson, John. "Central Plains Tradition Settlements in the Loup River Basin: The Loup River Phase." In *The Central Plains Tradition: Internal Development and External Relationships*, edited by Donald J. Blakeslee, 94–108. Iowa City, Iowa: Office of the State Archaeologist, report no. 11, 1978. Argues that the Loup River Phase was the intermediary between the Upper Republican Phase and the Lower Loup Phase protohistoric Pawnees. Explains that when Pawnee ancestors abandoned Upper Republican Phase villages because of drought, they likely migrated northward to the Loup River basin near present-day Fullerton, Nebraska.

203. ——. "Historic Indian Tribes: Ethnology and Archaeology." *NEBRASKAland* 72 (January–February 1994): 134–45. This excellent overview also appears in *Nebraska History* 75, no. 1 (Spring 1994). Gives a general history, then details on individual Nebraska tribes. Among the Pawnee topics are early villages, a protohistoric bison hunting camp in present-day Custer County, and the Pike-Pawnee village near Red Cloud. Beautifully illustrated with color photos. Most of the artifacts pictured are of Pawnee origin.

204. ——. "The Loup River Phase and the Origins of Pawnee Culture." Master's thesis, University of Nebraska, 1975. 154 pp. A highly specialized study that uses radiocarbon dating, ceramic trends, and material culture contents to trace the evolution of the Pawnee people. The study presents the hypotheses of two anthropological schools—one that argues that the early people of the Upper Republican River valley migrated to the panhandle region of Oklahoma and Texas, and one that argues that these people moved north and east to the Lower Loup River region and became the Pawnees and Arikaras. After comparing the data, Ludwickson concludes that the Republican to Loup River theory is correct.

205. Lydick, Beverly J. "Area Site Yields Ancient Campsite." *Fremont (Nebraska) Tribune*, 25 April 2002, 1–2. In 2002, road crews discovered the remains of a seventeenth-century Pawnee campsite, which was identified by food caches found there. Apparently, the same site later became an Otoe Indian burial ground. The remains of an Otoe child were also found, along with two skeletons believed to be of white trappers. This discovery was handled well. The Pawnee and Otoe tribes were notified immediately of the find.

206. McWilliams, K. Richard. "Investigation of the Popular History of the Arikara." In *Pathways to Plains Prehistory: Anthropological Perspectives of Plains Natives and Their Pasts*, edited by Don G. Wyckoff and Jack L. Hofman, 163–72. Oklahoma Anthropological Society, Memoir 3. The Cross Timbers Heritage Association, Contribution 1. Duncan, Oklahoma: Cross Timbers Press, 1982. A highly technical study of skulls from archaeological digs at various sites in Nebraska, South Dakota, and Missouri. The title is somewhat misleading; the bulk of the study attempts to prove that the Skidi Pawnees were of different origins than the Pawnee south bands.

207. Montgomery, Robert Lynn. "A Paleodemographic Comparison of a Protohistoric Pawnee Site (25NC3) with a Historic Pawnee Site (25PK1)." Master's thesis, Louisiana State University, 1986. 155 pp. In this carefully researched thesis, Montgomery analyzed the skeletal remains of 129 Pawnees from burials at the Wright Site, a protohistoric Lower Loup Pawnee village located just southwest of present-day Genoa, Nebraska, and the Clarks Site, a nineteenth-century Grand Pawnee village along the Platte River. After careful analysis, it was determined that the Wright location was the site of a massacre, but the study of the Clarks skeletons was inconclusive. It appears that the Pawnees at the Wright Site were in overall better health than those at Clarks, which was occupied during what the author refers to as a "period of decline." All of the data is carefully reproduced in maps, charts, and graphs.

208. O'Brien, Patricia J. *Archaeology in Kansas*. University of Kansas Museum of Natural History Public Education Series, no. 9. Lawrence: University of Kansas, 1984. 144 pp. On pages 69–72 is a brief but informative history of the Pawnee, focusing mainly on their residence in Kansas, which boasts two historic sites—the Bogan Site near Junction City and the preserved Pawnee Village in Republic County.

209. ———. "Evidence for the Antiquity of Women's Roles in Pawnee Society." *Plains Anthropologist* 36 (April 1991): 51–64. Based on findings at the C. C. Witt Site in Kansas, O'Brien asserts that male and female roles were defined as early as 1300 A. D. The burial mound at this site also revealed numerous arrowheads and the remains of a girl about twelve years old—evidence that a Morning Star Ceremony may have been performed there.

210. ———. "Prehistoric Evidence for Pawnee Cosmology." *American Anthropologist* 88 (October–December 1986): 939–46. Clearly written article which attempts to prove the antiquity of certain ideas associated with Pawnee cosmology. In excavating an earth lodge/burial complex of the Smoky Hill phase in Kansas, O'Brien discovered floral and faunal remains, evidence of an altar, and astronomical alignments indicating that this was the lodge of a Pawnee priest. Radiocarbon dating and other methods date this earth lodge at the C. C. Witt Site to about 1300 A. D., proving that Pawnee traditional cosmology existed before the historical period. Researchers in Pawnee material culture should consult this source.

211. O'Shea, John M. "Pawnee Archaeology." *Central Plains Archaeology* 1, no. 1 (1989): 49–107. Not merely limited to archaeology, this outstanding article is really a concise history of the Pawnee people, their ethnology, their settlement patterns, their sacred sites, and their material culture. This article is worth exploring just for the four-page history of investigations that pinpoints the locations of Pawnee sites and explains what excavations have been undertaken at each one. Contains nine pages of clear maps, charts, and tables that relate to the text.

212. ———. "A Simulation of Pawnee Site Development." In *Simulation Studies in Archaeology*, edited by Ian Hodder, 39–46. Cambridge: Cambridge University Press, 1978. Attempts to simulate the development and life span of Pawnee earth lodges, food caches, and other physical elements of a village by using available archaeological and ethnographical data. Results are illustrated by numerous charts and graphs.

213. ———. "Social Configuration and the Archaeological Study of Mortuary Practices: A Case Study." In *The Archaeology of Death*, edited by R. Chapman, I. Kinnes, and K. Randsborg, 39–52. New York: Cambridge University Press, 1981. Article analyzes mortuary practices at five Plains burial sites—two Pawnee, one Omaha, and two

Arikara. In discussing the Linwood Pawnee site, O'Shea notes that male and female bodies were oriented in different directions, that three clear rank levels were apparent within the burial complex, and that some incomplete skeletons were found buried separately. The Clarks Site burials revealed that most bodies faced north, and there were no separate burials of incomplete remains. Over time, the burials reflected changes in Pawnee society, with emphasis on changing social distinctions. Charts show these changes and indicate the age groups buried at each site.

214. O'Shea, John M., and Patricia S. Bridges. "The Sargent Site Ossuary (25CU28), Custer County, Nebraska." *Plains Anthropologist* 34 (February 1989): 7–21. Detailed analysis of a burial site containing at least twelve Indian crania discovered along the Middle Loup River in central Nebraska. Careful examination showed that these bones had been moved from the area where the deaths occurred. They were probably war victims removed from a battlefield and returned home for burial. Although the crania are not positively identified, the area where they were found was traditionally occupied by the Pawnees.

215. Peterson, John K. "Excavations at Three Burials at 25HW1, March 7 and 8, April 7 and 8, 1992." Report on File at the Bureau of Reclamation, Grand Island, Nebraska. 10 pp. In 1992, in preparation for the construction of the Fullerton Canal, experts from the University of Nebraska and the Bureau of Reclamation investigated three supposed Pawnee burials at the Palmer Site in Nance County. Two of the graves had been disturbed by pot hunters, but a third appeared to be intact. After consultation with representatives of the Pawnee Tribe, the Fullerton Canal route was changed and concrete caps were placed on all three burials. Soil was placed over the caps, and the area was reseeded after the completion of canal construction.

216. Peterson, John K., Danial R. Watson, and Amy Goedert. "A Pawnee Bone Grease Processing Area: Site 25HW75, Howard County, Nebraska." Technical Report 93-01. Lincoln: Nebraska Archaeological Survey, University of Nebraska State Museum, 1993. 21 pp. During excavation for the Fullerton Canal Project in north central Nebraska, a road grader uncovered a feature that was at first believed to be a Pawnee burial site. Analysis of the bones at the site showed them to be bison bones. This feature was a Pawnee bone grease processing area where marrow and grease were extracted from bison bones for use in

making pemmican and in tanning hides. Researchers will find this report difficult to obtain, and any text or maps that indicate the exact location of this feature will be either omitted or blacked out to protect the integrity of the site.

217. Reinhard, Karl J., and Karin L. Sandness. "Burial Investigations at 25HW1." Lincoln: University of Nebraska Department of Anthropology, 1992. 23 pp. This detailed report on three possible Pawnee burial sites near present-day Palmer, Nebraska was prepared for the Pawnee Tribal Council of Oklahoma. The researchers explain how they developed a profile of a skeleton from one of the burial sites. What they found in these burials is consistent with Pawnee mortuary traditions. Although this is a technical report, it is quite accessible for the non-expert.

218. Roper, Donna C. "Documentary Evidence for Changes in Protohistoric and Early Historic Pawnee Hunting Practices." *Plains Anthropologist* 37 (November 1992): 353–66. Article concludes that Pawnee seasonal hunts pre-dated the acquisition of horses, that these hunts occurred in both summer and winter, and that prior to horses, hunting camps were likely placed nearer kill sites. In addition, pressure from other tribes forced the Pawnees to expand their hunting ranges, especially in the early nineteenth century.

219. ———. *Historical Processes and the Development of Social Identity: An Evaluation of Pawnee Ancestry.* Washington, D.C.: Submitted to Repatriation Office, National Museum of Natural History, Smithsonian Institution, 1993.

220. ———. "John Dunbar's Journal of the 1834–5 Chaui Winter Hunt and Its Implications for Pawnee Archaeology." *Plains Anthropologist* 36 (August 1991): 193–214. The journal of John Dunbar, Presbyterian missionary to the Pawnees, is the earliest and best account of a Pawnee hunt. Using the journal as her source, Roper describes four stages of a hunt that can provide information for archaeologists—the route of the hunt, the number and duration of camps, the circumstances of encampment, and criteria for locating camps. This superb article is a must for researchers.

221. ———. "Lower Loup Phase Pottery in Great Bend Aspect Sites." *Plains Anthropologist* 45 (May 2000): 169–77. Article focuses on pottery from the Lower Loup Phase found at Great Bend aspect sites.

Indicates that from about 1575–1650 there was contact in the form of visitation and trade between the Pawnee South Bands (Lower Loup Phase) and the Wichita (Great Bend Phase).

222.   ——. "The Material Culture of 25DS21, A Lower Loup Hunting Camp in the Platte River Valley." *Central Plains Archaeology* 4, no. 1 (1994): 55–95. A very technical examination of a long-neglected Pawnee hunting camp of the Lower Loup Phase (protohistoric phase of Pawnee culture). The site lies in the floodplain of the Platte River and is crossed by Interstate 80 near present day Lexington in Dawson County, Nebraska. When this site was first excavated in 1963, it was tentatively identified as being part of the prehistoric Birdwood Culture. The site has been difficult to date, but it was probably already old when the Pawnees acquired horses. The article includes twenty pages of charts, graphs, and photos of stone artifacts and pottery from the site. A map on page 73 locates the site in relation to the Platte River.

223.   ——. *Protohistoric Pawnee Hunting in the Nebraska Sand Hills: Archaeological Investigations at Two Sites in the Calamus Reservoir.* A Report to the U. S. Department of the Interior, Bureau of Reclamation, Great Plains Region, 1989. 536 pp. The preface to this lengthy government document asserts that earlier archaeological investigations of the pre-horse period concentrated entirely on Pawnee village sites, ignoring the fact that protohistoric Pawnees spent much of their time in temporary hunting camps. This highly technical and detailed report deals with two such sites along the Calamus River. Argues that these sites represent a winter hunt base camp at a bison kill site and presents data that support the theory of extensive Pawnee buffalo hunting before the introduction of the horse.

224.   Schlesier, Karl H., ed. *Plains Indians, A. D. 500–1500: The Archaeological Past of Historic Groups.* Norman: University of Oklahoma Press, 1994. 479 pp. A monumental study of Plains Indians archaeology. Heavily illustrated and with many fine maps, this volume is an excellent source for a researcher with a background in archaeology, but it is a bit technical for the general reader. Divided into culture areas, with a closing chapter on the history of ethnic groups. Nearly every important Plains Indian scholar is cited, and the book has an eighty-eight page bibliography. Numerous references to the Pawnees are scattered throughout this volume.

225. Sheldon, Addison E. "Contributions to the Archaeology of the Upper Republican Valley." *Nebraska History* 15 (July–September 1934): 133–209. Data collected on Nebraska State Historical Society digs in south central Nebraska in the summer of 1934. Most of the Indian village and house sites investigated were of either prehistoric or historic Pawnee origin. Burial sites were also discovered. This lengthy article includes photographs, maps, and line drawings that are very helpful.

226. Steinacher, Terry L., and Gayle F. Carlson. *Nebraska Highway Archaeological and Historic Salvage Investigations, 1969–1975.* Nebraska State Historical Society Publications in Anthropology, No. 10. Lincoln: Nebraska State Historical Society, 1984. 191 pp., plus illustrations. This highway salvage report is a follow-up to an earlier investigation [171], and includes further information on Site 25BU1 (the Linwood Site) in Butler County. This site is believed to have been occupied at least twice by the Pawnees, perhaps as early as 1725 A. D. Surrounding the site are hills that were used as burial grounds during the various Pawnee occupations. During the 1969 excavation, archaeologists found the previously undiscovered grave of a newborn child. The artifacts found with this burial clearly show how dependent the Pawnees had become on white trade goods by the 1850s. Also discovered was a French medal, likely the first medal of French manufacture to be found at an Indian site in Nebraska.

227. Strong, William Duncan. *An Introduction to Nebraska Archaeology.* Smithsonian Miscellaneous Collections, vol. 93, no. 10. Washington, D.C.: Smithsonian Institution, 1935. 323 pp. This is a detailed summary of archaeological excavations in Nebraska prior to 1932. Strong discusses ten historic Pawnee sites and two sites believed to be protohistoric Pawnee.

228. ———. "The Plains Culture Area in the Light of Archaeology." *American Anthropologist* 35 (April–June 1933): 271–89. Strong believes the Pawnees tried to compromise between the agricultural and bison cultures and unfortunately failed at both. This article is now badly outdated in light of more recent archaeological findings, but it is still worthwhile. Much of this material would be published in Bureau of American Ethnology Bulletins.

229. "Uncover Pawnee Lodge in Kansas." *Kansas City Star*, 1 November 1967. Archaeology Department Clippings File, vol. 1, 1966–1981, 10–11. Kansas State Historical Society. An Indian village discovered

near Junction City proved to be a Pawnee village occupied briefly in the late 1700s and probably destroyed in a prairie fire. Because of the expense involved and the preservation of the larger Pawnee village near Republic, the Kansas State Historical Society and the Army Corps of Engineers decided not to preserve this site.

230. Wedel, Waldo R. *Central Plains Prehistory: Holocene Environments and Culture Changes in the Republican River Basin*. Lincoln: University of Nebraska Press, 1986. 280 pp. This is an outstanding source. Part history, part archaeology, part ethnography, and part environmental study, it covers all aspects of the Republican River basin as it relates to Native Americans. Covering a span of approximately 15,000 to 18,000 years, it explains how Native Americans, and later, whites, adapted to the changing environment of this important Plains region. The Pawnees are featured prominently throughout the book, which includes dozens of photos, line drawings, and maps.

231. ———. "Contributions to the Archaeology of the Upper Republican Valley." *Nebraska History* 15 (July–September 1934): 133–209. Report of an ambitious archaeological survey sponsored by the Nebraska State Historical Society in the spring of 1934. Village and house sites near Guide Rock, Red Cloud, and Holdrege, Nebraska, and along Red Willow and Medicine creeks were carefully investigated. Archaeologists discovered food caches and burial sites along with pottery, tools, and weapons. The researchers concluded that this Upper Republican culture was primarily horticultural, and that it occupied many areas in Nebraska later peopled by the historic Pawnees. Further, they concluded that this culture was directly ancestral to the Pawnees. An important paper for researchers in Pawnee origins.

232. ———. "Culture Sequence in the Central Great Plains." *Plains Anthropologist* 17 (August 1972): 291–353. A reprint of "Essays in Historical Anthropology of North America." *Smithsonian Miscellaneous Collections*, vol. 100. Washington, D.C.: Smithsonian Institution, 1940, 291–353. By dividing a huge span of time into four cultural periods, this classic article explains patterns of early Indian life on the Great Plains. Much of the study is based on prehistoric, protohistoric, and historic sites in Kansas and Nebraska, and the Pawnees and their ancestors receive considerable mention.

233. ———. "The Direct-Historical Approach in Pawnee Archaeology." *Smithsonian Miscellaneous Collections*, vol. 97, no. 7. Washington,

D.C.: Smithsonian Institution, 1938. 27 pp. Article attempts to resolve the argument regarding the inter-relation among the Oneota culture aspect, the Lower Loup Focus, and the historic Pawnees. Using archaeological findings, historic writings, early maps and Pawnee traditional lore, Wedel concludes that the historic Pawnees can be linked directly to the people of the Lower Loup focus. Includes a detailed comparison of traits associated with the three groups and a number of photographs of pottery and house sites to support his findings.

234. ———. "Holocene Cultural Adaptations in the Republican River Basin." In *The Great Plains: Environment and Culture*, edited by Brian W. Blouet and Frederick C. Luebke, 1–25. Lincoln: University of Nebraska Press and Center for Great Plains Studies, 1979. This essay is largely concerned with the environmental history of the Republican River basin, but it also traces the occupation of the area by Indian tribes before the historic Pawnee era. Spanish accounts locate the Pawnees in the Republican basin in the late eighteenth century, but by the early 1800s, they had moved their villages to the Platte River Valley, while continuing to hunt in the bison-rich Republican Valley.

235. ———. *An Introduction to Pawnee Archaeology*. Bureau of American Ethnology Bulletin 112. Washington, D.C.: Government Printing Office, 1936. Reprint. Lincoln, Nebr.: J and L Reprint Co., 1977. 122 pp. This classic work should be consulted by researchers interested in learning about protohistoric and historic Pawnee village sites. The sites are grouped according to the Pawnee bands that occupied them, and each village is carefully described. Objects found at the various sites also receive considerable attention. Plates, maps, and drawings support the text. In addition, there is an extensive bibliography, and an index guiding researchers to pertinent passages.

236. ———. *A Plains Archaeology Source Book: Selected Papers of the Nebraska State Historical Society*. New York: Garland Publishing, Inc., 1985. Reprint of five lengthy *Nebraska History* articles on archaeological digs in Nebraska between 1935 and 1939, most under the direction of Asa T. Hill.

237. ———. *Prehistoric Man on the Great Plains*. Norman: University of Oklahoma Press, 1961. 355 pp. This classic work includes scattered mentions of the Pawnees. The one substantial mention (pp. 122–25) points out that after 1800, Pawnee material culture seems to have deteriorated. Describes village formation, tools, weapons, pipes,

grave goods, and the lack of pot shards, indicating an increase in the use of metal pots and kettles. Wedel also points out that by the nineteenth century, some earlier traditions, such as orientation of earth lodges, were no longer followed.

238. ———. "Toward a History of Plains Archaeology." *Great Plains Quarterly* 1 (Winter 1981): 16–38. Wedel traces the development of Great Plains archaeology and profiles many of the men involved, including Asa T. Hill, who unearthed Pawnee graves near Red Cloud, Nebraska. Includes a lengthy, well-documented endnotes section with references to many works on Plains archaeology.

239. Weltfish, Gene. "The Question of Ethnic Identify: An Ethnohistorical Approach." *Ethnohistory* 6, no. 4 (1959): 321–46. Argues that the Pawnees can be identified as a distinct tribal group throughout time by using comparative ethnology, archaeology, linguistics, and the ethnic interpretation of history.

240. Weymouth, John. "A Magnetic Survey of the Palmer Site, 25HW1, on the Fullerton Canal Route." Report submitted to the U.S. Bureau of Reclamation, Grand Island, Nebraska, 1990. 19 pp. Results of a magnetic survey of a Skidi village site from the early nineteenth century to indicate whether village burial sites lay in the path of the Fullerton Canal. Much of this report is an explanation of the magnetic survey process, and the last eight pages are grids and drawings showing the survey results. This report is available from the Bureau of Reclamation in Grand Island.

241. Wood, W. Raymond, and Margot Liberty, eds. *Anthropology on the Great Plains*. Lincoln: University of Nebraska Press, 1980. 306 pp. Twenty-one essays by leading scholars cover many aspects of Great Plains anthropology, from pre-history to the Native American Church. Contains numerous references to the Pawnees, including the seldom-mentioned roles of women.

242. Zimmerman, Larry J. "Archaeological Evidence and Pawnee Claims for Human Remains and Burial Offerings in the Central Plains." Boulder, Colorado: Report to the Native American Rights Fund, 1990.

243. Zimmerman, Larry J., and Roger Echo-Hawk. "Ancient History of the Pawnee Nation: A Summary of Archaeological and Traditional Evidence for Pawnee Ancestry in the Central Great Plains." Boulder, Colorado: Native American Rights Fund, 1990.

244. Zimmerman, Mark E. "Circular Shrines in Quivira, and the Jehovah of the Ohio Mound Builder." *Collections of the Kansas State Historical Society*, vol. 17 (1926–1928), 547–58. Topeka: Kansas State Printing Plant, 1928. Ties the "White Pawnees" of Kansas to Hebrews, ancient freemasons, Celts, and Stonehenge. This confusing article should be read in conjunction with Zimmerman's article in *Collections of the Kansas State Historical Society*, vol. 16 [245].

245. ———. "The Pawnee Americans." *Collections of the Kansas State Historical Society*, vol. 16 (1923–1925), 463–75. Topeka: Kansas State Printing Plant, 1925. Highly speculative and unsubstantiated essay asserts that an undocumented group of Pawnees who lived in Kansas centuries ago may actually have been of Celtic origin and may have built stone box graves similar to those used by Druids and Scots in Britain. The author also ties these people to the ancient Hebrews through a serpent cult.

4
Myths, Legends, and Sacred Places

246. Blaine, Martha Royce. "Mythology and Folklore: Their Possible Use in the Study of Plains Caddoan Origins." *Nebraska History* 60 (Summer 1979): 240–48. Suggests that clues to the early Pawnees may be found in tribal myths and legends. From a selected group of tales from George A. Dorsey's *Pawnee Mythology*, Blaine points out that the Pawnee bands may all have built grass houses at some point in their histories, and mentions of or lack of references to bodies of water in these tales may provide clues to Pawnee migrations and early settlements.

247. Bouc, Ken. "The Legend of Pahuk." *NEBRASKAland* 55 (July 1977): 36–37, 47–48. Points out that the site of Pahuk, the Pawnees' most sacred animal lodge, is very close to land that at one time was considered as a location for Neapolis, the possible Nebraska state capital. The author explores the controversy over Neapolis and the history of Pahuk, both of which are near present-day Fremont.

248. Boye, Alan. *A Guide to the Ghosts of Lincoln*. 2d ed. St. Johnsbury, Vermont: Saltillo Press, 1987. 145 pp. Among the stories in this unique book is the tale of a Pawnee visionary who was buried near Lincoln, Nebraska. Since his burial site was disturbed during highway construction, Indian drums are sometimes heard in the morning, and witnesses have reported seeing the image of an Indian man who appears to be dancing.

249. Coons, Susan. "Baptiste Bayhylle and the Pawnee Removal." (Edited by Roger Echo-Hawk.) *Rolling Stock* 12 (1987): 11. Relates a charm-

ing story about interpreter Baptiste Bayhylle and his encounters with a "scalped" Pawnee as the last group of Pawnees were traveling from Nebraska to their new home in Indian Territory.

250. Cunningham, Don. "Pahuk Place." *NEBRASKAland* 63 (June 1985): 27–31. Modern story of a Nebraska doctor and his wife who bought the land on which "Pahuk," one of the most sacred Pawnee sites, is located. Originally intending to build a home there, they decided instead to preserve the site once they learned its history and lore. The site is now on the National Register of Historic Places.

251. DeVoe, Carrie. *Legends of the Kaw: The Folk-Lore of the Indians of the Kansas River Valley*. Kansas City: Franklin Hudson Publishing Co., 1904. 216 pp. The Pawnees are prominently featured in this somewhat unreliable and very ethnocentric work, which does include an interesting tale about a magical horse and a version of the Pahuk legend.

252. Dorsey, George A. *The Pawnee Mythology*. Washington, D.C.: Carnegie Institution Publication no. 59, 1906. Reprint. Introduction by Douglas R. Parks. Lincoln: University of Nebraska Press, 1997. 546 pp. This companion volume to Dorsey's *Traditions of the Skidi Pawnee* features 148 tales under the general categories of myths, hero tales, vision stories, and coyote (trickster) tales. Researchers should also consult Parks' excellent introduction to the reprint edition.

253. ———. "A Pawnee Personal Medicine Shrine." *American Anthropologist* 7 (April–June 1905): 496–98. Charming tale related by an elderly Kitkehaki Pawnee tells of a warrior who finds a mysterious "stone man" in a ravine. When he prays to the stone man, he has success in battle. Later, he shows an unlucky and unsuccessful fellow Pawnee where the stone shrine is located. Oddly, the stone man is gone, but the unlucky warrior prays anyway and leaves ashes where the man of stone once stood. He becomes a successful warrior, and is forever grateful to the warrior who first guided him to the "stone man."

254. ———. *Traditions of the Skidi Pawnee*. American Folklore Society Memoirs, No. 8. Boston: Houghton Mifflin Company, 1904. Reprint. New York: Kraus Reprint Company, 1969. 366 pp. An excellent collection of tales about Pawnee cosmology, heroes, medicine, and stories of animals and people who become animals. Dorsey recorded these tales in the late nineteenth century directly from Pawnee sources.

255. Echo-Hawk, Elmer. "The Horse and the Buffalo." *The Arrow* (February 14, 1908): n.p. Relates a Pawnee myth that the Milky Way resulted from a cosmic race between a horse and a buffalo. The horse won.

256. Echo-Hawk, Roger C. "Ancient History in the New World: Integrating Oral Traditions and the Archaeological Record in Deep Time." *American Antiquity* 65 (April 2000): 267–90. When the Native American Graves Protection and Repatriation Act (NAGPRA) became law in 1990, it listed oral traditions as a criterion for bridging the gap between ancient and modern Native Americans. Pawnee scholar Roger Echo-Hawk presents a framework within which scholars can integrate oral records with archaeological findings. He also traces the history of the Caddoan-speaking peoples' presence on the Great Plains, and the Pawnees are discussed at length.

257. ———. "Forging a New Ancient History for Native America." In *Native Americans and Archaeologists: Stepping Stones to Common Ground*, edited by Nina Swindler, Kurt Dongoske, Alan Downer, and Roger Anyan, 88–102. Walnut Creek, California: Alta Mira Press, 1997. Excellent article argues that oral tradition should play a larger role in the writing of ancient Native American history. Stressing Pawnee narratives, Echo-Hawk points out that this is especially important due to changes in archaeological methods since the passage of the Native American Graves Protection and Repatriation Act of 1990 (NAGPRA).

258. Flannery, Monica. "A Comparative Sketch of the Mythology of the Siouan and Caddoan Linguistic Stocks." Master's thesis, University of California, Berkeley, 1916.

259. Gilmore, Melvin R. "The Legend of Pahuk." Melvin R. Gilmore Papers. RG 3308. AM. Nebraska State Historical Society. 6 pp. Preserved on microfilm, this is the legend of Pahuk as told to Gilmore by the elderly Pawnee White Eagle when they toured Pawnee sites in Nebraska in 1914. This particular account gives the exact location of Pahuk, or "Sacred Ground," as it was sometimes called.

260. ———. *Prairie Smoke*. New York: Columbia University Press, 1929. Reprint introduction by Roger Welsch. St. Paul: Minnesota Historical Society Press, 1987. 225 pp. Much of this volume is devoted to Pawnee folklore and oral traditions. Included are tales of Pahuk, the

most sacred animal lodge, a legend involving Courthouse Rock, and stories about birds and the importance of corn to the Pawnees.

261. Grinnell, George Bird. "Development of a Pawnee Myth." *Journal of American Folklore* 5 (January–March 1892): 127–34. Relates the tale of a Kitkahahki Pawnee hero who saves his people from starvation by calling the buffalo, and explains the origins of this folk tale.

262. ———. "The Girl Who Was the Ring." *Harper's Monthly* 102 (February 1901): 425–29. Tale of a little girl kidnapped by buffalo and turned into a ring for a stick game. The clever coyote responsible for her abduction gathers a group of animals and birds which rescues and returns her to her home.

263. ———. "The Medicine Grizzly Bear." *Harper's Monthly* 102 (April 1901): 736–44. A poor, unhappy Pawnee boy is magically drawn to a sacred animal lodge, where a grizzly bear teaches the boy secret rituals and passes along his powers of healing.

264. ———. *Pawnee Hero Stories and Folk Tales, with Notes on the Origin, Customs, and Character of the Pawnee People.* New York: Forest and Stream Publishing Company, 1889. Reprint. Lincoln: University of Nebraska Press, 1961. 417 pp. Tales collected from leading Pawnees who feared that their stories would be lost to their descendants. Grinnell recorded the tales exactly as they were told to him. Any editorial comments are limited to explaining certain Pawnee terms.

265. ———. "Pawnee Mythology." *Journal of American Folklore* 6 (January–March 1893): 113–30. Discusses the hierarchy of Pawnee gods, tribal cosmology, and animal spirits. Explains the importance of the four cardinal directions and the history and meaning of sacred bundles. Also includes a lengthy creation story, and notes similarities between Pawnee religion and Christianity.

266. ———. "A Pawnee Star Myth. *Journal of American Folklore* 7 (January–March 1894): 197–200. Story of the son of a bright star and a Pawnee chief's daughter. After the death of his mother, the boy's father gives him supernatural powers and always protects him.

267. ———. *The Punishment of the Stingy and Other Indian Stories.* New York: Harper & Brothers, 1901. Reprint. Lincoln: University of Nebraska Press, 1982. 235 pp. A collection of tales from the Blackfeet, the Indians of the Northwest, and the Pawnees. Of the four Pawnee

myths, "The Girl Who Was the Ring" and "The Grizzly Bear's Medicine" were also published in *Harper's Monthly* in 1901 [262], [263].

268. ———. "The Young Dog's Dance." *Journal of American Folklore* 4 (1891): 307–13. Story of how the Young Dog's Dance (Sun Dance) came to the Pawnees via the Arikaras, as told to Grinnell by Pipe Chief, an elder of the Skidi band. Also gives Pipe Chief's account of participation in the Sun Dance.

269. "Grinnell Writes about the Pawnee." *Nebraska History* 3 (April–June 1920): 1–2. Grinnell recounts an undated, unprovoked attack on a Chaui Pawnee band by the Skidi while the two groups were completely separate. Grinnell's elderly Chaui informant told him that by using trickery, the Chaui and other bands avenged the attack, confiscated many Skidi horses, and forced Skidi women to marry into the other bands, this forging a band alliance. Letter gives more details about an event related in Grinnell's *Pawnee Hero Stories and Folk Tales*, 233–34 [264].

270. Gulliford, Andrew. *Sacred Objects and Sacred Places: Preserving Tribal Traditions*. Boulder: University Press of Colorado, 2000. 285 pp. This outstanding book examines the ways Native Americans are trying to preserve their cultures. It is beautifully illustrated and written in a style that makes it accessible to all readers. The Pawnees are featured twice: first, in a seven-page essay on the sacred bundle from Massacre Canyon that is being preserved by the Kansas State Historical Society; and second, in an essay on Pahuk, the Pawnee sacred site near Fremont, Nebraska, which tells the history of the site and explains how it is being preserved.

271. Harris, Earl R. "Courthouse and Jail Rocks: Landmarks on the Oregon Trail." *Nebraska History* 43 (March 1962): 29–51. Before emigrants along the Oregon Trail first saw Courthouse Rock, the Pawnees knew a colorful legend involving this famous landmark. Unfortunately, the author does not include the source of this beautiful Pawnee folk tale.

272. Harrod, Howard L. *The Animals Came Dancing: Native American Sacred Ecology and Animal Kinship*. Tucson: University of Arizona Press, 2000. 170 pp. Harrod incorporates a number of Pawnee myths and traditions into this study. The Pawnee origin tradition is explained, and he gives two examples of Pawnees marrying animals.

One version of a young boy receiving magical powers from animals is recounted, and he explains how the Pawnee yearly cycle is influenced by sacred bundles.

273. Hungate, Mary. "Religious Beliefs of the Nebraska Indian." *Nebraska History* 19 (July–September 1938): 207–25. The first half of this article relates creation stories of the Chaui and Skidi Pawnees, but neither offers any analysis, and neither includes sources.

274. Isakson, Doug. "Pawnees' Sacred Site Remains Untouched." *Fremont (Nebraska) Tribune*, 28 September 1991, A3. Profile of Dr. and Mrs. Louis Gilbert, who purchased the land containing Pahuk. In cooperation with the Nebraska State Historical Society, the Pahuk site will be kept in its natural state and preserved as a sacred site.

275. Leeming, David, and Jake Page. *The Mythology of Native North America*. Norman: University of Oklahoma Press, 1998. 209 pp. In their chapter on the cosmos, the authors relate two traditional Pawnee myths regarding the end of the world.

276. McKee, Jim. "A New Chapter on Robbers Cave." *Lincoln Journal Star*, 18 March 2001, 2K. Fascinating article about a cave in Lincoln, Nebraska, that some believe was used by the Pawnees to hold sacred rites and tribal councils.

277. Marriott, Alice, and Carol K. Rachlin. *Plains Indian Mythology*. New York: Thomas Y. Crowell Company, 1975. 194 pp. Selected myths, legends, and folk tales of Plains tribes, told by native women storytellers. Includes a Pawnee creation story, a tale of sacred songs, and an amusing tale of jealous cousins.

278. Miller, Dorcas S. *Stars of the First People: Native American Star Myths and Constellations*. Boulder, Colorado: Pruett Publishing Company, 1997. 346 pp. Pages 218–29 recount the Skidi Pawnee creation story and explain what a number of stars and constellations meant to the extremely spiritual Skidis. The author relies heavily on the works of Von Del Chamberlain and George A. Dorsey.

279. Moroney, Lynn. *The Boy Who Loved Bears*. Chicago: Childrens Press, 1994. 32 pp. Retells the inspiring story of the relationship between a young Pawnee and a bear who brought him back to life after he was killed in battle. Also explains the role of Pawnee bear doctors. Charles Chapman, who illustrated the book, is a Pawnee.

280. Osborne, Samuel. "Powhohatawa." *The Indian Leader* (May 1915): n.p. A student at Haskell Institute tells this myth of a Pawnee warrior who was killed by the Sioux and magically brought back to life by animals. He became the guardian of his people and protected them from harm.

281. "Pahuk." Melvin R. Gilmore Papers. RG 3308.AM. Nebraska State Historical Society. 4 pp. (Microfilm). Yet another variation of the Pawnee animal lodge oral tradition regarding this sacred place. It tells of a boy who receives magical powers from the animals and becomes a leading Pawnee medicine man. No source is identified for this version of the tale.

282. Parks, Douglas R. "Three Skiri Pawnee Stories." In *Coming to Light: Contemporary Translations of the Native Literatures of North America*, edited by Brian Swann, 377–402. New York: Random House, 1994. A modern linguist translates three tales told to him in 1965 by an elderly blind Pawnee storyteller named Harry Mad Bear. The first is a tale about riddles; the second tells of Pawnee war exploits, and the third is a typical coyote story in which the evil deeds of "Old Woman Rat" are undone by animal doctors.

283. ———. "An Historical Character Mythologized: The Scalped Man in Arikara and Pawnee Folklore." In *Plains Indian Studies: A Collection of Essays in Honor of John C. Ewers and Waldo R. Wedel*, edited by Douglas H. Ubelaker and Herman J. Viola, 47–58. Smithsonian Contributions to Anthropology, no. 30. Washington, D.C.: Smithsonian Institution Press, 1982. Explains the many roles of survivors of scalping in Arikara and Pawnee oral traditions. A "scalped man" was ostracized and forced to live outside the Indian community. In folklore, he is represented in turn as an actual person, a legendary figure with supernatural powers, a mythological character, and sometimes as a bogeyman or a comic. The article presents examples of tales showing the scalped man in his various roles.

284. Parks, Douglas R., and Waldo R. Wedel. "Pawnee Geography: Historical and Sacred." *Great Plains Quarterly* 5 (Summer 1985): 143–76. Excellent article focuses on Pawnee sacred sites and animal lodges. Points out that animal lodges taught Pawnee doctors the secrets of all animals, rather than single personal guardian spirits. Following an excellent essay on Pawnee historical geography, the authors discuss the purpose of animal lodges. In all, fourteen animal

lodges, or sacred sites, have been either positively or tentatively identified, and each one is discussed in detail. Also included are excellent maps and modern photographs of some of the sites.

285. Pound, Louise. "Nebraska Cave Lore." *Nebraska History* 29 (December 1948): 299–323. A survey of Nebraska's caves and the tales associated with them. Included are lengthy sections on the Pawnees' sacred Pahuk Cave near Fremont, and "Robbers Cave" in Lincoln, said to be at one time the site of Pawnee religious rites.

286. ———. *Nebraska Folklore*. Lincoln: University of Nebraska Press, 1987. 243 pp. Two of the cave legends in this collection, the stories of Pahuk Cave near Fremont and Lincoln's "Robbers Cave," have direct connections to the Pawnees. The chapter on "lovers' leaps" discusses a cliff near Fullerton in Nance County. It is believed that the Pawnees may have once driven buffalo over this cliff, but a romantic poem tells a tale of an Indian girl and a white boy who jumped to their deaths there.

287. ———. "Nebraska Legends of Lovers' Leaps." *Western Folklore* 8 (1949): 304–13. Despite white claims to the contrary, there are no Indian "lovers' leaps" in Nebraska. In Nance County, a legend was told of a Pawnee girl who fell in love with a white boy. Because they could not be together, the couple jumped off a clay bank near Fullerton to their deaths. Most Nance County natives refer to this site as Crazyman's Leap, or Buffalo Leap.

288. Real-McKeighan, Tammy. "Fremont Area Rich with Indian Lore." *Fremont (Nebraska) Tribune*, 6 September 1990, B3. Features three Fremont-area sites connected to Pawnee legends: Pahuk Hill, home of sacred animals; Skull Creek, where a Sioux massacre of Pawnees allegedly occurred; and Rawhide Creek, whose legend of a white man being skinned alive was a hoax. Also relates the story of the heroic Pawnee warrior Petalesharo.

289. Spence, Lewis. *The Myths of the North American Indians*. London: G. G. Harrop, 1914. Reprint. New York: Dover Publications, Inc., 1989. 393 pp. To illustrate Pawnee spirituality, Spence includes a sacred bundle tale and the story of a young man who is able to transform himself into a bear.

290. Thomas, Fred. "Family Preserves Pawnees' Sacred Ground." *Omaha World-Herald*, 3 May 1987, 1B. One of a series of articles by Thomas

on historical sites in Nebraska. While describing a local doctor's preservation of Pahuk, the Pawnees' most sacred site, he also recounts the history and legend surrounding this sacred animal lodge near Fremont.

291. Wake, C. Staniland. "Mythology of the Plains Indians: Magical Animals." *American Antiquarian and Oriental Journal* 28 (1906): 205–12. Contains animal myths and legends of several Plains tribes, adapted from George A. Dorsey's studies of the Arikara, Arapaho, Caddo, and Wichita tribes. Mentions a Skidi legend of "How the Buffalo Went South." Oddly, no source is credited for this animal legend. The researcher interested in Pawnee mythology would be wise to read Dorsey's original accounts.

292. ———. "Mythology of the Plains Indians: Nature Deities." *American Antiquarian and Oriental Journal* 27 (1905): 73–80. A rather disorganized article that tries to convey too much information on too many Plains tribes. The Pawnees are featured prominently, but this material is taken directly from works by George A. Dorsey and James R. Murie. Not the best source on Plains Indian religion.

293. Williamson, John W. "An Indian Legend." John William Williamson Manuscripts. MS 2710. Lincoln: Nebraska State Historical Society. (Microfilm). Pawnee agency farmer Williamson signed his name to this hero legend, but it was probably told to him by tribal elders. In the legend, a young outcast is aided by eagles and swans who give him the power to find buffalo to feed his starving people. The date on the manuscript is January 1924.

5
Language and Linguistic Studies

294. Campbell, Lyle, and Marianne Mithun, eds. *The Languages of North America: Historical and Comparative Assessment*. Austin: University of Texas Press, 1979. 1,034 pp. The sixty-nine page introductory essay discusses the work of past linguists and current studies, and suggests what needs to be done in the field of Native American linguistics. The introduction includes a fine bibliography, and each chapter is devoted to a particular Native American linguistic family. Much of the material in the chapter on Caddoan languages is quite technical and geared toward other linguists, but the authors do identify the most important Caddoan language studies.

295. Chafe, Wallace L. "Estimates Regarding the Present Speakers of North American Indian Languages." *International Journal of American Linguistics* 28 (1962): 162–71. Beginning in the fall of 1960, the Bureau of American Ethnology sent questionnaires to anthropologists, teachers, and members of Indian language groups, among others, to determine about how many Indians still speak their native languages. The survey showed that at that time, 400 to 600 people in Oklahoma spoke Pawnee. Chafe considered the Arikara language so closely related to Pawnee that he believed the 200 to 300 Indians in North Dakota who speak Arikara should be added to the Pawnee total.

296. ———. "Siouan, Iroquoian, and Caddoan." In *Current Trends in Linguistics*, vol. 10, 1164–1209. The Hague: Mouton, 1973. Reprinted in *Native Languages of the Americas*, edited by Thomas A. Sebeok, vol.

1, 527–72. New York: Plenum Press, 1976. A discussion of all the languages included in these Native American linguistic families. A short bibliographical essay traces studies on each language. Author asserts that there may be tenuous connections among the three language groups, and shows these similarities by using selected words and grammatical forms.

297. Dorsey, George A. "Pawnee Language Notebook." Manuscript in George A. Dorsey Papers. Chicago: Field Museum of Natural History, Department of Anthropology, 1907.

298. Grinnell, George Bird. "Two Pawnian Tribal Names." *American Anthropologist* (o.s.) 4 (April 1891): 197–99. This brief article was written to reinforce the theory that the name Pawnee ("Pani") comes from the Pawnee word "parika," or horn. Grinnell points out that in ancient times Pawnee men shaved most of their hair, leaving only a scalp-lock, which they stiffened with grease and clay and either wore upright or curved backward like a horn. Grinnell further argues that the tribal name Arikara means horns, or horned. This makes perfect sense if one believes, as he did, that the Arikaras were once part of the Skidi Pawnee band.

299. Hayden, Ferdinand V. "Brief Notes on the Pawnee, Winnebago, and Omaha Languages." Philadelphia: *Proceedings of the American Philosophical Society,* vol. 10, 1868. After erroneously assuring the reader that Indians cannot accurately recall their own history, Hayden lists fifteen pages of Pawnee words, numbers, and phrases, all with English translations. Before the alphabetical list of words is a Pawnee version of the "Lord's Prayer," also translated. Elvira Platt, longtime teacher among the Pawnees, helped with the word lists and translations.

300. Lesser, Alexander, and Gene Weltfish. "Composition of the Caddoan Linguistic Stock." *Smithsonian Miscellaneous Collections*, vol. 87, no. 6. Washington, D.C.: Smithsonian Institution, 1932. Provides brief coverage of the four Caddoan-speaking Plains tribes and the similarities and differences in their dialects. Much of the article discusses the three Pawnee dialects and the derivation of the four band names. Oddly, the Pawnees have no name for themselves as a nation, always referring to each other by their individual band names. This linguistic essay is clearly written and should be easily understood by non-linguists.

301. Lounsbury, Floyd. "A Semantic Analysis of the Pawnee Kinship Usage." *Language* 32 (1956): 158–94. Exhaustive and very complicated

analysis of Pawnee words used to denote family members. Ends with a short sociological profile of the Pawnees given to support the linguistic information. Difficult for anyone but a professional linguist.

302. Mallery, Garrick. *Pictographs of the North American Indians: A Preliminary Paper*. Fourth Annual Report of the Bureau of American Ethnology, 1882–1883. Washington, D.C.: Government Printing Office, 1886. 253 pp. The Pawnees are represented as the enemy nine separate times in Dakota winter counts interpreted by Dr. William H. Corbusier, an assistant surgeon with the United States Army. Among the pictographs is one from 1843–1844 showing the Cheyenne Medicine Arrows that the Sioux recaptured in a battle with the Pawnees.

303. ———. *Picture-Writing of the American Indians*. Tenth Annual Report of the Bureau of American Ethnology, 1888–1889. Washington, D.C.: Government Printing Office, 1893. 804 pp. Mallery's massive work contains scattered mentions of the Pawnees—from wooden "passports" inscribed in pictographs, to a description of a Skidi skull circle near the Platte River, and winter count illustrations of the Cheyenne Medicine Arrow taken from the Pawnees by the Sioux and traded back to the Cheyenne for 100 horses.

304. Murie, James R. "Pawnee Ethnographic and Linguistic Notes." Chicago: Field Museum of Natural History, Anthropological Archives, Box A1-2, 1902.

305. Parks, Douglas R. "George A. Dorsey, James R. Murie, and the Textual Documentation of Skiri Pawnee." In *Theorizing the Americanist Tradition*, edited by Lisa Philips Valentine and Regna Darnell, 227–44. Toronto: University of Toronto Press, 1999. Parks traces the history of the collaboration between Dorsey and Murie and their agenda to publish works on Skiri Pawnee mythology, ethnography, music, material culture, and linguistic texts. Unfortunately, some of the projects were never completed. Parks later worked with narratives told by an elderly Pawnee priest named Roaming Scout that had been recorded by Dorsey and Murie. Of interest to researchers in Pawnee star lore is Roaming Scout's account of the creation of the Pawnee sky chart.

306. ———. *A Grammar of Pawnee*. New York: Garland Publishing, Inc., 1976. 361 pp. This scholarly study of the Pawnee south band dialect is primarily intended for linguistic specialists, but it offers insight into Pawnee culture by demonstrating how the language was used.

307. ———. "The Importance of Language Study for the Writing of Plains Indian History." In *New Directions in American Indian History*, edited by Colin G. Calloway, 153–97. Norman: University of Oklahoma Press, 1988. A noted linguist and Native American historian argues that writers of Plains Indian history pay too little attention to the proper use of the languages of the peoples they are writing about. He points out that modern writers have perpetuated errors by earlier authors, and that Indian names are often improperly translated and incorrectly spelled. Many of the examples given are Pawnee, such as the names of leading chiefs and band names. A bit technical in places for the non-linguist, but a valuable study with an excellent bibliography.

308. ———. "Pawnee Texts: Skiri and South Band." In *Caddoan Texts.* International Journal of American Linguistics Native American Texts Series, vol. 2, no. 1. Chicago: University of Chicago Press, 1977. This volume contains samples of writings in five Caddoan languages—Arikara, Caddo, Kitsai, Pawnee, and Wichita. Parks collected the six Pawnee texts between 1965 and 1968. Each was told to him by an elderly Pawnee informant, recorded on tape and later transcribed. All but one belong to the fairy tale genre, and the first three are trickster tales. Each story is translated literally from the original Pawnee dialect in which it was told.

309. Parks, Douglas R., and Raymond J. DeMallie. "Plains Indian Native Literatures." In *American Indian Persistence and Resurgence*, edited by Karl Kroeber, 106–48. Durham, North Carolina: Duke University Press, 1994. This chapter is two essays, one by Parks on Pawnee literature and one by DeMallie on a Lakota text. Parks traces the history of the "Roaming Scout Texts," stories told by Roaming Scout, an elderly, mono-lingual Skiri (Skidi) religious leader and compiled by George A. Dorsey and James R. Murie. An appendix to the chapter gives a transcription and translation of one of Roaming Scout's Pawnee tales.

310. Powell, John Wesley. *Indian Linguistic Families of America North of Mexico*. Seventh Annual Report of the Bureau of American Ethnology. Washington, D.C.: Government Printing Office, 1891. Reprint. Lincoln: University of Nebraska Press, 1966. 141 pp. Divides North America into linguistic families, lists the tribes included in each group, and explains their geographical location. Powell separates the

Caddoan language family into three groups—northern (Arikara), middle (Pawnee), and southern (Caddo, Wichita, and Kitsai).

311. Taylor, Allen R. "The Classification of the Caddoan Languages." *Proceedings of the American Philosophical Society*, vol. 107, no. 1. Philadelphia: American Philosophical Society, 1963. Written in the form of a bibliographical essay, this article traces the history of the recording and classification of the Caddoan languages, which include Pawnee. Listed at the end of the article are all the primary Caddoan language sources known to the author when this essay was written.

312. ———. "Comparative Caddoan." *International Journal of American Linguistics* 20 (1963): 113–31. Extremely technical grammatical and pronunciation comparison among Caddoan languages. One conclusion drawn from this study is that contrary to the findings of some earlier linguists, the Arikara language most closely resembles Pawnee South Band dialects, not the dialect of the Skidi.

313. "The Tower of Babel is Tumbling Down—Slowly." *U. S. News and World Report*, July 2, 2001: 9. Statistics showing that in 2001 there were 184 world languages with fewer than ten speakers. Included among dying languages is Pawnee. This brief report lists only four people who still speak the Pawnee language.

314. Weltfish, Gene. *Caddoan Texts: Pawnee, South Band Dialect*. Publications of the American Ethnological Society, vol. 17. New York: G. E. Stechert & Co., 1937. 251 pp. A collection of over forty Pawnee folk tales and historical episodes related by native speakers and gathered by the author in the late 1920s. Includes both literal and free translations of each story.

315. ———. "The Linguistic Study of Material Culture." *International Journal of American Linguistics* 24 (1958): 301–11. Best understood by other linguists, but includes the story of a Pawnee boy who becomes an eagle. Includes a literal translation and grammatical analysis of the text.

316. ———. "The Vision Story of Fox-Boy, A South Band Pawnee Text." *International Journal of American Linguistics* 9 (1936–1939): 44–75. An abbreviated version of a longer tale told to the author by a Pawnee woman in 1929. Includes both a literal and free translation. Very technical, and intended for other experts in the field.

6
Social Organization

317. Bratton, Ethel Mae. "Sociological Effects upon the Pawnee Indians of the Interaction between White and Indian Cultures." Master's thesis, University of Texas, 1932. 105 pp. The first part of this study is a Pawnee history and ethnology, taken from classic sources. The second section explains how the Pawnees have changed over the years and how they adapted to and actually embraced white ways. A detailed table of contents makes finding topics easy and the appendix includes two survey forms that the author distributed to Oklahoma Pawnees to help gather data. Despite its age, this is a very useful source.

318. Chamberlain, Von Del. "The Chief and His Council: Unity and Authority from the Stars." In *Earth and Sky: Visions of the Cosmos in Native American Folklore*, edited by Ray A. Williamson and Claire R. Farrer, 221–35. Albuquerque: University of New Mexico Press, 1992. Discusses the importance of three constellations for Pawnee tribal organization and society. The first, called by the Pawnees "star-that-does-not-move" (Polaris) was considered the chief star that set the pattern for tribal government. A nearby circle of stars (the Corona Borealis), called by the Skidis the "Chief's Council," represented the circle in which leaders sat to discuss tribal issues. The cluster of stars known as Pleiades was a symbol of tribal unity. The Pawnee earth lodges were constructed so that these stars would be highly visible, and the smoke hole in the lodge's center was the route by which messages were received from the celestial deities. Much of this essay is taken from Chamberlain's longer study *When Stars Came Down to Earth* [404].

319. Dorsey, George A. "Social Organization of the Skidi Pawnee." *Proceedings of the International Congress of Americanists* 15 (1906): 71–77. Detailed discussion dealing with villages, families, marriage, pregnancy and birth, settling of disputes, and character flaws. This is a useful source for Skidi society and customs.

320. Dorsey, George A., and James R. Murie. *Notes on Skidi Pawnee Society*, edited by Alexander Spoehr, 65–119. Anthropological Series, vol. 27, no. 2. Chicago: Field Museum of Natural History, 1940. This very important source is concerned mostly with Pawnee societal groups and life stages, such as bands and villages, kinship, crime and punishment, and classes within Pawnee society, as well as important milestones in the lives of individuals. Unlike his predecessor, Ralph Linton, Spoehr does credit James R. Murie with his invaluable contributions to this work.

321. Grinnell, George Bird. "Marriage Among the Pawnees." *American Anthropologist* (o.s.) 4 (January 1891): 275–81. With the disclaimer that his information comes from Skidi informants, whose customs often differed from those of other Pawnee bands, Grinnell explains Pawnee courtship and marriage customs, especially the giving of gifts to the bride's family. After asking Pawnees about the practice of presenting marriage gifts, he concludes that in earlier times robes and horses were simply gifts, but over time brides' families came to expect expensive presents. As rival suitors raised the stakes, it appeared that young Pawnee men were buying their wives, leading to the belief that marriage was a commercial arrangement.

322. Kracht, Benjamin R. "The Effects of Disease and Warfare on Pawnee Social Organization, 1830–1859: An Ethnohistorical Approach." Master's thesis, University of Nebraska, 1982. 160 pp. A fine study of the social impact of Pawnee depopulation between 1830 and 1859 — a critical period in their tribal history. Areas discussed are settlement patterns, socio-political organization, marriage, residence patterns, and kinship systems. The conclusion is that disease and warfare were the primary reasons for Pawnee social change during this era.

323. Lesser, Alexander. "Levirate and Fraternal Polyandry among the Pawnee." *Man* 30 (June 1930): 98–101. Contrary to the custom in most North American tribes of men having sexual relations with and marrying their brothers' widows, among the Pawnees, sexual relations between a man and his living older brother's wife was socially

accepted without benefit of marriage. When a husband was absent for extended periods, his brother acted as his surrogate. Also discusses marriages to multiple sisters and living arrangements after marriage.

324. Lowie, Robert H. "Pawnee and Arikara." In *Plains Indian Age-Societies: Historical and Comparative Summary*, 890–94. Anthropological Papers of the American Museum of Natural History, vol. 11, 1916. A brief discussion of Pawnee warrior and sacred bundle societies, comparing them with the societies of other Plains tribes. In many ways, Pawnee societies were unique, but Lowie suggests that they may have influenced societies among the Arapaho, Oglala Lakota, and the Gros Ventres, and were certainly similar to some Arikara societies.

325. Murie, James R. "Pawnee Indian Societies." In *Societies of the Plains Indians*, edited by Clark Wissler, 545–644. New York: Anthropological Papers of the Museum of Natural History, vol. 11, part 7, 1914. Murie gathered all available information on Pawnee societies and the ceremonies connected with them. Included is information on bundle societies, medicine men's societies, and modern ceremonies. This is an important work by a reliable scholar, and should be consulted by all serious researchers.

326. "Pawnee Marriage Customs of the Old Days." *Indian School Journal* (February 1915): 299–301. Mixed-blood Pawnee ethnologist James R. Murie, testifying in a land dispute case in 1882, explains traditional Pawnee marriage customs and rules of inheritance. While Murie's actual account is probably accurate, the introduction to his testimony contains several errors.

327. Schmitt, Karl, and Iva Schmitt. *Wichita Kinship, Past and Present*. Norman: University of Oklahoma Book Exchange 1952. 72 pp. Because the Wichitas and Pawnees both speak Caddoan languages, and because the two tribes were closely affiliated at one point, this study includes a brief discussion comparing Wichita kinship systems to those of the Republican and Grand Pawnees. Kinship charts for the two bands are printed within the text.

328. Tate, Michael L. "Pawnee Political and Legal Traditions." In *The Encyclopedia of Native American Legal Tradition*, edited by Bruce E. Johansen, 240–44. Westport, Connecticut: Greenwood Press, 1998. A brief but informative essay explaining parts of Pawnee his-

tory, but focusing on tribal organization and government, especially among the Skidi band. Points out that although kinship lines were matrilineal, chieftainship passed through a male line.

329. Wishart, David J. "The Roles and Status of Men and Women in Nineteenth Century Omaha and Pawnee Societies: Postmodernist Uncertainties and Empirical Evidence." *American Indian Quarterly* 19 (Fall 1995): 509–18. Wishart argues that nineteenth-century observers such as the Reverend John Dunbar misunderstood the roles of Pawnee men and women when he called the women slaves and the men lazy. In his opinion, the observations of Alice Fletcher, and much later, Gene Weltfish, were closer to the truth. Weltfish referred to Pawnee society as "balanced," and Fletcher stated that women were "held in high regard." A good reassessment of Pawnee gender roles from a modern viewpoint.

7
Material Culture

330. "Ancient Pawnee Medal." *Nebraska History* 2, no. 2 (1919): 5. The curator of the Nebraska State Historical Society Museum describes the Petalesharo medal in detail, but misdates it. A letter from the Rev. Michael Shine tries to settle an argument regarding the Pawnee band affiliation of Petalesharo by pointing out that the two men with this name had each received medals, but belonged to different bands.

331. Ashworth, Kenneth A. "Pawnee Art, Style, and Culture." Master's thesis, Wichita State University, 1981. 153 pp. The first chapter provides background on Pawnee social and political structure and religion. The bulk of this work explains Pawnee works of art, which for the most part appear on apparel, ceremonial objects, pouches, cradle boards, and articles used in warfare. The Pawnee art style is discussed, and a section is devoted to the way this style reflects Pawnee religion and myths and the importance of the cosmos. Dozens of line drawings illustrate many of the objects discussed in the text.

332. Blasing, Robert. "The Seasonal Round." *NEBRASKAland* 72 (January–February 1994): 130. This essay also appears in *Nebraska History* 75 (Spring 1994). Explains the annual schedule by which Nebraska Indians obtained meat and grew crops. Early nineteenth-century witnesses wrote about both the Pawnee cycle and buffalo surrounds.

333. Bozell, John R. "Changes in the Role of the Dog in Protohistoric-Historic Pawnee Culture." *Plains Anthropologist* 33 (February 1988):

95–111. By using ethnohistorical and archaeological evidence, this author shows that prior to acquiring horses, the Pawnees had many large working dogs that served as pack animals and as an emergency food source. After the change to horse culture, the dog population decreased, and so did the size of the dogs. Dog breeding was virtually abandoned when horses took their places.

334. Buckstaff, Ralph N. "Stars and Constellations of a Pawnee Sky Map." *American Anthropologist* 29 (January–March 1927): 279–85. A detailed description and interpretation of the elk skin Skidi star chart in the Pawnee collection at the Field Museum of Natural History in Chicago, complete with drawings and diagrams. Buckstaff explains how he believes the Pawnees designed the map, and he seems certain that since the map is over three hundred years old, its production would not have been influenced by white culture. However, others have disputed the age of the star chart.

335. Bushnell, David I., Jr. *Burials of the Algonquian, Siouan, and Caddoan Tribes West of the Mississippi*. Bureau of American Ethnology, Bulletin 83. Washington, D.C.: Government Printing Office, 1927. Reprint. Nashville: Blue and Gray Press, 1972. 103 pp. Pages 79–82 of this study are devoted to a description of Pawnee burial methods, cemeteries, and mourning practices. In passages taken from John Dunbar's journal and Charles Augustus Murray's work on the Pawnees, Bushnell emphasizes the tenderness with which the Pawnees cared for the dying and the depth of their sorrow upon the death of a loved one. Also included is an old photo of a Pawnee cemetery.

336. ———. *Villages of the Algonquian, Siouan, and Caddoan Tribes West of the Mississippi*. Bureau of American Ethnology, Bulletin 77. Washington. D.C.: Government Printing Office, 1922. Reprint. Nashville: Blue and Gray Press, 1972. 211 pp. This contains excellent descriptions of Pawnee permanent and temporary villages, and points out that all four Pawnee bands constructed similar dwellings. Bushnell draws his material from the first-hand accounts of Pike, Irving, James, Fremont, Dunbar, DeSmet and Murray. This is an excellent synthesis of the writings of white observers.

337. "Cherished Relics." Omaha: Douglas County Historical Society. Pawnee Indian File. n.s., n.d. Article about a Pawnee artifacts display and a painted mural, both at the Genoa National Bank in Genoa, Nebraska, site of the Pawnees' Nebraska reservation.

338. *Cheyenne (El Reno, Oklahoma) Transporter*, 15 February 1885, 7. Untitled paragraph describes a Pawnee relic—a wooden war club about 2 feet long with a steel projection, which had by now rusted.

339. Cosentino, Andrew F. *The Paintings of Charles Bird King (1785–1862)*. Washington, D.C.: Smithsonian Institution Press, 1977. 214 pp. Only one chapter of this book is devoted to King's famous Indian portraits, but in that chapter, the Pawnees are well represented, with one color plate and several black and white reproductions of Pawnee subjects.

340. Culin, Stewart. *Games of the North American Indians*. Twenty-Fourth Annual Report of the Bureau of American Ethnology, 1902–1903, 3-809. Washington, D.C.: Government Printing Office, 1907. Pawnee games figure prominently in this lengthy report, with much of the information coming from the Field Museum in Chicago. Among the games discussed are gambling baskets and dice, the Pawnee hand game, arrow games, the ring and javelin game, and ball games. Much of the Pawnee information was gathered by George A. Dorsey, John B. Dunbar, and George Bird Grinnell. A number of the items at the Field Museum are pictured and include museum catalog numbers.

341. Echo-Hawk, Roger C. "Pawnee Mortuary Traditions." *American Indian Culture and Research Journal* 16, no. 2 (1992): 77–99. Superb article covering all aspects of Pawnee burials. Echo-Hawk conducted interviews with elderly members of different Pawnee bands and cites the works of many prominent ethnologists. The three pages Echo-Hawk devotes to "grave-tampering" are especially enlightening. This excellent source is part of an edition of this journal devoted to Native American reburials and repatriation.

342. Ewers, John C. "Charles Bird King: Painter of Indian Visitors to the Nation's Capital." Washington, D.C.: *Smithsonian Report, Publication 4168*, 1954, 463–73. A brief but thorough personal sketch of King, who has been both praised and criticized for his Indian paintings, many of which were destroyed in an 1865 fire at the Smithsonian. This little report may be most valuable for its list of King paintings, including the ones lost in the fire. The list includes each subject's tribal affiliation, name of the subject, date, and the location of each painting. Five of the works are of Pawnees.

343. ———."'Chiefs from the Missouri and Mississippi' and Peale's Silhouettes of 1806." *Smithsonian Journal of History* 1 (Spring 1966):

1–26. In 1805–1806, a delegation of western Indian chiefs traveled to the east coast to visit the "Great Father." In Philadelphia, artist Charles Willson Peale made paper silhouettes of some of the Indian delegates. This article reproduces and identifies the subjects of the silhouettes, two of whom were young Republican Pawnees. These silhouettes are probably the first likenesses of Pawnee Indians ever produced by a white artist.

344. ———. "Water Monsters In Plains Indian Art." *American Indian Art* 6 (Autumn 1981): 38–45. Water monsters permeate Plains Indian art, and take different forms for each tribe. The Skidi Pawnees created what was probably the largest representation of any creature by a Plains Indian tribe when they fashioned a sixty-foot-long, three-dimensional water monster for their annual Doctor's Lodge ceremony. Pawnee-Creek artist Acee Blue Eagle's tempera painting of a water monster being attacked by thunderbirds hangs in the reading room of the National Anthropological Archives at the Smithsonian Institution.

345. Feder, Norman. "George Catlin: Sometimes Accurate." *American Indian Art* 2 (Summer 1977): 72–75. Feder uses Catlin as an example of an early observer of Native American material culture. Most of this brief article focuses on Pawnee otter fur turbans and their depictions in Catlin's portraits. Two of Catlin's paintings are featured along with an excellent photograph of a beautiful Pawnee turban originally misidentified as either Seminole or Sioux.

346. ———. "Pawnee Cradleboards." *American Indian Art* 3 (Autumn 1978): 40–50. Beautifully illustrated article explaining the construction, decoration, and use of cradleboards among the Pawnees, and comparing their construction to those of the Poncas, Omahas, Wichitas, and Osages. Nearly every Pawnee cradleboard known to the author is pictured.

347. Gilmore, Melvin R. *Uses of Plants by the Indians of the Missouri River Region.* Thirty-Third Annual Report of the Bureau of American Ethnology. Washington, D.C.: Government Printing Office, 1919. Reprint. Lincoln: University of Nebraska Press, 1977. 109 pp. In this classic study, Gilmore lists over eighty plants used by Indians of the eastern Plains, along with their Indian names. Each plant is thoroughly described, and most were used by the Pawnees for food, for medical purposes, or put to practical use. Myths associated with certain plants are related as well.

348. Harrington, John P. "Pawnee Hogans." *Indians at Work* 6 (January 1939): 20–21. This brief article provides no new information on Pawnee earth lodges, but it does include an 1871 William Henry Jackson photograph of one of the last Pawnee earth lodges along the Loup River near Genoa, Nebraska. The Pawnees relocated to Indian Territory a few years after this photo was taken.

349. Healy, Don. "Flag of the Pawnee." *Flags of the Native Peoples of the United States.* user.aol.com/donh523/navapage/pawn.htm. Very informative internet article tracing the history of the flag of the Pawnee Nation and explaining its meaning. Each element of the flag has either historical or cultural importance. The article also describes a variation of this flag that is flown at the Oklahoma City Flag Plaza honoring the Indian tribes of Oklahoma. Traditional flags can be purchased from the Pawnee Nation via the internet.

350. Hogarth, Paul. "Off to the Plains!" *American West* 5 (November 1968): 5–17. Chronicles the career of British illustrator Boyd Houghton, who toured the American frontier in 1869–1870, producing dozens of drawings. With Indian Agent Jacob Troth as his guide, Houghton traveled to the Pawnee reservation in Nance County, Nebraska, and recorded scenes of Pawnee life. Two of these drawings, of a Pawnee camp and Indian gambling, are reproduced in the article.

351. Hurt, R. Douglas. *Indian Agriculture in America: Prehistory to the Present.* Lawrence: University Press of Kansas, 1987. 290 pp. This unique source surveys Indian agricultural methods and government policy dealing with Indian farming into the recent period. The Pawnees are only mentioned briefly, but this well-written and thoroughly researched study is a good overview of federal policy on Indian agriculture over the past 150 years.

352. Koch, Ronald P. *Dress Clothing of the Plains Indians.* Norman: University of Oklahoma Press, 1977. 219 pp. This book is divided into chapters by article of clothing and decoration. Hairstyles and dance costumes also receive a great deal of attention, and numerous line drawings and photographs provide added information. The Pawnees are briefly mentioned in nearly every chapter.

353. Kremens, John Benjamin. "A Survey of the Roached Hairdress Among the Indians of North America." Master's thesis, University of Pennsylvania, 1941. 48 pp. Since this is a survey, little time is spent

on any particular tribe, but the Pawnees are discussed. The name *Pawnee* itself may have been derived from the word *pariki*, indicating a horn, or roached hairstyle. According to Kremens, the Skidi Pawnees sometimes also wore decorated artificial roaches made of deer hair during the *Iruska* ceremony. All of the material in this brief thesis is derived from traditional ethnographic sources.

354. La Flesche, Francis. "The Past Life of Plains Indians." *Southern Workman* 34 (November 1905): 587–94. Although written by a mixed-blood Omaha, this detailed discussion of pre-reservation farming and hunting practices could apply to any number of Plains tribes, including the Pawnees.

355. Lillie, G. William. "Indian Burials." *American Antiquarian and Oriental Journal* 8 (1886): 28–30. Pawnee Bill of wild west show fame writes to the journal to describe burial practices among the Pawnees in the late nineteenth century. According to his observations, the ceremony accompanying burials differed depending on the decedent's rank within the tribe. Chiefs lay in state, were loudly mourned by the women, and took with them to the spirit world trade goods and symbolic items. Elderly women, on the other hand, were buried where they died, without ceremony or coffins.

356. Linton, Ralph. "Origin of the Plains Earthlodge." *American Anthropologist* (n.s.) 26 (April–June 1924): 247–57. Article argues that the Plains earth lodges, regardless of which tribe built them, began with a single early plan that originated in the lower Mississippi valley and was carried northward by tribal migrations. The Pawnees apparently adopted earth lodge construction rather late in their history.

357. Maurer, Evan M. *The Native American Heritage: A Survey of North American Indian Art.* Chicago: Art Institute of Chicago, 1977. 351 pp. This is the catalog for the Art Institute of Chicago's Native American Art exhibition of July through October 1977. The Plains/Plateau section includes a pair of elk leather leggings that belonged to Riding In, a Pawnee. Also depicted and belonging to Riding In is a necklace of otter fur and grizzly bear claws decorated with ribbon and glass beads. The leggings are dated c. 1870, the necklace c. 1865. The essay accompanying the Plains artifacts pages is introduced by a selection from the Pawnee *Hako* ceremony.

358. Moore, Robert J., Jr. *Native Americans, A Portrait: The Art and Travels of Charles Bird King, George Catlin, and Karl Bodmer.* New York: Stewart, Tabori & Chang, 1997. 279 pp. This beautiful, oversized book reproduces in full color nearly all of the paintings of these preeminent portrayers of Native American life and individual Indians. Each painting is carefully explained, often in the words of the artist, and the text tells the fascinating stories of King, Catlin, and Bodmer. Among the portraits of Pawnees are four by King and five by Catlin, including the book's dust cover.

359. Nabokov, Peter, and Robert Easton. *Native American Architecture.* New York: Oxford University Press, 1989. 431 pp. A marvelous resource for the researcher looking for information on Indian living quarters and ceremonial structures. Beautifully illustrated with black and white photos, color plates, and line drawings, the book covers North America from the southwestern United States to the Arctic region. A fifty-two page chapter (122–74) is devoted to Great Plains earth lodges, grass houses, and tipis. The Pawnee earth lodge receives considerable coverage, with a diagram and explanation of the cosmic symbolism of this type of dwelling. A series of photos records the building of a model Pawnee lodge at the St. Louis World's Fair in 1904.

360. Newman, Thomas N. "Documentary Sources on the Manufacture of Pottery by the Indians of the Central Plains and Middle Missouri." *Plains Anthropologist* 4 (July 1955): 13–20. This outdated article is basically a list of paragraphs describing pottery manufacture taken from earlier works. The three references to the Pawnees are from Dunbar, Grinnell, and Weltfish.

361. O'Shea, John M. *Mortuary Variability: An Archaeological Investigation.* New York: Academic Press, Inc., 1984. 338 pp. A highly detailed comparison of selected burial sites of the Omahas, Arikaras, and Pawnees. Attempts to equate the treatment of individuals in death to their social status in life. Numerous charts, graphs, and drawings consolidate the large amount of data from the various burial sites. Draws the conclusion that in some cases, social status did influence burial practices.

362. Paul, R. Eli. "Faces of the First Nebraskans." *Nebraska History* 69 (Summer 1988): 50–53. Article showcases an Indian exhibit that opened at the Nebraska State Historical Society Museum in 1987. Artifacts featured in the exhibit were Pawnee catlinite and stone pipes

and an exact copy of the Segesser hide painting of the Villasur battle with the Otoes and Pawnees in 1720.

363. "Pawnee Fashions for 1838." *Missouri Saturday News*, 25 August 1838. Reprint. *Missouri Historical Society Bulletin* 23, no. 4, part 1 (July 1967): 351–52. Reading like a fashion show runway commentary, this satirical article describes the appearance and dress of a Skidi Pawnee "princess" at a buffalo dance.

363a. "Pawnee Monument Rescued from Neglect." *Omaha World Herald*, 7 September 2003, 8B. Human interest story of a Cedar Bluffs, Nebraska, high school senior who restored a Pawnee historical marker and roadside park near Fremont as an Eagle Scout project. The marker is near the site of Pahuk, and marks the location of the last earth lodges built by the Pawnees before being relocated to their Nebraska reservation near Genoa.

364. "Skull Creek, Butler County." *Nebraska History* 5 (July–September 1922): 36–37. An early Butler County, Nebraska, settler writes about this Pawnee burial ground that the Pawnees, Otoes, and Omahas visited once a year to honor their dead. Valuable as an original source, but it does contain errors.

365. "Pawnee Sky Observations." *Hands-On Astrophysics*. hoa.aavso. org/pawn.htm, July 27, 2000. Interprets the Pawnee elk skin star chart and points out that the Pawnees, unlike many Plains tribes who worshiped the sun, conducted their lives according to the movements of the stars.

366. Spencer, Lillian White. "Fairy Tales of Archaeology—III." *Southwestern Lore* 3 (1937): 10–12. Reprints a letter from Luther North explaining that Petalesharo's silver medal awarded in 1821 was found in a plowed field by school children. Article then traces the medal from the Nebraska State Historical Society to the Heye Museum in New York, and on to the American Numismatic Society, where it was on display.

367. Tomblin, Marion N. "Pawnees Built Mud Lodges Before Coming of White Men." *Tulsa Daily World*, 13 April 1930, 9. Article traces the history of Pawnee earth lodges and includes photos of an earth lodge village in Nebraska and a reconstructed lodge at Pawnee Bill's ranch near Pawnee, Oklahoma. The author makes assumptions about Pawnee ancestry that have not yet been proven by scholars.

368. Viola, Herman J. *The Indian Legacy of Charles Bird King*. Washington, D.C.: Smithsonian Institution Press and Doubleday and Co., 1976. 152 pp. This book shows King's important role in the preservation of the history and ethnography of Native Americans. King painted portraits of Indian leaders from over thirty tribes, most of whom were members of delegations visiting Washington, D.C. A comparison of King's paintings to those of other artists indicates that his portraits were often idealized. Among King's Pawnee subjects were Peskelechaco, La-ke-too-nee-ra-sha, Le-shaw-loo-pa-le-hoo, Sharitarish, and the young hero Petalesharo. Also reproduced is the silver medal presented to Petalesharo for his rescue of an Indian girl during the 1817 Morning Star Ceremony.

369. Walker, Joel. "Tirawa, the Pawnee and Square Architecture." *Platte Valley Review* 15 (Spring 1987): 68–79. Rambling article that attempts to show that square earth lodges were built before the Pawnees adopted the idea of a supreme being. By using examples from Grinnell's *Pawnee Heroes and Folk Tales*, the author deduces that belief in animal deities preceded belief in Tirawa, and the building of circular lodges began after Tirawa became the Pawnees' supreme being.

370. Wedel, Waldo R. "House Floors and Native Settlement Populations in the Central Plains." *Plains Anthropologist* 24 (May 1979): 85–98. Analyzes changes in the size of Pawnee dwellings over time by using archaeological, anthropological, and historical evidence. Concludes that larger, multi-family lodges became more prevalent among the Pawnees in the post-white contact period, and provides a large amount of numerical data to support this argument.

371. Weltfish, Gene. "Coiled Gambling Baskets of the Pawnee and Other Plains Tribes." *Indian Notes* 7 (July 1930): 277–95. A study of small, non-decorative woven baskets used to hold dice in Indian games of chance. In 1929, two Pawnee women made baskets for the author, and she describes the technique used by each basket weaver.

372. White, Richard. "The Cultural Landscape of the Pawnees." *Great Plains Quarterly* 2 (Winter 1982): 31–40. Excellent article concerned mainly with the impact of horses on the Pawnees. Discusses acquisition of horses, their importance, their influence on buffalo hunts, and the conflicts they caused. One section deals with the difficulty of feeding thousands of horses, and explains the ways the Pawnees found to solve this problem.

373. Will, George F., and George E. Hyde. *Corn Among the Indians of the Upper Missouri*. St. Louis: William Harvey Miner Co., 1917. Reprint. Lincoln: University of Nebraska Press, 1964. 323 pp. Basing their research on archaeological findings and on accounts of eighteenth- and nineteenth-century travelers and missionaries, the authors discuss the most important agricultural societies of the Upper Missouri Valley — the Omaha, Pawnee, Arikara, Mandan, Hidatsa, Crow, Ponca, Otoe, and Iowa. They describe fifty varieties of Indian corn and provide photographs of many types. Included are dozens of references to Pawnee corn, agricultural techniques, and descriptions of how corn was prepared and used in Pawnee ceremonies. This work also provides glimpses of the differences in farming techniques and culture among the Pawnee bands.

374. Witty, Thomas A., and Wendell P. Frantz. "The Historic Uses of Dogs among the Plains Indians." *Kansas Anthropological Association Newsletter*, vol. 20, nos. 4 and 5, December 1953 and January 1954. 8 pp. This brief article cites a number of standard sources that mention the use of dogs by Plains tribes. There is conflicting data as to whether the Pawnees used dogs as beasts of burden after they acquired horses, but several sources state that they did eat dogs on ceremonial occasions and served them to honored guests.

8
Music and Dance

375. Beloff, Sandra B. "Music of the Pawnees (With Special Reference to Present Day Oklahoma Pawnees)." Master's thesis, University of California at Los Angeles, 1972. 214 pp. A bit technical for the non-musicologist, but a useful source that includes two chapters on Pawnee history and beliefs. Primarily, this work emphasizes more modern uses of Pawnee music. Thirty-six Pawnee songs are carefully analyzed.

376. Curtis, Natalie. "American Indian Cradle Songs." *Musical Quarterly* 7 (October 1921): 549–58. Contains the Indian and English lyrics and the music to seven lullabies, one of which is Pawnee. Other references to Pawnee culture are scattered throughout the article. Some of this material also appears in Curtis' *The Indians' Book* [377].

377. ———. *The Indians' Book: Songs and Legends of the American Indians.* New York: Harper and Brothers, 1907. Reprint. New York: Dover Publications, Inc., 1968. 584 pp. Includes brief overviews of Pawnee history and mythology, along with the music and English translations of ceremonial songs performed for the author by Pawnees in the early twentieth century.

378. Densmore, Frances. "Music of the American Indians at Public Gatherings." *Musical Quarterly* 17 (October 1931): 464–79. Explains several Indian dances and describes how a few games are played. Densmore attended and took part in Pawnee games. She includes the music to the Pawnee hand game, which consists of just two notes, played in a changing rhythm.

379. ——. *Pawnee Music*. Bureau of American Ethnology Bulletin 93. Washington, D. C.: Government Printing Office, 1929. 129 pp. This work begins with a technical comparison of Pawnee music to the music of six other tribes. In 1919 and 1920, Frances Densmore conducted research among the Oklahoma Skidi and Chaui bands of Pawnees and witnessed several important ceremonies. The eighty-six songs included in this collection were performed by ten Pawnee singers. Each song, along with its Pawnee lyrics, is reproduced and analyzed, and most include free translations by James R. Murie. For ease in accessing these songs, they are listed by serial and catalog number.

380. ——. "The Songs of Indian Soldiers during the World War." *Musical Quarterly* 20 (October 1934): 419–25. Among the World War I songs featured in this interesting essay is a "Song Deriding a Slacker." Both words and music are included. Also describes a ceremony celebrating the safe return of Pawnee soldiers, in which a pseudo-scalp dance was performed with a captured German helmet replacing an enemy scalp.

381. Evarts, Mark. "Music of the Pawnee Sung by Mark Evarts." Documentary Recording by Gene Weltfish. Washington, D.C.: Ethnic Folkways Library, 1967. One hour recording with extensive documentation. Includes numerous dances, descriptions of Pawnee games, and some folklore. For a further description and a scholarly review of this recording, see *Chronicles of Oklahoma* 43 (Autumn 1965): 353–54.

382. Fletcher, Alice C. *Indian Games and Dances, with Native Songs, Arranged from American Indian Ceremonies and Sports*. Boston: C. C. Birchard and Company, 1915. Reprint. Introduction by Helen Myers. 139 pp. Lincoln: University of Nebraska Press, 1994. Among the dances included in this collection is the procession in honor of the ceremonial corn planted first thing in the spring. Fletcher describes the costumes worn by the participants and the movements of the dance, and includes words and music to the two songs that are performed during this "Life of the Corn" dance. Also explains *I-oú-tin*, a guessing game played by the Omahas, Otoes, Poncas, and Pawnees.

383. ——. *Indian Story and Song from North America*. Boston: Small, Maynard and Company, 1900. Reprint. Introduction by Helen Myers.

126 pp. Lincoln: University of Nebraska Press, 1995. After hearing Omaha Indians sing their songs at the 1898 Trans-Mississippi Exposition, Alice Fletcher prepared for publication the words, music, and stories of the thirty songs that appear in this volume. Five of the songs are of Pawnee origin.

384. Hart, Mickey, and K. M. Kostyal. *Song Catchers: In Search of the World's Music*. Washington, D.C.: National Geographic Society, 2003. 172 pp. Among the "song catchers" profiled in this beautifully illustrated volume are Alice Fletcher and Frances Densmore, both of whom recorded Pawnee music on wax cylinders in the late eighteenth and early nineteenth centuries. Since 1979, the Library of Congress has been transferring the music on these fragile cylinders into digital form.

385. Hofmann, Charles, comp. and ed. *Frances Densmore and American Indian Music: A Memorial Volume*. Contributions from the Museum of the American Indian, Heye Foundation, Vol. XXIII. New York: Museum of the American Indian, Heye Foundation, 1968. 127 pp. A biography and collection of writings by and about Miss Densmore, who spent her career reproducing the music of Native Americans in manuscript form and in field recordings. Contains an excerpt (p. 43) from the Forty-First Annual Report of the Bureau of Ethnology (1919–1924) describing a visit to the Oklahoma Pawnees during which she was allowed to view the contents of the Morning Star sacred bundle.

386. Howard, Helen Addison. "Literary Translators and Interpreters of Indian Songs." *Journal of the West* 12 (April 1973): 212–28. Profiles of Alice C. Fletcher, Frances Densmore, and Natalie Curtis, all of whom did important work with Pawnee music.

387. Lillie, G. William. "Sacred Dances of the Pawnees." *American Antiquarian and Oriental Journal* 7 (1885): 208–12. Pawnee Bill draws on his experiences among the Pawnees to describe important dances—when they were performed, how they were performed, and who participated. Included are a lengthy explanation of the scalp dance, the pony dance, the medicine dance, the rarely performed but interesting white horse dance, the eagle and circle dances, war dances, the buffalo dance, and the important pipe dance.

388. McAllester, David P. *Peyote Music*. Viking Fund Publications in Anthropology, vol. 13, 1949. Reprint London: Johnson Reprint Com-

pany, Ltd., 1964. 168 pp. Traces the history of peyotism and explains the importance of music in the peyote ritual. Among the songs reproduced with music and Indian lyrics are three from the Pawnees. The author points out that the rhythms of Pawnee peyote songs are different than most. Ten sound recordings of Pawnee songs are among the collection in the Archives of Folk and Primitive Music at Indiana University.

389. "Music of the Papago and Pawnee." *Smithsonian Miscellaneous Collections*, vol. 72. no. 6, 1920, 102–7. In April 1920, Frances Densmore visited Pawnee, Oklahoma, and was allowed to briefly view the contents of the Pawnee Morning Star bundle. She listened to the Morning Star Ceremony from outside the sacred lodge and made manuscript notes of the songs, some of which were in two-part harmony. She also recorded Pawnee songs during this visit.

390. Rhodes, Willard, rec. and ed. "Plains: Comanche, Cheyenne, Kiowa, Caddo, Wichita, Pawnee." In *Folk Music of the United States*. Archive of Folk Song, Recording no. AFSL 39. Washington, D.C.: Library of Congress, Music Division Recording Laboratory, n.d. One of a series of long-playing records of music of the American Indians recorded for the Library of Congress. Side B features five Pawnee selections: a prayer song, Pawnee hand game songs, Pawnee ghost dance music, a flag song, and a recording of a Pawnee war dance song. All are performed by Pawnee singers and musicians.

391. Roberts, Helen H. "Ceremonial Songs of the Pawnee: Transcriptions of Music and Musical Analysis." Manuscript 1788, National Anthropological Archives. Washington, D. C.: Smithsonian Institution, 1922. This is a companion paper to *Ceremonies of the Pawnee*, by James R. Murie [440].

392. ———. "New Phases in the Study of Primitive Music." *American Anthropologist* 24 (January–March 1922): 144–60. This study is directed primarily toward experts in the construction of Indian music. Prominent among the examples are the Pawnee Skull Bundle Ceremony song, music to accompany the Morning Star Ceremony, and the White Beaver Ceremony song. Roberts emphasizes the similarities between Teton Sioux and Pawnee music, giving weight to the Pawnee argument that the Sioux borrowed the idea for their medicine societies from the Pawnee.

393. Sambrich, Marcella. *My Favorite Folk Songs*. Boston: Oliver Ditson Company, 1918. 138 pp. This collection of songs from around the world features two native American tunes—one Omaha and one Pawnee. The Pawnee love song is called "Laughing Water," and includes English lyrics and piano accompaniment.

394. *Songs of the Pawnee and Ute*. Smithsonian-Densmore Cylinder Collection, L 25. Recording Laboratory, Music Division of the Library of Congress, 1952. One of seven twelve-inch long-playing records of Frances Densmore's collection of Indian music. The recording is accompanied by a twenty-one-page booklet with the same title.

395. Weyland, Rudolph Harry. "A Study of the Musical Talent among Indian Children from the Pawnee Indian Agency Jurisdiction, Pawnee, Oklahoma." Master's thesis, Oklahoma Agricultural and Mechanical College, 1945. 56 pp. Two hundred sixty students ranging in age from ten to sixteen years from four schools—the Pawnee Indian Boarding School, the Pawnee, Oklahoma, elementary school, a school in White Eagle, Oklahoma, and the Red Rock, Oklahoma, school—were tested for musical ability using a complicated set of criteria. The conclusion drawn was that based on the author's test standards, Pawnee children have little musical talent. This study would be most useful to musicologists, since it is quite technical.

396. YellowHorse, Pawnee. *Look to the Stars*. This final recording from Pawnee YellowHorse features songs written in the Pawnee language by the late Vance Horsechief, Jr. Walter R. Echo-Hawk is a singer on this compact disc, available on the internet from Echohawks.com, an online store operated by members of the Echo-Hawk family.

397. ———. *Spirit of the Plains*. A compact disc of original music composed and sung in the Pawnee language. This recording includes a women's chorus. The compact disc is available on the internet at www.Echohawks.com.

9
Religion and Ceremonialism

398. Albers, Patricia, and Seymour Parker. "The Plains Vision Experience: A Study of Power and Privilege." *Southwestern Journal of Anthropology* 27 (Autumn 1971): 203–33. Notes that among Plains Indians engaging in horticulture as well as hunting, such as the Pawnees, the vision experience is more community related than personal. The more complex a society, the less likely that visions would be solely the property of individuals.

399. Alexander, Hartley Burr. *The Mystery of Life: A Poetization of "The Hako—A Pawnee Ceremony."* Chicago: Open Court Publishing Co., 1913. 81 pp. The forty-eight-page introduction is basically a retelling of Alice Fletcher's study of the Hako, and the remainder of the volume reprints parts of the actual Hako ceremony. Researchers should consult Fletcher's original work [415].

400. Benedict, Ruth Fulton. "The Vision in Plains Culture." *American Anthropologist* (n.s.) 24 (January–March 1922): 1–23. Nicely written article comparing and contrasting the spirituality of Plains tribes. The Pawnees receive considerable attention mainly because they took a different approach. Unlike many Plains tribes, the Pawnees did not practice self-torture. Women in mourning did cut their arms and legs, but Benedict asserts that in the huge body of literature on Pawnee ceremonialism, self-torture is never mentioned. Also setting the Pawnees apart is the absence of an actual "vision quest." Special powers among the Pawnees came from years of training—not from a single experience. Instead of

personal guardian spirits, the Pawnees have "above" and "below" spirits, represented respectively by the stars and animal medicine lodges. Apparently, animal lodges are found only among the Pawnee, Wichita, and Arikara tribes, making them a Caddoan phenomenon.

401. Blaine, Martha Royce. "The Pawnee Sacred Bundles: Their Present Uses and Significance." *Papers in Anthropology*, vol. 24. no. 2. Norman: University of Oklahoma Press, 1984. This is a very useful article that discusses the history of sacred bundles among the Pawnees and the closely related Arikaras, then tells the story of the bundles brought to Indian Territory in the 1870s. The sacred bundles are rarely the focal points of modern Pawnee ceremonies, but in the 1970s, Garland Blaine presided over a ceremony blessing the Pawnee bundles in the collections of Chicago's Field Museum of Natural History.

402. Blakeslee, Donald J. "The Origin and Spread of the Calumet Ceremony." *American Antiquity* 46 (October 1981): 759–68. Presents ethnohistorical and archaeological evidence that the calumet and its associated ceremonies originated in the Great Plains prior to 1634 A. D., and then spread eastward through trade and warfare. Cites several authors of respected works on the Pawnees, two of whom claim that the first use of the calumet was by the Pawnees.

403. Bruce, Robert. *Pawnee Naming Ceremonial Near Pawnee, Oklahoma, Armistice Day, November 11, 1932.* New York: Privately Published, 1933. 36 pp. In November 1932, Robert S. Ellison was given the Pawnee name Wyo-La-Shar in an elaborate name-changing ceremony conducted in the traditional way. This slim volume contains a great deal of other information, but it is completely disorganized. There are biographical sketches of prominent Pawnees, a photo of the Pawnee Supreme Council, a list of white men who have received Pawnee names, personal histories of everyone Bruce could think of, and even an abbreviated version of the Pawnee Naming Ceremony, taken from Alice Fletcher's Bureau of Ethnology report. A unique source that requires patience to use.

404. Chamberlain, Von Del. *When Stars Came Down to Earth: Cosmology of the Skidi Pawnee Indians of North America.* Los Altos, California: Ballena Press, 1982. 270 pp. An astronomer attempts to consolidate bits and pieces of Skidi mythology and star lore into an explanation of what this Pawnee band knew about the cosmos. He equates earth lodges to observatories, speculates about the identity of certain stars, and devotes twenty pages to the Pawnee star chart, now at Chicago's

Field Museum. This book has been criticized by other scholars such as Douglas R. Parks, whose review essay appears in *American Indian Culture and Research Journal* [444].

405. Clark, John Owen. "Diffusion Center vs. Melting Pot." *American Anthropologist* 29 (1927): 732–33. In this letter to the editor, Clark responds to Ralph Linton's earlier article on the origins of the Skidi Morning Star ceremony [434]. He takes Linton's theory one step further with the intriguing idea that perhaps the Indians of Mexico adopted certain rituals and characteristics of their ceremonies from tribes in the present United States.

406. Dorsey, George A. "One of the Sacred Altars of the Pawnee." Easton, Pennsylvania: International Congress of Americanists, Thirteenth Session, 1905, 67–74. The word "altar" in this title refers to a sacred bundle, in this case the bundle relating to the planting of corn. Dorsey carefully explains the preparations for opening the sacred bundle, then goes step by step through the actual ceremony. Of particular interest is the role played by women in this ritual.

407. ———. "A Pawnee Ritual of Instruction." *Anthropological Papers Written in Honor of Franz Boas. Boas Anniversary Volume*, 350–54. New York: G. E. Stechert & Co., 1906. A twenty-six-line ritual believed to have been recited by adults to children. Its reference is to the girl who was the earth's first human and to the events that occur during the Morning Star sacrifice. Each line of the ritual poem is fully interpreted in the accompanying notes.

408. ———. "The Skidi Rite of Human Sacrifice." *Proceedings of the International Congress of Americanists* 15: (1906): 65–70. Very detailed explanation of the Morning Star Ceremony as related by Skidi priest Roaming Scout and two women who observed the ritual when they were girls.

409. Dorsey, George A., and James R. Murie. "Pawnee Notes, Morning Star Folder." On file in the archives of the Department of Anthropology of the Field Museum of Natural History, Chicago, 1902.

410. ———. "The Pawnee: Society and Religion of the Skidi Pawnee." Manuscript notes and drafts on file in the archives of the Department of Anthropology of the Field Museum of Natural History, Chicago, 1907.

411. Druery, Mrs. Paul. "The Price Is Blood." *NEBRASKAland* 43 (August 1965): 38–39. Written on the occasion of a Genoa, Nebraska,

reenactment of the Morning Star Ceremony, this romanticized account tells of an undated earlier sacrifice, seen through the eyes of a young Sioux victim.

412. Duke, Philip, ed. "The Morning Star Ceremony of the Skiri Pawnee as Described by Alfred C. Haddon." *Plains Anthropologist* 34 (August 1989): 193–203. A British anthropologist's detailed description of a 1906 Morning Star ceremony performed in Oklahoma. All of the elements of the ceremony were present except the sacrificial victim. Haddon was the guest of George A. Dorsey, and James R. Murie and Roaming Scout participated in the ritual.

413. Farwell, Arthur. "The Artistic Possibilities of Indian Myth." *Poet-Lore* 15 (1904): 46–61. Includes a lengthy analysis of Alice C. Fletcher's *The Hako: A Pawnee Ceremony*.

414. Fletcher, Alice C. "Giving Thanks: A Pawnee Ceremony." *Journal of American Folklore* 13 (January–March 1900): 261–66. While visiting the Pawnees, anthropologist Fletcher witnessed a ceremony rarely seen by whites. A young Pawnee had tried to give a medicine man two horses for healing his wife. In this ritual, the medicine man opens a medicine bundle and asks forgiveness of Ti-rá-wa, the Great Spirit, for not accepting the ponies.

415. ———. *The Hako: A Pawnee Ceremony*. Twenty-Second Annual Report of the Bureau of American Ethnology. Washington, D.C.: Government Printing Office, 1904. Reprint. *The Hako: Song, Pipe, and Unity in a Pawnee Calumet Ceremony*. Lincoln: University of Nebraska Press, 1996. 368 pp. With the cooperation of an elderly Chaui informant and with James R. Murie as collaborator, Alice Fletcher was able to record the entire Hako Ceremony in 1898. The Hako, or Calumet Ceremony, focused on a sacred pipe with a feathered shaft, and promoted social unity both within and between tribes. All of the songs and rituals are presented and explained.

416. ———. "A Pawnee Ritual Used When Changing a Man's Name." *American Anthropologist* (n.s.) 1 (January 1899): 82–97. This ceremony was recorded directly from the words of an elderly Chaui Pawnee priest who had been a friend of the Omaha chief Joseph La Flesche. Pawnee scholar James R. Murie brought the priest to Washington, D. C., and also helped to interpret his words. This was a three-part ritual concluding with the discarding of an old name and the

acceptance of a new one. Following the explanation of the ritual is the text of the ceremony, first in Pawnee, then translated as closely as possible into English.

417.   ———. "Pawnee Star Lore." *Journal of American Folklore* 16 (January–March 1903): 10–15. Explains the role of stars and different types of winds in the Pawnee creation story and in their mythology. Each type of wind has a purpose and a connection to certain heavenly bodies.

418.   ———. "Star Cult Among the Pawnee—A Preliminary Report." *American Anthropologist* (n.s.) 4 (October–December 1902): 730–36. This brief article hints at the complexity of Skidi Pawnee star lore. It does briefly discuss the idea of male-female duality, the order in which star-related ceremonies were performed, and the cosmic symbolism of the Pawnee earth lodge. Numerous later works cover these topics in greater detail.

419.   Gill, Sam D. *Native American Religions: An Introduction*. Belmont, California: Wadsworth Publishing Company, 1982. 192 pp. Contains a short but effective description of the Pawnee sacrifice to the Morning Star, emphasizing the symbolism of blood in the ceremony.

420.   Golla, Susan. "Skidi Pawnee Religion: A Structural Analysis." Master's thesis, George Washington University, 1975. 95 pp. An excellent scholarly study of the complex religion and ceremonialism of the Skidi Pawnees. The major conclusions drawn are that Skidi religion is profoundly dualistic, and that Skidi social organization mirrors their cosmology. Line drawings and charts help to clarify these points.

421.   Good, Diane L. *Birds, Beads, and Bells: Remote Sensing of a Pawnee Sacred Bundle*. Anthropological Series, no. 15. Topeka: Kansas State Historical Society, 1989. 23 pp. This is a unique Pawnee source. In the early 1970s, the granddaughter of a Massacre Canyon survivor who had inherited her family's sacred bundle donated the bundle to the Kansas State Historical Society. Not wishing to dishonor Pawnee tradition by opening the bundle, experts, including the author, used Computerized Axial Tomography (CAT) scanning to determine its contents. This is the story of that particular bundle, which now occupies a place of honor at the Pawnee Village Museum in Republic, Kansas, but it is also a brief history of the Pawnees and a fine explanation of the meanings and uses of Pawnee sacred bundles in general.

422. ———. "Sacred Bundles: History Wrapped Up in Culture." *History News* 45 (August 1990): 13–14, 27. An abridged version of Good's *Birds, Beads, and Bells: Remote Sensing of a Pawnee Sacred Bundle*, published by the Kansas State Historical Society [421]. Discusses the bundle donated to the Society by a descendant of a Massacre Canyon survivor.

423. Hall, Robert L. *An Archaeology of the Soul: North American Indian Belief and Ritual*. Urbana: University of Illinois Press, 1997. 222 pp. Skiri (Skidi) Pawnee rituals and ceremonies figure prominently in this outstanding study of Indian religion. Chapters Eleven and Twelve are dedicated to the Morning Star Sacrifice and the Garden of the Evening Star, respectively. In each of these chapters, comparisons are made to Meso-American rituals.

424. Hanson, Jeffrey R. "Structure and Complexity of Medicine Bundle Systems of Selected Plains Indians Tribes." *Plains Anthropologist* 25, Part 89 (August 1980): 199–227. Shows that tribal medicine bundles of semi-sedentary horticultural tribes were more complex than the bundles of horse nomads, and that bundle complexity was directly linked to the degree of tribal organization. Of the seven Plains tribes included in this study, the Skidi Pawnees had the most elaborate tribal bundle system. Included are a detailed schedule of Pawnee sacred bundle ceremonies, and charts comparing contents and usage of tribal bundles.

425. Hodge, Gene Meany, comp. *Four Winds: Poems from Indian Rituals*. Santa Fe: The Sunstone Press, 1972. 32 pp. This slim volume contains eight excerpts from the Pawnee Hako Ceremony as translated by Alice C. Fletcher. There is nothing new here, and researchers should consult Fletcher's original work.

426. Howard, Helen Addison. "An Introduction to Pre-Missionary Indian Religion." *Journal of the West* 13 (January 1974): 9–24. While concentrating on Southwest Indians, two pages of this study concern the Hako Ceremony of the Pawnees. Most of this information is taken from Alice C. Fletcher's study, *The Hako: A Pawnee Ceremony*.

427. "Indian Incantations." *NEBRASKAland* 49 (March 1971): 15, 64. Brief essay relates the methods of healing employed by Omaha and Skidi Pawnee medicine men and explains how these healers achieved exalted status within their tribes.

428. "Indian Sacrifice." *Missouri Intelligencer and Boone's Lick Advertiser*, 19 October 1827, 1. Alphonso Wetmore recounts Indian agent John Dougherty's attempt to free a young girl chosen to be sacrificed to the Morning Star. Also includes a French description of the ceremony, in which the victim is referred to as "he," and mentions that the Pawnee women oiled their hoes with the victim's fat after he/she was burned.

429. Irwin, Lee. *The Dream Seekers: Native American Visionary Traditions of the Great Plains*. Foreword by Vine Deloria, Jr. Norman: University of Oklahoma Press, 1994. 306 pp. References to Pawnee religion, visions, and legends abound in this analysis of the role of visions among Plains Indians. A scholarly work, it is not geared toward the casual reader. This book receives a lukewarm review in *American Indian Culture and Research Journal* 19, no. 2 (1995): 191–95.

430. Jones, Dorothy V. "John Dougherty and the Pawnee Rite of Human Sacrifice: April 1827." *Missouri Historical Review* 63 (April 1969): 293–316. Heavily footnoted article explains the controversy arising from the Skidi Pawnees' continued performance of the Morning Star Ceremony and recounts Indian agent John Dougherty's unsuccessful attempt to rescue a young Cheyenne woman who was sacrificed in the spring of 1827.

431. Lesser, Alexander. "Cultural Significance of the Ghost Dance." *American Anthropologist* 35 (January–March 1933): 108–15. In this thoughtful article, Lesser shows how the Ghost Dance phenomenon revitalized a Pawnee culture that was in disarray. He argues that the decline of Pawnee culture prior to the Ghost Dance was primarily the result of the loss of the buffalo, since so many rituals revolved around that all-important animal. But with the Ghost Dance and its messages from dead ancestors, the Pawnees once more began to perform their rituals and play their traditional games. In his opinion, the time of the Ghost Dance was nothing short of a Pawnee cultural renaissance. For a more in-depth discussion of the Ghost Dance movement among the Pawnees, see Lesser's *The Pawnee Ghost Dance Hand Game* [432].

432. ———. *The Pawnee Ghost Dance Hand Game: Ghost Dance Revival and Ethnic Identity*. Vol. 16 of Contributions to Anthropology. New York: Columbia University Press, 1933. Reprint. Introduction by Alice Beck Kehoe. Lincoln: University of Nebraska Press, 1996.

340 pp. Following chapters on 19th century Pawnee history and the Ghost Dance of 1890, Lesser explains how the Ghost Dance combined with a revival of this hand game to restore hope and a sense of tradition to the dispirited Pawnees.

433. Linton, Ralph. *Annual Ceremony of the Medicine Men.* Leaflet no. 8. Chicago: Field Museum of Natural History, Department of Anthropology, 1923. 20 pp. By performing prescribed annual rituals, Pawnee medicine men renewed their special powers, drove diseases from the villages, and convinced their fellow Pawnees that the powers they claimed were real. The actual ceremonies are described in minute detail.

434. ———. "The Origin of the Skidi Pawnee Sacrifice to the Morning Star." *American Anthropologist* (n.s.) 28 (July–September 1926): 457–66. The first part of this article is a detailed explanation of the Morning Star Ceremony and its accompanying rituals. The second part is a rebuttal to Wissler and Spinden's theory that this Skidi ceremony had Aztec origins [462]. Linton admits that some aspects of the ritual were similar to Aztec sacrifices, but he argues that there were also many differences. His final opinion is that this ceremony involving human sacrifice developed north of the Rio Grande.

435. ———. *Purification of the Sacred Bundles, A Ceremony of the Pawnee.* Leaflet no. 7. Chicago: Field Museum of Natural History, Department of Anthropology, 1923. 11 pp. This is another detailed account of a Pawnee ceremony extracted by Linton, sometimes word for word, from the field notes of George A. Dorsey and James R. Murie. It is a valuable source, but Linton gives no credit to Murie.

436. ———. *The Sacrifice to the Morning Star by the Skidi Pawnee.* Leaflet no. 6. Chicago: Field Museum of Natural History, Department of Anthropology, 1922. 18 pp. In the final sentence of this creation legend and detailed description of the Morning Star Ceremony, Linton states that the article was compiled primarily from the unpublished field notes of George A. Dorsey. However, he fails to credit the second author, Pawnee ethnographer James R. Murie, and does not mention that much of the article was copied verbatim from Dorsey and Murie's notes.

437. ———. *The Thunder Ceremony of the Pawnee.* Leaflet no. 5. Chicago: Field Museum of Natural History, Department of Anthropology,

1922. 16 pp. Includes a brief history of the tribe and an introduction to Pawnee religion. The Thunder Ceremony, neither the most important nor the most elaborate of the Pawnee rituals, was however very important because it was the first ritual of the ceremonial year. The trigger for the performance of this rite was the first sound of thunder in the spring. Working from the field notes of George A. Dorsey and the research of the uncredited James R. Murie, Linton goes step by step through the ceremony, outlining the roles of Pawnee priests, chiefs, and the very minor role of women.

438. Lund, Ruth Ludington. *Down Ludington Lane*. Self-published, 1974. 66 pp. This unusual little volume is partly a family history and partly reminiscences about events in the Columbus, Nebraska, area. Much of the book is poetry by the author. Included among the events is an account of the Pawnee Morning Star Ceremony, along with a romanticized poem about Petalesharo's daring rescue of a young woman about to be sacrificed.

439. Mullin, Cora Phoebe. *Needle of Cedar: The Story of Pita-le-sharu and The Hako, A Pawnee Ceremony*. Omaha: The Citizen Printing Company, 1931. 72 pp. A collection of poems honoring and extolling the virtues of the Pawnee leader Petalesharo, who lived from 1823 to 1874. The poems are romanticized, and no sources are given for any of them. This small volume also includes an English version of the Hako ceremony taken from Alice Fletcher's work.

440. Murie, James R. *Ceremonies of the Pawnee. Part I: The Skiri, and Part II: The South Bands*. Edited by Douglas R. Parks. Smithsonian Contributions to Anthropology No. 27. Washington, D.C.: Smithsonian Institution Press, 1981. 497 pp. This is the most complete account of Pawnee ceremonialism ever published. Working under the direction of Clark Wissler, Murie spent a decade collecting the details of Pawnee rituals and ceremonies. Part 1 presents the annual cycle of Skiri (Skidi) ceremonial life in great detail and explains the roles and functions of Skiri sacred bundles. The second part includes accounts of three South Band ceremonies. Songs accompanying the ceremonies are included, with lyrics in both Pawnee and English. This manuscript had been in the archives of the Bureau of American Ethnology since 1921. It was finally prepared for publication by Douglas Parks, and contains translations, notes, an expanded bibliography, a biography of James Murie, and two indexes.

441. North, Luther H. "Fighting the Frontier Battles." *The Nebraska Farmer* (March 21, 1931): 8, 25. Eyewitness accounts of performances of Pawnee medicine men. One medicine man produced a live hawk out of thin air, and another grew a stalk of corn in thirty minutes. Several of North's Pawnee Scouts used sleight of hand to turn mud balls into turtles and to turn themselves into deer.

442. O'Brien, Patricia J. "Morning Star Sacrifices: Contradiction or Dualism?" *Plains Anthropologist* 32 (February 1987): 73–76. Article argues that because male/female dualism was so much a part of Pawnee culture, it is reasonable to assume that if females were sacrificed to the Morning Star (Mars), males were sacrificed to the Evening Star (Venus). Cites writers who used the word "he" when referring to a sacrificial victim.

443. O'Brien, Patricia J., and Diane M. Post. "Speculation About Bobwhite Quail and Pawnee Religion." *Plains Anthropologist* 33 (November 1988): 489–504. This article resulted from the discovery of four pairs of northern bobwhite wings in a storage pit of a Kansas earth lodge that has been identified as belonging to the Smoky Hill tradition, ancestors of the Pawnees. The authors argue that since the bobwhite had no economic value to these people, it must have played a symbolic role. The article presents arguments to support this hypothesis.

444. Parks, Douglas R. "Interpreting Pawnee Star Lore: Science or Myth?" *American Indian Culture and Research Journal* 9 (1985): 53–65. Highly critical review essay of Von Del Chamberlain's *When Stars Came Down to Earth*. Parks argues that Chamberlain often confuses star lore with astronomy and makes false assumptions regarding Pawnee knowledge and ceremonialism.

445. Parsons, Elsie Clews. "Ritual Parallels in Pueblo and Plains Cultures, with a Special Reference to the Pawnee." *American Anthropologist* 31 (July–September 1929): 642–54. Presents an argument that there are many more similarities between the Pueblo and Plains cultures than previously recognized. The author singles out the Pawnees as the Plains group whose rituals and beliefs most closely resemble those of the Pueblos. Aspects mentioned are bundle societies, tribal government, medicine lodges, and calendars. Rather technical for the non-anthropologist.

446. *The Peyote Road*. Produced by Gary Rhine. Written by Phil Cousineau, and narrated by Peter Coyote. San Francisco: Kifaru Productions, 1993. 60 minutes. In 1990, the U.S. Supreme Court ruled

that the first amendment to the constitution does not protect the Native American Church and its members' transportation and use of peyote, thus threatening the freedom of Indian religion. In 1994, President Clinton signed an amendment to once more allow the use of peyote for religious purposes. This film traces the history of the peyote religion and the stumbling blocks that have been placed in its way. Includes appearances by several peyote "road men" and other Native American Church members. The court decisions, missionary and Indian agents' impact, and other actions involving peyote religion are clearly explained by prominent Pawnee attorney Walter Echo-hawk. The film is illustrated throughout with stunning Native American art.

447. Richert, Bernhard E. "Plains Indian Medicine Bundles." Master's thesis, University of Texas, 1969. 209 pp. Divides the Plains Indians into nomadic tribes and semi-sedentary village tribes and discusses the medicine bundle system of each group. Devotes fifteen pages to a thorough explanation of Pawnee bundles, using respected anthropological sources.

448. Roper, Donna C. "A Note on the Quail and the Pawnee." *Plains Anthropologist* 39 (February 1994): 73–76. Argues that there is no concrete evidence to support the theory of O'Brien and Post [443] that the bobwhite quail represented the Pawnee people, and offers evidence to refute that theory.

449. "Sacred Family Bundle Donated to Society." *Kansas State Historical Society Mirror* 34 (November 1988): 1, 3. The sacred bundle that has a place of honor in the Pawnee Indian Village near Republic, Kansas, was donated to the Kansas State Historical Society in the summer of 1988. The article points out that it is unusual for a sacred bundle to be displayed publicly, but this bundle, which survived Massacre Canyon, has been blessed by the Pawnee and is displayed in its proper context.

450. Schenck, Sara Moffatt. "The Stars in the Culture of the American Indians." Master's thesis, University of California, Berkeley, 1925. 70 pp. Thesis divides Native Americans into geographic regions and explains the significance of stars to each group. The author concludes that stars played a larger role in the religion and mythology of Plains Indians than among any other tribes. Because of the Morning Star Ceremony, the Pawnees figure prominently in this study.

451. Thurman, Melburn D. "A Case of Historical Mythology: The Skidi Pawnee Morning Star Sacrifice of 1833." *Plains Anthropologist* 15

(November 1970): 309–11. Illustrates the way historical errors are perpetuated by comparing several accounts of Agent John Dougherty's attempted rescue of a Cheyenne captive. States that the correct date must be 1827, but it has been recorded variously as 1831, 1832, or 1833.

452. ———. "The Skidi Pawnee Morning Star Sacrifice of 1827." *Nebraska History* 51 (Fall 1970): 269–80. Presents evidence to support his argument that Indian agent John Dougherty's unsuccessful attempt to rescue a young Cheyenne woman scheduled to be sacrificed occurred in 1827, not in 1833, as often stated. There is no mention of this event in Dougherty's 1833 reports or correspondence, but he did report it in 1827.

453. ———. "The Timing of the Skidi-Pawnee Morning Star Sacrifice." *Ethnohistory* 30 (Fall 1983): 155–63. Argues convincingly that rather than being conducted randomly, the Morning Star sacrifice was scheduled only when certain cosmic conditions occurred involving Venus, Mars, and the crescent moon.

454. "Traveling in the Sacred Manner: The Pawnee Trail." In *On Kansas Trails: Traveling with Explorers, Emigrants, and Entrepreneurs.* Lawrence: University of Kansas Division of Continuing Education, 1986, 5–7. Explains that there were actually a number of Pawnee trails followed by bands as they traveled to the buffalo hunting grounds. Of value in this brief essay is a description of the cosmic connection in preparing for hunts.

455. Troike, Nancy Patterson. "Mesoamerican and Pawnee Arrow Sacrifice Ceremonies: A Comparative Analysis." Master's thesis, University of Texas, 1958. 101 pp. Troike concludes that the Pawnee Morning Star sacrifice very closely resembled the *Tlacaciliztli* rite of human sacrifice practiced in Mesoamerica, and therefore, represented a diffusion of the Mesoamerican ritual. This conclusion differs from those of some other writers, especially Ralph Linton [434], who believed that the Pawnees borrowed aspects of this rite from neighboring tribes, then combined them into the Morning Star Ceremony.

456. Ubelaker, Douglas H., and Waldo R. Wedel. "Bird Bones, Burials, and Bundles in Plains Archaeology." *American Antiquity* 40 (1975): 444–52. This general article on the non-economic uses of birds among Plains Indians briefly mentions the observations of several western travelers that the Pawnees stuffed bird skins with herbs and

roots—so-called medicine birds. More recent research on the Pawnee use of birds for ceremonial purposes can be found in O'Brien and Post [443] and Roper [448].

457. Wedel, Waldo R. "Native Astronomy and the Plains Caddoans." In *Native American Astronomy*, edited by Anthony Aveni. Austin: University of Texas Press, 1977, 131–45. Focusing on the Pawnees and Wichitas, this provocative essay points out that the Pawnees differed from nearly all other Plains tribes in that their religion and ritual were heavily interlaced with star lore. Wedel traces the Pawnee ethnographic record and describes the Morning Star Ceremony and earth lodge orientation. He criticizes the Presbyterian missionaries for failing to record tribal religious beliefs, and argues that the Pawnee sky map at the Field Museum of Natural History could not possibly be 300 years old, as claimed.

458. West, Elliott. *The Contested Plains: Indians, Goldseekers, and the Rush to Colorado*. Lawrence: University Press of Kansas, 1998. 422 pp. Among the references to the Pawnees in this book is an account of the Summit Springs battle, taken from James T. King's article on the Republican River Expedition in *Nebraska History* [860], but the most intriguing passage concerns the discovery in Kansas of an earth lodge perhaps belonging to a Native American priest who was a Pawnee ancestor. The remains of four bobwhite quail in a storage pit led West to suggest that the proto-Pawnee group to which this priest belonged may have thought of themselves as the Quail People. For a more in-depth study of this earth lodge and the possible bobwhite connection, see O'Brien and Post, "Speculations About Bobwhite Quail and Pawnee Religion" [443].

459. Williamson, Ray A. *Living the Sky: The Cosmos of the American Indian*. Boston: Houghton Mifflin Company, 1984. 366 pp. An entire chapter of this well-written and nicely illustrated book is devoted to the Skidi Pawnee Morning Star Ceremony and to a careful explanation of the Skidi leather star chart housed at the Field Museum of Natural History in Chicago. Williamson strongly supports astronomer Von Del Chamberlain's theories regarding Skidi cosmology, and many of his references are to Chamberlain's work. Also discusses the Pawnee earth lodge as a classic example of Native American cosmology, and explains that the structure of a lodge represented the Pawnee concept of heaven and earth.

460. Wissler, Clark. "Comparative Study of Pawnee and Blackfoot Rituals." *Proceedings of the Nineteenth International Congress of Americanists*, vol. 19, 1915. 5 pp. Highly speculative essay argues that some Pawnee rituals came from the Blackfoot tribe by way of the Mandans, Hidatsas, and Arikaras. Ceremonies involving corn may have come from the Pueblos of the Southwest, and Wissler believes strongly that the Pawnee Morning Star rite of human sacrifice was borrowed from the Aztecs. (See Wissler and Spinden, [462].)

461. ———. "The Sacred Bundles of the Pawnee." *Natural History* 20 (November–December 1920): 569–71. Discusses several of the Pawnee sacred bundles in the collections of the American Museum of Natural History and explains the difference between Indian doctors and priests. Features the Skidi Evening Star and skull bundles and the tribal bundles of the Kitkahaki (Kitkahahki) and Chaui bands.

462. Wissler, Clark, and Herbert J. Spinden. "The Pawnee Human Sacrifice to the Morningstar." *American Museum Journal* 16 (January 1916): 49–55. Using as their evidence several Mexican codices showing a similar ritual, Wissler and Spinden present the controversial argument that the human sacrifice during the Pawnee Morning Star Ceremony was borrowed from the Aztecs. The authors believe that the idea of the scaffold-type ceremony could have spread north in the very early 1500s. Others disagree with this theory, however [405], [434].

10
Relations with Other Tribes

463. "Ancient Indian Feuds." *Omaha Bee*, 30 November 1895. Explains that both the Sioux and the Pawnees attacked the Poncas when they lived on their Nebraska reservation just south of Dakota Territory, and argues that it was these attacks that convinced the government to move the Poncas to Indian Territory.

464. Bassett, S. C. "The Sioux-Pawnee War." *Nebraska History* 5 (April–June 1922): 30. Eyewitness account of the Pawnees' trek to the Republican River hunting grounds where many of them would die at the hands of the Sioux. This homesteader mentions that Pawnee survivors were returned to a point near their reservation on and in Union Pacific railroad cars.

465. Bent, George. "The Battle of the Medicine Arrows." *The Frontier* 4 (November 1905): 3–4. Story of the Pawnee theft of the Cheyenne sacred arrows, as told by the mixed-blood son of William Bent, founder of Bent's Fort in southeastern Colorado. By this account, one arrow was returned to the Cheyennes as a peace offering in 1835, and one was recaptured by the Sioux two years later and returned to its rightful owners. These arrows and two replacements are still with the Cheyennes in Oklahoma.

466. Bixby, J. F. "Last Hunt of the Pawnees." *Overland Monthly* (n.s.) 29 (1897): 52–61. Romanticized, undocumented account of the battle at Massacre Canyon. Although basically accurate, the flowery prose

detracts from the story. Not the best source of information on this 1873 Sioux-Pawnee confrontation.

467. Blaine, Garland James, and Martha Royce Blaine. "Pa-Re-Su A-Ri-Ra-Ke: The Hunters that Were Massacred." *Nebraska History* 58 (Fall 1977): 342–58. The story of Massacre Canyon told from Pawnee and Sioux viewpoints. Interviews with participants and relatives of participants add authenticity to this account, co-written by a Pawnee.

468. Blaine, Martha Royce. "The Pawnee-Wichita Visitation Cycle: Historic Manifestations of an Ancient Friendship." In *Pathways to Plains Prehistory: Anthropological Perspectives of Plains Natives and Their Pasts,* edited by Don G. Wyckoff and Jack L. Hofman, Oklahoma Anthropological Society, Memoir 3, 113–34. The Cross Timbers Heritage Association, Contribution 1. Duncan, Oklahoma: Cross Timbers Press, 1982. Includes a brief history of early Pawnee-Wichita contacts. Also explains the historic visitation cycle between the two tribes and describes traditional visitation events. Points out that the cycle continues today in Oklahoma, although in a modified form.

469. Bogner, Carl Wendell. "Indian Relations in the Nebraska Territory, 1854–1860." Master's thesis, University of Tulsa, 1964. 114 pp.

470. "Bound to Fight." *Omaha Daily Herald*, 15 August 1873, 4. Prints an account by Julius Meyer, who visited the Pawnees on their Loup River reservation shortly after the tragedy at Massacre Canyon. The Indians informed him that after a suitable period of mourning, they would seek revenge against the Sioux. Meyer also learned that the Pawnee felt betrayed by Sky Chief, their leader who died at Massacre Canyon, since they believed his negligence had led them into the ambush.

471. Brady, Cyrus Townsend. *Indian Fights and Fighters*. McClure, Philips & Co., 1904. Reprint. Introduction by James T. King. Lincoln: University of Nebraska Press, 1971. 423 pp. Many of the entries in this collection of accounts of frontier battles were related many years later by participants. Among the recollections is a colorful but error-strewn description of the 1869 Battle of Summit Springs. The former white scout who recalled this battle misidentified the Cheyenne Dog Soldier leader Tall Bull as a Sioux and greatly inflated the number of Indian dead and wounded. Fortunately, James King's excellent introduction cautions readers about errors in the text.

472. *Dances with Wolves.* Produced by Jim Wilson and Kevin Costner. Directed by Kevin Costner. Orion Pictures, 1990. 181 minutes. Oscar-winning film stars Kevin Costner as Lt. John Dunbar, an army officer assigned to a frontier outpost in 1863. Dunbar becomes acquainted with the Sioux and temporarily adopts their way of life. This film is ground-breaking in that every Indian role is played by an Indian, and the Lakota language is spoken extensively throughout the film. The problem with Costner's approach is that all of the Sioux are heroic, while the Pawnees are portrayed as stereotypical villains. Most accounts of Sioux-Pawnee relations see the Pawnees as victims of the more powerful Sioux.

473. "Destruction of a Pawnee Village." *Missionary Herald*, vol. 29. Boston: Crocker and Brewster, 1833, 369. In May 1833, a missionary to the Osages reported an attack by Osages on a Pawnee village, resulting in many Pawnee deaths and the taking of captives. Ironically, some of the goods taken from the Pawnees had been stolen earlier from Santa Fe traders.

474. Dorsey, George A. "How the Pawnee Captured the Cheyenne Medicine Arrows." *American Anthropologist* 5 (October–December 1903): 644–58. Dorsey relates two versions of the theft of the Cheyenne Medicine Arrows, told to him by Skidi Pawnee informants. Both versions tell basically the same story, although one is much more detailed than the other. The only major difference is the number of captured medicine arrows put into the Skidi Morning Star sacred bundle. These accounts differ slightly from those passed on by George Bird Grinnell [483].

475. ———. "Pawnee War Tales." *American Anthropologist* 8 (April–June 1906): 337–45. Two rather confusing stories about Pawnee relations with the Cheyenne and Arapaho, but especially with the Comanches. Told to Dorsey by an elderly Pawnee warrior called George Shooter.

476. *El Reno (Oklahoma) News*, 11 June 1897, 8. Reports that recently the Pawnees hosted a pipe dance four miles south of Pawnee, Oklahoma, in honor of visiting Osages. The members of each tribe dressed in all their finery, and according to witnesses, the dress of the Osages was gorgeous. This event was also reported in the *Kingfisher (Oklahoma) Free Press* on 10 June 1897, page 2.

477. Faust, Harold S. "The American Indian in Tragedy and Triumph." Presbyterian Historical Studies, no. 1. Reprinted from the *Journal of*

the Presbyterian Historical Society 22, nos. 3 and 4. Philadelphia: Presbyterian Historical Society, 1945. 73 pp. A Presbyterian minister recounts an attack on Iowa Indians by a Pawnee war party in 1843, and the Iowas' revenge.

478. Finney, James F. "Reminiscences of a Trader in the Osage Country." *Chronicles of Oklahoma* 33 (Summer 1955): 145–58. In 1872, Finney was a trader at the Osage Indian Agency in Oklahoma when the Pawnees, historic enemies of the Osages, arrived in Oklahoma from their Nebraska reservation. Relations between the tribes were mostly peaceful, and Finney recounts a horse-and-gun-stealing incident that ended amicably after a council between Osage and Pawnee leaders.

479. Fletcher, Alice C., and Francis La Flesche. The *Omaha Tribe*. Twenty-Seventh Annual Report of the Bureau of American Ethnology, 1905–1906. Washington, D.C.: Government Printing Office, 1911. Reprint Lincoln: University of Nebraska Press, 2 vols., 1992. 660 pp. Although this is an important study of the Omaha tribe, the index lists thirteen references to the Pawnees, which mainly refer to inter-tribal relations and comparisons of Omaha and Pawnee rituals, especially the calumet ceremony.

480. Forbes, Allen, Jr. "The Plains Agon—A Gross Typology." *Plains Anthropologist* 17 (May 1972): 143–55. Divides the Plains Indians' military complex into seven types of events: sacred symbol expeditions, major revenge expeditions, annual summer ceremonial expeditions, search-and-destroy missions, mourning expeditions, defense of hunting grounds, and horse raids. Includes an account of an Omaha sacred symbol expedition against the Pawnees, and two sacred symbol confrontations between the Pawnees and the Cheyennes.

481. Grinnell, George Bird. "Coup and Scalp among the Plains Indians." *American Anthropologist* 12 (1910): 296–310. Although primarily about the Cheyennes, and the Pawnees are mentioned just once, counting coup, taking scalps, and scalp dances were Pawnee customs as well, and the Pawnees and Cheyennes encountered each other many times in Plains warfare.

482. ———. *The Fighting Cheyennes*. New York: Charles Scribner's Sons, 1915. Reprint. Norman: University of Oklahoma Press, 1956. 450 pp. Includes numerous accounts of confrontations between the Cheyennes and the Pawnees, such as the Summit Springs battle in-

volving the North brothers and the Pawnee Scouts, and the fight during which the sacred Cheyenne Medicine Arrows were stolen. Other, more recent accounts of these events are perhaps more clearly written, but Grinnell's are special because they were related to him by Indian participants.

483. ———. "The Great Mysteries of the Cheyenne." *American Anthropologist* (n.s.) 12 (October–December 1910): 542–75. The "Great Mysteries" are the Cheyenne Medicine Arrows and the sacred Buffalo Hat. Grinnell explains the meaning of the sacred arrows, describes the arrow renewal ceremony, and recounts two versions of the capture of the arrows by the Pawnees—one account told by Cheyennes who were present at the battle that resulted in the arrow theft, and one told by a Skidi warrior and the daughter of the Skidi who led the Pawnees in this fight. These accounts of the battle differ somewhat from those passed on by Dorsey [474]. The Cheyennes attributed the many disasters that befell them in the nineteenth century to damage to the buffalo hat and the loss of the sacred arrows.

484. ———. "Prairie Battlefields." In *Frontier Days*. Edited by Oliver G. Swan, 195–201. Philadelphia: Macrae-Smith Company Publishers, 1928, 195–201. Grinnell relates the story of the battle between the combined Chaui, Pita-hau-í-rata (Pitahawiratas), and Kitka-hah-ki (Kitkahahki) bands of Pawnee and the Skidi band, which resulted in the Skidis joining and intermarrying with the other three bands. This tale was told to Grinnell by a Chaui elder, and has no date.

485. Hyde, George E. *Life of George Bent Written from His Letters*. Edited by Savoie Lottinville. Norman: University of Oklahoma Press, 1968. 389 pp. Correspondence from George Bent, mixed-blood son of William Bent, who founded Bent's Fort in southeastern Colorado, to author George E. Hyde. George Bent's mother was Owl Woman, daughter of a prominent Southern Cheyenne. Bent's letters describe several important events involving the Pawnees—among them the theft of the Cheyenne Medicine Arrows and the role played by Pawnee Scouts at the Battle of Summit Springs. Nicely written accounts told from a Cheyenne viewpoint.

486. ———. *Spotted Tail's Folk: A History of the Brulé Sioux*. Foreword by Harry H. Anderson. Norman: University of Oklahoma Press, 1974. 361 pp. The Pawnees and Brulé Sioux were deadly enemies, and in Hyde's work, the many battles between the two are always

Sioux victories. He covers the last Pawnee-Sioux battle, at Massacre Canyon, in some detail.

487. Inman, Henry. "Indian Fight on Lowrey's Island Opposite Larned in 1860." In *The Heart of New Kansas: A Pamphlet Historical and Descriptive of Southwestern Kansas*, edited by Bernard Bryan Smith, vol. 1, 68–74. Great Bend, Kansas: B. B. Smyth, Book and Job Printer, 1880. In this excerpt from the diary of Kansas Governor Isaac Sharp, printed earlier in the *Larned (Kansas) Chronoscope*, Inman provides a colorful account of a battle between a band of Pawnees and a group of Cheyennes led by Black Kettle. Sharp apparently played a role in this fight, carrying messages back and forth between the two Indian bands. This source is available at the Kansas State Historical Society in Topeka.

488. Lavender, David. *Bent's Fort*. Garden City, New York: Doubleday & Company, Inc., 1954. 450 pp. Exhaustive story of the events that swirled around the trading post built in 1833 by William and Charles Bent and Ceran St. Vrain and the later post established by William Bent. This is not a story of the Pawnees, but they are mentioned frequently as enemies of the Cheyennes. Lavender relates the tale of the loss of the Cheyenne Medicine Arrows and the later recovery of two of the arrows. In a footnote, he also explains how the Cheyenne dealt with possessing six medicine arrows after two of the originals were returned after replacements had been made.

489. "Massacre Canyon Number." *Nebraska History* 16 (July–September 1935): 131–84. Much of this issue is devoted to the tragic attack on Pawnee buffalo hunters and their families in 1873 near present-day Trenton, Nebraska. Featured articles are an historical account of the massacre, letters, documents, and interviews regarding the event, and an account of the efforts of the State of Nebraska to have a monument erected at the site of this last battle between the Sioux and the Pawnees.

490. Mathews, John Joseph. *The Osages: Children of the Middle Waters*. Norman: University of Oklahoma Press, 1961. 823 pp. The Pawnees appear mainly as enemies, but this book does include an account of Zebulon Pike's visit to a Pawnee village in 1806. Mathews notes that Osages also attended this meeting.

491. Newcomb, W. W., Jr. "A Re-Examination of the Causes of Plains Warfare." *American Anthropologist* 52 (July–September 1950): 317–30. Rejecting earlier theories that Plains Indians fought among themselves

because they were by nature warlike, Newcomb argues that individual Indians were warlike because their socio-economic systems forced them to be. He cites numerous economic reasons for inter-tribal warfare: competition for hunting grounds, acquisition of horses, the desire for European weapons, and competition for trade with whites. The Pawnees are not specifically mentioned, but much of this material would also apply to them.

492. Paul, R. Eli, ed. *Autobiography of Red Cloud, War Leader of the Oglalas.* Helena: Montana Historical Society Press, 1997. 220 pp. This "autobiography," which may or may not have been dictated by Red Cloud, relates the events of two Oglala attacks on the Pawnees—one in present-day Kearney County when Red Cloud was a boy of sixteen, and another undated raid on a Pawnee village on the Middle Loup River. During the latter raid, the Oglala chief suffered a near-fatal arrow wound that would trouble him for the rest of his life.

493. ———. "Lester Beach Platt's Account of the Battle of Massacre Canyon." *Nebraska History* 67 (Winter 1986): 381–407. One of only two known written eyewitness accounts of this confrontation near Trenton, Nebraska. (The other is the Williamson account [517]). Platt was a Yale divinity student who came west to visit his aunt and uncle who operated a trading post adjacent to the Pawnee Reservation. His rather romantic version of the events at Massacre Canyon was published in both *The Cosmopolitan* and the *Omaha World Herald* in 1888.

494. ———. *The Nebraska Indian Wars Reader, 1865–1877.* Lincoln: University of Nebraska Press, 1998. 245 pp. All but one of the articles in this collection are reprinted from *Nebraska History* magazine, and all concern the Indian wars in western Nebraska between 1865 and 1877. Topics include the Republican River Expedition, the Pawnee Scouts, Massacre Canyon, and the capture of Red Cloud and Red Leaf near Fort Robinson.

495. "Pawnees Kept the Arrows." *Kansas City Star*, 21 August 1905. Pawnee Indians Clippings File, vol. 1, 4. Kansas State Historical Society. Reports a visit to Pawnee, Oklahoma, by the Cheyenne Dog Soldiers in an attempt to recover the two sacred Medicine Arrows captured by the Pawnees in 1830 and still in the Pawnees' possession. The Pawnees agreed to "consider" returning the arrows, but this did not happen.

496. Phillips, Curtis J. "How Indian Logic Averted a Pawnee and Osage Massacre." *Tulsa Daily World Magazine*, 16 June 1929, 7. Recalls an encounter between the Pawnees and their Osage allies and a band of Cheyennes led by Stone Calf. The face-off took place in the Cherokee Strip in the late 1870s, and Osage leader Big Chief defused a tense situation by arranging a meeting the following year and promising that the Pawnees would return to the Cheyennes a "medicine flag" that had been captured years earlier.

497. Platt, Lester Beach. "A Story of the Plains." *Omaha Daily Herald*, 22 January 1888, 9–10. Account of the Massacre Canyon battle told by Platt, one of two white men who accompanied the Pawnees on the fateful hunt in August 1873. Reprinted from the popular magazine *The Cosmopolitan*, this may be the most detailed of all accounts.

498. Powell, Peter J. *Sweet Medicine: The Continuing Role of the Sacred Arrows, the Sun Dance, and the Sacred Buffalo Hat in Northern Cheyenne History*. 2 vols. Norman: University of Oklahoma Press, 1969. 935 pp. One chapter of volume one tells the story of the Pawnee capture of the Cheyenne's Sacred Medicine Arrows. Much of this material is taken from the works of George Bird Grinnell, George Bent, and George A. Dorsey.

499. "Reminiscences of a Range Rider." *Chronicles of Oklahoma* 3 (December 1925): 253–88. James C. Henderson, one of Oklahoma's pioneer cattlemen, wrote this memoir for his grandsons. Among his exciting tales is the story of a Pawnee who became separated from his friends while on a peace mission to an Osage camp. Unaware that peace had been declared, an Osage mourning war party found the lost Pawnee, killed and scalped him, and brought his scalp back to camp.

500. "Removal of Pawnee and Peace with Their Neighbors: A Memoir of Charles Chapin." *Nebraska History* 26 (January–March 1945): 43–48. This article is really two stories. The first describes a Pawnee parlay and feast with their former enemies, the Cheyennes, shortly after the Pawnees arrived in Indian Territory. The second is an amusing tale of a vain young Pawnee who is forced to cut his hair when he encounters an Osage mourning war party who wanted the hair to bury with a deceased member of their tribe.

501. Riley, Paul D. "The Battle of Massacre Canyon." *Nebraska History* 54 (Summer 1973): 221–49. Drawing on all known original sources,

and explaining events both before and after this tragic meeting between the Pawnees and the Sioux, this may be the best of all accounts of Massacre Canyon. Nicely written and well-documented.

502. ———. "Dr. David Franklin Powell and Fort McPherson." *Nebraska History* 51 (Summer 1970): 153–69. Includes a graphic description of the carnage at Massacre Canyon by an eyewitness to the aftermath. This account also appeared in the August 21, 1873, *Omaha World-Herald*.

503. ———, ed. "Red Willow County Letters of Royal Buck, 1872–1873." *Nebraska History* 47 (December 1966): 371–97. In two August 1873 letters to newspapers, Buck first simply reports the events at Massacre Canyon, then describes in great detail the carnage in the canyon. An excellent source of information on this tragic event.

504. Rollings, Willard H. *The Osage: An Ethnohistorical Study of Hegemony on the Prairie-Plains.* Columbia: University of Missouri Press, 1992. 320 pp. The Pawnees are mentioned frequently, mainly as enemies of the Osage, who formed a military alliance with their Kansa neighbors to keep the Pawnees north of the Osage hunting grounds. When small Pawnee bands did venture south of the Smoky Hill region, the Osage drove them away.

505. Sage, Rufus. *Rocky Mountain Life or Startling Scenes and Perilous Adventures in the Far West.* Chicago: Donohue Henneberry & Co., 1857. Included among the "startling scenes" is the story of the Pawnee-Sioux battle that occurred at Ash Hollow in 1835 and may have driven the Pawnees farther east in Nebraska.

506. Secoy, Frank Raymond. *Changing Military Patterns of the Great Plains Indians.* Seattle: University of Washington Press, 1953. Reprint Lincoln: University of Nebraska Press, 1992. 111 pp. Secoy divides the Plains into geographic areas and culture periods to explain how the acquisition of horses and guns changed inter-tribal dynamics in these areas. Although more recent studies have revised or expanded upon Secoy's fifty-year-old work, it is still often consulted.

507. Sheldon, Addison E. "Massacre Canyon: The Last Nebraska Battlefield of the Sioux-Pawnee War." *Nebraska History* 4 (October–December 1921): 53–60. In October 1921, accompanied by museum curator Elmer Blackman, Luther North, and John W. Williamson, who had been present at Massacre Canyon in 1873, Sheldon retraced the route

the Pawnees followed from their reservation on the Loup River to the rich buffalo grounds along the Republican. Once there, Williamson retold the story of this last battle between Indian tribes in Nebraska.

508. Sherk, Mary L. *Massacre Canyon: The Last Indian Battle.* Littleton, Colorado: Prairie Print, 1987. 12 pp. This slim pamphlet effectively tells the story of the Sioux attack on a Pawnee buffalo-hunting party on August 5, 1873, in the Republican River valley in southwestern Nebraska. Also included is George Bird Grinnell's description of a Pawnee buffalo hunt and its elaborate preparations.

509. Stands In Timber, John, and Margot Liberty. *Cheyenne Memories.* New Haven: Yale University Press, 1967. 330 pp. Among Stands In Timber's recollections are an attack by Cheyenne suicide warriors on a Pawnee camp, and a train wreck caused by Pawnees.

510. "Stones of Time." *NEBRASKAland* 44 (June 1966): 30–34. The first monument mentioned in this tour of Nebraska's historical markers is the pink granite obelisk near Trenton that marks the site of the 1873 Sioux massacre of Pawnee hunters and their families.

511. Taylor, William Z. "The Last Battle of the Pawnee with the Sioux." *Collections of the Nebraska Sate Historical Society,* vol. 16, 165–67. Lincoln: Nebraska State Historical Society, 1911. One of the few accounts of Massacre Canyon that explains how the bodies of the Pawnee people were disposed of. Taylor also claims to have found scaffold burials with the bodies of six Sioux who died in the attack. He includes among the dead a white woman named "Pawnee Mary."

512. Unrau, William E. *Indians of Kansas: The Euro-American Invasion and Conquest of Indian Kansas.* Topeka: Kansas State Historical Society, 1991. 112 pp. Brief, lavishly illustrated volume explains the interactions of Kansas Indian tribes, including the Pawnees, their reactions to the influx of whites, and their eventual expulsion from the State of Kansas. Much of the discussion on the Pawnees concerns their sometimes volatile relationship with the Kansas and the Osages.

513. ———. *The Kansa Indians: A History of the Wind People, 1673–1873.* Foreword by R. David Edmunds. Norman: University of Oklahoma Press, 1971. 244 pp. The Kansas and Pawnees lived close to each other and often claimed the same hunting grounds. Because of their adversarial relationship, the Pawnees receive considerable attention in this historical account, especially as it relates to tribal claims to the Republican River valley.

514. U.S. Congress. House. *Battle Monument of Last Indian Conflict*. 70th Cong., 1st sess., 1928. H. Rept. 1146. [Ser. 8837]. 4 pp. This report, which contains a few errors, accompanied a bill to provide funds for a monument at the site of the 1873 Massacre Canyon battle. The House Library Committee recommended passage of the bill, but with an amendment to reduce the appropriation amount.

515. White, Richard. "The Winning of the West: The Expansion of the Western Sioux in the Eighteenth and Nineteenth Centuries." *Journal of American History* 65 (September 1979): 319–43. Award-winning article explaining how inter-tribal warfare led to Lakota domination of the northern Plains before the mid-18th century. As enemies of the Sioux, the Pawnees receive considerable attention.

516. Wiegers, Robert Paul. "Osage Culture Change Inferred from Contact and Trade with the Caddo and the Pawnee." Ph.D. diss., University of Missouri, 1985. 229 pp. Attempts to explain how inter-tribal conflict changed Osage culture. Of special interest are a brief history of the Pawnees, a section on the Indian slave trade, and comparisons of Osage and Pawnee pottery and tools.

517. Williamson, J(ohn). W. "The Battle of Massacre Canyon: The Unfortunate Ending of the Last Buffalo Hunt of the Pawnees." *Trenton (Nebraska) Republican Leader*, 1922. 23 pp. In this pamphlet, written years after the events, the trail agent who accompanied the Pawnees on the hunt that resulted in the Massacre Canyon tragedy gives his eyewitness account of the battle.

518. ———. "Survivor Narrates Story of a Famous Indian Battle." In Thomas R. Armstrong. *My First and Last Buffalo Hunt*, 33–42. T. R. Armstrong, 1918. This version of the events at Massacre Canyon is quite similar to the Williamson account published by the *Trenton (Nebraska) Republican Leader* in 1922 [517].

519. Youngren, Harold. "Pawnee and Sioux—Mortal Foes." *Omaha World-Herald Sunday Magazine of the Midlands* 4 June 1967, 4–5. A colorful essay explaining how Pawnees posed as Sioux when committing depredations against white settlers in Nebraska. Quotes a number of letters from settlers who had been victimized, and includes photos of Sioux, Pawnees, and government officials.

11
White Contact to 1806

520. Bannon, John Francis. *The Spanish Borderlands Frontier, 1513–1821.* New York: Holt, Rinehart and Winston, 1963. Reprint Albuquerque: University of New Mexico Press, 1974. 308 pp. Study of the interaction among the Spanish, French, and Indians in the American Southwest and on the Plains. Spanish concerns regarding increased French influence among Plains Indians led to the ill-fated Villasur Expedition of 1720.

521. Blakeslee, Donald J. *Along Ancient Trails: The Mallet Expedition of 1739.* Niwot, Colorado: University Press of Colorado, 1995. 291 pp. Carefully researched reconstruction of the first successful overland expedition from French Illinois to Santa Fe. Includes numerous short references to the Pawnees, including band name origins, descriptions of sacred sites, and a brief account of the Villasur battle of 1720.

522. Blakeslee, Donald J., Robert K. Blasing, and Hector F. Garcia. *Along the Pawnee Trail: Cultural Resource Survey and Testing at Wilson Lake, Kansas.* Report to the Army Corps of Engineers, Kansas City District, 1986. 285 pp. Historic and cultural survey of Wilson Lake, in central Kansas, lying near the historic Pawnee Trail, which ran from the Pawnee villages in central Nebraska to the Great Bend of the Arkansas River. For the researcher of the Pawnees, the survey's greatest value is its detailed accounts of over a dozen military and exploring parties that used the trail. Included among the travelers' accounts are those of Villasur, Etienne de Bourgmont, Zebulon Pike, John C. Fremont, and

Charles Augustus Murray. Also includes excellent maps of the Pawnee Trail and surrounding areas.

523. Brugge, David M. "Some Plains Indians in the Church Records of New Mexico." *Plains Anthropologist* 10 (August 1929): 181–89. Contains tables showing the numbers, dates, and sites of Plains Indian baptisms and burials from the eighteenth and nineteenth centuries found in Catholic Church records. Some of these baptisms were voluntary, while others were forced baptisms of Indian slaves or captives. The records show thirty-four baptisms and nineteen burials of Indians identified as Pawnees.

524. Chávez, Thomas E. "The Segesser Hide Paintings: History, Discovery, Art." *Great Plains Journal* 10 (Spring 1990): 96–109. Traces the history of two hide paintings depicting the Villasur battle with the Pawnees and Otoes in 1720. Explains the political situation in the Great Plains at the time of the Villasur expedition and follows the paths of the artifacts, Segesser I and Segesser II, to Switzerland and back to New Mexico, where they are displayed in the Palace of the Governors in Santa Fe.

525. Diller, Aubrey. "Pawnee House: Ponca House." *Mississippi Valley Historical Review* 36 (September 1949): 301–4. Argues that Jean Baptiste Trudeau's trading post on the Upper Missouri River was only occupied for a short time and that it became known erroneously as "Pawnee House" rather than "Ponca House" due to an early edition of Lewis and Clark's journals. Clark referred to "Pania" house, which was construed as "Pawnee." The original error apparently stemmed from poor penmanship on a map drawn in 1796.

526. Dunbar, John B. "Massacre of the Villasur Expedition by the Pawnees on the Platte, in 1720." *Collections of the Kansas State Historical Society*, vol. 11. Topeka: Kansas State Printing Office, 1910, 397–423. Detailed account of the preparations for the Spanish expedition, the actual battle, and an analysis of what went wrong. Dunbar seems to have no doubt that French soldiers fought alongside the Pawnees, and he believes the Apache auxiliaries with Villasur had made a deal with the Pawnees that they would not be harmed.

527. Dunn, William E. "Spanish Reaction Against the French Advance toward New Mexico, 1717–1727." *Mississippi Valley Historical Review* 2 (December 1915): 348–62. Based on French and Spanish archival

sources, article presents the defeat of the Villasur Expedition as part of Spain's overall strained relations with France during the 1700s.

528.   Folmer, Henri. *Franco-Spanish Rivalry in North America, 1524–1763*. Glendale, California: Arthur H. Clark, 1953. 346 pp. Contains a three-page account of the Villasur Expedition and the battle with the Otoes and Pawnees, taken from Spanish correspondence and journals. The pages preceding this account explain why Villasur was sent to the Platte River region.

528a. "First Contact—Expanding Trade: Villasur Sent to Nebraska." *nebraskastudies.org*. www.nebraskastudies.org. 2 pp. An excellent explanation of the reasons for Villasur's expedition. Also identifies the people who accompanied him and his tiny army, and includes a map of his approximate route to the Loup River region.

529.   Hanson, James A. "Spain on the Plains." *Nebraska History* 74 (Spring 1993): 2–21. Analyzes Spain's relations with Indians and with other nations as she tried to retain control of the Great Plains territory and trade. The Pawnees are mentioned several times, and the 1720 Villasur Expedition is covered in detail.

530.   Hennepin, Father Louis. *A New Discovery, 1698*, ed. Reuben G. Thwaites. 2 vols. Chicago: A. C. McClurg & Co., 1903. 711 pp. Volume 2 contains an early reference to Pawnee tribal divisions. Hennepin locates the Pawnees near the Missouri and Osage rivers.

531.   Hotz, Gottfried. *Indian Skin Paintings from the American Southwest*. Translated by Johannes Malthaner. Norman: University of Oklahoma Press, 1970. 248 pp. Traces the history of the ill-fated Villasur Expedition of 1720, and examines in great detail the hide painting of the battle between Villasur's troops and the Pawnees. Each figure on the painting, known as Segesser II, is carefully analyzed. A copy of the hide painting can be viewed at the Nebraska State Historical Society Museum in Lincoln.

532.   John, Elizabeth Ann Harper. *Storms Brewed in Other Men's Worlds: The Confrontation of Indians, Spanish, and French in the Southwest, 1540–1795*. College Station: Texas A&M University Press, 1975. 805 pp. Drawn mainly from archival collections. Tells the story of the Plains and Southwest Indians caught up in the struggle between Spain and France to control Texas and the rest of the Southwest before the Louisiana Purchase. The Pawnees are mentioned fairly often, mainly as enemies of the Osages.

533. Loomis, Noel M., and Abraham P. Nasatir. *Pedro Vial and the Roads to Santa Fe*. Norman: University of Oklahoma Press, 1967. 569 pp. Fastidiously researched story of Pedro (Pierre) Vial, a previously obscure explorer who may have been the first person to travel the Santa Fe Trail. Includes an account, in letter and diary form, of Vial's journeys to the Pawnee country in 1804, 1805, and 1806 on behalf of Spain to gather information on American activities—especially those of Lewis and Clark—along the Missouri River and among the Indians.

534. McDermott, John Francis. *Tixier's Travels on the Osage Prairies*. Translated by Albert J. Salvan. Norman: University of Oklahoma Press, 1940. 309 pp. The journal of the young French explorer Victor Tixier, as he travels through Osage country and spends considerable time with that tribe. Tixier considers the Pawnees the most dangerous enemy of the Osages. He provides a short but vivid account of a Pawnee horse-stealing raid, and describes their method of making war. According to this account, the Osages were in awe of Pawnee horse stealing skills and believed they may have performed their thievery by using magic.

535. Moulton, Gary E., ed. *Atlas of the Lewis & Clark Expedition*. (The Journals of the Lewis and Clark Expedition, Vol. 1). A Project of the Center for Great Plains Studies, University of Nebraska-Lincoln. Lincoln: University of Nebraska Press, 1983. 23 pp. and 151 pp. of plates. The only maps in this wonderful collection that mention the Pawnees are a few drawn before the expedition (especially Plates 4 and 5), Plate 6, from 1804, which shows "Territory of divers Tribes of Panises," and Plate 13, a detailed map of the region including the Council Bluff, near present-day Fort Calhoun, Nebraska. Plates 32 a, b, and c are versions of a detailed map drawn by William Clark and dated 1805. Possibly the finest map is Plate 126, a post-expeditionary chart of the entire Lewis and Clark route, dated 1814, which clearly places Pawnee villages north and south of the Platte River, and lists village populations.

536. ———. *Journals of the Lewis and Clark Expedition*. 13 vols. Lincoln: University of Nebraska Press, 1986–2001. The definitive edition of these all-important journals. Fully annotated and complete, it is far superior to the earlier edited *Journals* by Elliott Coues (1893) and Reuben Gold Thwaites (1904–1905). Volume one is the atlas of the Lewis and Clark Expedition [535], volumes two through twelve contain the journals themselves, and volume thirteen is a fine index which includes numerous references to the Pawnees, both as a group and as individual bands.

537.   Nasatir, Abraham P, ed. *Before Lewis and Clark: Documents Illus-
       trating the History of the Missouri, 1785–1804.* 2 vols. St. Louis: St.
       Louis Historical Documents Foundation, 1952. Reprint Lincoln: Uni-
       versity of Nebraska Press, 1990. 853 pp. The most important collec-
       tion of primary documents pertaining to Indian trade and inter-tribal
       relations in the Missouri River region prior to Lewis and Clark. Taken
       from French, Spanish, and American archives, most of the letters and
       reports are annotated and identified. Nasatir begins the book with a
       115-page overview of this time period. Researchers will find dozens
       of references to the Pawnees in the excellent index.

538.   Norall, Frank. *Bourgmont, Explorer of the Missouri, 1698–1725.*
       Lincoln: University of Nebraska Press, 1988. 192 pp. Etienne de
       Bourgmont spent years with the Indians of the Missouri River re-
       gion, and may have been the first white man to explore this region
       and record his findings. Bourgmont locates the Pawnees along the
       Platte River, with the Panimahas (Skidi Pawnees) farther along the
       Platte. Bourgmont probably did not travel along the Platte, and his
       information on the Pawnees was most likely second-hand. Had he
       spent time with the Skidis, he would not have stated that they wor-
       shipped the sun.

538a. "First Contact—Expanding Trade: Recording the Massacre."
       www.nebraskastudies.org. A brief interpretation of the scenes de-
       picted on the Segesser hide painting of the 1720 Villasur massacre
       on the Loup River. Also identifies individuals shown in the painting.

539.   Savage, James W. "A Visit to Nebraska in 1662." *Nebraska State His-
       torical Society Transactions and Reports*, vol. 2. Lincoln: State Jour-
       nal Company, Printers, 1887, 114–32. Presents arguments to support
       his theory that a Spanish expedition under Don Diego Penalosa
       crossed the Platte River in 1662. Also includes colorful versions of
       Pawnee culture and states that rather than being in Kansas, the leg-
       endary land of Quivera was on the Loup River near present-day
       Columbus, Nebraska. At the request of Nebraska Senator Charles
       Manderson, this essay was also printed and distributed to United
       States Senators as S. Misc. Doc. 14, 53rd Cong, 2nd sess., 1893 [Ser.
       3167].

540.   Shine, Michael A. "In Favor of the Loup Site." *Nebraska History* 7
       (1924): 82–87. Monsignor Shine presents evidence, including a map,
       to support his contention that the Villasur massacre of 1720 occurred

along the Loup River in present-day Platte County, Nebraska. This is a rebuttal to the location theory of Alfred Barnaby Thomas [542].

541. Thomas, Alfred Barnaby, ed. and trans. *After Coronado: Spanish Exploration Northeast of New Mexico, 1696–1727, Documents from the Archives of Spain, Mexico, and New Mexico.* Norman: University of Oklahoma Press, 1935. 2d ed., 1966. 307 pp. Included in the testimony and correspondence in this volume are three accounts of the 1720 Villasur massacre at the hands of Pawnees in present-day Nebraska. Two are in letters to the Spanish viceroy and one is part of the court testimony of a Spanish settler and former soldier. A note on pages 278–79 explains the controversy over the Villasur battle site and traces the literary history of the argument.

542. ———. "The Massacre of the Villasur Expedition at the Forks of the Platte River August 12, 1720." *Nebraska History* 7 (July–September 1924): 68–81. By tracing the route and calculating mileage distance from Spanish records, Thomas argues that the Villasur Expedition's confrontation with the Pawnees occurred on the Platte River near present-day North Platte, Nebraska, not on the Loup River near the town of Columbus. For a rebuttal to his argument, see Michael Shine, [540].

543. Thomas, Fred. "Art Depicts Spanish-Indian Conflict." *Omaha World-Herald*, 13 July 1998, 31. One of a series of articles on historic sites in Nebraska. Thomas nicely summarizes the Pawnee-Villasur battle and discusses the hide painting of the conflict, which is the oldest depiction of a Nebraska scene.

544. Troike, Rudolph C. "A Pawnee Visit to San Antonio in 1795." *Ethnohistory* 11 (Fall 1964): 380–93. Describes a little-known event in early 1795. A group later identified as Skidi Pawnees visited the Spanish authorities asking for peace and protection from Americans. The Pawnee delegation also gave to Spaniards the names of thirty-three other Indian tribes who might entertain friendly relations with Spain. Not all of the tribal names have been identified.

544a. "First Contact—Expanding Trade: The Battle." *www.nebraskastudies.org.* An outstanding account of the events prior to, during, and immediately following Villasur's brief battle with Oto and Pawnee warriors near present-day Columbus, Nebraska. Includes an image of a portion of the hide painting of the battle.

545. Villiers, Marc de. "Massacre of the Spanish Expedition of the Missouri (August 11, 1720)," Translated by Addison E. Sheldon. *Nebraska History* 6 (January–March 1923): 3–31. English translation of this somewhat inaccurate account of the destruction of Villasur's force.

546. Wedel, Mildred Mott. "The Identity of La Salle's Pana Slave." *Plains Anthropologist* 18 (August 1973): 203–17. In 1682, explorer Robert La Salle received as a gift a "Pana" boy who had been held captive by four different Indian tribes. Writings have suggested that the Pana may have been Pawnee, Ponca, Arikara, or Apache. Basing her argument on linguistic, cultural, and historical accounts, Wedel concludes that this captive was a Wichita.

12

Explorers, Emigrants, and Soldiers from 1806

547. Anderson, William Marshall. *The Rocky Mountain Journals of William Marshall Anderson: The West in 1834*. Edited by Dale L. Morgan and Eleanor Towles Harris. San Marino, California: Huntington Library, 1967. Reprint. Lincoln: University of Nebraska Press, 1987. 430 pp. Adventurer William Anderson originally planned to accompany a unit of army dragoons escorting traders along the Santa Fe Trail, but changed his mind and rode along with fur trader William Sublette to a rendezvous in the Rocky Mountains. On the way west, Anderson and his party encountered Pawnees near present-day Grand Island, Nebraska, and on the return trip by a different route, met leaders of several Pawnee bands along the Loup Fork, near modern Columbus, Nebraska. This expertly edited journal is one of the earliest of its kind. Included in this volume are reprints of three 1837 articles that Anderson contributed to the monthly periodical *American Turf Register and Sporting Magazine*.

548. Belden, George P. *Twelve Years Among the Wild Indians. Chiefly from the Diaries and Manuscripts of George P. Belden, the Adventurous White Chief, Soldier, Hunter, Trapper, and Guide*. Edited by James S. Brisbin. St. Louis: Anchor Publishing Company, 1881. Reprint. Athens, Ohio: Ohio University Press, 1974. 541 pp. Firsthand account of Belden's adventures among the Indians of the West, his adoption into a Yankton Sioux band, and his marriages to two Yankton women. Although not specifically concerned with the Pawnees, this memoir is full of details of Plains Indian life and customs and does include ac-

counts of two battles between the Pawnees and the Sioux, both of which the Pawnees won.

549. Brooks, George R., ed. "George C. Sibley's Journal of a Trip to the Salines in 1811." *Bulletin of the Missouri Historical Society* 21, no. 3 (1965): 167–207. Actually a letter from Sibley, trader at Fort Osage, to his father. Sibley spent a week with the Republican and Skidi Pawnees, and about ten pages of this excellent account are devoted to descriptions of the Indian villages, earth lodges, and terrain along the Platte River. Also discusses Zebulon Pike's visit to the Pawnee villages in 1806, as related to him by a Skidi chief. Excerpts from this letter also appear in *Chronicles of Oklahoma* [605].

550. Carleton, J. Henry. *The Prairie Logbooks: Dragoon Campaigns to the Pawnee Villages in 1844, and to the Rocky Mountains in 1845.* Edited by Louis Pelzer. Chicago: Caxton Club, 1943. Reprint. Lincoln: University of Nebraska Press, 1983. 295 pp. Well-written and often humorous daily account of a cavalry regiment's campaign from Fort Leavenworth to visit the Pawnees and to hold a peace council with the tribe. Carleton's diary contains vivid descriptions of the Pawnees and their way of life as well as valuable information on the waterways and wildlife of what would soon become Nebraska Territory.

551. Carpenter, Helen. "A Trip Across the Plains in an Ox Wagon, 1857." In *Ho for California! Women's Overland Diaries from the Huntington Library*, edited by Sandra L. Myres, 93–188. San Marino, California: Huntington Library, 1980. On June 13, Mrs. Carpenter reported arriving at Fort Kearny, where many destitute Pawnees were trying to sell the dried meat from a recent buffalo hunt to emigrants—at high prices.

552. Chittenden, Hiram Martin. *History of Early Steamboat Navigation on the Missouri River: Life and Adventures of Joseph La Barge, Pioneer Navigator and Indian Trader for Fifty Years*, vol. 1. New York: Francis P. Harper, 1903. Reprint. Minneapolis: Ross and Haines, 1962. 461 pp. In 1832, at the age of seventeen, La Barge signed on as an employee of the American Fur Company, serving at Cabanne's trading post, just north of modern-day Omaha. He describes the Pawnee villages and corn fields, and gives a brief account of Agent John Dougherty's attempt to rescue a girl scheduled to be sacrificed to the Morning Star. On one occasion, La Barge was captured by a Pawnee war party, but came to no harm, since he could speak to them in their native tongue.

553. Clayton, William. *William Clayton's Journal: A Daily Record of the Journey of the Original Company of 'Mormon' Pioneers from Nauvoo, Illinois, to the Valley of the Great Salt Lake.* Salt Lake City: *The Deseret News*, 1921. Reprint. New York: Arno Press, 1973. 376 pp. Clayton was named an official historian by Brigham Young when the Mormons left Winter Quarters in 1847. His journal of the trek from the Missouri River to Utah is a valuable record of early western history. Clayton's journal entries for February 21–24 are among the best descriptions of the construction of a Pawnee earth lodge and the terrain in the vicinity of the Pawnee villages on the Loup Fork of the Platte River. He also describes Pawnee horse corrals and food caches.

554. Cooke, Philip St. George. *Scenes and Adventures in the Army or Romance of Military Life.* Philadelphia: Lindsay & Blakiston, 1857. Reprint. New York: Arno Press, 1973. 432 pp. On page 110, Cooke recalls a group of Pawnee warriors who visited Fort Leavenworth and performed a dance in which each man told of his bravest deed.

555. Cordeal, John F. "Historical Sketch of Southwestern Nebraska." *Nebraska State Historical Society Collections*, vol. 17, 1913, 16–47. Highlights important historical events in Nebraska west of the 100th meridian. Most of the vignettes are of explorers and settlers, but mention is made of Massacre Canyon and the defeat of the Cheyenne Dog Soldiers at Summit Springs.

556. Cornwall, Bruce. *Life Sketches of Pierre Barlow Cornwall.* San Francisco: A. M. Robertson, 1906. 87 pp. Written by his son from his father's memoirs, this tells the story of a New Yorker who crossed the Plains in 1848. Contains a lengthy account of the Cornwall party's capture by and escape from a Pawnee band near the Platte River's Loup Fork.

557. Coues, Elliott, ed. *The Expeditions of Zebulon Montgomery Pike.* 2 vols. Minneapolis: Ross & Haines, Inc., 1965. 955 pp. This expertly edited edition of Pike's journals of his travels is a reprint of the original 1810 edition. Students of the Pawnees would be most interested in Pike's second expedition, during which he visited the Pawnees at their now famous and controversial "Pike-Pawnee Village" near the Kansas/Nebraska border. One of the folded maps in the second volume locates Pawnee villages along the Platte and Loup rivers and estimates the number of warriors at each one.

558. Cummings, Mariett Foster. "A Trip Across the Continent." In *Covered Wagon Women: Diaries and Letters from the Western Trails*, vol. 4, edited by Kenneth L. Holmes, 117–68. Glendale, California: Arthur H. Clark Company, 1985. Reprint. Lincoln: University of Nebraska Press, 1997. Mariett Cummings and her husband, William, left Illinois in April 1852, bound for California. By late May, they had reached the Platte River, where they encountered a sizable band of Pawnees involved in a running battle with about a dozen Sioux. According to Mrs. Cummings' diary, the Sioux routed the Pawnees. Her journal also mentions a deserted Pawnee village with a square or circle of horse skulls. Many overland travelers mentioned this particular site.

559. Dale, Harrison C., ed. *The Ashley-Smith Exploration and the Discovery of a Central Route to the Pacific in 1822–1829*. Cleveland: Arthur H. Clark Company, 1918. 352 pp. In November 1824, Ashley reached the Pawnee villages on the Loup Fork, but found that the Indians had left on their winter hunt. When Ashley located the hunting parties, they were very helpful, advising him not to proceed west until spring. Ashley insisted on going forward, and the Pawnees told him where to find wood, and even sold him supplies and twenty-three horses that they really could not spare.

560. Dillon, Richard, ed. *California Caravan: The 1846 Overland Trail Memoirs of Margaret M. Hecox*. San Jose, California: Harlan-Young Press, 1966. 70 pp. Mrs. Hecox recalls several unpleasant encounters with the Pawnees, including their terrifying performance of a war dance by the light of a blazing campfire. The next morning, the travelers were missing numerous articles, and they discovered that the Pawnees had removed the bolts from their wagons.

561. Dodge, Richard Irving. *Our Wild Indians: Thirty Years Personal Experience Among the Red Man of the Great West*. Hartford: A. D. Worthington & Co., 1883. Reprinted as *Thirty-three Years Among Our Wild Indians*. Freeport, New York: Books for Libraries Press, 1970. 653 pp. The Pawnees are only mentioned briefly, but this is an excellent travelogue of the Plains and their Indian inhabitants by an early traveler.

562. Donaldson, Thomas. *The George Catlin Indian Gallery in the U.S. National Museum (Smithsonian Institution),with Memoir and Statistics*. Washington, D.C.: Government Printing Office, 1887. 939 pp. Pages 68–72 of this massive work contain a list of Catlin's thirteen

Pawnee paintings separated by band affiliation. Also includes three pages of "notes" on the location and condition of the Pawnees when he visited them in 1833 and 1834.

563. Evans, Hugh. "The Journal of Hugh Evans, Covering the First and Second Campaigns of the United States Dragoon Regiment in 1834 and 1835." Edited by Fred S. Perrine and Grant Foreman. *Chronicles of Oklahoma* 3 (September 1927): 175–215. A cavalry regiment under the command of Col. Henry Dodge left Jefferson Barracks to meet with Indians farther west, including the Pawnees. Sgt. Hugh Evans was most likely Col. Dodge's orderly, and his account of the peace council and prisoner exchange is nearly identical to the account in the journal kept by Lt. T. B. Wheelock [616]. The editors believe that either Evans had access to Wheelock's journal, or Wheelock received his information from Evans.

564. *Explorer on the Northern Plains: Lieutenant Gouverneur K. Warren's Preliminary Report of Explorations in Nebraska and Dakota, in the Years 1855–'56–'57.* Introduction by Frank N. Schubert. Washington, D.C.: Historical Division, Office of Administrative Services, Office of the Chief of Engineers, Engineer Historical Studies Number 2, 1981. Originally printed as part of the Report of the Secretary of War in 1858, this report very briefly mentions the Pawnees, but it does give an excellent description of the Platte River, and estimates the cost of bridges and improved river crossings and ferries.

565. Fackler, Herbert V. "Cooper's Pawnees." *American Notes and Queries* 6 (October 1967): 21–22. Argues that rather than being romanticized, James Fenimore Cooper's descriptions of his fictional Pawnees in *The Prairie* were very similar to accounts by explorers such as Edwin James and Lewis and Clark.

566. Fuller, Harlin M., and LeRoy R. Hafen, eds. *The Journal of Captain John R. Bell, Official Journalist for the Stephen H. Long Expedition to the Rocky Mountains, 1820.* Glendale, California: Arthur H. Clark Company, 1957. 337 pp. Part 2 of this beautifully written journal provides an excellent description of the terrain and streams on the way to the Pawnee villages along the Loup Fork. Upon arrival at the Pawnee settlements, Captain Bell vividly records details of the villages and the Pawnee people.

567. Gregg, Josiah. *The Commerce of the Prairies.* New York: H. G. Langley, 1844, 2 vols. Reprint. Reuben Gold Thwaites, ed. *Early Western*

Travels, vols. 19–20. Cleveland: Arthur H. Clark Company, 1905. Reprint. Milo M. Quaife, ed. Lincoln: University of Nebraska Press, 1967. 343 pp. A trader along the Santa Fe Trail from 1831–1844, Josiah Gregg recounts two Pawnee horse-stealing raids.

568. Hamilton, W. T. *My Sixty Years on the Plains*. New York: Forest and Stream Publishing Company, 1905. Reprint. Columbus, Ohio: Long's College Book Co., 1951. 244 pp. A band of Pawnees stole 100 horses and mules while Hamilton and his trading partners were camped at a Sioux village on the South Platte River. He relates in colorful detail the pursuit of the horse thieves and the recovery of the stolen stock.

569. "History of Fort Kearny." *Publications of the Nebraska State Historical Society*, vol. 21. Lincoln: Nebraska State Historical Society, 1930, 215–36. A 1928 University of Nebraska master's thesis by Lillian Willman, an address by State Historical Society Director Addison E. Sheldon, plus numerous military and civilian documents pertaining to both Nebraska forts named in honor of Stephen Watts Kearny. Most of the publication deals with "New" Fort Kearny on the Platte River, but contains little information on the Pawnees, who claimed the land on which the fort would be located. Includes brief mention of the treaty ceding the land, but other references to the Pawnees pertain to the new fort's ability to control them, since it was located between their permanent villages and their hunting grounds.

570. "Hugh Evans' Journal of Colonel Henry Dodge's Expedition to the Rocky Mountains in 1835." Edited by Fred S. Perrine. *Mississippi Valley Historical Review* 14 (June 1927–March 1928): 192–214. Sergeant Evans' account of the First Dragoons' meeting with the Grand Pawnees in June 1835 lacks the detail of the events related by Captain Lemuel Ford [590], but is similar in many ways.

571. *In Search of the Oregon Trail*. Documentary coproduced by Oregon Public Broadcasting and Nebraska Public Television. Narrated by Stacy Keach. Approximately three hours. An ambitious educational television project that tells the "true" story of the Oregon Trail and traces its entire length from Missouri to Oregon. Much of the narrative is taken from emigrant diaries. The filmmakers point out that much of the trail passed through Pawnee land along the Platte River in Nebraska. Pawnee historian James Riding In discusses the importance of corn and the buffalo to his ancestors. He explains that the Platte River was the center of Pawnee culture and that the loss of the

buffalo herds marked the beginning of the end of the Pawnee presence in Nebraska. Pawnee scholar Roger Echo-Hawk served as an advisor in the filming of this outstanding documentary.

572. Irving, John Treat, Jr. *Indian Sketches, Taken during an Expedition to the Pawnee Tribes*. Philadelphia: Carey, Lea and Blanchard, 1835. Reprint. New York: G. P. Putnam's Sons, 1888. Reprint. John Francis McDermott, ed. Norman: University of Oklahoma Press, 1955. 275 pp. Considered by many to be one of the finest accounts of Pawnee villages and life. Irving, nephew of Washington Irving, accompanied Treaty Commissioner Henry Ellsworth to Pawnee camps in modern-day Nance County in 1833. His vivid descriptions of Pawnee towns, the Indians' appearance and behavior, and their customs should be read by all serious researchers.

573. Irving, Washington. *A Tour on the Prairies*. Edited by John Francis McDermott. Norman: University of Oklahoma Press, 1956. 214 pp. Irving began his prairie tour late in 1832. One of his companions colorfully explained Pawnee fighting methods. As they entered Pawnee territory, another told exaggerated tales of Pawnee warriors' prowess with bows and arrows and, at one point, the travelers came upon a fresh trail identified as Pawnee by the moccasin tracks.

574. James, Edwin. *Account of an Expedition from Pittsburgh to the Rocky Mountains, performed in the Years 1819, 1820 . . . under the Command of Maj. S. H. Long*. In *Early Western Travels*, vols. 14–17. Edited by Reuben G. Thwaites. Cleveland: Arthur H. Clark Company, 1905. Written during Stephen Long's topographical exploration of the Great Plains, James' descriptions of Plains Indian tribes are some of the finest ever written. While the Pawnees do not receive as much attention as some of the others, in vol. 14, James describes an attack on a group of Long's men by Republican Pawnees and a later meeting at Council Bluff between Long and several tribes, including the Pawnees.

575. Jensen, Richard E., ed. "Soldiers' Letters from Fort Childs, 1848–49." *Nebraska History* 82 (Fall 2001): 122–29. In letters to his brother, Private William Ingraham gives a vivid description of Old Fort Kearny, on the Missouri River, and mentions the Pawnees in each of his letters from Grand Island, which would be the location of Fort Childs, later the second Fort Kearny. The Pawnees were in poor physical condition, and were being victimized by the Sioux, who burned a Pawnee village after stealing the contents of their food caches.

576. _____. "The Wright-Beauchampe Investigation and the Pawnee Threat of 1829." *Nebraska History* 79 (Fall 1998): 133–43. R. P. Beauchampe, subagent for the Upper Missouri Indian Agency, and infantry officer George Wright traveled up the Missouri River in 1829 to investigate reports that the Pawnees planned to go to war with the whites. Basing their findings on interviews with traders and other Indians, along with a lengthy letter from trader Lucien Fontenelle, the investigators determined that the Pawnees had no war plans, but the government should take action to stop Pawnee raids.

577. Dougherty, John, to Elbert Herring, October 29, 1831. In *Correspondence on the Subject of the Emigration of Indians*, vol. 2, Document 512. Washington, D.C.: Duff Green, 1835, 718–19. Dougherty reports that when he visited the Pawnees, they were in terrible condition. Many of their young people had died of smallpox, and the rest were starving. The Pawnees asked to be paid for land that had been given to the Delawares.

578. Jones, Ivan E. "Steamboating on the Nebraska Shore." *Nebraska History* 8 (January–March 1925): 11–13. Brief account of Major Stephen Long's 1819 encounter with Missouri River tribes at Engineer Cantonment north of present-day Omaha. On October 9, Pawnees performed a dance, and five days later, four Pawnee chiefs made speeches.

579. "Letter from General Atkinson to Colonel Hamilton." *Nebraska History* 4 (January–March 1921): 9–11. Atkinson briefly recounts his 1825 expedition west of the Mississippi to forge treaties with the Plains tribes. He reports that at the time there were 1,100 Grand Pawnees, 700 Pawnee Loups (Skidis), and 300 Republican Pawnees.

580. Long, Stephen H. *Account of an Expedition from Pittsburgh to the Rocky Mountains.* Introduction by Howard R. Lamar. Barre, Massachusetts: Imprint Society, 1972. 547 pp. An abridged version of the original 1823 edition. Retains the accounts of the Pawnee attack on members of Long's party and the later council with the Pawnees [574].

581. Lowe, Percival G. *Five Years a Dragoon ('49 to '54) and Other Adventures on the Great Plains.* Kansas City: Franklin Hudson Publishing Company, 1906. Reprint. Norman: University of Oklahoma Press, 1965. 336 pp. One of the few frontier army journals written by an enlisted man. Among his adventures in Nebraska were an 1849 skirmish with a small group of Pawnees on an island in the Platte River and at-

tempts to bring all the Pawnees back to Fort Kearny for peace talks. The Skidis were reluctant to come in.

582. McDermott, John Francis, ed. *An Artist on the Overland Trail: The 1849 Diary and Sketches of James F. Wilkins.* San Marino, California: The Huntington Library, 1968. 143 pp. Contains an anecdote that illustrates how destitute the Pawnees were in 1849. Near Wilkins' camp, a family of six Indians found an ox that had been dead for two weeks. They were so hungry that they ate it anyway, barely warming the rancid meat over a fire. An informant at Fort Childs told Wilkins that fifty-five Pawnees had starved to death the preceding winter. Also contains Wilkins' trail sketches, including a drawing of a deserted Pawnee village.

583. _____. "Isaac McCoy's Second Exploring Trip in 1828." *Kansas Historical Quarterly* 13 (August 1945): 400–462. In 1828, Baptist missionary and explorer Isaac McCoy took groups of Indians west to inspect lands on the frontier. The journals and letters from this trip include several mentions of the Pawnees, almost always portraying them as warlike and disruptive. According to McCoy, the Osages were at war with the Pawnees, and he records in his journal an idealistic plan to establish peace between the two tribes. Although McCoy takes credit for this plan, an editorial note attributes the scheme to trader Auguste Chouteau.

584. Mattes, Merrill J. *The Great Platte River Road.* Lincoln: Nebraska State Historical Society, 1969. Reprint. Lincoln: University of Nebraska Press, 1987. 583 pp. Most of the references to the Pawnees in this award-winning study are from emigrants' and soldiers' diaries. The general consensus among western travelers seemed to be that while the Pawnees were accomplished thieves, they posed no great threat to people on the Oregon Trail.

585. Mead, James R. *Hunting and Trading on the Great Plains, 1859–1875.* Edited by Schuyler Jones. Norman: University of Oklahoma Press, 1986. 276 pp. Mead dictated his adventures in Kansas to a stenographer in the 1890s. His chapter entitled "With the Indians on the Plains" includes an excellent account of Pawnee horse-stealing operations, resulting in a general hatred of the Pawnees by other tribes. Mead also describes several encounters with Pawnee horse thieves who shared his camp and his food as they returned from unsuccessful forays.

586. _____. "The Pawnees as I Knew Them." *Transactions of the Kansas State Historical Society*, vol. 10. Topeka: Kansas State Printing Office, 1908, 106–111. Mead gave this address at the 100th anniversary celebration for the Pike-Pawnee Village. He mainly spoke of the Pawnees' prowess as horse thieves.

587. Miner, Donald D. "Western Travelers in Quest of the Indian." In *Travelers on the Western Frontier*, edited by John Francis McDermott, 267–89. Urbana: University of Illinois Press, 1970. 267–89. Profiles four adventurers who journeyed among the Plains Indians, two of whom spent considerable time with the Pawnees. Charles Augustus Murray [591] began his journey with a preconceived notion of the Pawnees as "noble savages," but as he came to know them, he discovered a much different truth. Unlike Murray, John Treat Irving [572] did not actually live among the Pawnees, but he did observe them carefully during peace conferences.

588. Morgan, Dale L. *Jedediah Smith and the Opening of the West*. Indianapolis: Bobbs-Merrill Company, Inc., 1953. Reprint. Lincoln: University of Nebraska Press, 1964. 458 pp. The index lists only one reference to the Pawnees, but it is significant. In December 1825, William Ashley's party encountered Pawnees near the Platte River's Loup Fork. The Indians advised Ashley not to continue on, but to winter there until spring. But Ashley decided to go on, and the Skidi Pawnees traded horses and provisions to enable him to continue his journey.

589. Morton, J. Sterling. "From Nebraska City to Salt Creek in 1855." *Transactions and Reports of the Nebraska State Historical Society*, vol. 4, 1892, 11–18. Having been assured that crops could not grow west of Otoe County, Nebraska, Morton and four others set out to prove otherwise. As they traveled west, they were shadowed by Pawnees watching their movements, begging for supplies, and even threatening to scalp the members of the exploring party when one of them set up surveying instruments to mark a possible town site.

590. Mumey, Nolie. *March of the First Dragoons to the Rocky Mountains in 1835: The Diaries and Maps of Lemuel Ford*. Denver: Eames Brothers Press, 1957. 109 pp. One of the many accounts of the cavalry march commanded by Colonel Henry Dodge. Ford and his fellow soldiers met a number of Indian tribes on their march. The Pawnees are mentioned numerous times, but there are no lengthy passages describing them.

591. Murray, Charles A. *Travels in North America During the Years 1834, 1835 & 1836, Including a Summer Residence with the Pawnee Tribe of Indians in the Remote Prairies of the Missouri, and a Visit to Cuba and the Azore Islands.* 2 vols. London: Richard Bentley, 1839. Reprint. New York: Da Capo Press, 1974. Murray, the grandson of the last British colonial governor of Virginia, came to the United States on business in 1834, and stayed for nearly three years. An eager sightseer, he made his way west, and in July 1835, set off from Fort Leavenworth with a party of Pawnees, bound for the Indian villages. Murray devotes nearly ten chapters of the first volume of his travels to his summer visit with the Pawnees. This is one of the most detailed accounts of the Pawnees by an early western traveler, and should be consulted by all researchers. Murray's adventures with the Pawnees are condensed in W. H. G. Armitage. "The Honorable Charles Augustus Murray among the Pawnees: 1835." *Mid-America* (n.s.) 21 (July 1950): 189–201.

592. Myers, John Myers. *Pirate, Pawnee and Mountain Man: The Saga of Hugh Glass.* Boston: Little, Brown and Company, 1963. Reprint. *The Saga of Hugh Glass: Pirate, Pawnee and Mountain Man.* Lincoln: University of Nebraska Press, 1976. 237 pp. Tells the almost mythical story of this ultimate survivor who was captured by a Pawnee band and lived with them for a time, adopting many of their customs.

593. Nichols, Roger L. ed. "General Henry Atkinson's Report of the Yellowstone Expedition of 1825." *Nebraska History* 44 (June 1963): 65–82. Atkinson provided a profile of each of the tribes he and Indian agent Benjamin O'Fallon encountered on their treaty expedition up the Missouri River. He gave the locations and populations of three Pawnee bands and said they were "at peace with the surrounding tribes, enemies to the Sioux, Osages, and other distant tribes."

594. Nichols, Roger L., and Patrick Halley. *Stephen Long and American Frontier Exploration.* Newark, Delaware: University of Delaware Press, 1980. 276 pp. Concentrates on the years 1816 through 1824—the years that Stephen Long traveled the West as the leader of exploring parties. The Pawnees are discussed on several occasions, especially in connection with the explorer's attempt to vaccinate them against smallpox with vaccine that had fallen into the Missouri River and was worthless. Pawnee leaders warned Long of the dangers ahead if he continued across the Plains.

595. "Notes on the Missouri River, and Some of the Native Tribes in Its Neighborhood—By a Military Gentleman Attached to the Yellowstone Expedition in 1819." *Analectic Magazine* (n.s.) 1 (April 1820): 293–313; (May 1820): 347–75. This account, probably written by Lt. Thomas Kavanaugh, includes a fascinating description of the Missouri River, and explains the Pawnees' tribal organization, their trade, their horse-stealing prowess, their appearance and hygiene, and several of their rituals, including an inaccurate version of the Morning Star Ceremony.

596. Oehler, Gottlieb F., and David Z. Smith. "Description of a Journey and a Visit to the Pawnee Indians." *Moravian Church Miscellany* (1851–52). Reprint. Fairfield, Washington: Ye Galleon Press, 1974. 32 pp. Slim volume contains a fine description of the Nebraska Territory between Bellevue and the Pawnee villages along the Platte River. The last six pages, written by Brother David Smith, describe the Pawnees, their lodges, their hunting and farming methods, their burial customs, and their mode of dress. Also contains important information on Samuel Allis and his work among the Pawnees.

597. Parker, Samuel. *Journal of an Exploring Tour Beyond the Rocky Mountains Under the Direction of the A. B. C. F. M. in the Years 1835, '36, and '37.* Ithaca, New York: Mack, Andrus and Woodruff, 1842. 408 pp. The American Board of Commissioners for Foreign Missions sent a group, including Parker, to meet the Indian tribes west of the Mississippi and to determine how to "civilize" them. On the Loup Fork, Parker and his party met the Pawnees, who treated the travelers very kindly, inviting them to feasts. Parker describes the Pawnees as being in a "degraded" condition, and he expresses his hope that missionaries Allis and Dunbar can be effective.

598. Pattie, James O. *The Personal Narrative of James O. Pattie of Kentucky.* In *Early Western Travels, 1748–1846,* vol. 18, edited by Reuben Gold Thwaites, 25–324. Cleveland: Arthur H. Clark Co., 1905. James Ohio Pattie was a third generation frontiersman who set off from Missouri in 1824 on a six-year journey that would take him and his party to the Pacific Ocean and then into Mexico. Early in the journey, Pattie spent time with the Republican and Loup (Skidi) Pawnee bands, both of which he described as friendly. He wrote of two events in particular: a Skidi celebration after a successful raid; and the negotiations with a chief to free a child taken captive during

that raid. The enemy tribe raided is not identified, but Pattie's account of the celebration is colorful and detailed.

599. Paul, R. Eli, ed. "George Wilkins Kendall, Newsmen, and a Party of Pleasure Seekers on the Prairies, 1851." *Nebraska History* 64 (Spring 1983): 35–80. Kendall and his fellow travelers originally intended to watch the Fort Laramie Treaty ceremonies, but because of delays, went instead with an army unit to visit and council with the Pawnees. Kendall's letters to his newspaper, the *New Orleans Picayune*, are colorful, full of humor, and informative. While visiting the Pawnees, he observed a peace council with the Grand Pawnee band, and explained how Captain Wharton, the chief army negotiator, convinced the Skidi Pawnees to return items stolen earlier from white traders.

600. Pelzer, Louis, ed. "Captain Ford's Journal of an Expedition to the Rocky Mountains." *Mississippi Valley Historical Review* 12 (March 1926): 550–579. On their march through the Platte River valley, companies of Colonel Henry Dodge's First Regiment of Dragoons were escorted into a Grand Pawnee village near present-day Grand Island, Nebraska. Ford describes a Pawnee "grand parade," the Indian village, and the people in it. Agent John Dougherty and army officers held a council with the Pawnees at this time, but Ford, being ill, did not participate in it. These events also appear in Hugh Evans' journal [563].

601. Reid, Russell, and Clell G. Gannon, eds. "Journal of the Atkinson-O'Fallon Expedition." *North Dakota Historical Quarterly* 4 (October 1929): 5–56. In 1825, a military expedition led by General Henry Atkinson and Indian agent Benjamin O'Fallon traveled by keel boat up the Missouri River from St. Louis to the mouth of the Yellowstone River. One of the goals was to sign treaties with as many Missouri Valley tribes as possible. The excellent introduction concludes with the general terms of the treaty signed by each tribe and a chronological list of the signing dates and locations. The Pawnee treaty was signed at Fort Atkinson on September 13, 1825. The original expedition journal is at the Missouri Historical Society.

602. "Reminiscences of Hugh Cosgrove." *Oregon Historical Quarterly* 1 (1900): 253–69. In his memoirs of the Overland Trail, Cosgrove gives a humorous account of two incidents involving Pawnee warriors near "Castle Rock." First, a group of about forty Pawnees attempted to steal the emigrants' cattle and horses, but were driven off. That same day, Pawnees surrounded two members of Cosgrove's party while

they were hunting, and forced them to undress. The two returned to camp naked except for their boots.

603. Schallenberger, Moses. "Overland in 1844." In *The Opening of the California Trail: The Story of the Stevens Party*, edited by George R. Stewart, 46–84. Berkeley: University of California Press, 1953. Moses Schallenberger was seventeen years old when he began his trek across the continent with a group of about fifty emigrants known as the Stevens Party. In an undated entry, he tells of finding a Pawnee village with only women, children, and old men—the young men having all been killed by a Sioux raiding party. The travelers were sure that the Pawnees were no threat.

604. Schetter, Adrienne Estelle. "The Indians on the Oregon Trail, 1845–1849; With Emphasis on the Kansas, Pawnees, and Sioux, Especially in 1846." Master's thesis, University of California, Berkeley, 1933. 115 pp. The chapter entitled "Relations with the Pawnees" is basically excerpts from a number of emigrant journals. Ethnocentric in tone, and not particularly well written. The concept is good, but there are better sources.

605. Sibley, George C. "Extracts from the Journal of Major Sibley." *Chronicles of Oklahoma* 5 (June 1927): 196–220. In May 1811, Sibley and fourteen others set out for Indian country to make peace among several tribes, including the Pawnees. He speaks of being cordially welcomed by a Republican Pawnee chief. Sibley provides a good explanation of how an earth lodge was constructed, and offers a less-than-flattering physical evaluation of the Pawnees themselves. Also relates a version of Zebulon Pike's visit to the Pawnee villages that had occurred a few years earlier. Some proper Indian names are misspelled, but Sibley's description of the Platte River near the Pawnee villages is masterful [549].

606. Stolley, William. "History of the First Settlement of Hall County, Nebraska." Translated by Harry Weingart. *Nebraska History* Special Issue (April 1946): 61–70. Chapter 10 is a delightful recollection of Stolley's overall good relations with the Pawnees. He relates tales of trade, dog feasts, his role as a doctor to the Indians, and an antelope hunt that could have turned deadly. Also includes a list of Pawnee words and numbers, translated into both German and English.

607. Tappan, William Henry. "'A Great Place for Gambling Whiskey Drinking & Roguery': A Fort Childs Diary, 1848." Edited by Ellen F. Tappan

and Richard E. Jensen. *Nebraska History* 82 (Fall 2001): 90–121. Artist William Tappan spent nearly six months in Nebraska with the Missouri Mounted Volunteers who were building Fort Childs (later Fort Kearny) along the Platte River. During his stay, he had several opportunities to observe the Pawnees, visit their villages, and even attend councils between the Indians and army officers. His description of a Pawnee village and a chief's lodge are excellent. Illustrating the article are several of Tappan's drawings and paintings.

608. Thayer, John M. "My Very First Visit to the Pawnee Village in 1855." *Proceedings and Collections of the Nebraska State Historical Society*, vol. 10, 1907. Lincoln: Jacob North & Co., Printers, 1907, 119–27. In 1855, General Thayer was asked by Nebraska Territorial Governor Mark Izard to travel to the Pawnee villages with a small party to warn the Indians that they must stop harassing white settlers or a military expedition would be sent to stop their depredations by force. After a council with the Pawnee chiefs, during which the chiefs promised to control their young men, Thayer and his companions returned to their wagons to find that Pawnees had stolen all their provisions, including a bottle of aged brandy. In 1859, Thayer and volunteer troops would confront the Pawnees after a series of particularly destructive raids.

609. Unruh, John D., Jr. *The Plains Across: The Overland Emigrants and the Trans-Mississippi West, 1840–60*. Urbana: University of Illinois Press, 1979. 565 pp. As emigrants crossed the Plains in ever-increasing numbers, Indian entrepreneurs devised clever ways to charge travelers for crossing their lands. At Shell Creek, in eastern Nebraska, the Pawnees demanded a twenty-five-cent toll for crossing the stream, even though the bridge there had been built by emigrant companies. When the bridge over Shell Creek washed away in an 1851 flood, the Pawnees refused to allow the emigrants to rebuild it. Later, in 1852, a group of pioneers refused to pay the Pawnees for crossing their territory and attacked the Indians, killing several of them.

610. U.S. Congress. House. *Colonel Dodge's Journal*. 24th Cong., 1st sess. 1836. H. Doc. 181. [Ser. 289]. 38 pp. In the late spring and early summer of 1835, Colonel Henry Dodge and three companies of cavalry marched 1600 miles from Fort Leavenworth to the Rocky Mountains and back, holding peace councils with each Indian tribe along the way. In late June, Dodge met with chiefs of the Pawnee bands. The journal includes speeches made by several leading Pawnees. A

valuable source of information on the Indians, as well as the territory through which Dodge and his men traveled. Also appears in 24th Cong., 1st sess., 1836. S. Doc. 209. [Ser. 281].

611. _____. *Message from the President of the United States, Transmitting a Report of the Secretary of War.* 18th Cong., 1st sess., 1824. H. Doc. 85. [Ser. 97]. 5 pp. The Quartermaster General informed John C. Calhoun, Secretary of War, that 200 horses needed to transport troops from Council Bluffs to Oregon could be purchased from the Pawnees for $25 to $30 each, in either cash or merchandise.

612. _____. Stokes, M., Henry L. Ellsworth, and J. T. Schermerhorn. *Report to the Secretary of War.* 23d Cong., 1st sess., 1834, 78–103. H. Rept. 474. [Ser. 263]. When the three Indian Commissioners filed their report on the status of Indian tribes west of the Mississippi, they were concerned about the difficulties between the Pawnees and the newly transplanted Delawares, who both claimed the same lands. Ellsworth and his fellow commissioners convinced the Pawnees to surrender the land, thus defusing the situation. The commissioners also recommended that a fort be built along the Platte River above the Grand Pawnee village.

613. U. S. Congress. Senate. Fremont, John C. *A Report of an Exploration of the Country Lying Between the Missouri River and the Rocky Mountains on the Line of the Kansas and Great Platte Rivers.* 27th Cong., 3d sess., 1843. S. Doc. 243. [Ser. 416]. Reprint. Fairfield, Washington: Ye Galleon Press, 1996. 243 pp. Contains only scattered mentions of the Pawnees, but Fremont's descriptions of Nebraska, especially the Platte and Loup River regions, are full of detail. The reprint edition is enhanced by Michael L. Tate's outstanding biographical profile of Fremont and a detailed fold-out map of his frontier explorations.

614. _____. *Report of the Secretary of War, Communicating, in Answer to a Resolution of the Senate, a Report and Map of the Examination of New Mexico, Made by Lieutenant J. W. Abert of the Topographical Corps, 1846–1847.* 30th Cong., 1st sess., 1848. S. Exec. Doc. 23. [Ser. 506]. 132 pp., plus illustrations. Also published as *Abert's New Mexico Report, 1846–47.* Albuquerque: Horn and Wallace, 1962. 182 pp. Abert and his company had almost completed their fact-finding mission when they encountered a band of Pawnees near the Arkansas River. When his mules disappeared, Abert suspected that the Indians had stolen them. The Pawnees offered to sell Abert new mules—at a very high price.

615. Wharton, Clifton. "The Expedition of Major Clifton Wharton in 1844." *Collections of the Kansas State Historical Society*, vol. 16 (1923–1925). Topeka: Kansas State Printing Plant, 1925, 272–305. In August 1844, the United States Army's First Dragoon Regiment under the command of Major Wharton left Fort Leavenworth for the Pawnee villages on the Platte River, then on to visit Missouri River tribes. Wharton held separate councils with the Pawnee bands, urging them to move north of the Platte River, as they had agreed to do a few years earlier, and the Pawnees presented their grievances against the Sioux. Well-written journal describes in great detail the country through which the cavalry unit marched and the poor condition of the Pawnees at the time.

616. Wheelock, T. B. "Journal of Colonel Dodge's Expedition from Fort Gibson to the Pawnee Pict Village." *American State Papers*, Military Affairs, vol. 5, 22d Cong., 1st sess., 1834, 373–82. Detailed journal of the first visit of a United States military unit to the Pawnees. In council with the Indians, Colonel Henry Dodge negotiated a prisoner exchange and tried to persuade Pawnee chiefs to visit the "Great Father" in Washington [563].

617. Wilhelm, Paul, Duke of Württemberg. *Travels in North America, 1822–1824.* Translated by W. Robert Nitske. Edited by Savoie Lottinville. Norman: University of Oklahoma Press, 1973. 456 pp. As part of his journey up the Missouri River in 1823, the duke made a side trip to visit the Grand Pawnees along the Loup Fork of the Platte River. Plagued by a dishonest interpreter, Paul Wilhelm nevertheless provided a colorful profile of the Pawnees—their villages, their numbers, and their appearance. Like several other early travelers, he noted that the Pawnees were clever thieves.

618. Young, F. G., ed. "Journal Kept by Dr. Marcus Whitman of His Tour of Exploration with Rev. Samuel Parker in 1835 Beyond the Rocky Mountains." *Oregon Historical Quarterly* 28 (1927): 239–57. In early July, on their way west from St. Louis, Whitman, Parker, and their party passed the villages of three Pawnee bands on the Loup Fork of the Platte River. Most of the Indians had gone on their summer hunt, but Samuel Allis and a few Skidis greeted the party and invited them to share several meals. On July 5, Whitman continued west with a few Pawnees who refused to let the emigrants travel ahead of them for fear they would frighten away the buffalo.

13

The Pike-Pawnee Village

619. Allan, Tom. "Bingo Billy Protects the Heritage of Pawnee Braves, Explorer Pike." *Omaha World-Herald*, 13 May 1962, 6B. Human interest story about a young boy from Guide Rock, Nebraska, whose "playground" was the area near the famous Pike-Pawnee Village where Zebulon Pike met with the Pawnees and persuaded them to exchange a Spanish flag for an American one. Also discusses the events of that 1806 meeting and the site's discovery by Asa T. Hill in 1925.

620. "Archaeological 'Digging' Tells Some of Pawnee Indian Story." *Belleville (Kansas) Telescope*, 12 August 1965. Archaeology in Kansas Clippings, vol. 3, 205–7. Kansas State Historical Society. Report that excavation had begun at the Pawnee Indian Village just west of Republic, Kansas. Describes the general layout of the village, its fortified wall, and the two earth lodges that would be excavated. Today, the Pawnee Indian Village Museum stands at the site and incorporates an excavated earth lodge.

621. "Archaeologists' Report Verifies Indian's Words." *Belleville (Kansas) Telescope*, 21 October 1926. Republic County Clippings, 1931–1950, vol. 2, 160–61. Kansas State Historical Society. Many years ago, an elderly Pawnee stated that his people were buried near Republic, Kansas. Article argues that the Pike-Pawnee Village was indeed in Kansas, and the arguments included were the basis for the Kansas State Historical Society's decision that Pike met the Pawnees in Kansas—not in Nebraska.

622. Burke, Bill. "Republic County Hasn't Forgotten the Pawnee." *Salina* (*Kansas*) *Journal*, 18 May 1980. Pawnee Indians Clippings File, vol. 1, 26–27. Kansas State Historical Society. A Republic, Kansas, farmer and amateur historian tried for years to pinpoint the actual site of the Pike-Pawnee Village. He believed the marked site was incorrect. Along with his story is an excellent description of a typical Pawnee earth lodge.

623. Burleigh, D. R. "Pike-Pawnee Site." *Nebraska History* 17 (January–March 1936): 75–76. Praises the work of Asa T. Hill and others in identifying the correct location of the Republican Pawnee village visited by Zebulon Pike, and encourages the placing of a monument at the site near Red Cloud, Nebraska.

624. Isley, Bliss. "Kansas Pioneers: Kiwiktaka, Chief of Pawnees, Deserves Place in History." *Medicine Lodge* (*Kansas*) *Index*, 21 October 1937. Pawnee Indian Clippings File, vol. 1, 12–13. Kansas State Historical Society. Describes the role of a little-known Pawnee chief in the raising of the American flag at the Pawnee village near present-day Republic, Kansas. This story is valuable only as local color, since the Pawnee village visited by Zebulon Pike was later identified as one across the state line in Nebraska.

625. Jackson, Donald, ed. *The Journals of Zebulon Montgomery Pike with Letters and Related Documents*. 2 vols. Norman: University of Oklahoma Press, 1966. 913 pp., plus maps. This is the first publication of Pike's complete journals since 1895, and Pike's maps and papers captured by the Spanish and held in Mexico for 100 years are included, along with Spanish official correspondence. The index lists many references to the Pawnees, including several accounts of his encounters with them at the Pike-Pawnee Village near the Republican River, and accurate descriptions of Pawnee villages and life. Originally printed in 1810, much of this material was also published in Elliot Coues, ed. *The Expeditions of Zebulon Montgomery Pike, To Headwaters of the Mississippi River, Through Louisiana Territory, and in New Spain, During the Years 1805–6–7*. 2 vols. Minneapolis: Ross & Haines, Inc., 1965.

626. ———. "Zebulon Pike and Nebraska." *Nebraska History* 47 (December 1966): 355–69. Outstanding essay using portions of his book on Zebulon Pike [625]. Explains events at Pike-Pawnee village and agrees with Nebraska researchers that the proper location of Pike's meeting with the Pawnees was in Nebraska, not Kansas.

627. "Kansas and the Flag." *Transactions of the Kansas State Historical Society*, vol. 7 (1901–1902). Topeka: W. Y. Morgan, State Printer, 1902, 261–317. Collection of addresses given either at the July 1901 laying of the cornerstone of the monument at the Pike-Pawnee Village near Republic, Kansas, or at the dedication of the monument in September of the same year. Although the speeches contain much Kansas boosterism, some do give valuable information on Zebulon Pike and the Pawnees.

628. "Kansas and Nebraska Both Lay Claim to Site of Pawnee Republic Birth." n.s., n.d. Kansas History Clippings File, vol. 6, 133–34. Kansas State Historical Society. Article written at about the same time the debate over the true location of the Pike-Pawnee Village flared up again. The author—a Kansan—challenges Nebraska to prove that the Republic, Kansas, site is incorrect.

629. "Medals Found in Pawnee Indian Graves." *Numismatist* 39 (March 1926): 139–40. Briefly addresses the controversy over the location of the Pike-Pawnee Village and describes Spanish, English, and American medals found in Pawnee graves on the Asa T. Hill farm, east of Red Cloud, Nebraska.

630. Morehouse, George P. "Pike's Pawnee Village." In *Kansas State Historical Society Twenty-Fifth Biennial Report, 1925–1926*. Topeka: Kansas State Printing Plant, 1927, 50–55. Writes in support of the site near Republic, Kansas, as the correct Pawnee village visited by Zebulon Pike in 1806, but argues that the actual village may have been in the Republican River valley, not on the bluff where the museum and historical marker now stand. Also includes a history of the Kansas State Historical Society's acquisition of the site.

631. "More Remains to Be Learned about Pawnee Indian Tribe." *Kearney (Nebraska) Daily Hub*, 7 June 1956. Pawnee Indians Clippings File, vol. 1, 20–21. Kansas State Historical Society. Points out that most of the Indian graves at the Pike-Pawnee Village near Red Cloud, Nebraska, had been examined, but many of the houses had not. Much of the site had been disturbed when the fields were cultivated. However, "good samples" had been obtained, and now other Nebraska historical sites had higher priority.

632. Munday, Frank J. "The Pike-Pawnee Village Site." *Nebraska History* 23 (October–December 1942): 261–62. Munday emphasized the

importance of the Pike-Pawnee Village and urged the creation of a society to publicize the site and secure a monument to commemorate Pike's visit.

633. "One Hundred Years under the Flag: The Centennial Celebration at Pike's Pawnee Village." *Transactions of the Kansas State Historical Society,* vol. 10 (1907–1908). Topeka: Kansas State Printing Office, 1908, 15–159. Collection of speeches delivered on the 100th anniversary of the raising of the American flag over the supposed Kansas site of the Pike-Pawnee Village. Most of the speeches deal with explorers and the early history of Kansas.

634. "Pawnee Indian Village Celebration Friday Next, Sept. 29th." n.s., n.d. Republic County Clippings File, 1931–1950, vol. 2, 159. Kansas State Historical Society. Reprints a letter from Pawnee scholar James R. Murie confirming that the Pawnee village near Republic, Kansas, was the site of Pike's visit in 1806.

635. "Pawnee Village." Topeka, Kansas: KTWU/Channel 11, Washburn University, 1995. ktwu.wuacc.edu/journeys/scripts/802a.html. Transcript of a television interview with Thomas Witty, retired state archaeologist, and Pike-Pawnee Village Museum curator Richard Gould. Witty and Gould share their knowledge of the Pawnee village near Republic, Kansas, and the people who lived there.

636. "Pawnee Village Site Near Red Cloud Top Historical Find." *Kearney (Nebraska) Daily Hub,* 6 June 1956. Pawnee Indians Clippings File, vol. 1, 19–20. Kansas State Historical Society. Describes the artifacts found in and around graves at the actual Pike-Pawnee Village near Red Cloud. Also recalls Asa T. Hill's purchase of the site and his role in its excavation. Especially poignant is the description of the grave of a privileged Pawnee child who was buried along with an eagle.

637. "Pawnee Indian Village Museum State Historic Site." www.kshs.org/places/pawneeindian. Web site profiles this historic site and museum near Republic, Kansas. Also provides links to the history of the village and to information on the Pawnee sacred bundle housed at the museum. Included are directions and hours of operation.

638. "Pike's Camp to Be Historically Chosen Tuesday." *Topeka Capital,* 17 October 1939. Republic County Clippings, 1931–1950, vol. 2, 165–66. Kansas State Historical Society. Reports that an announcement will be made in a few days as to whether the Kansas or Nebraska

Pawnee Indian village was visited by Zebulon Pike, and presents both states' arguments.

639. "Pike's Visit to Nebraska Historically Important." *Omaha World-Herald*, 9 November 1998, 30. Travel article provides a brief but excellent account of Zebulon Pike's meeting with Pawnees near Guide Rock, Nebraska, and describes attempts by the State Historical Society to attain funds for a Pawnee museum and burial vault at the site. The Historical Society was protecting and preserving the property, which was being farmed.

640. Roberts, Ricky L. "The Archaeology of the Kansas Monument Site: A Study in Historical Archaeology on the Great Plains." Master's thesis, University of Kansas, 1978. 189 pp. Outstanding study of the artifacts recovered from the Republic County site that the State of Kansas once believed marked the Pawnee village visited by Pike in 1806. Besides carefully identifying and explaining the artifacts, the introduction to this thesis clearly explains the dispute between Kansas and Nebraska over the actual Pawnee village location, and points out the importance of this village on the southern periphery of Pawnee lands.

641. Ryan, Leo J. "Doesn't Play Golf So Digs Up History." *Omaha World-Herald*, 13 September 1925, Social Events Section, 10. Explains how amateur archaeologist Asa T. Hill located the likely site of the Pike-Pawnee village by comparing landmarks just east of Red Cloud, Nebraska, to entries in Zebulon Pike's journals. While excavating, Hill unearthed a British medal matching a description given by Pike. On occasion, he invited the public to join him in searching for artifacts and burials on his land.

642. Sanborn, Theo A. "The Story of the Pawnee Indian Village in Republic County, Kansas." *Kansas Historical Quarterly* 39 (Spring 1973): 1–11. Discussion of the argument between Kansas and Nebraska over the actual site of the Pawnee village visited by Zebulon Pike. Also describes the 1967 construction of the Pawnee Village Museum near Republic, Kansas.

643. Vaughn, Harry. "Lost Pawnee Village Found Near Guide Rock, Nebraska." *Guide Rock (Nebraska) Signal*, 5 August 1926, 1. A local account of Asa T. Hill's discovery of the Pike-Pawnee village six miles from Guide Rock. Describes the home sites, burial grounds, and artifacts uncovered by Hill.

644. "Village Reveals Secrets." *Wichita (Kansas) Sunday Eagle & Beacon,* 7 August 1966. Archaeology Department Clippings File, vol. 1, 1966–1981, 1–2. Kansas State Historical Society. Explains the look of the Pawnee Village Museum and how it would be constructed. In discussing the site, archaeologist Thomas Witty seemed convinced that the Indians who lived there left in an orderly fashion, since the food caches were empty. But it is also evident that the village was burned.

645. "The War Between Nebraska and Kansas: Both Sides of the Dispute over the True Location of the Pike-Pawnee Indian Village Where the Spanish Flag Came Down and the Stars and Stripes Went Up." *Nebraska History* 10 (July–September 1927): 159–258. Entire volume dedicated to the Nebraska-Kansas controversy over the exact location of the Republican Pawnee village visited by Zebulon Pike in 1806. Articles include an autobiography of Asa T. Hill, a review of the evidence favoring Nebraska's claim to the site, Lewis and Clark's description of the Pawnee nation, references to the Pawnees by other explorers, and a lengthy investigative article by a committee representing the Kansas State Historical Society arguing that the Pike-Pawnee village was in Kansas.

646. Witty, Thomas A. "The Pawnee Indian Village Museum Project." *Newsletter, Kansas Anthropological Association* 13 (January 1968): 1–5. Gives a thorough explanation of the archaeological work that was done to prepare for the building of a museum at the Pike-Pawnee Village site in Republic County, Kansas. Although this site proved not to be the actual meeting place, it is the only preserved Pawnee village in the Central Plains.

647. "Writes Data about 'Republic of Pawnee'." *Belleville (Kansas) Telescope,* 20 January 1955. Pawnee Indians Clippings File, vol. 1, 15–16. Kansas State Historical Society. Contents of a chatty letter written in anticipation of the 150th anniversary of the alleged American flag raising at the Pawnee village near Republic, Kansas. Identifies local farmers who later owned the land where the village was located, and ends with a suggestion that the site be set aside as a tourist attraction.

648. Zimmerman, Mark E., and Edward Park. "Some Archaeological Investigations Made in Republic County, Kansas and in Webster County, Nebraska." *Twenty-fifth Biennial Report of the Kansas State*

Historical Society, 1926–1928, 72–74. A committee representing the Kansas State Historical Society investigated the two sites claiming to be where Zebulon Pike met with the Pawnees in 1806. After weighing the evidence, they decided that the Pawnees moved to the Nebraska site after Pike visited their village in northern Kansas, thus supporting Kansas' claim to the Pike-Pawnee Village.

14

Depredations and Claims

649. Covington, James W., ed. "A Robbery on the Santa Fe Trail, 1827." *Kansas Historical Quarterly* 21 (Autumn 1955): 560–63. Reprints a letter from seven Santa Fe traders to Congress asking payment for livestock stolen by Pawnee raiders on October 12, 1827, along the Arkansas River in Kansas. The request for payment was denied.

650. "Murder in Greeley County." *Columbus* (*Nebraska*) *Journal Extra*, 18 March 1874, 1. From Albion, Nebraska, comes a report of the murder of a trapper, allegedly by Pawnees claiming to be Sioux.

651. "Murder of Joseph Dillo." *Columbus* (*Nebraska*) *Journal*, 25 March 1874, 3. Agent William Burgess presents evidence to show that the trapper allegedly murdered by Pawnees was actually killed by renegade Sioux. Apparently the party who originally accused the Pawnees also retracted his statement.

652. "Pawnee Indians." *Omaha Nebraskian*, 25 November 1856, n.p. Strongly worded editorial complaining about Pawnee horse thefts and interference with surveyors, which the editor claimed prevented white settlement in Nebraska Territory. He urged the government to either protect Nebraska settlers from the Pawnees or to exterminate these "red rascals."

653. "The Pawnee Sensation." *Columbus* (*Nebraska*) *Journal*, 2 September 1874, 4. Article reprinted from the *Lincoln Journal* expressing

outrage over the false reporting of the whipping and dismemberment of a Colfax County settler by Pawnees.

654. U.S. Congress. House. *Thomas Talbot and Others*. 28th Cong., 1st sess., 1844. H. Rept. 370. [Ser. 446]. 3 pp. The Committee on Indian Affairs ruled that because of the wording of treaties with the Pawnees, the government could not withhold annuities to pay for about 100 horses stolen from traders in October 1827. The government refused to accept responsibility for the traders' losses.

655. ———. *Bent, St. Vrain, & Co*. 28th Cong., 2d sess., 1845. H. Rept. 194. [Ser. 468]. 9 pp. The trading company of Bent, St. Vrain, & Co. submitted a claim to the Indian Affairs Committee for repayment for goods stolen by a band of Pawnees in 1838. Despite the Pawnees' admission of guilt and several documents supporting the claim, the government refused to pay, since the theft occurred outside of the United States, in Mexican Territory.

656. ———. *Thomas Talbot and Others*. 30th Cong., 1st sess., 1848. H. Rept. 299. [Ser. 525]. 5 pp. After further consideration, the Committee on Indian Affairs recommended that the government pay Talbot and his fellow traders for their losses at the hands of the Pawnees 21 years earlier [654].

657. ———. *M. M. Marmaduke and Others*. 35th Cong., 1st sess., 1858. H. Rept. 293. [Ser. 965]. 2 pp. Using the claim of Thomas Talbot [656] as a guide, the Committee on Indian Affairs recommended that Marmaduke and other traders be paid for horses, mules, and donkeys stolen by the Pawnees along a government trade route in 1828.

658. ———. *William D. Latshaw*. 36th Cong., 1st sess., 1860. H. Rept. 631. [Ser. 1070]. 2 pp. A surveyor whose oxen were stolen by the Pawnees was paid for his stock and was now seeking damages for lost wages. The claim was denied.

659. ———. *Indian Depredations*. 41st Cong., 2d sess., 1869. H. Misc. Doc. 20. [Ser. 1431]. 7 pp. Includes a detailed list of stolen property, deaths, injuries, and destroyed homes in Kansas as the result of Indian raids in 1867 and 1868. According to this report, twenty-four of these depredations were by Pawnees, acting either alone or with Cheyenne allies.

660. ———. *Russell S. Newell*. 49th Cong., 2d sess, 1887. H. Rept. 3678. [Ser. 2500]. 1 p. Supports a bill to repay trader Russell Newell for

merchandise stolen from him by Pawnees in 1858. The bill presented to Congress by Newell totaled $3,150.

661. ———. *Russell S. Newell.* 51st Cong., 1st sess., 1890. H. Rept. 2989. [Ser. 2815]. 2 pp. In 1890, the Committee on Indian Affairs recommended that Newell be paid for his losses [660], but in the amount of $2,000, not the over-$3,000 originally requested.

662. U. S. Congress. Senate. *Memorial of the Legislature of Missouri.* 20th Cong., 2d sess., 1829. S. Doc. 52. [Ser. 181]. 3 pp. Citing loss of trade goods and loss of life, the State of Missouri asked the government to build a military post near where traders bound for Santa Fe crossed the Arkansas River. There had been numerous Indian raids in that area, and the Pawnees were quoted as vowing to kill any white man who passed that way. The memorialists also requested that British traders be barred from United States territory, since they incited the Indians.

663. ———. *Report from the Secretary of War in Compliance with a Resolution of the Senate, in Relation to the Establishment of a Line of Military Posts from the Missouri to the Oregon or Columbia River.* 26th Cong., 1st sess., 1840. S. Doc. 231. [Ser. 358]. 3 pp. Secretary of War Joel Poinsett recommended building three forts, in addition to Fort Leavenworth, along the westbound trade route. The first military post would be built at the junction of the north and south forks of the Platte River, where it could help control the Pawnees, Poncas, and Kansas.

664. ———. *Mr. Atchison, from the Committee on Indian Affairs, Made the Following Report.* 29th Cong., 1st sess, 1846. S. Doc. 54. [Ser. 473]. 1 p. Response to a claim by Indian sub-agent Elijah White that he was robbed of over $1,000 worth of goods by Pawnees in the vicinity of Grand Island. Since the Pawnees had no annuities from which White could be compensated, the Indian Affairs Committee recommended that he be reimbursed by the government.

665. ———. *Mr. Atchison, from the Committee on Indian Affairs, Made the Following Report.* 29th Cong., 2d sess., 1847. S. Doc. 45. [Ser. 494]. 1 p. One year after originally recommending that the government reimburse sub-agent Elijah White for losses at the hands of the Pawnees [664], the Indian Affairs Committee once again submitted its recommendation.

666. ———. *In the Senate of the United States, Mr. Atchison Made the Following Report*. 29th Cong., 2d sess., 1847. S. Doc. 75. [Ser. 494]. 2 pp. For the fifth time, trader Thomas Talbott petitioned the government for indemnity for goods and cash stolen by Pawnees in 1826. This time, he asked the government if he could take matters into his own hands. After reviewing the case, the Committee on Indian Affairs urged the government to pay the roughly $4,000 claim.

667. ———. *In the Senate of the United States*. 43d Cong., 1st sess., 1874. S. Rept. 59. [Ser. 1586]. 1 p. Sarah Brooks, a Kansas resident, claimed that she was taken prisoner by six Pawnees in 1868, after which she was raped and forced into slavery. She was allegedly freed by George Armstrong Custer in 1869. Her claim for damages was denied for lack of supporting evidence of any kind.

668. ———. *In the Senate of the United States, Mr. Atchison Made the Following Report*. 30th Cong., 1st sess., 1847. S. Rept. 11. [Ser. 512]. 2 pp. Eleven months after his last report, Senator Atchison once more asked the government to repay Thomas Talbot for his losses to the Pawnees twenty-one years earlier.

669. Whiting, Albe B. "Some Western Border Conditions in the 50s and 60s." *Collections of the Kansas State Historical Society*, vol. 12, 1912. Topeka: Kansas State Printing Office, 1912, 1–10. Includes an account of an Indian attack on a wagon train along the Republican River in May 1857. Settlers claimed that the Indian raiders were normally friendly Pawnees who believed that either the Sioux or the Cheyennes would be blamed for the depredations.

15
Treaties and Land Cessions

670. Coffin, Haskell. *Painting Commemorating the Signing of the Table Creek Treaty in 1857—Whereby the Pawnee Indians Ceded Their Land in Nebr. to the U.S.* Painted in 1897 and located on the second floor landing of W. Sterling Morton's Arbor Lodge in Nebraska City, Nebraska, this approximately five-foot by thirteen-foot oil painting depicts the council at which the Pawnees gave up their remaining Nebraska lands and agreed to locate on a reservation on the Loup Fork of the Platte River. Table Creek is located just a few miles north of Arbor Lodge.

671. "Commission Findings. Docket no. 10. *Pawnee Indian Tribe of Oklahoma v. the United States.*" In *Pawnee and Kansa (Kaw) Indians*, 281–451. New York: Garland Publishing, Inc., 1974. Document from the Indian Claims Commission addresses each of the Pawnee claims corresponding to the tribe's four land cessions, and presents the commission's findings. The Pawnee case actually came before the Claims Commission twice. The original finding was dated 1953, and in June 1957, a revised finding was issued. For a detailed discussion of this case, see David J. Wishart, "The Pawnee Claims Case, 1947–64" [710].

672. "Experts Back Indian Claim." *Omaha World-Herald*, 22 April 1959, 3. Brief article announcing that experts were in the city testifying in support of the Pawnee case before the Indian Claims Commission. Much of the information on the value of Pawnee lands would be presented by William G. Murray of Ames, Iowa, whose appraisals are annotated elsewhere in this category [677].

673. "From Washington." *Nebraska City (Nebraska) News*, 16 January 1858, 1. A report from the nation's capital on a delegation of sixteen Pawnees currently in the city with their agent. The plan was for them to tour the city, meet the president, and discuss the terms of their recent treaty establishing a Pawnee reservation in north-central Nebraska.

674. "Indian Treaty Ceded Lands." *Nebraska City (Nebraska) News-Press*, 14 November 1954, 1B. Poorly worded article that confuses the March 1854 Omaha Indian treaty with the 1857 Treaty of Table Creek, by which the Pawnees gave up all their land north of the Platte River except their reservation in present-day Nance County. Includes a few recollections of local settlers and a reproduction of the Haskell Coffin painting that now hangs near the staircase in Nebraska City's Arbor Lodge.

675. "Indians Reject $8 Million U.S. Offers for Lost Land." *Topeka Capital*, 28 February 1961. Pawnee Indians Clippings File, vol. 1, 25. Kansas State Historical Society. The attorney for the Pawnees of Oklahoma states that the Indian Claims Commission award amounts to about thirty-seven cents per acre. The tribal council believes the Pawnees should receive triple that amount.

676. Malin, James C. *Indian Policy and Westward Expansion*. Bulletin of the University of Kansas, vol. 22, Humanistic Studies, vol. 2. Lawrence: University of Kansas, 1921. 108 pp. Analyzes the government's reasons for wanting to move Indian tribes either north or south of the Platte River Road and the routes of the soon-to-be-built railroads. Since westward-moving pioneers and the Union Pacific Railroad would be going through their lands, the Pawnees and other Nebraska Indians figure prominently in this study.

677. Murray, William G. *Appraisal of Pawnee Tracts in Nebraska, 1833, 1848, 1857, 1875; in Kansas, 1833.* New York: Clearwater Publishing Co., 1973. 143 pp. Originally printed by the U.S. Department of Justice in 1959, this important source regarding the value of Pawnee lands ceded to the government in the nineteenth century is available on microfiche at major research libraries. Murray's appraisals are listed under Indian Claims Commission Part B, Testimony, Docket 10, and take into consideration soils, availability of timber and water, climate, and use of the lands when they were ceded.

678. *Pawnee Indian Lands.* March 3, 1893. 27 *Statutes at Large,* 644. Executive agreement to pay the Oklahoma Pawnees up to $80,000 for

their lands between the Cimarron and Arkansas rivers. In keeping with the terms of the 1892 Jerome Agreement, this land would be opened to white settlement.

679. "The Pawnees: Important Council at Grand Island." *Platte Journal*, 31 July 1872, 1. Columbus, Nebraska, newspaper reports the signing of an agreement whereby the Pawnees sold 50,000 acres of reservation land north of Silver Creek, Nebraska. The Pawnee chiefs signed the agreement on the condition that the money for the land would be turned over to their trusted agent, Jacob Troth, for distribution.

680. "The Pawnees: Their Removal to the Indian Territory." *Columbus (Nebraska) Journal*, 18 November 1874, 1. Reprints the document in which the Pawnees agreed to sell their reservation in Nebraska and move to a new 300-square-mile reservation in Indian Territory. Article 4 requests that no tribal funds be used for the trip south, and that any government employees who go south with them will draw only their regular salaries.

681. Royce, Charles C., comp. *Schedule of Indian Land Cessions in the United States*. Eighteenth Annual Report of the Bureau of American Ethnology, 1896–1897, Part 2. Washington, D.C.: Government Printing Office, 1899. Reprint. New York: Arno Press, 1971. 997 pp. Excellent source listing all the treaties that affected Pawnee lands. A brief synopsis of each treaty is provided, and maps in the appendix show the exact areas ceded by the Pawnees in the nineteenth century.

682. Sarchet, Corb. "Pawnee Suit Against U.S. Revived by Court Ruling." *Wichita Morning Eagle*, 4 June 1953. Clippings, Alphabetical File. Kansas State Historical Society. Reports a Supreme Court ruling that the Pawnees could continue their claim for repayment for Kansas and Nebraska lands sold to the government in nineteenth-century treaties. Also states that because they once occupied the region, the Pawnees claimed a share in Red River Valley oil revenues.

683. Sheldon, Addison E. "Land Systems and Land Policies in Nebraska." *Publications of the Nebraska State Historical Society*, vol. 22. Lincoln: Nebraska State Historical Society, 1936. 337 pp. Chapters entitled "Indian Land Tenure and Its Extinction" and "Indian Reservations Lands" address the history of Indians in Nebraska. A table of Indian land cessions with an accompanying map clearly documents the land losses. The sale of Pawnee Reservation lands, mostly to white speculators, is ex-

plained in detail. Included is a list of those people who purchased over 1,000 acres of the former Pawnee reserve between 1878 and 1884.

684. "Treaties with Several Tribes." *American State Papers*: 2, *Indian Affairs*, 15th Cong., 2d sess., 1818, no. 155, 164–80. Pages 171–72 contain four Pawnee treaties of peace and friendship. Signing for the government on all these treaties were William Clark and trader Auguste Chouteau. These agreements can also be found in 7 *Statutes at Large* 172–75, and are reprinted in Charles Kappler, ed. *Indian Laws and Treaties*, vol. 2, 156–59.

685. "Treaties with Several Tribes." *American State Papers*: 2, *Indian Affairs*, 19th Cong., 1st sess., no. 226, 1826, 595–609. Reprints the texts of the treaties procured by Brig. General Henry Atkinson and Indian agent Benjamin O'Fallon on their Missouri River expedition. The Pawnee treaty, signed at Council Bluff in September 1825, appears on pages 603–604. The Pawnee treaty can also be found in 7 *Statutes at Large* 279, and is reprinted in Charles Kappler, ed. *Indian Laws and Treaties*, vol. 2, 258–60.

686. "Treaty with the Pawnee, 1833." 7 *Statutes at Large* 448. Reprinted in Charles Kappler, ed. *Indian Laws and Treaties*, vol. 2, 416–18. By this treaty, signed on October 9, 1833, at the Grand Pawnee village on the Platte River, the four bands of Pawnees agreed to surrender all of their land south of the Platte.

687. "Treaty with the Pawnee—Grand, Loups, Republicans, etc., 1848." 9 *Statutes at Large* 949. Reprinted in Charles Kappler, ed. *Indian Laws and Treaties*, vol. 2, 571–72. On August 6, 1848, the Pawnee bands agreed to cede a narrow strip of land south of the Platte River near Grand Island, which would become the site of Fort Childs, later Fort Kearny. The treaty text includes a plat of the ceded area.

688. "Treaty with the Pawnee, 1857." 11 *Statutes at Large* 729. Reprinted in Charles Kappler, ed. *Indian Laws and Treaties*, vol. 2 , 764–67. At Table Creek, just north of Nebraska City, Nebraska, on September 24, 1857, the Pawnees ceded all of their remaining Nebraska lands except the area on the Loup Fork of the Platte River that would become their Nebraska reservation. The Pawnees were expected to move to their reservation within one year, at no cost to the government.

689. "Tribe Asks Price Hike for Land Sold Long Ago." *Kansas City Star*, 22 April 1959. Pawnee Indians Clippings File, vol. 1, 24. Kansas

State Historical Society. A Denver appraiser researched the sale of Pawnee lands during the 1800s, and appeared as a witness before the Indian Claims Commission. This article does not include his actual testimony or his opinions as to the land's nineteenth-century value.

690. U.S. Congress. House. *Estimates—Treaty Stipulations with Pawnee Indians*. 35th Cong., 1st sess., 1858. H. Exec. Doc. 134. [Ser. 959]. 8 pp. Reprints the September 1857 treaty with the Pawnees and urges that the appropriation provided for in the treaty be provided immediately.

691. ———. *Appropriations for Indian Treaties*. 40th Cong., 2d sess., 1868. H. Exec. Doc. 124. [Ser. 1337]. 2 pp. Commissioner of Indian Affairs N. G. Taylor informed the Interior Secretary of amounts necessary to purchase goods to fulfill treaty obligations. The appropriation for the Pawnees was $30,000.

692. ———. *Appropriations for Pawnee Indians*. 42d Cong., 2d sess., 1872. H. Exec. Doc. 47. [Ser. 1510]. 3 pp. The Quaker agent at the Pawnee Reservation requested an additional $8,400 to meet treaty obligations to educate Pawnee children. The money would be used to build school houses and dormitories and to pay staff.

693. ———. *Sale of Certain Lands in Nebraska*. 42d Cong., 3d sess., 1873. H. Exec. Doc. 79. [Ser. 1565]. 2 pp. A request for $20,000 to defray the costs of appraising and selling Nebraska lands belonging to the Omaha, Pawnee, Otoe and Missouria, and Sac and Fox Indians.

694. ———. *Fort Kearney [sic] Military Reservation*. 43d Cong., 2d sess., 1874. H. Exec. Doc. 12. [Ser. 1644]. 1 p. Reports that Fort Kearny was abandoned in 1871. Because the land for the fort was purchased from the Pawnees by treaty in 1848, the land must now be transferred from the War Department to the Department of the Interior before it could be sold.

695. ———. *Pawnee Indians*. 43d Cong., 2d sess., 1874. H. Exec. Doc. 36. [Ser. 1644]. 3 pp. Important document regarding the Pawnees' move from Nebraska to Indian Territory. The acting Commissioner of Indian Affairs asked for $300,000 to purchase a new reservation, that amount to be repaid from the proceeds of the Pawnees' Nebraska reserve. Also includes a brief overview of events leading to the Pawnee request for removal and a copy of the bill authorizing the sale of the Nebraska reservation. This document also appears as 43rd Cong., 2d Sess., 1874. S. Misc. Doc. 35. [Ser. 1630].

696. ———. *Pawnee Indians*. 43d Cong., 1st sess., 1874. H. Exec. Doc. 42. [Ser. 1606]. 3 pp. Because of a surveyor's error when the Pawnees' Nebraska reservation was established, the reservation was 4,800 acres smaller than what the 1857 treaty stipulated. This document is a request for $6,000 ($1.25 per acre) to pay the Pawnees for the land they did not receive.

697. ———. *Pawnee Indian Lands in Nebraska*. 43d Cong., 2d sess., 1875. H. Rept. 140. [Ser. 1657]. 2 pp. The Committee on Indian Affairs gave its wholehearted approval to a proposal to move the entire Pawnee tribe to Indian Territory, to temporarily reside with the Wichitas on their large reservation. Reviews the desperate Pawnee situation in Nebraska and notes that the Pawnees expressed their desire to relocate.

698. ———. *Pawnee Indian Reservation in Nebraska*. 51st Cong., 1st sess., 1890. H. Rept. 1175. [Ser. 2810]. 2 pp. The House Committee on Indian Affairs recommended passage of a bill to force those speculators who had purchased over 60,000 acres of land on the Nebraska Pawnee Reservation to pay the total price within two years of the bill's passage or forfeit the land. This congressional action was prompted by complaints by citizens of Nance County that the county was being deprived of tax income from those lands.

699. ———. *Providing for the Disposition of Judgment Funds Now on Deposit to the Credit of the Pawnee Tribe of Oklahoma*. 88th Cong., 2d sess., 1964. H. Rept. 1566. [Ser. 12619-3]. 3 pp. Report accompanying a bill to distribute, on a per capita basis, the $6,439,088 awarded to the Pawnees by the Indian Claims Commission. States the 1864 Pawnee tribal population and its distribution throughout twenty-eight states.

700. U.S. Congress. Senate. *Letter from the Secretary of the Interior*. 42d Cong., 2d sess., 1872. S. Misc. Doc. 41. [Ser. 1481]. 4 pp. Because their annuities proved to be inadequate, former Indian Superintendent Samuel Janney and Interior Secretary Delano urged Congress to allow the Otoes, Omahas, and Pawnees to sell part of their reservations to raise money for "improvements." The Sac and Fox Indians wished to sell their entire small reservation and move to the Indian Territory. In order to purchase farm equipment, the Pawnees hoped to sell 50,000 acres.

701. ———. *Message from the President of the United States*. 52d Cong., 2d sess., 1893. S. Exec. Doc. 16. [Ser. 3055]. 14 pp. Important document transmitting the agreement between the Pawnees of Oklahoma

and the Cherokee (Jerome) Commission by which the Pawnees agreed to cede their reservation to the government and take allotments in severalty. Included are supporting documents and the names of all the Pawnees who signed the agreement.

702. ———. *Agreement with the Pawnee Tribe of Oklahoma.* 61st Cong., 2d sess., 1909. S. Doc. 358. [Ser. 5657]. 2 pp. Executive agreement by which the Pawnees of Oklahoma exchanged their $30,000 permanent annuity provided in Article 2 of their 1857 treaty for a lump sum payment of $600,000, to be divided pro rata among enrolled members of the tribe. The government agreed to continue to provide at least $10,000 per year to maintain schools for Pawnee children

703. ———. *Claims of Pawnee Tribe of Indians.* 61st Cong., 2d sess., 1910. S. Rept. 768. [Ser. 5584]. 2 pp. In this invaluable report, Interior Secretary R. A. Ballinger provided a complete history of Pawnee treaties and agreements with the United States government and listed Pawnee claims that the government had not satisfied. It was Ballinger's judgment that these agreements should be taken to the U.S. Court of Claims for adjudication.

704. ———. *The Pawnee Tribe of Indians.* 66th Cong., 3d sess., 1920. S. Doc. 311. [Ser. 7794]. 11 pp. Findings and conclusions of the U.S. Court of Claims regarding the series of claims made by the Pawnees in 1910. Reports the court's finding on each claim, and provides complete background information. All but one of the Pawnee claims were denied. The court agreed that the proceeds plus interest from surplus lands mentioned in the Jerome Agreement had never been paid. Principle plus interest was over $315,000.

705. ———. *Pawnee Tribe of Indians, Oklahoma.* 66th Cong., 3d sess., 1921. S. Doc. 395. [Ser. 7794]. 3 pp. Letters from the Treasury Secretary, the Secretary of the Interior, and the Assistant Commissioner of Indian Affairs, all supporting the findings of the U.S. Court of Claims in the Pawnee case. However, due to an error in calculating surplus acreage, the amount of the payment would be reduced by $2,965.76, to $312,811.27.

706. ———. *Providing for the Disposition of Judgment Funds now on Deposit to the Credit of the Pawnee Tribe of Oklahoma.* 88th Cong., 2d sess., 1964. S. Rept. 1351. [Ser. 12616-4]. 4 pp. The Indian Claims Commission awarded the Pawnees $7,316,197, with $876,897 being deducted for legal fees. The Interior Secretary recommended that

these funds be distributed to the Pawnees on a per capita basis and that the money not be subject to state or federal income taxes. Part of this report was also printed as 88th Cong., 2d sess. H. Rept. 1566. [Ser. 12619-3].

707. Wishart, David J. "Buying Nebraska from the Indians." *NEBRASKA-land* (March 1990): 15–19. Nicely sums up the Nebraska Indians' land losses of the nineteenth century. With their several treaties and eventual removal to Indian Territory, the Pawnees figure prominently in this story. Included is a map showing Indian land cessions and the per-acre price the native people of Nebraska received for their lands.

708. ———. "Compensation for Dispossession: Payments to the Indians for Their Lands on the Central and Northern Great Plains in the Nineteenth Century." *National Geographic Research* 6 (Winter 1990): 94–109. Traces nineteenth-century Indian land cessions in the Great Plains and explains the problems involved in purchasing the land and the variations in amounts paid by the government. A two-page chart lists details of land purchases in chronological order. References to the Pawnees appear throughout the article. Pawnee land sales and later claims for added compensation are discussed in greater detail in Wishart's "The Pawnee Claims Case, 1947–64" [710].

709. ———. "The Dispossession of the Pawnee." *Annals of the Association of American Geographers* 69 (September 1979): 382–401. Explains the nineteenth-century decline of the Pawnees due to Sioux attacks and white encroachment on their lands. Pawnee treaties and land cessions receive considerable attention, as does the Nebraska reservation period. In 1874, conditions in Nebraska had become so intolerable for the Pawnees that they chose to migrate to Indian Territory.

710. ———. "The Pawnee Claims Case, 1947–64." In *Irredeemable America*, edited by Imre Sutton. Albuquerque: University of New Mexico Press, 1985, 157–86. Excellent chapter tracing the history of *Pawnee Indian Tribe of Oklahoma v. the United States*, an early case heard by the Indian Claims Commission, in which the Pawnees claimed that they had lost title to over 40,000,000 acres of land through fraud and duress. Originally, the Commission rejected most of the Pawnee claims, but on appeal, the Commission found for the tribe, and after adjustments, the Pawnees received a little over $7,000,000 in compensation for land purchased by the government in the nineteenth century for about ten cents an acre.

16
Missionaries and Teachers

711. Adams, Zu. "Biography of John Brown Dunbar." *Transactions of the Kansas State Historical Society,* vol. 10. Topeka: Kansas State Printing Office, 1908, 99–106. The first six pages of this biography are an excellent history of the Presbyterian mission to the Grand and Skidi Pawnees in the 1830s. Contains much information on Samuel Allis and on John Dunbar, father of John Brown Dunbar.

712. Allis, Samuel. "Forty Years Among the Indians and on the Eastern Borders of Nebraska." *Transactions and Reports of the Nebraska State Historical Society,* vol. 2. Lincoln: State Journal Company, Printers, 1887, 133–66. In 1834, Allis and the Rev. John Dunbar arrived in Nebraska as missionaries to the Pawnees, Dunbar going to the Grand Pawnees and Allis to the Skidi band. Most of this biography is about the Pawnees—their daily lives, hunts, their earth lodges, courtship customs, and methods of making war. The writings of Allis and Dunbar are extremely valuable first-hand accounts of the Pawnees in the pre-reservation period.

713. Brendel, J. G. "A Memorable Week among the Pawnee Indians." In *Our Home Field.* Nashville: Home Mission Board, Southern Baptist Convention, n.d.

714. Clark, John A. "The Pawnee Missionaries." In *The Christian Keepsake and Missionary Annual.* Philadelphia: William Marshall and Co., 1839, 25–29. Editor of *The Christian Keepsake and Missionary Annual* relates the tragic story of Dr. Benedict Satterlee and his young

wife Martha, contemporaries of John Dunbar and Samuel Allis, who came to Nebraska from New York in the 1830s to serve as Protestant Episcopal missionaries to the Grand Pawnees. Martha Satterlee died of illness before reaching the Pawnee villages and her husband died alone on the prairie from unknown causes and was apparently eaten by wild animals.

715. "Communications from Messrs. Dunbar and Allis." *The Missionary Herald at Home and Abroad* 32 (February 1836): 68–70. Primarily a report from Samuel Allis, missionary to the Skidi Pawnees, in which he complained about being invited to too many feasts. Touches briefly on buffalo meat versus beef, gives the locations of the various Pawnee bands, then expresses his concern that the Indians will die "heathens."

716. Dunbar, John. "The Presbyterian Mission among the Pawnee Indians in Nebraska, 1834 to 1836." *Collections of the Kansas State Historical Society*, vol. 11. Topeka: Kansas State Printing Office, 1910, 323–32. Valuable history of the Presbyterian mission to the Pawnees, told by one of its participants. Dunbar also provides insights into Pawnee society and chieftainship, and he expresses doubt that these people will ever adopt Christian ways. His description of a buffalo hunt is superb. This document can also be found in *Collections of the Nebraska State Historical Society*, vol. 16, 1911, 268–87. The Nebraska document includes an addendum in the form of a letter from B. S. Dunbar, a son of Rev. John Dunbar.

717. Dunbar, John B. "Wild Life in the Early Days of Nebraska." *Omaha World-Herald* (28 August 1910), 2M. Written expressly for the *World-Herald* by a son of Presbyterian missionary John Dunbar. Most of the events actually occurred before the author was born. He remembers a beautiful otter-skin coat presented to his father and tells some humorous anecdotes, describes frightening and tragic events, and shares his version of the Morning Star sacrifice. Also includes an unflattering report concerning Sir Charles Augustus Murray's stay among the Pawnees [591].

718. Elvira Platt to Unidentified Correspondent, n.d. Platt Family Papers. RG 0907.AM, Box 1, Folder 1. 3 pp. Nebraska State Historical Society. Hand-written letter in response to Mrs. Platt's corespondent's query regarding the location of the Pawnee mission near Genoa, Nebraska. Mrs. Platt also provides the names of the streams in the vicinity and locates the villages of the Pawnee bands. A map of north-central Nebraska accompanies the letter.

719. Elvira G. Platt to William E. Connelley, n.d. Platt Family Papers. RG 0907.AM, Box 1, Folder 3. 4 pp. Nebraska State Historical Society. Mrs. Platt gives the Pawnee names for a number of Nebraska rivers and streams, and explains how the Pawnees arrived at those names. In 1844, it was the wild potatoes growing along the Loup Fork that kept the Pawnees alive after Otoes and Omahas raided their food caches while the villages were unattended.

720. Elvira G. Platt to William E. Connelley, August 22, 1899. Platt Family Papers. RG 0907.AM, Box 1, Folder 3. 3 pp. Nebraska State Historical Society. In a letter to the editor of volume 3 of the Nebraska State Historical Society *Proceedings and Collections*, Mrs. Platt states that the word "Nebraska" is from an Otoe word, not a Pawnee word, and it does not mean "shallow water," as mentioned in that volume. According to Mrs. Platt's informant, who lived among the Otoes, the Otoe word "Nebrathka" means "weeping water." She also calls attention to stream names in Nebraska that had been changed or interchanged, such as Plum Creek and Council Creek, both near Genoa.

721. "Extracts from the Journal of Doct. Satterlee." *The Missionary Herald at Home and Abroad* 33 (February 1837): 74–75. Dr. Benedict Satterlee and the Rev. John Dunbar accompanied the Pawnees on their summer hunt in 1836, where they experienced several violent thunderstorms. While out on the prairie, Satterlee treated a Pawnee hunter who had been wounded in an encounter with the Sioux.

722. "Extracts from the Journal of Mr. Dunbar." *The Missionary Herald at Home and Abroad* 31 (September 1835): 343–49; (October 1835): 376–81; (November 1935): 417–21. Dunbar speaks of his first contact with the Pawnees in 1834 and his arrival at the Genoa Pawnee village. Also describes earth lodge construction, Pawnee medicine, and a winter buffalo hunt. Indian feasts receive attention, as do the traditional roles of men and women. Dunbar criticizes the Pawnees for their "heathen" religion, which to him makes no sense. Although this journal has a definite Christian bias, it is an invaluable eyewitness account of Pawnee life.

723. Jensen, Richard E. "Bellevue: The First Twenty Years, 1822–1842." *Nebraska History* 56 (Fall 1975): 339–74. Concerned mostly with early Bellevue's trading posts and traders, this earliest of Nebraska towns was also home at times to John Dunbar and Samuel Allis, missionaries to the Pawnees.

724. ——. "The Pawnee Mission, 1834–1846." *Nebraska History* 75 (Winter 1994): 301–10. Excellent account of the years John Dunbar and Samuel Allis spent among the Pawnees. Discusses the Pawnees' reluctance to adopt white ways and the Christian God, and explains the schisms that developed between white factions at the Pawnee mission.

725. John Dunbar to Joseph V. Hamilton, October 19, 1839. John Dunbar Papers. MS 0480, Box 1, Folder 1. 2 pp. Nebraska State Historical Society. Rev. Dunbar forwarded his assessment of the area around the Loup Fork of the Platte River where the Pawnees planned to build their new villages to comply with the terms of their 1837 treaty. Accompanying the letter is a sketch showing the locations of the villages and a list of the number of each Pawnee band's lodges. Dunbar's chief concern with the new location seemed to be the scarcity of timber.

726. "Letter from Mr. Dunbar, Dated June 8, 1838." *The Missionary Herald at Home and Abroad* 34 (1838): 383–85. States that the Pawnees are in very poor condition, having lost people to the Sioux and to smallpox. Repeats a version of the Morning Star Ceremony told to him by an unnamed eyewitness, mentions the attempted rescue of a sacrificial victim by the Indian agent (John Dougherty), and speaks of a sacrifice performed in the spring of 1838.

727. "Letters Concerning the Presbyterian Mission in the Pawnee Country, Near Bellevue, Neb., 1831–1849." *Collections of the Kansas State Historical Society*, vol. 14. Topeka: Kansas State Printing Plant, 1918, 570–784. Primary source on the Presbyterian mission in the form of letters sent from the Plains by John Dunbar and Samuel Allis to their superiors and other correspondents on the east coast. No serious researcher of the missionary period can afford to overlook this rich source. Most of these letters were reprinted with a new introduction in Waldo R. Wedel, ed. *The Dunbar-Allis Letters on the Pawnee*. New York: Garland Publishing, Inc., 1985.

728. Mankowski, Linda. "Allis and Dunbar." In *"La Belle Vue": Studies in the History of Bellevue, Nebraska*, edited by Jerold L. Simmons, 164–87. Marceline, Missouri: Walsworth Publishing Company, 1976. The story of the early Presbyterian mission to the Pawnees, told mostly from the letters and reports of John Dunbar and Samuel Allis. Although quotes and extracts from primary sources are printed in bold type, this chapter has no footnotes, making it impossible to clearly identify the sources.

729. "Pawnees on the Platte River." In *Twenty-Fifth Annual Report of the American Board of Commissioners for Foreign Missions*. Boston: Crocker & Brewster, 1834, 119–20. Describes the chain of circumstances that brought John Dunbar and Samuel Allis to Nebraska as missionaries to the Pawnees. Their original intent was to minister to tribes farther west.

730. Platt, Elvira G. "How Did the Pawnees Receive Us?" Platt Family Papers. RG 0907.AM, Box 1, Folder 3. 9 pp. Nebraska State Historical Society. In a long letter to her friend William Connelley, Mrs. Platt lovingly recalls many of her favorite Pawnees, both men and women, and relates anecdotes of each one. This is an invaluable glimpse into the daily lives and personalities of individual Pawnees.

731. ———. "Le-shar-o Pit-ko." Platt Family Papers. RG 0907.AM, Box 1, Folder 3. 3 pp. Nebraska State Historical Society. Recollections of a Pawnee leader whose name translates into "Twice a Chief." When he left Nebraska to go to Indian Territory, he left a precious red pipestone tablet with Mrs. Platt for safekeeping.

732. ———. "Reminiscences of a Teacher Among the Nebraska Indians, 1843–1885." *Transactions and Reports of the Nebraska State Historical Society*, vol. 3, 1892, 125–43. Mrs. Platt recalls her adventures from the time she and her husband traveled to the Pawnee villages to her widowhood and retirement to a home in Iowa. Her description of the flora and fauna found between Bellevue and the Pawnee villages is amazing, and she also carefully describes the territory around the villages on the Loup River. This is a priceless account of a woman's life among the Indians. See also: Platt, Elvira G. "Some Experiences as a Teacher among the Pawnees." *Collections of the Kansas State Historical Society*, vol. 14, 784–94 [733] for a similar account.

733. ———. "Some Experiences as a Teacher among the Pawnees." *Collections of the Kansas State Historical Society*, vol. 14. Topeka: Kansas State Printing Plant, 1918, 784–94. A wonderful glimpse of Pawnee reservation life during the 1830s and 1840s. Writing decades later, Mrs Platt recalls Sioux attacks, special students, Indian agents both good and bad, and Pawnees who became her friends.

734. ———. "Why Did I Go to Teach the Pawnees?" Platt Family Papers. RG 0907.AM, Box 1, Folder 3. 6 pp. Nebraska State Historical Society. Explains the conditions under which Mrs. Platt and her husband

came to be Pawnee teachers, and describes the successes and failures of their school. Also gives her opinion of the quality and character of three Pawnee agents during the 1840s.

735. Potter, Gail DeBuse. "A Note on the Samuel Allis Family: Missionaries to the Pawnee, 1834–46." *Nebraska History* 67 (Spring 1986): 1–7. Provides insight into the personal life of Allis. His request to teach school and act as agency farmer angered the Presbyterian Board of Missions which had hired him as a missionary and did not want him holding government jobs.

736. Ranney, T. E. "On the Character and Customs of the Pawnees." *Archives of Science* 1 (October 1870): 3–17. Ranney served as a missionary to the Pawnees for three years, and he describes, in ethnocentric language, the dwellings, customs, religion, and medicine of the Indians he served. His account is interesting, even entertaining, but lacks objectivity. This is certainly not the best source for Pawnee culture, since Ranney obviously felt contempt for his Indian charges, often referring to them as "fools" and "heathens."

737. Tuttle, Sarah. *History of the American Mission to the Pawnee Indians*. Sabbath School Society, 1938.

17
The Pawnees and the Quakers

738. "Agency Matters: A Communication from the Agent." *Columbus (Nebraska) Journal*, 10 September 1874, 2. Quaker agent William Burgess refutes an article from the *Omaha Republican* inferring that he encouraged the Pawnees to meet with white citizens of Columbus, Nebraska, to arrange for the Pawnees' move south to Indian Territory. He insists that he did not call the meeting, and simply happened to be in Columbus at the time the meeting took place.

739. Chapman, Berlin B. "Pawnee Pilgrimage." *Tulsa Sunday World*, 10 May 1953, 31. Describes the Pawnee Reservation in Oklahoma as it appeared when the Pawnees relocated there from Nebraska in 1875. The entire text is excerpted from the journals of Quaker Indian superintendent Barclay White, who oversaw the Pawnee removal [1270].

740. "A Double Pawnee Wedding."*Platte Journal*, 12 July 1871, 2. This Columbus, Nebraska, newspaper reports the weddings of two young Pawnee couples on the Fourth of July. Both couples were students at the Pawnee school, and the Quaker ceremony was held in one of the classrooms.

741. *The Friends and the Indians: Report of Barclay White, Late Superintendent of Indian Affairs in the Northern Superintendency, Nebraska.* Oxford, Pennsylvania: Published for the Convention, 1886. White, a former Indian superintendent, described the general condition of the Nebraska tribes when the Hicksite Friends began their tenure as agents, then explained the progress toward "civilization" of each

tribe. He was shocked that the Pawnee children rounded up to attend their day school arrived at the school nude. He also introduced an ambitious Quaker agenda to promote civilization among the Indians under their care.

742. Gerlach, Gail Brooks. "Samuel McPherson Janney: Quaker Reformer." Master's thesis, University of Utah, 1977. 265 pp. Well-written biography of the first Quaker Indian superintendent in Nebraska, taken primarily from Quaker sources and Janney's memoirs. Nearly half of the thesis deals with Quaker attitudes and actions toward the Pawnees and other tribes in the Northern Superintendency.

743. Illick, Joseph E. "'Some of Our Best Indians Are Friends . . .' Quaker Attitudes and Actions Regarding the Western Indians during the Grant Administration." *Western Historical Quarterly* 2 (July 1971): 283–94. Overview of the work done by both orthodox and liberal Quakers among the Indians of the Central and Northern Superintendencies. Contains one brief mention of the Pawnees, describing them as "industrious," and listing their population at 2,398.

744. "Indian Report." *Friends' Intelligencer* 30 (December 6, 1873): 650–53. Lengthy report is almost entirely concerned with the Pawnees. White settlers near the Pawnee Reservation called for the removal of Agent William Burgess due to poor agency management, but an enclosed report clears him of wrongdoing. The agency schools are discussed, as is the tragedy at Massacre Canyon. An excellent account of Pawnee Agency affairs in 1873.

745. "The Indians." *Friends' Intelligencer* 26 (May 8, 1869): 145–46. Excerpt from a letter written by Quaker leader Benjamin Hollowell in which he explains the proposal made to President Grant to set up an Indian Superintendency in Nebraska led by Friends and with all Quaker agents. The proposal also suggested an oversight committee of friends to visit each agency once or twice a year. According to Hollowell, the president informally approved the project at the time it was suggested.

746. "The Indians." *Friends' Intelligencer* 27 (July 9, 1870); 295. Samuel Janney reports a meeting with Oglala chief Red Cloud to try to arrange peace between the Sioux and the Pawnees. The Pawnees had agreed to a cease-fire, but Red Cloud reminded Janney that Pawnee Scouts had killed many Sioux.

747. "The Indians: Noble Vindication of the Quaker Policy." *Omaha Weekly Herald*, 24 November 1869, 1. Part of an address given in Philadelphia by Episcopal Bishop Robert Clarkson, in which he praises the work of the Quakers among the Indians of Nebraska.

748. Janney, Samuel M. "The Indians." *Friends' Intelligencer* 26 (July 10, 1869): 299–300. Superintendent Janney cautions people back east that "civilizing" the Indians of Nebraska will be a slow process. Among the three tribes he had visited, he believed the Pawnees to be the least civilized and most warlike, but he praised them for not using alcohol or allowing it on their reservation.

749. ———. "Letter from Samuel M. Janney to the Convention of Friends, Held at Philadelphia, on Indian Concerns." *Friends' Intelligencer* 27 (June 11, 1870): 233–34. A report on conditions at the Nebraska Indian agencies. By 1870, many Pawnee men were working in the fields, and some of the underused Indian ponies had been put to work pulling plows. The Manual Labor School now had seventy-five pupils.

750. ———. *Memoirs of Samuel M. Janney.* Philadelphia: Friends Book Association, 1881. 309 pp. In 1869, as part of President Grant's Peace Policy, the aging Samuel Janney took over the Northern Superintendency, which included the Pawnees and other Nebraska tribes. In chapter twenty-two, Janney gives a brief, partially accurate history of the Pawnees. The rest of the material on the Pawnees is a discussion of the widely publicized Yellow Sun murder case (see chapter 19).

751. ———. "To the Editors of *Friends' Intelligencer*." *Friends' Intelligencer* 26 (June 12, 1869): 230–31. Janney, the new head of the Northern Superintendency, reports the arrival of all the Quaker agents in Omaha. Among them was Jacob Troth, who would be the first Quaker Pawnee agent. This letter includes flattering descriptions of 1869 Omaha.

752. "Letter from S. M. Janney, Superintendent." *Friends' Intelligencer* 28 (June 10, 1871): 235–37. Janney reports that Brulé Sioux chief Spotted Tail was willing to sign a peace treaty with the Pawnees, but was reluctant to do so without the concurrence of the other Sioux bands.

753. Milner, Clyde A., II. "Off the White Road: Seven Nebraska Indian Societies in the 1870s—A Statistical Analysis of Assimilation, Population, and Prosperity." *Western Historical Quarterly* 12 (January

1981): 37–52. Using charts and graphs, article expertly analyzes the progress, or lack of progress, among the seven Indian tribes on the six reservations of the Northern Superintendency in Nebraska while under the control of Hicksite Friends. According to the statistics, none of the tribes was assimilating to the degree that the Quakers had expected. Of the seven tribes, the Pawnees had the sharpest population decline between 1868 and 1882.

754. ———. *With Good Intentions: Quaker Work among the Pawnees, Otos, and Omahas in the 1870s.* Lincoln: University of Nebraska Press, 1982. 238 pp. Beginning in 1869 with President Ulysses S. Grant's Peace Policy, members of the Society of Friends (Quakers) became Indian agents and superintendents. One group of Quakers, the Hicksites, took control of the Northern Superintendency, which was responsible for six Indian reservations in Nebraska. This comparative study of the fates of the Pawnees, Otos, and Omahas during the Quaker regime points out the good intentions and ultimate failure of the Quaker program. One of the best sources on this chapter in Nebraska Indian history.

755. "Pawnee Agency." *Friends' Intelligencer* 28 (February 10, 1872): 794. Neither the writer nor the recipient of this letter is identified, but the writer was associated with the Pawnee school. Some of the students' parents asked that their children be allowed to stay in school rather than go along on the winter hunt. The writer also chats about the progress of several favorite students.

756. Powell, Joseph. "Council with the Pawnees." *Friends' Intelligencer* 26 (August 7, 1869): 358–59. Recounts a meeting at the Pawnee Agency in Genoa, Nebraska, on July 21, 1869, between Quakers, three Pawnee chiefs, and about fifty Pawnee "braves." During the conference, the three chiefs all spoke, explaining that their people were hungry, and would like permission to hunt buffalo. One chief asked the Quakers to intervene on behalf of Pawnee prisoners in Omaha, who had been arrested for allegedly killing a white man. This refers to the purported murder of Edward McMurty by Yellow Sun and other Pawnees (see chapter 19).

757. ———. "The Indians." *Friends' Intelligencer* 26 (October 9, 1869): 500–1. Apparently written by a member of the Quaker oversight committee, this report enumerated the many obstacles that needed to be overcome before the Nebraska Indians could become productive

Christians. Powell was especially appalled by what he perceived to be poor treatment of Indian women.

758. "The Quaker Indian Policy." *Omaha Weekly Herald*, 10 November 1869, 1. A *Herald* writer heaps praise on the Quaker Indian agents and on Superintendent Samuel Janney for their fair and honest dealings with Nebraska Indians, and predicts that under Quaker influence, Indian hostilities will soon end.

759. "The Quaker Indian Policy: Interesting Debate in the United States Senate." *Platte Journal*, 22 June 1870, 1. This Columbus, Nebraska, newspaper reprints a debate over whether the Quakers in charge of the Northern Superintendency should be given an additional appropriation of $30,000 to make improvements on the Nebraska reservations. The arguments are mostly against the funding, since these Indians had already received all the money agreed to in their treaties.

760. "Quaker Report on Indian Agencies in Nebraska, 1869." *Nebraska History* 54 (Summer 1973): 151–219. Reprint of the important 1869 report serialized in the *Friends' Intelligencer* in November and December 1869 [771].

761. "Report of Barclay White, for the Pawnee Agency under the Joint Care of Baltimore and Illinois Yearly Meetings." *Friends' Intelligencer* 34 (November 3, 1877): 577–81. Although the Pawnees were reassigned to the Central Superintendency after their removal to Indian Territory, they remained under the supervision of Hicksite Quakers for the time being. This report is a complete accounting of all aspects of the new Pawnee Reservation in Indian Territory. White collected data on acreage, location of agency buildings, and Pawnee band locations, as well as information on supplies delivered to the new agency. In White's opinion, Pawnee removal from Nebraska was a disaster. He estimated that during the first two years in Indian Territory, 900 Pawnees had died. No one researching the topic of Pawnee removal should neglect this report.

762. "Report of Convention at Omaha." *Friends' Intelligencer* 27 (September 10, 1870): 442–44. Quaker agents shared their ideas with Superintendent Janney at this August 1870 meeting. Agent Troth reported that the Pawnees were willing to sell a portion of their reservation south of the Loup Fork. It was also suggested that the Indians could grow broom corn and manufacture brooms for sale.

763. "Report of the Indian Committee." *Friends' Intelligencer* 30 (June 21, 1873): 265–68. Pages 265–66 discuss the Pawnees. The Sioux have continued their raids, resulting in the loss of 200 horses in the first half of the year. The major topic included is the theft of timber from the Pawnee Reservation by white men. Many of the men who stole wood agreed to pay for it, and those who refused to pay were arrested.

764. "Report of the Indian Committee of Baltimore Yearly Meeting." *Friends' Intelligencer* 28 (November 25, 1871): 619–20. Includes a basically positive report from Agent Troth. Donations of food and clothing were received, the Pawnees' hunt was a success, and their harvest was good. The school continued to flourish, but two young Pawnee men were killed in October by the Sioux.

765. "Report of the Indian Committee of Baltimore Yearly Meeting." *Friends' Intelligencer* 29 (December 14, 1872): 668–71; (December 21, 1872): 686–87. Includes an update on Pawnee agriculture, the Industrial and Day Schools, and the announcement of the resignation of Jacob Troth. William Burgess, a Pennsylvanian, would be his replacement. Fifty thousand acres of Pawnee land south of the Loup Fork had been sold, and was currently being surveyed.

766. "Report of the Indian Concern." In *Minutes of the Standing Committee on the Indian Concern of Baltimore Yearly Meeting of Friends*, October 24, 1873. Swarthmore, Pennsylvania: Friends Historical Library, Swarthmore College. 8 pp. Informative report of an especially eventful year for the Pawnees. Includes results of an investigation into poor performance by a Quaker agent, a report on the manual labor and day schools, a mention of the events at Massacre Canyon, and a report that the survey of Pawnee lands to be sold would not be completed until spring.

767. "Report on the Indian Concern." In *Minutes of the Standing Committee on the Indian Concern, of Baltimore Yearly Meeting of Friends*, October 22, 1875. Swarthmore, Pennsylvania: Friends Historical Library, Swarthmore College. 7 pp. This is the first committee report after the Pawnees relocated to Indian Territory. The Hicksite Friends believed that the Pawnees would now be part of the Central Superintendency, but this was not the case, and they would continue as Pawnee agents. Includes a glowing report on the new agency, and the committee members who visited the new reservation claimed to see a great change for the better among the Pawnees now that they were far removed from the Sioux.

768. "Report on the Indian Concern." In *Minutes of the Standing Committee on the Indian Concern, of Baltimore Yearly Meeting of Friends*, October 24, 1876. Swarthmore, Pennsylvania: Friends Historical Library, Swarthmore College. The committee reports that the Pawnees were transferred to the Central Superintendency in May 1876, but they would remain in the care of the Hicksite friends, with their agent reporting to the Central Superintendent.

769. "Report on the Indian Concern." In *Minutes of the Standing Committee on the Indian Concern, of Baltimore Yearly Meeting of Friends*, October 26, 1877. Swarthmore, Pennsylvania: Friends Historical Library, Swarthmore College. Announces the resignation of William Burgess, the agent who accompanied the Pawnees to Indian Territory. A tribal census shows that from 1875 to 1877, the Pawnee population had decreased by 677, mostly due to malaria. Also discusses land under cultivation, Indian rations, and the progress of the schools.

770. "Report on the Indian Concern." In *Minutes of the Standing Committee on the Indian Concern, of Baltimore Yearly Meeting of Friends*, October 1878. Swarthmore, Pennsylvania: Friends Historical Library, Swarthmore College. Barclay White gives the Pawnee schools high marks, but reports that all is not well at the agency. The Pawnees have had three agents in one year, and an agency clerk is suspected of undermining his superiors. The Hicksite friends informed the president that if their agents could not choose their own employees, they would leave the Pawnee Agency.

771. "Report of the Joint Delegation Appointed by the Committee on the Indian Concern, of the Yearly Meetings of Baltimore, Philadelphia, and New York, respectively, to visit the Indians under the care of Friends, in the Northern Superintendency, State of Nebraska, Seventh and Eighth Months, 1869." *Friends' Intelligencer* 26 (November 13, 1869): 577–81; (November 20, 1869): 593–98; (November 27, 1869): 609–14; (December 4, 1869): 625–28. An important report conveying to the Society of Friends the general condition of the Nebraska Indians in 1869. The Joint Delegation visited all of the Nebraska reservations. Pages 578–81 pertain specifically to the Pawnees.

772. "Report of the Standing Committee of Baltimore Yearly Meeting on the Indian Concern." October 23, 1874. Swarthmore, Pennsylvania: Friends Historical Library, Swarthmore College. This report is almost entirely concerned with the Pawnees. The sale of part of the Pawnee

reserve had not been approved, the schools were fairly successful, the Indian crops had been destroyed by grasshoppers, and more and more Pawnees seemed determined to leave Nebraska and relocate among the Wichitas in Indian Territory.

773. "Report of the Standing Committee of Baltimore Yearly Meeting on the Indian Concern." *Friends' Intelligencer* 32 (December 18, 1875): 676–79. Explains to the Society of Friends the Pawnee removal to Indian Territory and events shortly before and after the relocation. This report is quite clear and informative, and should be consulted for the Quaker view of Pawnee removal.

774. "A Trip to the Pawnee Agency." *Friends' Intelligencer* 29 (November 9, 1872): 589–91. The writer of this letter, identified only by initials, gives an excellent description of a trip from the Santee Agency to Genoa and the Pawnee reserve. Describes the Pawnee Industrial School and explains the construction of an earth lodge.

775. Troth, Jacob M. "Letter from the Pawnee Agency." *Friends' Intelligencer* 27 (May 28, 1870): 198. Thanks the Friends of the town of Pipe Creek for their recent contributions of clothing for the students at the Pawnee Industrial School. Points out that the school is under-funded, and stresses the importance of contributions such as theirs.

776. ——. "Letter from the Pawnee Agency." *Friends' Intelligencer* 27 (December 31, 1870): 694–95. Thanks a person with the initials R. T. for a contribution of food and clothing for the Pawnees, but Agent Troth complains that some of the packages were incorrectly addressed and had to be forwarded at his expense. He emphasizes the need for a reservation doctor, and reports that the Pawnees have used annuity money to buy farm equipment.

777. Walton, Samuel B. "Indian Marriages." *Friends' Intelligencer* 27 (November 26, 1870): 617. Walton passed along the news of two Pawnee couples married in Christian ceremonies, one at the Manual Labor School and one at the home of the agency farmer.

778. ——. "Pawnee Agency, Genoa, Platte Co., Nebraska, 9th mo. 12, 1869." *Friends' Intelligencer* 26 (October 2, 1869): 483–85. Wonderful letter to the Quaker journal from a Pawnee Agency employee describing the prairie around the Pawnee reservation, the wildlife in the area, the Pawnee Industrial School, and the Pawnees themselves. He

also gives a vivid account of the marriage of a fifteen-year-old Pawnee girl and an older Indian widower.

779. ———. "The Pawnees." *Friends' Intelligencer* 27 (April 9, 1870); 86. Walton claims that many Pawnees would like to change their way of life, but would have difficulty doing so, due to "ignorance and superstition." He recounts a literary evening at the Pawnee school during which students read and recited in English. He also praises the Pawnees for their temperance and good nature, but he is concerned about their general health.

18
Nebraska Reservation
Period (1859–1875)

780. "The Accident at the Agency." *Platte (Columbus, Nebraska) Journal*, 14 January 1874, 2. Agent William Burgess reported a freak accident at the Pawnee Agency in Genoa, Nebraska. A loaded gun fell out of the pocket of the assistant agency farmer and discharged, killing the agency farmer.

781. Aldrich, J. J. "Diary of a Twenty Days' Sport: Buffalo Hunting on the Plains with the Pawnees." *Omaha Weekly Herald*, 19 August 1868, 1; 26 August 1868, 1, 3. Aldrich tells of his adventures on a hunt on the Republican River with a large band of Pawnees. Major Frank North was in overall command of the hunt. Aldrich got more than he bargained for—storms, difficult river crossings, and an attack by Sioux that resulted in several deaths. Aldrich is not identified; apparently he was along strictly for the sport.

782. Beadle, Erastus F. *Ham, Eggs, and Corn Cake: A Nebraska Territorial Diary.* New York: New York Public Library, 1923. Reprint. Lincoln: University of Nebraska Press, 2001. 130 pp. Erastus Beadle came west to make his fortune, and in 1857, he became part of a real estate group developing the town of Saratoga, Nebraska, between Omaha and Florence. His diary, covering about seven months, includes several mentions of the Pawnees. As his journal progresses, his attitude toward the Pawnees changes from disgust to pity and understanding.

783. Bell, John T. *History of Washington County, Nebraska: Its Early Settlement and Present Status, Resources, Advantages and Future*

Prospects. Omaha: Herald Steam Book and Job Printing House, 1876. Reprint. Blair, Nebraska: Washington County Historical Association, 1985. 64 pp. Early county history contains a chapter (pp. 12–23) on the nearly bloodless "Pawnee War" of 1859, which was begun when settlers in northeastern Nebraska overreacted to Pawnee raids. One of several contemporary accounts of this non-event, the prose is sometimes humorous and always ethnocentric.

784. Bollman, C. P. "Describes Visit to Indian Village." *Albion (Nebraska) Argus,* 15 March 1923, 1. A former editor of the *Albion Argus* recalls his first visit with his father to a Pawnee village in 1871, when he was seventeen years old. He remembers the Indians who came to the agency trading post and gives a good description of a Pawnee earth lodge.

785. Burke, Marguerette R., ed. "Henry James Hudson and the Genoa Settlement." *Nebraska History* 41 (September 1960): 201–35. In 1857, westbound Mormons founded the town of Genoa, Nebraska, on the Loup River, only to discover two years later that their town was included in the area set aside as the reservation for the Pawnees in their 1857 treaty. Reproduces a speech by Hudson after the Mormons were forced to vacate their Genoa settlement. In it, he expresses anger and bitterness at his people's treatment by the government, and especially by the Pawnee agent.

786. Curtis, Earl G. "John Milton Thayer." *Nebraska History* 28 (October–December 1947): 225–38. Discusses an 1855 council with Pawnee chiefs. During this meeting, Thayer's Pawnee guides stole the peace delegation's provisions. Also recounts Thayer's role in the 1859 "Pawnee War" to punish the Indians for livestock thefts.

787. Dinesen, Wilhelm. "A Dane's Views on Frontier Culture: 'Notes on a Stay in the United States,' 1872–1874, by Wilhelm Dinesen." Trans. Donald K. Watkins. *Nebraska History* 55 (Summer 1974): 265–89. For two years, Dinesen lived near Columbus, Nebraska, in close proximity to the Pawnees. In his insightful notes, he comments on the Nebraska countryside and the inevitable fate of Native Americans. There are numerous references to the Pawnees, whom he obviously admired.

788. Dudley, Edgar S. "Notes on the Early Military History of Nebraska." *Transactions and Reports of the Nebraska State Historical Society,* vol. 2. Lincoln: State Journal Company, Printers, 1887, 166–85. Most

of this article is concerned with Nebraska forts and military roads, but the last four pages are an account of the causes and the campaign of the "Pawnee War" of 1859.

789. "General John M. Thayer." *Nebraska History* 5 (July–September 1922): 41–46. Biographical sketch of the Nebraska militia officer who led a volunteer force of frontiersmen against marauding Pawnees in the 1859 "Pawnee War."

790. Gerrard, Ernest A. "A Gruesome War Dance: A Deer-Hunting Experience Among the Pawnee Indians." *Outing* 39 (October 1901–March 1902): 404–407. Undated account of a confrontation between white hunters and Pawnees over a deer shot by one of the hunters. Lack of documentation makes it impossible to tell if this event really happened.

791. Hazen, R. W. "The Pawnee Indian War, 1859." *Transactions and Reports of the Nebraska State Historical Society,* vol. 3. Fremont, Nebraska: Hammond Brothers Printers, 1892, 279–86. A colorful account of General John M. Thayer's nearly bloodless punitive expedition against the Pawnees, told by one of his volunteer militia officers. Reprinted from the *Omaha Bee,* 17 February 1890.

792. McKee, Jim. "The Mormons, the Pawnee and the History of Genoa." *Lincoln Journal Star,* 14 July 2002, 2K. Brief but informative piece tracing the history of Genoa's short-lived Mormon settlement and the treaty that brought the Pawnees to the Genoa area. Most useful is the history of the U. S. Indian School at Genoa, formerly the Pawnee Industrial School.

793. ———. "Hartsuff Example of Early Fort." *Lincoln Journal Star,* 27 January 2002, 2K. Short history of this outpost on the North Fork of Nebraska's Loup River which was only in use as a fort for seven years (1874–1881). Built to protect both settlers and the Pawnees from Sioux attacks, the fort became irrelevant when the Pawnees were relocated to Indian Territory and the Sioux were placed on reservations in the Dakotas.

794. North, J. E. "The Elkhorn-Battle Creek Campaign." *Nebraska History* 18 (July–September 1937): 193–95. Recounts his adventures as part of the militia force sent to the Columbus, Nebraska, area to put a stop to depredations by hungry Pawnees who had been stealing livestock. This was a virtually bloodless military campaign, with the only casualty a horse belonging to an Omaha Indian.

795. "Our Letter from Genoa." *Platte Journal*, 26 November 1873, 2. Unidentified correspondent's report to the Columbus, Nebraska, newspaper from the Pawnee Reservation is mostly about the difficulties encountered in teaching the Indian children a new language and showing them how to be clean. It also gives an example of Pawnee honesty, which the author claims was rare.

796. Paine, Bayard Henry. *Pioneers, Indians, and Buffaloes*. Curtis, Nebraska: The Curtis Enterprise, 1935. 192 pp. Relates the story of a Pawnee woman who worked for several families in Grand Island, Nebraska, and refused to go on the ill-fated August 1873 buffalo hunt. Briefly mentions the battle at Summit Springs and the role of the Scouts, and also tells the tale of the Pawnees' last successful buffalo hunt. The events of this hunt were recorded by Captain Luther North and George Bird Grinnell, who accompanied the Indians to the Republican River region. Excellent account of the hunt and its preparations.

797. Paul, R. Eli. "Pawnee Camp Equipage. A Letter by John W. Williamson." *Museum of the Fur Trade Quarterly* 21 (Summer 1985): 1–3. Reprints a letter in answer to a query by Addison E. Sheldon of the Nebraska State Historical Society regarding the weight of baggage and food items carried by the Pawnees on an 1873 buffalo hunt and on their move south to Indian Territory from their Nebraska reservation. Williamson accompanied the Pawnees on both of these occasions.

798. "The Pawnee Ordeal." *NEBRASKAland* 62 (January–February 1984): 14. Brief essay explains the obstacles faced by the Pawnees after they moved to their reservation along the Loup River. Points out that dishonest agents and idealistic Quaker agents compounded their problems. About one-third of the essay is devoted to Massacre Canyon.

799. "Pawnee Reservation: 1859 Survey." *Nebraska History* 19 (July–September 1938): 266. In 1938, the Nance County, Nebraska, surveyor requested the exact boundaries of the former Pawnee Reservation. The Nebraska State Historical Society provided seventy-five typewritten pages of information, which are now part of the Nance County records.

800. "The Pawnees." *Platte Journal*, 6 July 1870, 2. Lengthy article in the Columbus, Nebraska, newspaper describes conditions on the Pawnee

Reservation, explains the workings of the Indian School, describes a program presented by Pawnee school children, then reprints the terms of the 1857 Table Creek treaty that established the Pawnees' Nebraska reservation along the Loup River.

801. "The Pawnees." *Platte (Columbus, Nebraska) Journal*, 28 January 1874, 4. Report of violence erupting over white settlers' thefts of timber from the Pawnee Reservation. Destitute settlers had been taking wood with no repercussions, but now men perfectly able to pay were stealing wood as well. Concludes with a notice from Agent William Burgess informing whites that the wooded land had not been sold, and still belonged to the Pawnees.

802. "The Pawnees: Their Removal to the Indian Territory." *Columbus (Nebraska) Journal*, 18 November 1874, 1. Reprinted from the *Omaha Daily Herald*. Discusses an October 8 Pawnee council during which the chiefs approved the terms of their move to Indian Territory. Article includes the terms of the removal agreement.

803. "A Pawnee Wedding." *Platte Journal*, 9 November 1870, 2. A Columbus, Nebraska, newspaper correspondent identified only as "Tee" sends this report of the wedding of mixed-blood interpreter Baptiste Bayhille and Belle Neiper, a student at the Pawnee Mission School in Genoa, Nebraska. The affair was unusual in that white residents of the reservation served the wedding meal to the Indians.

804. "Proposal for the Construction of Two Frame Buildings at the Pawnee Indian Agency." *Platte Journal*, 5 July 1871, 3. Public notice submitted to the Columbus, Nebraska, newspaper by Agent Jacob Troth asking for bids on the construction of two buildings. Measurements, desired completion date, and other specifics are included in the notice.

805. Reiger, John F., ed. *The Passing of the Great West: Selected Papers of George Bird Grinnell*. New York: Winchester Press, 1972. Based on Grinnell's memoirs and articles he wrote for *Forest and Stream* magazine. The index lists numerous references to Frank and Luther North. Grinnell's wonderful description of the Pawnees moving out on their summer buffalo hunt is a high point of the book.

806. "The Reserve Indians." *Omaha Weekly Herald*, 21 December 1870, 3. Gives a glowing report of the progress of the Pawnees, who are obedient and industrious, farming successfully, and sending their children to the manual labor school on the reservation.

807. Seymour, Silas S. *Incidents of a Trip Through the Great Platte Valley, to the Rocky Mountains and Laramie Plains in the Fall of 1866, with a synoptical statement of the various Pacific railroads, and an account of the great Union Pacific Excursion to the One Hundredth Meridian of Longitude*. New York: D. Van Nostrand, 1867. 129 pp. In late 1866, to celebrate being ahead of schedule, officials of the Union Pacific Railroad invited dignitaries to ride the rails to the 100th meridian, near present-day Cozad, Nebraska. At a stop near Columbus, the excursionists were entertained on successive days by a staged Pawnee war dance and a sham Indian battle, with Pawnees playing the roles of the Sioux. Although entertaining, this account is ethnocentric and condescending, referring often to the Pawnees as squaws, papooses, and uncouth savages. The account of this excursion is reprinted in *Nebraska History* 50 (Spring 1969): 27–53.

808. Thayer, John M. "The Pawnee War of 1859." *Proceedings and Collections of the Nebraska State Historical Society*, vol. 5. Lincoln: Jacob North & Co, Printers, 1902, 231–46. On January 10, 1900, General Thayer addressed the Nebraska State Historical Society. In a very entertaining fashion, Thayer recalled his volunteer army's march to the Pawnee villages and the Indians' surrender.

809. "A Trip to the Reserve." *Platte (Columbus, Nebraska) Journal*, 10 July 1872, 2. Undated account of the correspondent's trip from Columbus, Nebraska, to the nearby Pawnee Reservation. Describes the agency and Indian farms, the Pawnee School, a deserted village (the Indians were hunting), and the lovely area on and around the reservation.

810. U.S. Congress. House. *Civilization of the Pawnee Indians*. 43d Cong., 1st sess., 1874. H. Exec. Doc. 55. [Ser. 1606]. 2 pp. Quakers, the Indian Commissioner, and the Interior Secretary request that $8,530.01 left over from fiscal year 1873 be added to the 1874 appropriation and used for the purpose of "civilizing" the Pawnees.

811. ———. *Indian Reservations in the Northern Superintendency*. 42d Cong., 2d sess., 1872. H. Exec. Doc. 84. [Ser. 1510]. 6 pp. Asked the House of Representatives to appropriate $100,000 for the tribes of the Northern Superintendency to be paid back through the sale of portions of reservations. The Committee of Friends reported that the Pawnees wished to sell 50,000 acres of their reserve so they could purchase farm equipment.

812. ———. *Mechanics at Pawnee Agency*. 43d Cong., 1st sess., 1874. H. Exec. Doc. 79. [Ser. 1607]. 2 pp. Requests from the Interior Secretary, Indian Commissioner, and Quaker agents for Congress to provide $1,600 for the fiscal year ending June 30, 1875, to pay the salaries of a carpenter and a shoemaker to teach the Pawnees their trades.

813. ———. *Pawnee Indian Lands in Nebraska*. 43d Cong., 2d sess., 1875. H. Rept. 140. [Ser. 1657]. 2 pp. Report from the Committee on Indian Affairs. In light of the Pawnees' indication that they would like to move to Indian Territory, the committee recommends that arrangements be made for the relocation. States the present condition of the Pawnees and gives reasons for supporting the move.

814. ———. *Salary for Matron at Pawnee Indian Agency*. 42d Cong., 3d sess., 1872. H. Exec. Doc. 28. [Ser. 1565]. 1 pp. A request to add to the Indian appropriation bill $800 for the annual salary of a matron for the Manual Labor School.

19
The Yellow Sun Murder Case

In May 1869, a white settler named Edward McMurty was killed near the Pawnee Reservation in north-central Nebraska. This grisly homicide and the incarceration and trial of the Pawnees accused of McMurty's murder would fascinate the public and the press for two years. Three of the four Indians accused of the murder insisted that Yellow Sun, a Pawnee medicine man, had been the killer. For that reason, the events are often referred to as the "Yellow Sun murder case." Included in this brief chapter are the trial citation, a scholarly article, and a master's thesis, plus a sampling of the newspaper reports of the murder, arrests, and trial. Pawnee scholar James Riding In's doctoral dissertation [133] also covers these events in great detail. No attempt has been made to include all newspaper mentions; most are from the *Omaha Weekly Herald*, which followed the case very closely. The newspaper entries on this murder case are listed in *chronological order*, to make the events of the arrests and trial of the alleged Pawnee perpetrators easier to follow.

815. *United States v. Sa-Coo-Da-Cot, et al*. 27 Fed. Cases 16212. Circuit Court, Nebraska, 1870, 924. The Pawnee Sa-Coo-Da-Cot (Yellow Sun) and his co-defendants had been convicted by a federal court of murdering Edward McMurty near the Pawnee reservation in Nance County, Nebraska. Because of a question of legal jurisdiction, federal judges John Dillon and Elmer Dundy later ruled that the convicted men should be turned over to a federal marshal. If the State of Nebraska did not issue arrest warrants within twenty-one days, the prisoners were to be set

free and allowed to return to the Pawnee Reservation. There is no record that they were ever re-tried.

816. Price, David H. "The Public Life of Elmer S. Dundy, 1857–1896." Master's thesis, University of Nebraska at Omaha, 1971. 158 pp. Years before he presided over *Standing Bear v. Crook*, four Pawnees accused of murdering Edward McMurty were tried in Judge Dundy's court. Thesis briefly explains the trial and Dundy's role in turning the case over to the Nebraska state courts.

817. Wishart, David J. "The Death of Edward McMurty." *Great Plains Quarterly* 19 (Winter 1999): 5–21. Using National Archives records, newspaper clippings, land records, and his own previous research, Wishart pulls together the threads of this bizarre murder that occurred near Columbus, Nebraska, and was allegedly committed by Pawnees.

818. Murder of Mr. McNulty [sic] by the Pawnees." *Omaha Weekly Herald*, 19 May 1869. One of the first reports of the murder of a settler named Edward McMurty on an island in the Platte River near the Pawnee reservation. Circumstantial evidence pointed to a group of Chaui Pawnees as his killers. At the time this article was written, McMurty's body had not been located.

819. "Murder of McMurty by the Pawnee Indians."*Omaha Weekly Herald*, 30 June 1869, 1. Follow-up to the report of May 19 stating that McMurty's body had not been found. Six weeks later, settlers found his mutilated body on an island in the Platte River. A coroner's jury ruled that he had been killed by Chaui Pawnees, and local citizens urged the United States marshal to arrest the Indians suspected in the murder.

820. "The McMurty Murder Trial." *Omaha Weekly Herald*, 11 August 1869, 4. On this day of the military investigation into the murder, it was decided that five of eight Pawnee prisoners would remain in custody and the other three would be released after posting bond. Several Pawnee chiefs spoke, promising that their people would not bother any whites when they went on their summer hunt.

821. "The Condemned Indians: Horse Driver and Little Wolf Attempt to Commit Suicide." *Omaha Weekly Herald*, 10 November 1869, 4. Reports that two of the Pawnee murder suspects had unsuccessfully tried to kill themselves with pointed sticks. They were then placed in irons.

822. "The Murder Trial." *Omaha Weekly Herald*, 10 November 1869, 3. Coverage of the arraignment of Yellow Sun, Little Wolf, Horse Driver, and Blue Hawk, the Pawnees charged with murdering Edward McMurty six months earlier. Also covers jury selection and testimony of witnesses for the defense and prosecution.

823. "The Murder Trial: Proceedings of the Last Day—The Testimony Concluded." *Omaha Weekly Herald*, 10 November 1869, 4. Report of the last day of the McMurty trial. Includes closing arguments and Judge Elmer Dundy's instructions to the jury.

824. "Guilty!" *Omaha Weekly Herald*, 10 November 1869, 4. After deliberating for five hours, a jury found four Pawnees guilty of the murder of Edward McMurty. Two prisoners escaped while being returned to jail. One was recaptured when he returned for his blanket. The other remained at large.

825. "The Indian Trial and Mr. Janney." *Omaha Weekly Herald*, 17 November 1869, 1. The *Herald* rallied to the defense of the Quaker Indian Superintendent in his handling of the investigation into the murder of Edward McMurty.

826. "The Blue Hawk Emergency." *Omaha Weekly Herald*, 24 November 1869, 1. Criticizes the hundreds of vigilantes who volunteered to hunt down Blue Hawk, one of the Pawnees convicted of the McMurty killing. He had escaped, wanting to die "among his own people."

827. "The Condemned Pawnees." *Omaha Weekly Herald*, 22 December 1869, 3. Recounts a visit to the jail cell of the four convicted Pawnees by a group of women, one of whom was a former reservation teacher who spoke Pawnee. Little Wolf, Blue Hawk, and Horse Driver expressed their desire to go home, and said that the "old medicine man," Yellow Sun, was the guilty party.

828. "The Condemned Indians." *Omaha Weekly Herald*, 11 May 1870, 4. Reprints the decision by Federal District Judge John Dillon that the federal courts had no jurisdiction in the trial of the four Pawnee men convicted of murdering Edward McMurty, since the crime was committed off the Pawnee reservation, on state land. The judge ruled that the prisoners be kept in custody for another twenty days. If the state did not issue warrants for the men's arrests, they would be set free at the end of the twenty-day period.

829. "The Trial of the Pawnee Indians." *Omaha Weekly Herald*, 26 October 1870, 4. Brief paragraph announcing that the four Pawnees tried earlier in federal district court were to be re-tried in a state court. A change of venue, perhaps to Douglas or Cass County, was considered likely.

830. "The Pawnee Indian Case." *Omaha Weekly Herald*, 9 November 1870, 2. A plea to the courts to release the Indians charged with the McMurty murder eighteen months earlier. Argues that keeping them in custody is inhumane.

831. "Murder." *Omaha Weekly Herald*, 30 November 1870, 2. An opinion by the *Herald* that at least three of the Pawnees being held in the Douglas County, Nebraska, jail were innocent and that by delaying their second trial until the spring of 1871, the state was slowly killing the incarcerated Pawnees.

832. "The Pawnee Indian Mockery." *Omaha Daily Herald*, 30 April 1871, 2. Very similar to an article appearing in the *Omaha Weekly Herald* three days later [833], this editorial criticizes the prosecutor in the McMurty murder case, points out that the accused Pawnees have been in jail for two years, and calls the handling of the case a "most cruel farce."

833. "The Pawnee Indian Mockery." *Omaha Weekly Herald*, 3 May 1871, 2. The state trial of the four Pawnees charged with murdering Edward McMurtry in 1869 was again postponed, in part because the prosecuting attorney could not produce his witnesses.

834. "The Pawnee Prisoners." *Omaha Weekly Herald*, 14 June 1871, 2. On June 13, 1871, the Pawnees accused of killing Edward McMurty were released on $5,000 bail with the understanding that they would present themselves at the next court session in Lincoln. The prisoners returned to the reservation to wait.

20
The North Brothers
and the Pawnee Scouts

835. Bain, David Howard. *Empire Express: Building the First Transcontinental Railroad*. New York: Viking Press, 1999. 797 pp. The new Union Pacific Railroad passed through their country, so the Pawnees are discussed on several occasions in this lengthy study. To keep the good will of the usually friendly Pawnees, railroad officials allowed the Indians to ride the trains at no charge, as long as they stayed out of the passenger cars. Includes a brief but excellent profile of Frank North and his Pawnee Scouts and their role as protectors of railroad workers, and an account of the death of the only scout ever lost while serving under North.

836. Bouc, Ken. "Pawnee Scouts: Guardians of the Union Pacific." *NEBRASKAland* 59 (April 1981): 20–23, 45–48. Written for a general audience, this excellent essay on the Pawnee Scouts covers nearly all of their campaigns under the command of Major Frank North, while concentrating on their role as protectors of the railroad. Points out the problems the scouts encountered as they worked for the government and also tried to support their families. Several photos of scouts accompany the article.

837. ———. "Pawnee Scouts: The Invincible Battalion." *NEBRASKAland* 58 (July 1980): 34–37, 45–47. Excellent coverage of both the Powder River Expedition and the Republican River Campaign, which culminated in the defeat of the Cheyenne Dog Soldiers at Summit Springs. Emphasizes the bravery of the Pawnee Scouts and the terrible conditions under which they fought. Although written for a general audience

and having no documentation, this is an extremely interesting account of the Pawnee Scouts' finest hours.

838. Bruce, Robert. *The Fighting Norths and the Pawnee Scouts: Narratives and Reminiscences of Military Service on the Old Frontier*. Lincoln: Nebraska State Historical Society, 1932. 73 pp. Based on the author's correspondence with Luther H. North over a four-year period, this unique source contains a wealth of information on Pawnee history and personalities, the lives of the North Brothers, and the work of the Pawnee Scouts. The accounts are very disorganized, and there is no index, but the patient researcher will be richly rewarded.

839. Burnett, F. G. "History of the Western Division of the Powder River Expedition." *Annals of Wyoming* 8 (January 1932): 569–78. Detailed day-by-day account of the 1865 Powder River Expedition under the command of General Patrick Conner, told by a civilian who accompanied the troops. Much discussion of Major Frank North and the ninety Pawnee Scouts assigned to the campaign. According to Burnett, the Pawnees were extremely clever and brave fighters who set traps for Sioux raiders and never took prisoners. In his opinion, had General Conner been able to continue the Powder River campaign, the Great Sioux War would have ended years earlier than it did, and many lives would have been saved.

840. "Captain of the Famous Pawnee Scouts, Omaha Citizen." *Omaha World-Herald*, 2 October 1910, M3. One of a number of published interviews with Luther North, former Pawnee Scout captain. He recalls the bravery and loyalty of his Pawnee soldiers, including an incident when they saved his life.

841. Cody, William F. *The Life of Hon. William F. Cody, Known as Buffalo Bill, the Famous Hunter, Scout, and Guide: An Autobiography*. Hartford, Connecticut: Frank E. Bliss, 1879. Reprint. Foreword by Don Russell. Lincoln: University of Nebraska Press, 1978. 365 pp. There has been controversy as to whether this book was ghost-written or actually written by William Cody. In his excellent foreword, Cody biographer Don Russell argues that except for a few sections, it is a true autobiography. For Pawnee researchers, pages 249–62 deal with the Pawnee Scouts and the Battle of Summit Springs.

842. Danker, Donald F., ed. "The Journal of an Indian Fighter—The 1869 Diary of Major Frank J. North." *Nebraska History* 39 (June 1958): 87–177. North writes of outfitting his Pawnee Scouts for the Repub-

lican River campaign, then describes in his terse style the Battle of Summit Springs. Numerous editorial notes explain his references to people, places, and events.

843.   ———. *Man of the Plains: Recollections of Luther North, 1856–1882.* Foreword by George Bird Grinnell. Lincoln: University of Nebraska Press, 1961. 350 pp. In 1925, an aging Luther North completed his memoirs, which his friend George Bird Grinnell had urged him to write. Because Luther North and his older brother, Frank, grew up near Columbus, Nebraska, and for years led the Pawnee Scouts, this work is filled with references to the Pawnees. North's memoir is sometimes self-serving and always protective of his brother's image, but it is a valuable source on nearly thirty momentous years on the Great Plains.

844.   ———. "The North Brothers and the Pawnee Scouts." *Nebraska History* 42 (September 1961): 161–79. Superb, well-researched article tracing the history of the Pawnee Scouts from the first recruits to their final mustering out of the army. Includes coverage of all their major military campaigns and their role as protectors of the Union Pacific Railroad.

845. Downey, Fairfax, and Jacques Noel Jacobsen, Jr. *The Red Bluecoats.* Fort Collins, Colorado: Old Army Press, 1973. 204 pp. The chapter on the Pawnee Scouts is highly romanticized and contains numerous errors. However, it does include brief recollections of Rush Roberts (Ahrekahrard), the youngest Pawnee Scout during General Crook's capture of Red Cloud and Red Leaf in 1876. The book's greatest value is the dozens of photographs and drawings of Indian scouts and their equipment.

846. Dunlay, Thomas. "The Indian Scouts." *NEBRASKAland* 62 (January–February 1984): 87. Brief overview of the history and role of the Pawnee Scouts. For Dunlay's more complete account of the Scouts, see his *Wolves for the Blue Soldiers* [847].

847.   ———. *Wolves for the Blue Soldiers: Indian Scouts and Auxiliaries with the United States Army, 1860–90.* Lincoln: University of Nebraska Press, 1982. 304 pp. In his chapter entitled "The Pawnee Wolves," Dunlay writes an outstanding account of the history and military campaigns of the famous Pawnee Scouts and their leader, Frank North. Where this account stands out from many others is in its coverage of the reasons why Pawnees joined the Scouts, the types of Indians attracted to scouting, and the controversy within the Pawnee tribe

over scouts leaving their people to join the army. Dunlay also presents the personal side of Frank North's relationship with his scouts.

848. "Early Days in Nebraska: A Running Fight with the Leader of a Band of Desperadoes." *Transactions and Reports of the Nebraska State Historical Society,* vol. 3. Fremont, Nebraska: Hammond Brothers Printers, 1892, 287–91. Amusing report of the attempted robbery of an army ambulance and its passengers en route to Genoa, Nebraska, with mustering-out pay for a group of Pawnee Scouts.

849. Echo-Hawk, Brummett. "Last of the Pawnee Scouts." *Omaha World-Herald Sunday Magazine*, 27 July 1958, 24–25. Reprinted from the *Tulsa World Sunday Magazine*. A tribute to Fancy Eagle (Rush Roberts), the last surviving Pawnee Scout, upon his death at the age of 99. Echo-Hawk recounts the eventful life of Fancy Eagle, and in doing so, tells a great deal of Pawnee history.

850. Filipiak, Jack D. "The Battle of Summit Springs." *Colorado Magazine* 41 (Fall 1964): 343–54. Much of this well-written account is concerned with events preceding the battle between Pawnee Scouts and General Carr's Fifth Cavalry and the Cheyenne Dog Soldiers. The Battle of Summit Springs has been the subject of several articles, and Filipiak draws heavily on earlier accounts by King [859], [860], and Reckmeyer [871].

851. Fisher, John R. "The Royall and Duncan Pursuits: Aftermath of the Battle of Summit Springs, 1869." *Nebraska History* 50 (Fall 1969): 293–308. After the defeat of the Cheyenne Dog Soldiers, troops, always accompanied by Pawnee Scouts, scoured the Upper Republican River valley, looking for survivors of the Summit Springs battle. Though not as dramatic as the actual battle with the Dog Soldiers, this follow-up operation demonstrated the army's determination to rid the area of hostile Indians.

852. "Frank North." *Forest and Stream*, March 19, 1885, 1. Lengthy obituary, published just five days after Major North's death at Columbus, Nebraska, is a tribute to the man who led the Pawnee Scouts. Included in the obituary are many anecdotes from North's days with the Scouts.

853. "From the Indian Campaign: Gallant Exploits of the Pawnee Scouts Under Lieut. Beecher." *Omaha Weekly Herald*, 21 July 1869, 2. Report from Lieutenant Beecher to Major Frank North describing a 130-mile scouting mission to track and locate Oglala Sioux bands. The Pawnees killed several Sioux and captured a few mules and horses.

854. Greene, Jerome A. "The Surrounding of Red Cloud and Red Leaf 1876: A Preemptive Maneuver of the Great Sioux War." *Nebraska History* 82 (Summer 2001): 69–75. Army units led by Colonel Ranald Mackenzie, and including the North Brothers and their Pawnee Scouts, surrounded, disarmed, and dismounted Oglala and Brulé Sioux under Red Cloud and Red Leaf, who had left the agency to camp along Chadron Creek, northeast of Fort Robinson. The Scouts played a major role in this peaceful operation that probably prevented future bloodshed.

855. Grinnell, George Bird. *Two Great Scouts and Their Pawnee Battalion*. Cleveland: Arthur H. Clark Company, 1928. Reprint. Foreword by James T. King. Lincoln: University of Nebraska Press, 1973. 299 pp. Traces the careers of Frank and Luther North from their Nebraska boyhood through their days as leaders of the Pawnee Scouts. Grinnell and the North Brothers were friends, and Frank and Luther North provided much of the material for this book. Researchers should also consult James T. King's excellent foreword.

856. Holmes, Louis A. *Fort McPherson, Nebraska, Fort Cottonwood, N. T.: Guardian of the Tracks and Trails*. Lincoln: Johnsen Publishing Company, 1963. 108 pp. Fort McPherson, formerly Fort Cottonwood, played a pivotal role in the Platte Valley Indian wars of the later nineteenth century, and was the home base of the Pawnee Scouts. A valuable military history, largely written from post records. Among the events are an aborted 1864 peace council between the Pawnees and Sioux, a buffalo hunting excursion under the protection of the Pawnee Scouts, the Beecher Island Battle of 1868, the Battle of Summit Springs, and Massacre Canyon. Also touches on the building of Fort Hartsuff near the Pawnee Reservation. On December 31, 1870, two companies of Pawnee Scouts mustered out of the army at Fort McPherson.

857. "The Indian Captives Free." *Omaha World-Herald*, 26 September 1867, 1. Two months earlier, the Sioux had captured three white girls and six-year-old twin boys just east of Kearney, Nebraska. Reports that the children were freed in exchange for Indians taken prisoner by Pawnee Scouts.

858. King, James T. "Forgotten Pageant: The Indian Wars in Western Nebraska." *Nebraska History* 46 (September 1965): 177–92. Divides the Nebraska Indian wars into four periods and points out that despite

their importance, these conflicts have received little attention from historians. Includes a brief discussion of Fort McPherson, General Eugene Carr's Fifth Cavalry, and the Pawnee Scouts.

859. ———. "The Republican River Expedition, June–July, 1869." Master's thesis, University of Nebraska, 1957. 127 pp. One of the high points in the history of the Pawnee Scouts, this military operation under the command of Brevet Major General Eugene Carr culminated in the defeat of the Cheyenne Dog Soldiers at the Battle of Summit Springs in northeastern Colorado. This is probably the definitive account of this important military campaign that opened the Republican River valley to white settlement.

860. ———. "The Republican River Expedition, June–July, 1869. Part 1: On the March." *Nebraska History* 41 (September 1960): 165–99, and "Part 2: The Battle of Summit Springs." *Nebraska History* 41 (December 1960): 281–97. This is an abbreviated version of King's fine Master's thesis [859].

861. ———. *War Eagle: A Life of General Eugene A. Carr.* Lincoln: University of Nebraska Press, 1963. 323 pp. Includes an account of the Republican River expedition and the 1869 Battle of Summit Springs in which Carr's Fifth Cavalry, along with the North brothers and their Pawnee Scouts, defeated the Cheyenne Dog Soldiers. Much of this material also appears in King's article in *Nebraska History* [860].

862. Liddic, Bruce R., and Paul Harbaugh, eds. *Camp on Custer: Transcribing the Custer Myth.* Spokane, Washington: Arthur H. Clark Company, 1995. 189 pp. A collection of interviews by Little Bighorn historian Walter M. Camp with army officers and enlisted men who served with George Armstrong Custer during the Indian wars. In Chapter 7, Luther H. North relates his experiences with the Pawnee Scouts at the Battle of Summit Springs.

863. "Life of Major Frank North, the Famous Pawnee Scout." *Platte Valley Times*, 30 May 1896 through 30 January 1897. Appears on page one of each edition. Serialized in ten chapters in this Columbus, Nebraska, newspaper, this is a very detailed biography of North that includes much material on the Pawnees. The *Platte Valley Times* is available on microfilm from the Nebraska State Historical Society. Unfortunately, some of the installments are missing.

864. North, Luther H. "My Military Experiences in Colorado." *Colorado Magazine* 11 (March 1934): 68–70. Brief account of the Summit

Springs Battle written sixty-four years after the event. Speaks well of the Pawnee Scouts, and emphasizes his and his brother Frank's roles in the defeat of the Cheyenne Dog Soldiers.

865. "The North Memorial Magazine." *Nebraska History* 15 (October–December 1934): 258–314. Entire issue devoted to the North Brothers and the Pawnee Scouts. Included are letters from Luther North to his uncle, John Calvin North, a reprint of a 1934 speech by Addison E. Sheldon entitled "The North Brothers and the Pawnee Nation," the surround and capture of Red Cloud and Red Leaf on Chadron Creek, and a memorial tribute to Luther North.

866. O'Donnell, Jeff. *Luther North, Frontier Scout*. Lincoln. Nebraska: J & L Lee Co., 1995. 209 pp. This biography of North recounts all the high points of his career as a leader of the Pawnee Scouts—guarding the Union Pacific Railroad, the Battle of Summit Springs, the capture of Red Cloud, the Powder River campaign, and the Dull Knife fight. Includes numerous photographs and several maps, but unfortunately, no footnotes.

867. "Old Indian Camps and Battlefields." *Nebraska History* 14 (April–June 1933): 82–86. In 1933, Captain Luther H. North, photographer Frank Shoemaker, and historian Addison E. Sheldon set out on an expedition to visit ancient Indian camps and battlefields in western Nebraska. They visited the site of the 1876 surround of Red Cloud and Red Leaf on Chadron Creek, the Pawnee Surrender Field near Battle Creek, and made an unplanned trip to the Summit Springs battlefield in eastern Colorado. Luther North and the Pawnee Scouts had played major roles in the Chadron Creek events and the Battle of Summit Springs.

868. Palmer, H. E. "History of the Powder River Indian Expedition of 1865." *Transactions and Reports of the Nebraska State Historical Society*, vol. 2. Lincoln: State Journal Company, Printers, 1887, 197–229. A former cavalry officer shares his colorful recollections of this important military campaign against the Sioux and Cheyenne. Contains numerous references to Major Frank North and the Pawnee Scouts, including a description of a Pawnee victory dance.

869. "Pioneering with Capt. Luther H. North." *Winners of the West* 11 (September 1934): n.p. Chatty letter from North to the editor of this journal reminiscing about recruiting Pawnee Scouts for the Powder River expedition, the surround of Red Cloud and Red Leaf near Fort

Robinson, and the Summit Springs battle. Writing in his old age, North's memory of events and names is not always sharp, but this is still a useful original source.

870. Price, George F. *Across the Continent with the Fifth Cavalry*. New York: Antiquarian Press, Ltd., 1959. 705 pp. Includes a detailed account of the Pawnee Scouts' role in the Republican River Expedition and the climactic battle at Summit Springs. Over half of the book is devoted to the military records of Fifth Cavalry officers, but since they were not officially attached to the unit, Frank and Luther North are not included.

871. Reckmeyer, Clarence. "The Battle of Summit Springs." *Colorado Magazine* 4 (November 1929): 211–20. The writer toured the Summit Springs battlefield in 1929 with former Pawnee Scout leader Luther North. This version of the events of that decisive battle is a bit self-serving on North's part, as he insists that it was his brother Frank, not Buffalo Bill Cody, who fatally shot Dog Soldier leader Tall Bull.

872. Russell, Don. *The Lives and Legends of Buffalo Bill*. Norman: University of Oklahoma Press, 1960. 514 pp. Probably the most authoritative biography of William F. Cody. One high point is the discussion of Cody's role in the Battle of Summit Springs. Russell points out that many published accounts of the battle are based on the testimony of Luther H. North, who perhaps because of jealousy or to protect the reputation of his older brother, Frank, trivialized Cody's role in this important campaign. Russell illustrates that North told many versions of the same story and that writers such as George Bird Grinnell faithfully recorded them all.

873. Smits, David D. "Fighting Fire with Fire: The Frontier Army's Use of Indian Allies in the Trans-Mississippi Campaigns, 1860–1890." *American Indian Culture and Research Journal* 22, no. 1 (1998): 73–116. Excellent history of Indian scouts from many tribes, explaining the army's rationale for using Indians to fight other Indians. Contains extensive coverage of the Pawnee Scouts and their campaigns.

874. Sorenson, Alfred. "A Quarter of a Century on the Frontier, or The Adventures of Major Frank North, the 'White Chief of the Pawnees.'" Frank J. North Papers. MS 448, Box 1, Series 4, Folder 1. Nebraska State Historical Society, Lincoln, Nebraska. 197 pp. Beginning with his boyhood and ending with his ranching operation in partnership

with Buffalo Bill Cody, Frank North tells his life story. The seventeen-chapter typescript includes much detailed information on the Pawnee Scouts and their military campaigns with Major North as their commander.

875. Sparks, Ray G. *Reckoning at Summit Springs*. Kansas City: Lowell Press, 1969. 52 pp. Written for the Logan County, Colorado Historical Society on the 100th anniversary of the death of Susanna Alderdice, a captive of the Cheyenne killed at the Battle of Summit Springs in 1869. Focuses on the life of Mrs. Alderdice and her fate at the hands of the Cheyenne Dog Soldiers.

876. U.S. Congress. House. *Resolution of the Legislature of Nebraska Asking Relief for Captain James Murrie* [sic]. 42d Cong., 1st sess., 1871. H. Misc. Doc. 52. [Ser. 1467]. 2 pp. A request by the State of Nebraska that Congress allocate funds to help support the family of James Murie, Pawnee Scout leader and father of mixed-blood Pawnee scholar James R. Murie. Captain Murie became mentally ill, and at the time of the resolution, was confined to a mental hospital. Because Murie had commanded Indians, there were no provisions for him to receive a disability pension.

877. Utley, Robert M. *Frontier Regulars: The United States Army and the Indian, 1866–1891*. New York: McMillan Publishing Co, Inc., 1973. Reprint. Lincoln: University of Nebraska Press, 1984. 462 pp. Among the army operations of 1868–1869 on the Plains was the Republican River Expedition, which began at Fort McPherson, Nebraska, and culminated in the decisive battle at Summit Springs in Colorado. The Pawnee Scouts were instrumental in this military campaign.

878. ———. *Frontiersmen in Blue: The United States Army and the Indian, 1848–1865*. New York: McMillan Publishing Co., Inc, 1967. Reprint. Lincoln: University of Nebraska Press, 1981. 384 pp. Offers a brief overview of the 1865 Powder River Expedition and the role of the Pawnee Scouts in this campaign.

879. Vaughan, Richard. "'Broad Are Nebraska's Rolling Plains': The Early Writings of George Bird Grinnell." *Nebraska History* 83 (Spring 2002): 36–46. Inside this general study of Grinnell's early days on the Great Plains are an account of his long-lived friendship with Frank and Luther North, and an excellent description of the physical appearance of two Pawnee Scouts who rode with Buffalo Bill Cody.

880. Ware, Eugene F. *The Indian War of 1864.* Introduction by Clyde C. Walton. New York: St. Martin's Press, 1960. Reprint. Lincoln: University of Nebraska Press, 1963. 483 pp. Told by an officer of the Seventh Iowa Cavalry, which spent the Civil War years fighting Indians on the Plains. He recounts an almost humorous attempt at a peace council between a band of Sioux and the Pawnee Scouts, and describes the Pawnees' lack of military discipline and inventive uses for army uniform parts. In Ware's opinion, the scouts were poor excuses for soldiers. Included is an 1864 muster roll with the Pawnee names of seventy-seven of Major North's scouts.

881. Werner, Fred H. *The Dull Knife Battle: Doomsday for the Northern Cheyennes.* Greeley, Colorado: Werner Publications, 1981. 119 pp. Written in a rather florid style almost entirely from secondary sources and poorly edited, this work sheds no new light on the role of the Pawnee Scouts in this decisive battle between the United States Cavalry and the Northern Cheyenne.

882. ———. *The Summit Springs Battle, July 11, 1869.* Greeley, Colorado: Werner Publications, 1991. 185 pp. The Pawnee Scouts are portrayed as bloodthirsty killers in this self-published, poorly written account of the final defeat of the Cheyenne Dog Soldiers. Direct quotes are not footnoted, and the sources of several primary documents included in the appendixes are not identified.

883. Wheeler, Keith. "Indians in Uniform." In *The Scouts.* Alexandria, Virginia: Time-Life Books, 1978, 112–47. Nicely done history of Indian scouts written for a general audience. Because of their military importance and longtime service, the Pawnees and the North brothers are central to this chapter. Anecdotal accounts of Pawnee bravery add color to this interesting essay.

884. White, Lonnie J. "Indian Raids on the Kansas Frontier, 1869." *Kansas Historical Quarterly* 38 (Winter 1972): 369–88. Among the raids and battles detailed are the Battle of Summit Springs and the role of the Pawnee Scouts in that fight and the "mop-up" operations, and a brief mention of the January 1869 deaths of six Pawnees who were allegedly discovered stealing cattle near Mulberry Creek, 14 miles from Salina, Kansas [1029].

885. Wilson, Ruby E. *Frank J. North: Pawnee Scout Commander and Pioneer.* Athens, Ohio: Swallow Press, 1984. 334 pp. Written in the first

person in journal form, this biography of Frank North incorporates newspaper clippings, personal interviews, military records, diaries of North's brothers, Luther and James, and two military campaign diaries kept by Frank North, which are now in the archives of the Nebraska State Historical Society. Includes many passages recalling the activities of the Pawnee Scouts.

21
The Pawnees in Oklahoma

886. Blaine, Martha Royce. *Some Things Are Not Forgotten: A Pawnee Family Remembers*. Lincoln: University of Nebraska Press, 1997. 274 pp. Author's husband was Garland James Blaine, a Pawnee leader who became head chief of the Pitahawirata band in 1964. Part one tells of the Blaine grandparents' generation and their experiences in Nebraska and later, in Indian Territory. Part two contains Blaine's memories of his people and his culture. Most of the material is from the Garland J. Blaine and Martha R. Blaine research notes, housed at the Oklahoma Historical Society in Oklahoma City.

887. Buchta, Shari. "Tribal Elders to Visit Sites in Nebraska." *Fremont (Nebraska) Tribune*, 8 June 1994, A1–2. In 1994, Cherrie Clarke, program director for the Pahuk historic site, arranged for a group of Pawnee elders from Oklahoma to tour Nebraska's Pawnee landmarks. It had been eighty years since any Pawnee had visited Pahuk, and whites in the region donated food, lodging, and money to make the tour a success.

888. Clark, Joseph Stanley. "Irregularities at the Pawnee Agency." *Kansas Historical Quarterly* 12 (November 1943): 366–77. Agent William Burgess was accused of conspiracy and misuse of funds for the Pawnee Agency when weights of cattle purchased for the Indians were tampered with. Burgess resigned, and charges were later dropped.

889. ———. "A Pawnee Buffalo Hunt." *Chronicles of Oklahoma* 20 (December 1942): 387–95. Reprints an account of a buffalo hunt in West

Texas that first appeared in the *Chicago Tribune* on July 17, 1879, and was probably written by one of the army officers escorting the Pawnees on their final hunt. Entertaining, but full of nineteenth-century slang and ethnocentric comments about the Pawnees.

890. ———. "The Ponca Indian Agency." Ph.D. diss., University of Wisconsin, 1940. Discusses dissension, dishonesty, and ineptness among government officials and employees in charge of both the Pawnee and Ponca Agencies. Based almost entirely on government documents, this important work covers the period from the Pawnees' removal from Nebraska to the allotment of their lands. Chapter 2 is also the topic of an article in *Kansas Historical Quarterly* [888].

891. Collier, John. "Present Status of Oklahoma Indians." *Harlow's Weekly* 43 (July 28, 1934): 13. Although concerned primarily with the Osages, Collier includes acreage figures on other Oklahoma tribes. According to this chart, all but about 38,000 acres of the Pawnees' original Oklahoma lands had been allotted by 1934. Those remaining lands continued under restrictions.

892. *Edmond (Oklahoma) Sun-Democrat,* 16 April 1894, 2. Announced that the Pawnee Mining Company had been chartered, and that capital stock was valued at $50,000.

893. *El Reno (Oklahoma) News,* 29 May 1896, 6. Hawk Chief, an elderly, blind Pawnee died days after a suicide attempt. Before citizenship, suicide was unknown among the Pawnees, but since 1893, four members of the tribe had taken their own lives.

894. *El Reno (Oklahoma) News,* 19 June 1896, 2. Brief report that a Pawnee Indian was caught trying to pass pieces of cardboard, stamped like a silver half-dollar, to pay a bill.

895. *El Reno (Oklahoma) News,* 20 November 1896, 2. Untitled article discusses perjury trials being conducted in the town of Pawnee. A grand jury had earlier indicted the county clerk and a Pawnee Indian attorney for giving false affidavits regarding pensions to Pawnees.

896. *El Reno (Oklahoma) News,* 18 June 1897, 6. In 1897, the Pawnee Indians had 16,000 acres of the very best land in Payne County. One thousand acres were leased to white men, twelve acres were farmed by Indians, and the rest lay idle.

897. *El Reno (Oklahoma) News*, 22 July 1898, 6. Four Pawnees were rejected for service in the Spanish-American War because they had too many bone fractures from breaking wild horses.

898. *Executive Orders Relating to Indian Reservations from July 1, 1912 to July 1, 1922*. Washington, D.C.: Government Printing Office, 1922, 64. Extends the trust period for Pawnee lands in Oklahoma to 1927.

899. Farnum, Allen L. *Pawnee Bill's Historic Wild West: A Photo Documentary of the 1900–1905 Show Tour*. Photos by Harry V. Bock. West Chester, Pennsylvania: Schiffer Publishing, Ltd., 1992. 129 pp. Photo essay covering the life of Gordon William Lillie—Pawnee Bill—and the history of his wild west show. The photos are from long-lost negatives given to the author's father by photographer Harry Bock.

900. Franks, Kenny A., and Paul F. Lambert. *Pawnee Pride: A History of Pawnee County*. Oklahoma Heritage County History Series. Edited by Odie B. Faulk. Oklahoma City: Western Heritage Books, 1994. 298 pp. Includes both a cultural and a political history of the Pawnee Indians, as well as a chapter on the North brothers and the Pawnee Scouts. Drawn from a few secondary sources, this is a useful, quick overview of the Pawnees. Included at the end of the text is an alphabetical list of Indian allotments in Pawnee County.

901. "Government Agent Visits the Pawnees." *The Daily (Oklahoma City) Oklahoman*, 19 December 1908, 8. Special Agent Campbell of the Indian Service made an inquiry as to the capitalization of the Pawnees. The government proposed to deposit $600,000 to the credit of the Pawnee tribe at five per cent interest. The amount accruing annually would be about $30,000.

902. "Harvey to Be Removed." *Oklahoma City Weekly Times Journal*, 9 October 1903, 1. Samuel Brosius of the Indian Rights Association recommended that Superintendent George Harvey be removed from his position for malfeasance in office, especially for his alleged whipping of a Pawnee girl with a leather belt. Harvey vowed to fight the charges.

903. "Indian Population by Tribes." *Harlow's Weekly* 16 (January 22, 1919): 7. Lists 1918 estimates or census figures for each tribe in Oklahoma. The Pawnee population at this time was 716. Also reprints a table from the report of the Commissioner of Indian Affairs listing numbers of Oklahoma acres allotted to Indians and the number of allottees. By 1918, 829 Pawnees had received 112,701 acres of land. This figure is larger than the population census numbers.

904. "In the New Country." *Edmund (Oklahoma) Sun-Democrat*, 24 January 1896, 1. Pawnees reportedly had left their farms and moved into tepees on Black Bear Creek, and had begun to make medicine and dance the Ghost Dance.

905. "Is Probably Hot Air." *The Daily (Oklahoma City) Oklahoman*, 26 December 1901, 5. Newspapers in Oklahoma City doubted the truth of this Associated Press report that a Pawnee buffalo dance had led to threats against whites on and around the reservation. The commotion began when "Pawnee Bill" gave the Indians a badly wounded buffalo that had to be killed.

906. "Items from the Pawnee Agency New Era." *Cheyenne (El Reno, Oklahoma) Transporter*, 28 April 1884, 1. An update on Pawnee Agency news, this column discussed allotments, leasing, and the role of missionaries among the Indians.

907. "Leasing Indian Lands." *The Indian Chieftain*, 2 March 1893, 2. This Vinita, Oklahoma, newspaper ran an article stating that the Interior Department had advertised the Pawnee Reservation for lease, and cattlemen were now bidding on the lands. If the leases were made, the reservation could not be opened to settlement for the period of the leases. The Cherokee Strip Settlers Association protested the government action.

908. Loper, Ethel Violet. "The Alienation and Utilization of the Pawnee Lands, 1874–1921." Master's thesis, University of Oklahoma, 1955. 96 pp. Concentrates on the period after the tribe's removal to Oklahoma. Based almost entirely on the reports of the Commissioners of Indian Affairs and Pawnee materials at the Oklahoma Historical Society, this thesis is informative, but it also contains errors, especially in the historical background chapters.

909. "McGuire Works Per Cent." *Lawton (Oklahoma) Weekly Enterprise*, 22 January 1904, 5. Reports charges and countercharges in a Pawnee Indian annuity payment scheme. The principals involved were Pawnee Superintendent George Harvey, Congressman Bird McGuire, and the heirs to a Pawnee land allotment.

910. "Oklahoma City, Feb. 6." *Blackwell (Oklahoma) Sunday Tribune*, 7 February 1932, 10. Governor W. H. Murray had issued an order making all records of the State Historical Society available to the Pawnee Tribe.

911. "Pawnee Agency." *Cheyenne (El Reno, Oklahoma) Transporter*, 26 February 1883, 4. Upbeat letter to the editor pointing out all the good

things happening to the Pawnees on their reservation. The writer refers to the Pawnees at this time as "a jolly people."

912. "The Pawnee Agency." *Purcell (Oklahoma) Register*, 16 January 1903, 7. Reprints Superintendent George Harvey's report to the Oklahoma governor on the status of the Pawnees. Along with routine business, Harvey expressed his opinion that the large annuities received by the Pawnees made them lazy and encouraged alcohol abuse.

913. "Pawnee Agency Locals." *Cheyenne (El Reno, Oklahoma) Transporter*, 26 January 1883, 1. Update citing repairs to the Pawnee School, receipt of annuities, births, and a recently held dance.

914. "Pawnee Agency Locals." *Cheyenne (El Reno, Oklahoma) Transporter*, 28 May 1883, 1. Column mentions grazing leases, allotments, the capture of horse thieves, and the forthcoming payment for Pawnee lands in Nebraska. The writer praises Pawnee agent Lewellyn Woodin and the head of the industrial boarding school. Also reports the death of Spotted Horse, who was shot in a nearby town while resisting arrest.

915. "Pawnee Dances Honor Indian Soldiers." *The Daily (Oklahoma City) Oklahoman*, 29 August 1920, B2. The Pawnees held a week-long celebration honoring Indian veterans of World War I, as well as Pawnee veterans of earlier wars. Parades and speeches by prominent Pawnees were daily features of the festival. In the parades, recent veterans and young chiefs rode on horseback, while Civil War veterans and those who had served in the Indian wars rode in automobiles.

916. Rainey, George. *The Cherokee Strip*. Guthrie, Oklahoma: Co-Operative Publishing Co., 1933. 504 pp. Profiles each Indian tribe that came to occupy the "Cherokee Strip" in north-central Oklahoma. This land was officially opened to white settlement in 1893 and later divided into seven counties. An easy-to-understand Pawnee history found on pages 97–107 explains all the Pawnee treaties and agreements with the government from 1818 through the Jerome Agreement of 1891, which provided for the allotment of Pawnee lands in Oklahoma.

917. Randolph, N. F. "Pawnee—In an Agricultural Paradise." *Sturm's Oklahoma Magazine* 8 (May 1909): 91–92. Describes the town of Pawnee, Oklahoma, in the early 1900s, and mentions that the entire annuity paid to the Pawnees made its way into the coffers of merchants in the new town.

918. *Stillwater (Oklahoma) Gazette*, 29 September 1893, 6. A number of bodies, charred beyond recognition, were found on the Pawnee Reservation after a rash of prairie fires.

919. Towers, Lem A. *Pawnee Indian Agency Program: Pawnee, Ponca, Tonkawa, Otoe & Kaw Reservations.* U.S. Bureau of Indian Affairs, Typescript dated March 22, 1944. 20 pp., including map. Rich source of information about the Indian tribes under the jurisdiction of the Pawnee Agency in Oklahoma. It contains data on tribal enrollments, school populations, natural resources, crops, heirship lands, leasing of pasture lands, tribal economies, and federal services provided to these five tribes. Also included is a future plan for this agency and a map of the area. A copy of this report is on file at the Kansas State Historical Society.

920. Underhill, Lonnie E., and John H. Battle. "Classification of Oklahoma Indian Tribes: Language Stocks, Population, and Localities." *Chronicles of Oklahoma* 48 (Summer 1970): 197–208. Report consists of detailed charts breaking Oklahoma's Indian population down by language groups, dialects, numbers of native speakers, total numbers, and residency on allotted lands on or near reservations. According to now thirty-year-old estimates, there were 2,080 Pawnees (Skidi and South Band) living in Oklahoma, 412 of whom spoke their native language.

921. U.S. Congress. House. *Indians of the Northern Superintendency.* 43d Cong., 2d sess., 1875. H. Exec. Doc. 92. [Ser. 1646]. 2 pp. Reprints a bill of June 10, 1872, that provided funds for Nebraska tribes, and amends the bill to strike funds to the Pawnees, who since their removal to Indian Territory, had been under the Central Superintendency.

922. ———. *Pawnee Indians.* 44th Cong., 1st sess., 1876. H. Rept. 241. [Ser. 1708]. 12 pp. The Committee on Indian Affairs transmits correspondence, all of which supports the removal of the Pawnees from Nebraska to Indian Territory. Of special importance are letters from Superintendent Barclay White and members of the Friends committee who had recently visited the Pawnees.

923. ———. *Pawnee Indians.* 44th Cong., 1st sess., 1876. H. Exec. Doc. 154. [Ser. 1689]. 12 pp. An exchange of letters, telegrams, and reports among Indian superintendents, government officials, and members of the Board of Indian Commissioners, all pointing out the destitute condition of the Oklahoma Pawnees and urging Congress to provide them

with emergency rations. Vendors are asked to provide beef and other supplies for the Indians without a government purchase order. Also discussed is the sale of the Pawnee Reservation in Nebraska, with the proceeds going to help the Pawnees in their new home. Contains important information regarding the early Oklahoma period.

924. ———. *Pawnee Indians in Nebraska.* 44th Cong., 1st sess., 1876. H. Exec. Doc. 80. [Ser. 1687]. 11 pp. The Secretary of the Interior explains the plight of the Pawnees since their removal to Indian Territory. Includes the terms for the sale of their Nebraska reservation and an authorization to purchase emergency supplies for the starving Pawnees.

925. ———. *Pawnee Indian Reservation in Indian Territory.* 47th Cong., 1st sess., 1882. H. Exec. Doc. 218. [Ser. 2031]. 3 pp. Permission is granted by President Chester A. Arthur to enlarge the Pawnee reservation in Oklahoma. Because of indistinct boundaries, sixty Pawnees had broken land and begun to farm well beyond the reservation borders. Since these land sections had not been assigned to any other tribe, it was decided to add them to the Pawnee Reserve.

926. ———. *Pawnee Indian Reservation in Nebraska.* 51st Cong., 1st sess., 1890. H. Rept. 1175. [Ser. 2810]. 2 pp. Purchasers of land on the former Pawnee reservation in Nebraska would be forced to either pay for the land in full within two years of the passage of this bill or forfeit the land. Over 60,000 acres had been bought by speculators who were still holding it for future sale. Also shows the status of sales of Pawnee Reservation lands as of June 30, 1889. This document also appears as S. Report 421, 51st Cong., 1st sess., 1890. [Ser. 2704].

927. ———. *Pawnee Tribe of Indians of Oklahoma.* 74th Cong., 1st sess., 1935. H. Rept. 286. [Ser. 9886]. 2 pp. An error in surveying the Pawnee reservation in Oklahoma resulted in a shortage of 4,800 acres. In 1934, $6,079.50 was appropriated to repay the Pawnees for this land at the rate of $1.25 per acre. But it was discovered that an 1876 law set the price for reservation land at no less than $2.50 per acre. When the land was sold, it brought an average price of $4.25 per acre. With that in mind, the Secretary of the Interior endorsed a bill to pay the Pawnees $20,479.50 for the acreage. This included the 5% interest accrued since 1878.

928. ———. *Report with Respect to the House Resolution Authorizing the Committee on Interior and Insular Affairs to Conduct an Investigation of the Bureau of Indian Affairs.* 82d Cong., 2d sess., 1952. H.

Rept. 2503. [Ser. 11582], 5 pp. Provides historical and statistical information on the Pawnees and many other tribes. Lists treaties, population, and other tribal data, including payments to the tribes by the Court of Claims and tribal funds on hand as of June 30, 1951.

929. ———. *Conveying the Reversionary Interest of the United States in Certain Lands to the City of Pawnee, Oklahoma.* 83d Cong., 2d sess., 1954. H. Rept. 2610. [Ser. 11743]. 2 pp. Bill to deed over to the City of Pawnee 88.43 acres of land that had originally been part of the Pawnee reservation. It had earlier been sold to the City of Pawnee as a school site, but the city had never received clear title to the land. This information is also included in S. Report 2485, 83rd Cong., 2d sess, 1954 [Ser. 11732].

930. ———. *Declaring that the United States Holds Certain Lands in Trust for the Pawnee Indian Tribe of Oklahoma.* 90th Cong., 1st sess., 1967. H. Rept. 747. [Ser. 12753-5]. 7 pp. Argues that lands formerly set aside for the Pawnee Agency and school should be held in trust by the government for the benefit of the Pawnees. This would allow the Pawnees to develop these lands. This information is also included in S. Report 831, 90th Cong., 1st sess., 1967. [Ser. 12750-5].

931. ———. *Declaring that the United States Holds Certain Lands in Trust for the Pawnee Indian Tribe of Oklahoma.* 90th Cong., 2d sess., 1968. H. Rept. 1894. [Ser. 12795-7]. 2 pp. Conference report clarifying and removing amendments from an earlier report stating that lands formerly set aside for the Pawnee Agency and school should be held in trust for the Pawnees, allowing development on those lands.

932. "U.S. to Help Indian Agency." *The Daily (Oklahoma City) Oklahoman*, 20 June 1928, 18. Pawnee Indian Agency superintendent announced that his request for $5,000 for improvement and repairs of the girls' dormitory at the school and $2,000 to build an addition to the present agency office building at Pawnee had been granted. The addition was necessary because of the consolidation of the Kaw, Otoe, Ponca, and Tonkawa agencies with the Pawnee Agency.

933. "Washington Notes." *Hennessey (Oklahoma) Clipper*, 21 July 1893, 2. Allotments to the Pawnees in Indian Territory were formally approved by the acting Secretary of the Interior. The schedules embraced allotments covering 112,710 acres, leaving a surplus of 170,320 acres to be thrown open to settlement.

22
Pawnee Personalities

934. "Acee Blue Eagle Exhibits Work in Washington, D.C." *Bacone Indian*, 9 December 1936, 1. Announcement that Blue Eagle (Pawnee-Creek), art director at Bacone College, was planning a trip to Washington to attend an exhibition of his paintings at the Arts Club there.

935. "Acee Blue Eagle, Indian Artist." *Smoke Signals* (November 1952): 7–8. Brief article mentions that Blue Eagle had begun working in media other than painting, such as silk screening, jewelry, and ceramics.

936. Ball, Helen W. "The Pawnee Rough Rider." *Midland Monthly* 10 (December 1898): 452–53. Written shortly after the end of the Spanish–American War, this is a highly romanticized account of William Pollack, the Pawnee who distinguished himself as a member of Theodore Roosevelt's Rough Riders.

937. "Blind Indian 'Chief' Employed at Plane Plant." *Wichita (Kansas) Morning Eagle*, 5 April 1956. Pawnee Indians Clippings File, Vol. 1, 17–18. Kansas State Historical Society. Profiles Charles Shunatona, a blind Pawnee who worked at the Boeing Aircraft plant in Wichita in the 1950s. A World War II veteran, Shunatona became blind after a serious illness in 1947, but despite his handicap, he continued to organize Indian events and ceremonies.

938. "Blue Eagle Mural Restoration." *Smoke Signals* 47–48 (Winter-Spring 1966): 29. Creek Indian artist Fred Beaver completed the

restoration of a 1942 mural by the late Pawnee artist Acee Blue Eagle in the Coalgate, Oklahoma, post office.

939. Bouc, Ken. "World's Greatest Horse Thief." *NEBRASKAland* 57 (September 1979): 39–42. Big Spotted Horse was one of the first Pawnees to travel to Indian Territory in the 1870s, and on his recommendation, many of his fellow tribesmen and women followed him. However, this article focuses on the prominent Pawnee's prowess as a horse thief, especially his theft of hundreds of ponies from the Cheyennes in one successful raid.

940. Caldwell, Richard M. "Ace Among Indian Painters." *Christian Science Monitor Magazine Section*, 8 February 1941, 12. Article praising the art and intellectual accomplishments of Acee Blue Eagle. Although condescending in places, this is a good overview of Blue Eagle's life and work.

941. "Canvasser." *The American* 123 (April 1937): 103. Brief biographical sketch of Acee Blue Eagle. Between 1932 and 1937, he painted 400 works, twelve of which were purchased by Alfonso, former king of Spain.

942. "Curley Chief Dead." *The El Reno (Oklahoma) News*, 27 August 1897, 6. Report of the death of Curley Chief, a prominent Pawnee who was over 100 years old. He had participated in many of the Indian wars.

943. "Death of a Good Indian." *Kansas City Star*, 12 March 1899. Pawnee Indians Clippings File, vol. 1, 1–3. Kansas State Historical Society. A lengthy illustrated obituary honoring the famous Pawnee "Rough Rider" William J. Pollack, who died at the age of 28. Highlights Pollack's academic career at Haskell Institute and the University of Kansas, his artistic ability, and his military career serving under Theodore Roosevelt. Of special interest is a detailed description of Pollack's traditional Pawnee funeral.

944. DeFord, B. D. Dale. "Petalesharo, Bravest of the Brave Pawnees." *Mankind* (1973): 21–25; 62–65. Rather romanticized biography of the famous warrior who rescued a Comanche girl during the Morning Star ceremony in 1817. Follows his career until his disappearance from history about 1833, and relates the circumstances of the recovery of the medal he received in Washington, D.C. in 1821.

945. Deskins, Earl. "Acee Blue Eagle and His Native Art." *Design* 41 (April 1940): 8–10, 22. Brief biography of Blue Eagle traces his successful

artistic and educational career, including exhibitions of his paintings in Europe and a series of lectures on Native American art in England. Also includes an analysis of his painting style.

946. Diffendal, Anne. P., ed. "Fred 'Bright Star' Murrie: Pawnee Roller Skater." *Nebraska History* 70 (Summer 1989): 158–63. Biography of a Pawnee whose family relocated to the East Coast when he was a teenager. Murree came to the public's attention as a speed skater in the 1870s, but spent most of his career as a trick skater performing in Indian costume under the name "Bright Star."

947. ———. *Great North American Indians: Profiles in Life and Leadership*. New York: Van Norstrand Reinhold Co., 1977. 386 pp. Perhaps because it was published twenty-five years ago, this collection features only one Pawnee—Petalesharo—but his profile does include a very good reproduction of the silver medal presented to him in Washington, D.C. in 1821.

948. Dunbar, John B. "Lone Chief and Medicine Bull." *Magazine of American History* 8 (November 1882): 754–56. Flattering biography of Lone Chief, a Skidi chief who Dunbar claims died from grief after losing his family to malaria shortly after their arrival in Indian Territory. Contains a less positive portrait of Medicine Bull, who Dunbar describes as a failed medicine man. Portraits of both men appear to illustrate differences in appearance among Pawnees.

949. ———. "Pitalesharu—Chief of the Pawnees." *Magazine of American History* 5 (November 1880): 343–45. Profiles the son of Petalesharo, the Chaui leader who opposed the Morning Star human sacrifice. He resisted Pawnee removal to Indian Territory, and died of a gunshot wound in 1874.

950. *El Reno (Oklahoma) News*, 13 May 1898, 6. Reported that William Pollack, talented Pawnee musician and artist and Haskell Institute graduate, had been called up with his cavalry unit to fight in the Spanish–American War.

951. Finney, Frank F. "William Pollack: Pawnee Indian Artist and Rough Rider." *Chronicles of Oklahoma* 33 (Winter 1955–1956): 509–11. Story of the talented Pawnee artist who also fought bravely with Theodore Roosevelt in the Spanish–American War. He died of pneumonia in Pawnee, Oklahoma, in 1899 at the age of 28.

952. Fuller, Todd. *60 Feet Six Inches and Other Distances from Home: The (Baseball) Life of Mose Yellow Horse*. Duluth, Minnesota: Holy Cow! Press, 2002. 165 pp. Masterful account in poetry, prose, and cartoons of the baseball career of the Pawnee pitcher who may have been the first full-blood Indian to play major league baseball. Yellow Horse pitched for the Pittsburgh Pirates in 1921–22 and ended his career in 1926 with the Omaha team of the Western League. In 1994, thirty years after his death, he was elected to the American Indian Athletic Hall of Fame.

953. Gilmore, Melvin R. "Trip with White Eagle Determining Pawnee Sites, Aug. 27–29, 1914." Melvin R. Gilmore Papers. RG 3308.A M, Series 1, Folder 1. Nebraska State Historical Society. Account of an automobile trip to Pawnee sites in Nebraska with the last man still living who was a chief during the Nebraska Reservation period. On the three-day trip, White Eagle reminisced about sites in present-day Saunders County, the Pahuk sacred site near Fremont, the villages of the Pawnee bands near Genoa, and "Burnt Village," near Fullerton.

954. Hodge, F. W. "Pitalesharu and His Medal." *Masterkey* 24 (1950): 111–19. Account of the exploits of this young Pawnee warrior taken from several versions of his story. Also includes the history of the silver medal he was awarded and gives the exact location of the grave in which it was found.

955. Hyson, Frank B. *Pakee, Boy from Black Bear Creek: Reflections of the Last Sixty Years*. Albuquerque: AVC, Inc., 1977. Hyson, a mixed-blood Pawnee, wrote this story of his life and his family for his grandchildren. Growing up in Pawnee, Oklahoma, he became a local sports celebrity, playing football, baseball, and basketball. He was also a star at Central State College in Edmond, Oklahoma, and later became a coach. This is a rare Pawnee autobiography and family history.

956. "Indian G. I. Is Internationally Famous Artist." *Christian Science Monitor Magazine Section*, 10 March 1945, 18. Emphasizes Acee Blue Eagle's role as artist and soldier. Mentions famous world figures who collected his works and points out that his paintings could be found on the walls of an officers' club in Washington State and aboard the ill-fated battleship Oklahoma.

957. "James Murie and the Skidi Pawnee." *Nebraska History* 4 (January–March 1921): 16. A short biographical sketch of this mixed-blood Pawnee ethnologist. Mentions that his mother was Pawnee and his father commanded a company of Pawnee Scouts.

958. "James Riding In." *Who Owns the Past?: The American Indian Struggle for Control of Their Ancestral Remains.* www.pbs.org/wotp/tribes/james_riding_in. Located on the PBS web site for the documentary "Who Owns the Past? The Struggle of American Indians for Burial Rights [1046]," this is an up-to-date professional biography of an accomplished Pawnee scholar. Includes his research, many of his writings, and his consulting work.

959. Johnson, Jim. "From the Heavens 2 Eagles Came Flying." *Daily (Oklahoma City) Oklahoma Orbit*, 8 February 1970, 10. Laudatory essay on the life of the now deceased hereditary Pawnee chief Garland James Blaine. Explains his band affiliation and his efforts to preserve the Pawnee language and culture. A fine article about one of the more prominent modern Pawnees.

960. Kaff, Al. "Yellow Horse Hitches to Post of Ponca City Groundskeeper." *The Sporting News*, 16 July 1947, 42. After playing for the Pittsburgh Pirates and a number of baseball teams in the minor leagues during the 1920s, Pawnee pitcher Moses Yellow Horse applied for a job as a coach with the Ponca City, Oklahoma, affiliate of the Brooklyn Dodgers. Instead, he was hired as a groundskeeper for the stadium.

961. Lucas, Jim. "Nationally Known Indian Artist to Display Paintings at Bacone College." *Muskogee (Oklahoma) Daily Phoenix*, 15 May 1938, 3B. Excellent article about Acee Blue Eagle and his approach to Indian art. Written in conjunction with an exhibition of forty-one of Blue Eagle's paintings at Bacone College, where he was art director.

962. Malinowski, Sharon, ed. *Notable Native Americans.* Detroit: Gale Research, Inc., 1995. 492 pp. Fine collection of short biographies. Entries are listed in the front of the book by tribe and occupation, and in the back are both tribal and alphabetical lists. At the conclusion of each entry are sources to consult and writings by the profiled person, if applicable. Included are biographies of Pawnees John and Walter Echo-Hawk and a lengthy profile of Petalesharo.

963. "One-Man Show by Albin Jake." *Smoke Signals* (August 1957): 9–10. Announcement of a show by this award-winning Pawnee artist and a description of his painting style.

964. Parks, Douglas R. "James R. Murie: Pawnee Ethnographer." In *American Indian Intellectuals*, edited by Margot Liberty, 75–89. St. Paul: West Publishing Co., 1978. Using mainly sources from Hampton Institute, Parks pieced together a biography of Murie, one of Hampton's

most accomplished graduates. Through the years, Murie collaborated with Alice Fletcher, George A. Dorsey, and Clark Wissler, doing ethnographical work on the Pawnees and the Arikaras. He was largely responsible for Chicago's Field Museum having one of the major Pawnee collections in the United States. Unfortunately, Murie's contributions have been underappreciated, with other ethnographers sometimes taking credit for his work.

965. "Pawnee Rice Killed." *Stillwater (Oklahoma) Eagle-Gazette*, 30 March 1894, 1. Report that one of the wealthiest members of the Pawnee tribe had accidentally shot and killed himself a week earlier. But a conflicting report one day earlier on page one of the *Indian Journal* said that Rice was murdered when he was caught rustling cattle. On April 6, the *Edmond (Oklahoma) Sun-Democrat* printed a report also suggesting that he had been shot and killed by a settler.

966. Roberts, George H. "Ancestry of Latakuts Kalahar (Fancy Eagle)." Annotated by George E. Hyde. *Nebraska History* 40 (March 1959): 67–73. His son traces the family lineage of the Skidi Pawnee leader Fancy Eagle (Rush Roberts). As Rush Roberts, he was recruited into the Pawnee Scouts, serving for about a year.

967. Stephenson, Malvina. "Daughter of Hereditary Chief of Pawnees Pursues Career as Modern Indian Princess." *Tulsa Daily World*, 14 June 1936, Sec. 4, 10. Profiles Vivian Roberts, a full-blood Pawnee and the daughter of Rush Roberts (Fancy Eagle). Miss Roberts, a recent graduate of the University of Oklahoma, represented Native Americans at gatherings throughout the United States, sometimes wearing a beaded dress handed down through generations of Pawnee women.

968. Wunder, John R. "Walter Echo-Hawk." In *The New Warriors: Native American Leaders since 1900*, edited by R. David Edmunds, 299–321. Lincoln: University of Nebraska Press, 2001. Nicely done biography of a high-profile modern Pawnee. Discusses Echo-Hawk's childhood, education, and his early days as an Indian activist, but is primarily concerned with his career as a senior staff attorney for the Native American Rights Fund.

969. Wydeven, Joseph, and Clem Klaphake. "Art and Eloquence." *NEBRASKAland* 62 (January–February 1984): 102–10. Profiles six Indian artists with ties to Nebraska. Among them is Brummett Echo-Hawk, a Pawnee from Oklahoma who works in several media and often depicts incidents from his Pawnee heritage.

23
Pawnee Education

970. Ahern, Wilbert A. "'The Returned Indians': Hampton Institute and Its Indian Alumni, 1879–1893." *Journal of Ethnic Studies* 10 (Winter 1983): 101–24. Although this excellent article primarily features Hampton alumni of the Omaha tribe, the relatively few Pawnees who attended the school would have had similar experiences.

971. Bayhylle, Louis. "Letter." *Red Man and Helper* (December 5, 1902): 21. Bayhylle responded to criticism by an Indian agent that Indian boarding school graduates were lazy and chose to live on their annuities. He cited examples of Pawnee graduates of Carlisle Indian School, including himself, who were productive citizens with families.

972. *Chilocco Indian School Lands in Trust for the Kaw, Otoe-Missouria, Pawnee, Ponca, and Tonkawa Tribes of Oklahoma*. Public Law 99-283, 1986. 100 *Statutes at Large* 404. In accordance with a 1985 agreement among the tribes, the nearly 6,000 acres of Oklahoma land at the Chilocco Indian School would be held in trust for these five tribes, plus the Cherokee Nation. Also held in trust would be mineral income from the Chilocco School reserve.

973. "$80,000 Fund Seen for Indian School." *The Daily (Oklahoma City) Oklahoman*, 26 January 1931, 13. The outlook for additional funds for school buildings at the Pawnee Indian Agency was brighter following receipt of a telegram from Senator Elmer Thomas, advising that Vice President Charles Curtis had agreed to permit consideration of an amendment providing $85,000 for new structures and improvements.

974. *El Reno (Oklahoma) News*, 24 June 1898, 6. Announced that the children of the Pawnee Indian School would be giving an entertainment, the proceeds to go to the Red Cross Society. The students designed their own programs.

975. "Exhibition at the Pawnee School." *Platte (Columbus, Nebraska) Journal*, 29 March 1871, 2. Report of a program held at the Pawnee Reservation school to show the progress of Indian students. The program included music, recitations, and a gymnastics routine. The reporter was pleasantly surprised to see Pawnee chiefs in the audience.

976. "Fire at Pawnee School." *The Purcell (Oklahoma) Register*, 23 January 1904, 2. Fire destroyed the large stone dormitory and school building of the Indian school on the Pawnee Reservation. The total loss was estimated at $25,00–$30,000. The fire was also reported in the *Lawton (Oklahoma) Weekly Enterprise* on January 29, 1904.

977. Foreman, Grant. "Transitional Progress at Bacone to Reflect in New Building Plans." *Muskogee (Oklahoma) Daily Phoenix*, 15 September 1935, 9. Lengthy article on the past, present, and future of Bacone College includes a paragraph in praise of 1930 graduate Acee Blue Eagle, citing his recent art lectures at Oxford University.

978. Lee, Jodi Rave. "A School of Assimilation." *Lincoln Journal Star*, 13 August 2001, A1–2. Brief history of the United States Indian School in Genoa, Nebraska, that evolved from the Manual Labor School on the Pawnee Reservation. Includes a timeline of important events in the life of the school, which was closed in 1934.

979. Little Chief, Lucy. "How Pawnees Celebrate Christmas." *The Indian Leader* 12 (December 20, 1907): 2. A Pawnee student at Haskell Institute in Lawrence, Kansas reports that Christmas is celebrated in much the same way as Thanksgiving in Pawnee, Oklahoma. The celebration includes prayers by both Indian leaders and the missionary, a Christian sermon, then dancing and a gift exchange.

980. Lomawaima, K. Tsianina. *They Called It Prairie Light: The Story of Chilocco Indian School*. Lincoln: University of Nebraska Press, 1994. 205 pp. Students from dozens of tribes attended Chilocco School in north central Oklahoma over nearly a one-hundred-year period beginning in 1884. Although no special emphasis is placed on the Pawnees, the school was established near the Pawnee Reservation, and Pawnees were among its first students. Their experiences would

have been similar to those of the former students interviewed by the author.

981. "The Nation's Wards." *Philadelphia Inquirer*, 24 March 1882, 3. Students of Virginia's Hampton Institute were introduced at a public meeting in Philadelphia on March 23. Among the students addressing the crowd was Pawnee James R. Murie, who explained the divisions within his tribe, explained how he spent his time at Hampton, and expressed his opinion that money provided to the Pawnees should be used to buy farm equipment.

982. "The Pawnee Indian School." Broken Claw. *BrokenClaw.com*. www.brokenclaw.com/native/pawnee.html. Brief capsule history and description of the Pawnee Indian School campus in Pawnee, Oklahoma, on the web site of Broken Claw, whose father attended the Pawnee School. Broken Claw conducts a written and visual tour of the campus as it is today, and includes recent photographs of the main buildings. Also recounts some of his father's experiences as a student, and mentions that in 1930, the Pawnee School sponsored the first all-Indian Girl Scout troop in the United States.

983. Pratt, Jennie. "An Indian Christmas Story." *The Indian Leader* 26 (December 29, 1922): 8. As an English class assignment at Haskell Institute, students were asked to share their Christmas experiences. This story tells of a Christmas Eve dance among the Pawnees that continued on the afternoon of Christmas Day.

984. Ricketts, Herman. "An Indian Christmas Celebration." *The Indian Leader* 26 (December 29, 1922): 9. Haskell Institute student recalls a 1920 Oklahoma Christmas celebration and reunion. Dinner was followed by dancing, drumming, and speeches by the chiefs.

985. Roberts, Henry. "The Indian Story." *The Indian Leader* 6 (January 9, 1903): n.p. Charming conversational story written by a Pawnee fourth grade student at Haskell Institute. He touches on buffalo hunting, his father running away from the Genoa Indian School in Nebraska, life in Oklahoma, and a herd of buffalo belonging to Pawnee Bill's Wild West Show.

986. Roberts, Vivian. "Christmas Story." *The Indian Leader* 26 (December 29, 1922): 8. Tells the story of a Pawnee Christmas long ago, when drummers drummed through the night, everyone shared a feast, and the old men told traditional Pawnee tales.

987. Snider, John Henry. "A Study of Indian Education in Pawnee County, Oklahoma." Master's thesis, University of Oklahoma, 1932. 97 pp. Detailed but dated study compares the costs of educating Indian children at the Pawnee Boarding School with educating them in Pawnee County public schools, and discusses the academic achievement of children in the two settings. These results are then compared to the same findings for white children in Pawnee County public schools. Over three dozen tables illustrate the results, which show that Indian students on the average had slightly lower IQs than white students, but Indian students in public schools tend to achieve at a higher level than their counterparts in boarding school.

988. Snyder, A. R. "Pawnee Boarding School." *Oklahoma Indian School Magazine* 1 (March 1932): 16. In this brief report, the Pawnee Boarding School superintendent updated the status of the school's physical plant and student enrollment, academic progress, and health. Some of the Indian students were attending public school, pending the completion of a new building at the boarding school. In the same column of the journal is a brief article about the Boy Scout troop of the Pawnee School, organized in 1925.

989. Stewart, Roy P. "Pawnee Indian School." *The Daily (Oklahoma City) Oklahoman*, 30 May 1948, D-9. Describes activities at the Pawnee School, explains how the school dealt with budget cuts, and gives the current value of the school's land and physical plant.

990. "32 Indian Tribes Represented at Bacone." *Muskogee (Oklahoma) Daily Phoenix*, 4 October 1925, 14. Written on the occasion of the forty-fifth anniversary of Bacone College. States that in 1925, the Pawnees ranked fourth among Oklahoma tribes in the number of students attending the school.

991. Trandahl, Edward. "Pawnee Indians Tell of Braid Dispute." *Omaha World-Herald*, 23 August 1973, 8. The sons of Lloyd Cummings of Pawnee, Oklahoma, wore their hair in long braids when attending school, in violation of dress codes. The family was threatened and their property damaged. At the time this article was written, the Cummings and their opponents were waiting to see if the U.S. Supreme Court would hear the case [996].

992. *Twenty-two Years' Work of the Hampton Normal and Agricultural Institute at Hampton, Virginia: Records of Negro and Indian Graduates*

and Ex-Students. Hampton, Virginia: Normal School Press, 1893. Microfiche Edition, 1987, vol. 265. The Record of Returned Indian Students in this volume profiles eight Pawnees, including James Murie and his younger brother Alfred. Part of James Murie's profile is in his own words. He tells of his life after Hampton—including his plan to study for the ministry and his disappointment when the promise of a job teaching at the Pawnee School never materialized. The Hampton profile mistakenly lists the Murie brothers as full-blood Pawnees.

993. U.S. Congress. House. *Remodeling Pawnee Indian School Plant, Pawnee Okla.* 69th Cong., 1st sess., 1926. H. Rept. 514. [Ser. 8532]. 2 pp. Bill to provide funds to remodel and repair the Pawnee School buildings received the support of the Committee on Indian Affairs. Since the school was considered necessary and the buildings were badly deteriorated, the Interior Secretary also approved the bill, with a slight change in its wording.

994. U.S. Congress. Senate. *Letter from the Secretary of the Interior in Response to Senate Resolution of February 28, 1891, Forwarding Report Made by the Hampton Institute Regarding Its Returned Indian Students.* 52d Cong., 1st sess., 1892. S. Exec. Doc. 31. [Ser. 2892]. 87 pp. Contains a wealth of information. Each student is profiled, and the report includes a fifty-five-page statistical analysis of former students that states each student's school name, Indian name, blood quantum, age, father's name, tribe, agency, date of arrival and departure, reason for departure, marital status, and date of death, if applicable. A second analysis of the same students lists education prior to arriving at Hampton, current occupation, present location, cost per year to educate, and place of "outing(s)" while at Hampton Institute. Of the 639 students listed, only twelve are Pawnees.

995. ———. *Providing for the Remodeling, Repairing, and Improving the Pawnee Indian School Plant, Pawnee, Oklahoma, and Providing an Appropriation Therefor.* 69th Cong., 1st sess., 1926. S. Rept. 176. [Ser. 8524]. 2 pp. The Pawnee School buildings had been allowed to deteriorate, and were badly in need of repair. After slight changes in the wording, it was recommended that an appropriation request for $22,000 be presented to Congress.

996. Zeaman, Janeice. "Long Haired Indians Win." *The Daily Oklahoman,* 2 May 1972, 1, 2. Citing tribal traditions, a U.S. District Judge or-

dered the Pawnee, Oklahoma, school system to reinstate three Indian boys who had been suspended when it was determined that their collar-length hair violated the school dress code. The boys' attorney argued that forcing them to cut their hair would violate their first and fourteenth amendment rights [991].

24

Graves Protection and Repatriation

997. "Assessment of the Cultural Affiliation of the Steed-Kisker Phase for Evaluation by the National Museum of Natural History Native American Repatriation Review Committee." *Smithsonian National Museum of Natural History Repatriation Office.* www.nmnh.si.edu/anthro/repatriation/steedrep.html. Report prepared to comply with the National Museum of the American Indian Act in response to a 1994 request by the Pawnee Tribe of Oklahoma. The original assessment that Indian remains from the Steed-Kisker Site in Missouri could have been associated with any of a number of tribal groups was rejected by the Pawnees, who contended that the evidence indicated that these are the remains of Pawnees, Arikaras, and Wichitas. Upon review, the Repatriation Review Committee recommended that the remains be returned to the Pawnees, with the condition that other interested tribes be given notice of that action. Five tribes eventually agreed to a joint repatriation, which took place in October 1997.

998. Baugh, Timothy G., and Stephanie Makseyn-Kelley. *People of the Stars: Pawnee Heritage and the Smithsonian Institution.* Washington, D.C.: Repatriation Office, National Museum of Natural History, Smithsonian Institution, 1992. 44 pp. In August 1988, Lawrence Goodfox, Jr., of the Oklahoma Pawnees requested an investigation regarding twelve sets of skeletal remains housed either at the National Museum of Natural History or the National Museum of Health and Medicine, formerly the Army Medical Museum. This

excellent report resulted from that investigation. Maps and text provide information on how these remains came to be in Washington.

The researchers concluded that all the remains were Pawnee and that they should be repatriated to the Pawnee tribe.

999. Bieder, Robert. *A Brief Historical Survey of the Expropriation of American Indian Remains.* Boulder, Colorado: Native American Rights Fund, 1990. 73 pp. Traces the history of disinterring Indian remains for scientific and pseudo-scientific purposes. Discusses the grave plundering of anthropologists such as Franz Boas and George A. Dorsey, who provided the Smithsonian, the American Museum of Natural History, and Chicago's Field Museum with a steady supply of Native American skeletons and crania. Military surgeons serving on the Plains also sent skulls of western Indians, including the Pawnees, to the Army Medical Museum. The cover photo of this report is of a skeleton from the Indian "burial pit" near Salina, Kansas, and is possibly the remains of a Pawnee.

1000. ———. "Collecting of Bones for Anthropological Narratives."*American Indian Culture and Research Journal* 16 (1992): 21–35. Traces the history of the practice of procuring skeletons, and especially skulls, for "research." Nineteenth-century grave robbers, respected anthropologists, and army surgeons serving on the frontier all contributed remains for these studies. Although Bieder makes no mention of the Pawnees, they were one of the Plains Indian groups whose remains were displayed and studied at various institutions.

1001. Billeck, William T., et al. *Inventory and Assessment of Human Remains and Associated Funerary Objects Potentially Affiliated with the Pawnee in the National Museum of Natural History.* Case Report No. 88-117. Washington, D.C.: Repatriation Office, National Museum of Natural History, Smithsonian Institution, 1995. 111 pp. Important report done at the request of the Pawnee Tribe of Oklahoma includes historical, archaeological, and ethnographic evidence linking a number of sets of skeletal remains at the National Museum of Natural History to either the Pawnees or the Central Plains Tradition. Each set of remains is carefully described, and its history recorded. Along with these descriptions is a great deal of Pawnee history and pre-history. Based on their data, the writers of this report recommended that twenty-five sets of remains be repatriated to the Pawnees.

1002. Bozell, John R. "Nebraska State Historical Society NAGPRA Implementation." In *Native American Graves Protection and Repatriation Act of 1990 (NAGPRA) Compliance Workshop Proceedings*, edited by Myra J. Giesen, 29–33. Lawrence, Kansas: Haskell Indian Nations University, 1995. Most of the Nebraska State Historical Society's repatriation efforts have involved the Pawnee Tribe. Bozell traces the acrimonious history of LB340, Nebraska's 1989 repatriation act, then explains how this law and NAGPRA have been implemented by the society. Bozell points out that a major stumbling block to complying with NAGPRA is trying to determine the tribal affiliation of curated remains and burial goods. This is an excellent source on the inner workings of an historical society.

1003. Bristow, Edgar T. "Update on Kansas Reburial Legislation." *Native American Rights Fund Legal Review* (Fall 1989): 16–17. Explains the negotiations that resulted in the 1989 "Treaty of Smoky Hill" [1043] that closed the Indian "burial pit" near Salina, Kansas, and provided that Indian remains there be buried with respect *in situ* at state expense. Bristow praises several Kansas groups for their sensitivity and cooperation.

1004. Brower, Montgomery, and Conan Putnam. "Walter Echo-Hawk Fights for His People's Right to Rest in Peace—Not in Museums." *People Weekly* (September 4, 1989): 42–44. Interview with a senior staff attorney for the Native American Rights Fund. Includes Echo-Hawk's opinions on the treatment of Indian remains, and cites as examples the Indian "burial pit" in Salina, Kansas, and the quarrel with the Nebraska State Historical Society over the return of Pawnee remains and artifacts.

1005. Cowley, Geoffrey, et al. "The Plunder of the Past." *Newsweek* (June 26, 1989): 58–60. General article about the traffic in Native American artifacts and the desecration of Indian graves. Presents the argument between advocates of reburial of skeletal remains and those who want to continue to warehouse them for future research. Cites closing of the Salina, Kansas, "burial pit" and Nebraska's 1989 law requiring the State Historical Society to return thousands of remains and grave goods.

1006. Echo-Hawk, Roger C., and Walter R. Echo-Hawk. *Battlefields and Burial Grounds: The Indian Struggle to Protect Ancestral Graves in the United States*. Minneapolis: Lerner Publications Company, 1994.

80 pp. This excellent overview of the entire Indian reburial issue presents a brief history of Indian grave desecrations, but most of the book concentrates on Pawnee burial practices and efforts to reclaim Pawnee skeletons and burial items. Good coverage of the Salina, Kansas, Indian "burial pit," the legacy of amateur archaeologist Asa T. Hill, and the battle with the Nebraska State Historical Society over Pawnee remains. Numerous photographs help tell the story.

1007. Echo-Hawk, Walter R. "Sacred Material and the Law." In *The Concept of Sacred Materials and Their Place in the World*, edited by George P. Horse-Capture, 67–81. Cody, Wyoming: The Plains Indian Museum, Buffalo Bill Historical Center, 1988. Walter Echo-Hawk presented this paper at the annual Plains Indian Seminar in 1985. Though not concerned specifically with the Pawnees, it is included here because of Pawnee attorney Echo-Hawk's importance in the repatriation issue. His paper deals with laws governing various methods of acquiring and accessing Native American remains. Numerous court cases and laws are cited in the notes.

1008. ———. "Tribal Efforts to Protect Against Mistreatment of Indian Dead: The Quest for Equal Protection of the Laws." *Native American Rights Fund Legal Review* 14 (Winter 1989): 1–5. Calls the Kansas Indian "burial pit" offensive, and criticizes the Nebraska State Historical Society's refusal to return Pawnee skeletons and funerary objects. Includes a number of court cases supporting the position of the Native American Rights Fund, and asks for the support of citizens of Kansas and Nebraska.

1009. Echo-Hawk, Walter R., and Roger Echo-Hawk. "Repatriation, Reburial, and Religious Rights." In *Handbook of American Indian Religious Freedom*, edited by Christopher Vecsey, 63–80. New York: Crossroad Publishing Company, 1991. A case study by two prominent Pawnees regarding the disinterment and reburial of Pawnee remains. They argue that the removal of Indian bodies from graves and the keeping of these bodies in museums violates Pawnee religious scruples pertaining to treatment of the dead. They also document the efforts of the Pawnee Tribe of Oklahoma to repatriate and rebury the bones of their ancestors.

1010. Fine-Dare, Kathleen S. *Grave Injustice: The American Indian Repatriation Movement and NAGPRA*. Lincoln: University of Nebraska Press, 2002. 250 pp. The author devotes two pages of her chapter on the 1980s repatriation movement (101–102) to the Pawnee-Nebraska State Historical Society conflict over Indian remains, the passage of Nebraska's Unmarked Burial Sites law (LB 340), and the eventual reburial of Pawnee remains and artifacts in Genoa, Nebraska.

1011. "A Good Wish." In Sharman Apt Russell. *When the Land Was Young: Reflections on American Archaeology.* Lincoln: University of Nebraska Press, 2001. 159–85. Pawnee scholar Roger Echo-Hawk figures prominently in this thought-provoking chapter on the needs of archaeologists versus the beliefs of Native Americans.

1012. Gulliford, Andrew. "Bones of Contention: The Repatriation of Native American Human Remains." *Public Historian* 18 (Fall 1996): 119–43. Also a chapter in Gulliford's *Sacred Objects and Sacred Places* [270]. Traces the history of the misappropriations, grave-robbing, and improper displays associated with Indian human remains. Nearly every example is given; among them is a discussion of the operation and closing of the Salina, Kansas, Indian "burial pit." Also discusses successful efforts to repatriate Indian remains. The one illustration is a reprint of a January 1989 political cartoon from the *Lincoln (Nebraska) Journal* [1135].

1013. Harjo, Suzan Shown. "Free at Last: Spirits of Plains Indians Can Rest after Reburial." *Wichita (Kansas) Eagle*, 8 April 1990, A 12. Written about a week after the Salina, Kansas, "burial pit" was closed, editorial identifies the Indians found there, explains the pit's operation, then describes the solemn ceremony conducted prior to reburying the remains.

1014. Harris, David J. "Respect for the Living and Respect for the Dead: Return of Indian and other Native American Burial Remains." *Washington University Journal of Urban and Contemporary Law* 39 (Spring 1991): 195–224. Presents the controversy between Native Americans and museums and historical societies, with special emphasis on the 1989 *National Museum of the American Indian Act* providing for the establishment of the museum in Washington, D.C. Harris also points out problems with identification of remains and weaknesses in current laws. He suggests that the federal government should use state laws such as Nebraska's 1989 statute as models. Article is heavily footnoted, and by carefully reading the notes, a researcher will find many references to other sources. The Pawnee are specifically mentioned only in the footnotes, but this is an article well worth exploring.

1015. Hicks, Nancy, and Lisa Prue. "For Indians, Bones Are Issue of Rights, Respect." *Omaha World-Herald*, 8 September 1998, 1–2. In September 1998, representatives of at least seventeen Indian tribes met at the University of Nebraska-Lincoln to discuss the return of Indian remains. Pawnee scholar Roger Echo-Hawk is quoted extensively in this nicely written article.

1016. "Indian Burial Pit Near Salina Draws Huge Crowds." *Topeka Capital-Journal*, 7 September 1958. Archaeology in Kansas Clippings, vol. 3, 155–57. Kansas State Historical Society. Reading like a public relations piece, this article mentions the increase in attendance at this popular Kansas "tourist attraction." Rather ethnocentric in tone, it includes a photo of a small boy viewing the Indian remains at the site.

1017. McPhilimy, Glennys. "Time to Close the Burial Pit." *Boulder (Colorado)Daily Camera*, 25 May 1989, A12. Associate editor recalls visiting this roadside attraction near Salina, Kansas, as a child, and is relieved to hear that the state is buying the site so that the human remains there can be properly reburied.

1018. Marsh, Gene A. "Walking the Spirit Trail: Repatriation and Protection of Native American Remains and Sacred Cultural Items." *Arizona State Law Journal* 24 (Spring 1992): 79–133. The first section of this article discusses issues involved with Native American remains; the second explains the 1990 Native American Graves Protection and Repatriation Act and its ramifications; and the third is case studies of laws protecting burial sites in four states. There is, however, no mention of the Pawnees and their battle with the Nebraska State Historical Society over the remains of their ancestors.

1019. Monroe, Dan L., and Walter Echo-Hawk. "Deft Deliberations." *Museum News* (July–August 1991): 55–58. Short history of the deliberations and compromises that led to the 1990 Native American Graves Protection and Repatriation Act (NAGPRA). Lists in clear language the four main provisions of the act. No Indian tribe is specifically mentioned, but Walter Echo-Hawk is a Pawnee, and the terms of the legislation have had a direct impact on the disposition of Pawnee remains.

1020. Otis, George A. *List of the Specimens in the Anatomical Section of the U.S. Army Medical Museum*. Washington, D.C.: Gibson Brothers,

1880. 194 pp. Page 122 lists one Pawnee skeleton that was received in exchange from the Smithsonian Institution and seven Pawnee crania procured for the Army Medical Museum by Army surgeon B. E. Fryer, who was stationed in Kansas. Each entry was assigned an acquisition number, and all measurements were carefully recorded.

1021. "Pawnee Tribe Makes Effort to Rebury Its Dead." *Pawnee (Oklahoma) Chief*, 23 February 1989, 1. Reprints a statement by attorney Walter Echo-Hawk explaining the status of pending legislation in Nebraska and Kansas regarding Pawnee skeletal remains and burial goods. Also announces the proposed "Treaty of Smoky Hill," which would close the Indian "burial pit" near Salina, Kansas.

1022. Preston, D. J. "Skeletons in Our Museums' Closets." *Harper's* 278 (February 1989): 66–75. Discusses the skeletal collections of various important museums and presents both sides of the argument regarding repatriation versus research. The Pawnees are not mentioned specifically, but Walter Echo-Hawk is quoted in the article.

1023. Price, H. Marcus, III. *Disputing the Dead: U.S. Law on Aboriginal Remains and Grave Goods*. Columbia: University of Missouri Press, 1991. 136 pp. Although it does not directly mention the Pawnees, this is an excellent general overview of legislation at both the federal and state level regarding treatment of Indian remains and artifacts and their repatriation. The book is divided into two parts: the first deals with general law; and the second discusses, in alphabetical order, state laws treating these issues. The Nebraska, Kansas, and Oklahoma entries would be of special interest to those researching the Pawnees.

1024. Quade, Vicki. "Who Owns the Past? How Native American Indian Lawyers Fight for Their Ancestors' Remains and Memories: *Human Rights* interview with Walter Echo-Hawk." *Human Rights* 16 (Winter 1989–90): 24–29, 53–55. Native American Rights Fund staff attorney Walter Echo-Hawk explains his mostly pro-bono work on behalf of Native Americans, especially a group in Alaska and his own Pawnee people. He also expresses his views on repatriation and reburial of Indian skeletal remains in the possession of the Nebraska State Historical Society, the Indian "burial pit" in Salina, Kansas, and the Pawnee crania held by the Smithsonian Institution. This interview was conducted shortly after the passage of Nebraska's landmark repatriation and reburial law (LB 340), but before Pawnee remains and artifacts were actually returned to his people, and at about the same time the State of Kansas closed down the roadside attraction near Salina.

1025. Riding In, James T. "Murder, Justifiable Homicide, or Head Hunting? The Killing and Decapitation of Former Pawnee Scouts by U.S. Soldiers and Citizens." 1989. 36 pp. A draft copy of this manuscript is on file at the Indian Law Library, Native American Rights Fund, Boulder, Colorado. Excellent article delves deeply into the prevailing nineteenth-century attitude toward Indians in the United States in general, and in the State of Kansas in particular, that allowed these Pawnee Scouts to be murdered and decapitated and their killers and mutilators to go unpunished. Should be read in conjunction with Riding In's "Report Verifying the Identity of Six Pawnee Scout Crania at the Smithsonian Institutions and the National Museum of Health and Medicine" [1029].

1026. ———. "Our Dead Are Never Forgotten: American Indian Struggles for Burial Rights and Protections." In *They Made Us Many Promises: The American Indian Experience 1524 to the Present.* 2d ed., edited by Philip Weeks, 291–323. Wheeling, Illinois: Harlan Davidson, Inc., 2002. From Thomas Jefferson to the present, this outstanding chapter traces the history of disrespect for buried Indians. All of the incidents involving Pawnee remains are discussed: the murder and decapitation of discharged Pawnee Scouts; the Salina, Kansas, "burial pit"; controversies with institutions in Nebraska; and even the fate of a Pawnee who died in Sweden.

1027. ———. "Pawnee Repatriation Initiatives." In *Native American Graves Protection and Repatriation Act of 1990 (NAGPRA) Compliance Workshop Proceedings,* edited by Myra J. Giesen, 49–52. Lawrence, Kansas: Haskell Indian Nations University, 1995. Pawnee scholar Riding In represented his people at this workshop, and his paper traces the history of desecration of Pawnee burial sites and disrespect for the Pawnee dead. Three major points presented are: the Pawnees' removal from Nebraska to Indian Territory in the 1870s made it impossible for the people to protect their Nebraska cemeteries, leaving them vulnerable to looters; the states of Kansas and Nebraska reacted differently to Pawnee repatriation requests, with Kansas cooperating and Nebraska fighting repatriation; and lack of funds has made it difficult for the Pawnees to finance repatriation efforts.

1028. ——. "Repatriation: A Pawnee's Perspective." *American Indian Quarterly* 20 (Spring 1996): 238–50. Pawnee activist explains his reasons for supporting repatriation of Native American remains and briefly traces the history of the repatriation movement and opposition to it. This essay also appears in Devon A. Mihesuah, ed. *Repatriation Reader: Who Owns American Indian Remains?* Lincoln: University of Nebraska Press, 2000, 106–120.

1029. ——. "Report Verifying the Identity of Six Pawnee Scout Crania at the Smithsonian Institution and the National Museum of Health and Medicine." Boulder, Colorado: Native American Rights Fund, 1990. 16 pp. Following a brief history of the Pawnee Scouts, this investigative report describes the events near Mulberry Creek in Kansas that resulted in the killing and decapitation of six former scouts by soldiers of the U.S. Army. Using primary sources, Riding In presents all sides of the story. Included are military records showing where each decapitation occurred and the accession numbers used by the Army Medical Museum and the National Museum of Natural History to identify the six crania. Report leaves no doubt that these crania are Pawnee and that they were collected by an army surgeon.

1030. ——. "Six Pawnee Crania: Historical and Contemporary Issues Associated with the Massacre and Decapitation of Pawnee Indians in 1869." *American Indian Culture and Research Journal* 16, no. 2 (1992): 101–19. Riding In relates the sordid story of former Pawnee Scouts who were massacred by U.S. soldiers, then decapitated and their skulls sent to the Army Medical Museum in Washington. Riding In follows the acquisition trail of the skulls from the Army Medical Museum to the National Museum of Natural History and even provides the acquisition number for each skull. In 1990, Riding In prepared a report for the Native American Rights Fund verifying the identities of the six Pawnee Scout crania [1029]. When this article was written, the skulls had not yet been returned to the Pawnee people, but they were repatriated in 1995 [1040].

1031. ——. "Without Ethics and Morality: A Historical Review of Imperial Archaeology and American Indians." *Arizona State Law Journal* 24 (Spring 1992): 11–34. Beginning with Thomas Jefferson and including phrenologists, scholars, and the military, Riding In follows the trail of grave desecration in the United States, then briefly addresses Indian efforts to protect their burial sites. Although much of the abuse of Indian dead ended with the passage of the Native American Graves

Protection and Repatriation Act, he states that more needs to be done. There are scattered references to the Pawnees throughout the article.

1032. Roper, Donna C. "A Culture-History of the Pawnee." Draft Report Prepared for the Repatriation Office, National Museum of Natural History, Smithsonian Institution, 1993.

1033. ———. "Historical Processes and the Development of Social Identity: An Evaluation of Pawnee Ancestry." Washington, D.C.: Report Submitted to the Repatriation Office, National Museum of Natural History, Smithsonian Institution, 1993.

1034. Schniedeler, John. "Salina Indian Artifacts Find Haven Back 'Home.'" *Salina (Kansas) Journal*, 26 September 1971. Archaeology Department Clippings File, vol. 1, 1966–1981, 30–31. Kansas State Historical Society. The original developers of the Salina, Kansas, "burial pit" decided to turn their collection of Indian artifacts over to the Kansas State Historical Society. They transported them from Everett, Washington, in a camper.

1035. *Science or Sacrilege: Native Americans, Archaeology, and the Law*. Berkeley: University of California Extension Center for Media and Independent Learning, n.d. (appr. 56 minutes). This film presents both sides of the controversy over the 1990 Native American Graves Protection and Repatriation Act (NAGPRA), in which prominent Pawnees played important roles.

1036. "Study at Indian Burial Pit." *Kansas State Historical Society Mirror* 36 (April 1990): 2. Explains the difficulties encountered by archaeologists when they tried to conduct an in-depth study of the remains at the Salina, Kansas, "burial pit." Now a National Historic Landmark, the site remains under state ownership, but is closed to the public.

1037. Svingen, Orlan J. *History of the Expropriation of Pawnee Indian Graves in the Control of the Nebraska State Historical Society*. Boulder, Colorado: Native American Rights Fund, 1989. 41 pp. This is Dr. Svingen's written testimony in support of LB340, Nebraska's repatriation law, which was passed in 1989. His testimony follows the history of the removal of bodies and grave goods from Pawnee cemeteries and explains how the Nebraska State Historical Society came to possess many of these remains. Thwarted for months by the Historical Society's refusal to allow access to records, Svingen finally gained access to the materials he needed after Nebraska's attorney general ordered the society to turn them over. Also included with the testimony are a number of photographs of Pawnee burial sites and human remains being treated with disrespect.

1038. ———. "The Pawnees of Nebraska: Twice Removed." *American Indian Culture and Research Journal* 16, no. 2 (1992): 121–37. The title refers to the removal of the Pawnees to Oklahoma in the 1870s and the desecration of the graves they left behind in Nebraska. Svingen explores the possible reasons for the Pawnee departure from Nebraska, then discusses the history of "grave robbing" in their former home. Asa T. Hill's desecration of the Pike-Pawnee Village near Red Cloud, Nebraska, receives considerable attention, as does the destruction of Pawnee grave sites near Genoa, site of the tribe's Nebraska reservation.

1039. Thomas, David Hurst. *Skull Wars: Kenewick Man, Archaeology, and the Battle for Native American Identity.* New York: Basic Books, 2000. 326 pp. Beautifully written and thought-provoking work on the battle between Native Americans and archaeologists for the control of Indian remains. The Pawnees are mentioned only once, but this brief section (57–58) discusses the Kansas murders and later decapitations of six Pawnees, whose skulls became part of a shipment of twenty-six Indian skulls sent to the Army Medical Museum for study.

1040. Thornton, Russell. "Who Owns Our Past? The Repatriation of Native American Human Remains and Cultural Objects." In *Native American Voices*, edited by Susan Lobo and Steve Talbot, 303–17. Upper Saddle River, New Jersey: Prentice Hall, 2001. The final pages of this superb essay give a moving account of the repatriation and burial of the crania of the six Pawnee Scouts believed to have been murdered and decapitated in Kansas. Includes the 1995 repatriation ceremony in Washington, D.C., and Senator John McCain's apology to the Pawnees.The Scouts' skulls were buried in Genoa, Nebraska, with other recently repatriated Pawnee remains.

1041. Thornton, Russell, et al. "Recommendations Regarding the Dispute between the Pawnee Tribe of Oklahoma and the National Museum of Natural History Repatriation Office over the Steed-Kisker Phase Human Remains and Funerary Objects." Washington, D.C.: Submitted to Secretary I. Michael Heyman, Smithsonian Institution, 1995. For an assessment of the cultural affiliation of these remains, see [997].

1042. Tomsho, Robert. "Indian Burial Site Becomes Big Issue in Little Salina, Kansas." *Wall Street Journal*, 17 May 1989, A1, 9. Focuses on the Kansas Indian "burial pit" and the controversy surrounding it. Highlights Indian objections to this roadside attraction.

1043. "Treaty of Smoky Hill." February 1989. 5 pp. This is the agreement among landowners, next of kin, local government, and preservation agencies providing for the sale of the land near Salina, Kansas, containing the Indian "burial pit," and for the proper reburial of Indian remains that had been displayed there. A final draft copy of this document, written by Walter R. Echo-Hawk of the Native American Rights Fund, is on file at the Kansas State Historical Society in Topeka. Photocopies are available upon request.

1043a. "Tribes Reclaim, Bury Remains." *Lincoln Journal Star*, 23 August, 2003, 2B. On August 19, 2003, representatives of the Ponca Tribe of Oklahoma and the Pawnee Nation accompanied the skeletal remains of nearly 600 of their ancestors for reburial in a Ponca cemetery along the Niobrara River in northern Nebraska. The remains were reclaimed from the University of Nebraska-Lincoln.

1044. Trope, Jack F., and Walter Echo-Hawk. "The Native American Graves Protection and Repatriation Act: Background and Legislative History." *Arizona State Law Review* 24 (Spring 1992): 35–77. Covers every aspect of NAGPRA: the origins of the repatriation movement, early failures of the legal system to protect Indian burial sites, and both state and federal legislation prior to NAGPRA. The second part covers the act itself—its passage, its terms, its limitations, and its enforcement. The controversy surrounding the passage of Nebraska's Graves Protection Act is discussed, and there are scattered references to the Pawnees throughout the article. This article can also be found in Devon A. Mihesuah, ed. *Repatriation Reader: Who Owns American Indian Remains?* Lincoln: University of Nebraska Press, 2000, 123–68.

1045. U.S. Congress. House. *Establishment of the National Museum of the American Indian: Joint Hearings Before the Committee on Interior and Insular Affairs, House of Representatives and the Subcommittee on Libraries and Memorials*. 101st Cong., 1st sess., 1989. H. Rept. 2668. Washington, D.C.: Government Printing Office, 1992. Includes thirty-one pages of testimony by Pawnee attorney Walter R. Echo-Hawk, of the Native American Rights Fund. Echo-Hawk speaks generally in favor of establishing the National Museum of the American Indian, but he has concerns regarding Native American rights and the treatment of Indian skeletons and burial goods.

1046. "Who Owns the Past? The American Indian Struggle for Control of Their Ancestral Remains." Produced and directed by N. Jed Riffe, 2000. This film, which aired on PBS in the fall of 2001, traces the history of mistreatment of Native American skeletal remains from the time of the Pilgrims to the 1990s. The Pawnees figure prominently in this story. The murders of discharged Pawnee Scouts in 1869 are discussed, along with the Indian "burial pit" in Salina, Kansas. Walter Echo-Hawk recounts the Pawnee struggle to force the Nebraska State Historical Society to turn over to the tribe its collection of Pawnee remains, and Blackfeet filmmaker George Burdeau covers the repatriation and reburial of the skulls of the murdered Pawnee Scouts. A complete transcript of the contents of this film is available on the PBS web site.

1047. Witty, Thomas A. "New Law to Protect Unmarked Burial Sites in Kansas." *Kansas Preservation* 11, no. 6 (1989): 3. Report on the history and terms of the Kansas Unmarked Burial Sites Preservation Act, passed in 1989. The act was prompted in part by outrage over the Indian "burial pit" near Salina. As a result of the act, the burial pit was purchased by the state, filled in, and sealed with a concrete cap.

1048. Zontek, Terry A. "Compliance with the Native American Graves Protection and Repatriation Act by the Great Plains Region of the Bureau of Reclamation." In *Native American Graves Protection and Repatriation Act of 1990 (NAGPRA) Compliance Workshop Proceedings,* edited by Myra J. Giesen, 57–65. Lawrence, Kansas: Haskell Indian Nations University, 1995. Since the passage of NAGPRA, the Bureau of Reclamation has tried hard to comply with the 1990 law, and between 1990 and 1995, there was only one case of intentional disturbing of Indian remains in the Great Plains Region. In 1992, the Palmer Site, a national Historic Landmark in Nebraska, was excavated during the construction of the North Loup Project. This Skidi Pawnee village had great historical significance, since it was probably where Petalesharo rescued a Comanche girl during a Morning Star ceremony. The Bureau disturbed as little of the Palmer Site cemetery as possible, and the one body that was disinterred was reburied close to its original burial site, following guidelines determined in consultation with the Pawnee Tribe. The new grave was sealed with a cement cap and continues to be monitored and protected.

25
Nebraska Legislative Bills (LB) 612 and 340

In the late 1980s, two bills regarding the return of Pawnee (and other tribes') skeletal remains and grave goods in the possession of the Nebraska State Historical Society came before the Nebraska State Legislature. Legislative Bill (LB) 612 did not pass, but LB 340 (Nebraska Unmarked Human Burial Sites and Skeletal Remains Protection Act), introduced by State Senator Ernie Chambers of Omaha on January 11, 1989, became law in May of that year. The controversy between the Pawnees and the leadership of the Nebraska State Historical Society before and after the passage of this bill was eagerly followed and thoroughly reported by Lincoln and Omaha newspapers. This chapter begins with a number of fine general articles on Nebraska's precedent-setting law, most of which were written by Robert Peregoy, a senior staff attorney for the Native American Rights Fund (NARF), who represented the Pawnee Tribe of Oklahoma. These entries are followed by newspaper articles on the failed LB 612 and the successful LB 340. Lincoln and Omaha newspapers' reports are listed separately and are in *chronological order* to aid researchers. Most have page numbers, but in the case of the *Omaha World-Herald*, no distinction is made between morning and evening editions.

1049. Cunningham, Jim. "Indian Remains Question One of Dignity, Not Historical Curiosity." *The Catholic Voice*, 16 December 1988. Presents the Nebraska Catholic Conference's stand on the Pawnee repatriation issue, and gives reasons why Catholics in Nebraska should

support the Pawnees' effort to have their skeletal remains and artifacts returned.

1050. Fell, Paul. "More 'Whispers from the Prairie'." Political Cartoon,
Lincoln Journal-Star, 24 January 1989. Pictures an Indian scaffold
burial and the words "Let my ancestors go," a reference to the Nebraska controversy over Pawnee remains.

1051. Peregoy, Robert M. "The Legal Basis, Legislative History, and
Implementation of Nebraska's Landmark Reburial Legislation."
Arizona State Law Journal 24 (1992): 329–89. Using government
and Nebraska State Historical Society (NSHS) documents,
testimony, Nebraska state laws, and newspaper reports, Peregoy
has written perhaps the most complete history of the bitter fight
between the Pawnees and the NSHS over the fate of Pawnee
remains and burial goods in the possession of the Historical
Society.

1052. ———. "Nebraska Lawmakers Enact Precedent-Setting Indian Burial Legislation." *Native American Rights Fund Legal Review* (Fall
1989): 15. Brief but informative acknowledgment of the passage of
Nebraska Legislative Bill (LB) 340, written by one of the attorneys
deeply involved in the issue. Traces the controversy over the reburial bill, criticizes those who had opposed it, and briefly states the
provisions of the new law.

1053. ———. "Nebraska's Landmark Repatriation law: A Study of Cross-
Cultural Conflict and Resolution." *American Indian Culture and Research Journal* 16, no. 2 (1992): 139–95. In 1989, the State of Nebraska enacted the Unmarked Human Burial Sites and Skeletal
Remains Protection Act, the nation's first repatriation statute, but the
period preceding its passage was a time of bitter acrimony between
the Pawnee Tribe of Oklahoma and the NSHS, which held thousands
of Pawnee skeletons and grave goods. Peregoy's article covers the
entire law-making process, from the conflicting interests of the
Pawnees and the Historical Society, to the floor fights in the Nebraska Unicameral, to the final passage and implementation of the
new law. This is one of the finest articles available on this
groundbreaking legislation, and it should be utilized by any researcher of modern Pawnee history, culture, and legal issues.

NEBRASKA LEGISLATIVE BILL (LB) 612

Lincoln Newspapers (Arranged Chronologically)

1054. Schmidt, J. L. "Opponents of Grave-Protection Bill Labeled Hysterical By Its Supporters." *Lincoln Journal-Star*, 15 February 1988, 6. An early argument over the graves protection issue in Nebraska. University of Nebraska anthropology professor Roger Welsch, State Senator Ernie Chambers, and others who supported Nebraska LB 612, which did not pass, believed that opponents, especially State Historical Society Director James Hanson, were overreacting to this bill that would mandate reburial of Indian skeletons and grave goods, many of which were Pawnee.

1055. Reist, Margaret. "Tribal Chairman Requests Return of Skeletal Remains." *Lincoln Journal-Star*, 25 June 1988, 5. In a statement to the Executive Board of the NSHS, Pawnee tribal chairman Lawrence Goodfox requested that all Pawnee remains being held by the Society be returned for reburial. The Board denied Goodfox's request, and attorney Robert Peregoy threatened to sue the society if the remains were not returned voluntarily.

1056. Schwartzlander, David. "Historical Society Head Labeled Racist." *Lincoln Journal-Star*, 5 October 1988, 16. As part of the verbal battle between Native Americans and the NSHS over the return of Pawnee remains, Reba White Shirt, Executive Director of the Nebraska Indian Commission, called Historical Society Director James Hanson an "institutional racist" because he loaned Pawnee remains to the Smithsonian Institution but would not allow the Indians themselves to do research on the skeletons.

1057. ———. "Indian Leaders Get Access to Records." *Lincoln Journal-Star*, 7 October 1988, 11. An opinion issued by the Nebraska attorney general's office stated that attorneys for the Pawnees could see NSHS accession records, but agreed to protect the confidentiality of artifact donors and the exact locations of archaeological sites.

1058. Laukaitis, Al J. "Decision Delayed on Indian Remains." *Lincoln Journal-Star*, 9 October 1988. 1B, 5B. Excellent piece presenting both sides of the Pawnee reburial issue. Historical Society Board member

Roger Welsch, attorney Walter Echo-Hawk, Nebraska Indian Commission leader Reba White Shirt, Society Director James Hanson, and two Smithsonian anthropologists are quoted in the article.

1059. "Burden on Historical Society in Keeping Pawnee Remains." *Lincoln Journal-Star,* 18 October 1988, 10. Editorial stating that unless there are compelling reasons not to, the NSHS should return Pawnee skeletons and burial goods to the tribe.

1060. Hanson, James A. "Letter to the Editor." *Lincoln Journal-Star,* 22 October 1988, 10. In this angry rebuttal to the *Journal-Star's* editorial of October 18, 1988, Hanson called the newspaper editor dead wrong, and argued that the Pawnee remains and artifacts are invaluable research tools. He also questioned the role of Colorado lawyers (referring to the NARF, based in Boulder) in "stripping" millions of dollars worth of artifacts from Nebraska.

1061. Schwartzlander, David. "Rule Cited in Reburial Case Doesn't Exist." *Lincoln Journal-Star,* 26 October 1988, 22. Attorneys for the Pawnees argued that a law forbidding the repatriation of Indian skeletons and burial goods excavated with federal funds was merely suggested and was never enacted. NSHS Director James Hanson had cited this law in his arguments against returning Pawnee bodies and artifacts.

1062. "Indian Rights Group Hires Prominent Local Lobbyists." *Lincoln Journal-Star,* 16 November 1988, 31. NARF attorney Robert Peregoy defends the decision to hire lobbyists to persuade the Nebraska Unicameral to pass legislation requiring the return of Indian burial goods. Other museums in Nebraska also held Indian artifacts, and Peregoy argued that the Historical Society could not make law for the entire state.

1063. Schwartzlander, David. "Spire Says Compromise Best Solution for Remains." *Lincoln Journal-Star,* 14 December 1988, 4. In an eleven-page opinion, Nebraska Attorney General Robert Spire suggested that Pawnee burial goods and skeletons held by the NSHS be returned to the tribe, but only after "legitimate research" was completed — possibly in three years.

1064. ———. "Pawnee Remains Motion Approved." *Lincoln Journal-Star,* 17 December 1988, 1, 7. The NSHS Board approved by a vote of 10-1 a proposal to return artifacts to the Pawnees, but set conditions on the return that had previously been rejected by the tribe.

1065. ———. "Board Approves Plan for Remains." *Lincoln Journal-Star*, 18 December 1988, 1C. Pawnee attorney Walter Echo-Hawk expressed disappointment in the decision by the NSHS board to return only skeletal remains to the Pawnees and in its placing of unacceptable conditions on those returns. The idea of storing the remains in a waterproof vault, as required by the Society, conflicts with Pawnee religious beliefs and burial practices.

1066. "Indian Position Ignored." *Lincoln Journal-Star*, 20 December 1988, 10. Editorial criticizing the NSHS for its decision to return some Pawnee remains under conditions unacceptable to the Indians.

1067. "Board Member: Historical Society Should Be a Regular State Agency." *Lincoln Journal-Star*, 26 December 1988, 11. Roger Welsch, a strong advocate of returning all Pawnee remains and burial goods to the tribe, recommended that the NSHS should become part of state government and that, in the future, the Society's director should be appointed by the governor.

1068. Schwartzlander, David. "Society Asked to Reconsider Action on Remains." *Lincoln Journal-Star*, 5 January 1989, 6. Based on a letter from the Bureau of Indian Affairs disclaiming any interest in the Pawnee remains and grave goods held by the NSHS, attorneys for the Pawnees urged the Society to reconsider their decision putting strict conditions on any repatriated items.

Omaha Newspapers (Arranged Chronologically)

1069. Thomas, Fred. "Hanson Blasts Bill on Indian Burial Sites." *Omaha World-Herald*, 10 February 1988, 1. NSHS Director James Hanson listed the reasons why LB 612 should not be passed. Hanson pointed out that the bill would require the Society to give up silver medals brought to Nebraska by Lewis and Clark because they were found with a burial.

1070. ———. "Society Head's Opposition to Bill Called Proper." *Omaha World-Herald*, 9 March 1988, 35. The chairman of the Executive Board of the NSHS stated it was within James Hanson's discretion to oppose LB 612. State Senator Ernie Chambers, sponsor of the bill, assured Hanson that the original version would be heavily amended.

1071. ———. "Indian Tribes Request Remains for Reburial." *Omaha World-Herald*, 26 March 1988, 53. Through their attorney, three Indian tribes—the Pawnees, Omahas, and Winnebagoes—formally requested the return of Indian skeletal remains in the hands of the NSHS, which were, at that time, on loan to the Smithsonian Institution. Of the 500 skeletons involved, about 100 were Pawnee.

1072. ———. "Tribes Threaten to Sue to Get Skeletal Remains." *Omaha World-Herald*, 25 June 1988, 15, 17. Excellent article on the meeting between Indian representatives and the Executive Board of the NSHS, held at Fort Robinson, Nebraska. At this meeting, the board ruled against the return of Pawnee and other Indian remains, and was then threatened with a lawsuit.

1073. "Anthropologist Blasts Skeleton Reburial Plan." *Omaha World-Herald*, 25 June 1988, 17. Because of their research value, a University of Wyoming anthropologist urged the NSHS not to give up its collection of human skeletal remains. He states that in Wyoming, Native American students actually do research on skeletons of their people.

1074. Thomas, Fred. "Dispute on Indian Remains May Flare." *Omaha World-Herald*, 3 October 1988, 13. The attorney representing the Pawnees planned to make one last presentation to the NSHS Executive Board before filing a lawsuit to force the return of Pawnee remains. The Society allegedly unearthed a federal law prohibiting it from turning over artifacts excavated with federal funds.

1075. "Indians Given Access to Papers on Remains." *Omaha World-Herald*, 7 October 1988. After months of wrangling between the NSHS and the Pawnee tribe, Nebraska's attorney general ruled that the Indians may have access to some Society records on human skeletal remains. The Historical Society director claimed the ruling as a victory as well, since it provided confidentiality of grave sites, donors, and scientific research.

1076. Thomas, Fred. "Tribe's Plea for Remains Put on Hold by Society." *Omaha World-Herald*, 17 October 1988, 1, 13. Outstanding article explaining the arguments for and against returning both skeletal remains and burial goods to the Pawnees. Although a motion was made to return the remains and goods, it died for lack of a second. Thomas identifies the persons on both sides of the issue and gives the reasons for their opinions.

1077. ———. "Hanson: Indians Seek Precedent on Remains." *Omaha World-Herald*, 20 October 1988, 7. The NSHS board accused the Pawnees and their attorneys of trying to force Nebraska to give up existing collections—an act not required by law in any other state.

1078. ———. "Indians Hire Lobbyists in Bid for Items." *Omaha World-Herald*, 16 November 1988, 22. NSHS Director James Hanson blasted NARF attorneys for hiring Nebraska lobbyists to plead the Pawnees' case with the state legislature, calling it an act of desperation.

1079. "Talks Canceled: Pawnees Upset." *Omaha World-Herald*, 20 November 1988, 4B. Citing bad weather in western Nebraska, the NSHS Board canceled its November 18 meeting during which a vote was scheduled on the Pawnee remains, angering attorneys for the Pawnee Tribe.

1080. "Pawnee Tribe Rejects Plan." *Omaha World-Herald*, 6 December 1988, 33. A compromise proposal by NSHS Board member Frederick Luebke to return only Pawnee skeletal remains at this time was rejected by tribal attorneys, who saw skeletal remains and burial goods as a unit, to be returned together.

1081. Thomas, Fred. "Date Set for Meeting on Remains Criticized." *Omaha World-Herald*, 6 December 1988, 33. NSHS Board member Roger Welsch, a strong supporter of the repatriation of Pawnee remains and grave goods, harshly criticized Director James Hanson for scheduling a special Board meeting on the remains issue at a time when Welsch could not attend. Attorneys for the Pawnees stated that holding the meeting without Welsch's input would be unfair to the tribe.

1082. ———. "Historical Society Chief Answers Barb." *Omaha World-Herald*, 8 December 1988, 18. In his rebuttal to criticism over a scheduled meeting time, NSHS Director James Hanson replied that Board member Roger Welsch knew that the society's board president, not the director, sets meeting dates. Hanson also argued that he, like Welsch, is an Indian expert.

1083. ———. "Sides Prepare Burial-Goods Arguments." *Omaha World-Herald*, 13 December 1988, 16. NSHS Director James Hanson and NARF attorney Robert Peregoy continued their verbal sparring prior to the rescheduled Society meeting to vote on the return of Pawnee skeletons and grave goods. Among other things, Hanson wanted to know who was paying the Rights Fund attorneys, since the Pawnee Tribe could not afford their fees.

1084. ———. "Historical Board Members Exchange Verbal Volleys." *Omaha World-Herald*, 25 December 1988, 9B. Members of the NSHS Board resorted to insults and name-calling in a heated discussion over the repatriation of Pawnee skeletal remains and artifacts.

1085. ———. "Tribal Lawyer Wants New Vote by Society on Indian Remains." *Omaha World-Herald*, 6 January 1989. Citing the reason that Pawnee remains and grave goods had been excavated using federal funds and were therefore the property of the government, the NSHS Board voted to give up only part of their Pawnee collection. Tribal attorney Walter Echo-Hawk received a letter from the Bureau of Indian Affairs waiving any federal interest in the Pawnee remains. Based on this information, Echo-Hawk wanted a new vote.

1086. ———. "Tribal Lawyer Criticizes Board President." *Omaha World-Herald*, 11 January 1989, 27. In another war of words, an attorney for the Pawnees criticized the president of the NSHS Board, and questioned whether the repatriation controversy could be ended under the board's present leadership.

NEBRASKA LEGISLATIVE BILL (LB) 340

Lincoln Newspapers (Arranged Chronologically)

1087. "Historical Society Chief Backs Bill to Return Indian Remains." *Lincoln Star*, 31 January 1989, 16. After receiving a letter from the widow of a Pawnee tribal leader, NSHS Director James Hanson tentatively agreed to support Nebraska LB 340, a second repatriation measure sponsored by State Senator Ernie Chambers of Omaha. However, Hanson had reservations about the bill, and wanted assurances that certain agreements would be worked out.

1088. Knapp, Fred. "Historical Director Now Backs Remains Bill." *Lincoln Journal*, 31 January 1989, 1, 12. Announces that NSHS Director James Hanson will support LB 340 if some questions are addressed. Representatives of the Pawnee Tribe also expressed a willingness to compromise on some issues.

1089. Stoddard, Martha. "Historical Society Board Backs LB 340 if Amended." *Lincoln Journal*, 4 February 1989, 1, 9. By a vote of five to three, the Executive Board of the NSHS agreed to support LB 340 if it was amended to address the concerns of the Society. This vote allowed the bill to advance to the floor of the legislature for debate.

1090. Howard, Ed, and J. L. Schmidt. "Hanson 'Reneged' on Remains Bill." *Lincoln Journal*, 7 February 1989, 3. In an apparent about-face, the NSHS director withdrew his support for LB 340, causing the bill's sponsor and its chief legislative supporter to question his motives and his integrity.

1091. "Hanson Says He Didn't Break Promise." *Lincoln Journal-Star*, 8 February 1989, 39. The NSHS director claimed that in withdrawing his support for LB 340, he was simply following the wishes of the Society's Executive Board.

1092. "Medals Stirring Dispute About Skeletal Remains." *Lincoln Journal*, 11 February 1989, 7. A group calling itself "Citizens to Save Nebraska's History" expressed concern that a Spanish medal and a medal brought to Nebraska by Lewis and Clark could possibly be reburied under the terms of LB 340.

1093. Knapp, Fred. "Indian Skeletal Remains Bill Is Advanced 25-7." *Lincoln Journal*, 1 March 1989, 1. The Nebraska Legislature gave first-round approval to LB 340 after amendments regarding burial goods were defeated. Included at the end of the article is the legislative vote on the bill.

1094. "Niobrara Man Links Firing, Opposition to Burial Bill." *Lincoln Journal*, 1 March 1989, 18. A teacher at the Nebraska Indian Community College claimed that he lost his job because he criticized the wording of LB 340 and allowed his name to be used on mailings sent by an organization opposed to the bill.

1095. "Pawnee Tribe, Society Agree to Compromise." *Lincoln Journal*, 14 March 1989, 15. Additional talks between the Pawnees and NSHS representatives produced three amendments to LB 340 to tighten its language and change certain deadlines and rules regarding public display of human skeletal remains.

1096. Schmidt, J. L. "Remains Debate Draws Students from Oklahoma." *Lincoln Journal*, 17 March 1989, 21. Two Indian students from Pawnee (Oklahoma) High School attended the Nebraska Legislature's round two debate on LB 340. According to the students, they were not treated well by Historical Society officials.

1097. Knapp, Fred. "Legislature Continues LB 340 Debate Regarding Return of Indian Remains." *Lincoln Journal*, 24 March 1989, 4. Members of the Nebraska Unicameral spent several hours debating amendments to LB 340, but recessed for the weekend without voting on the bill.

1098. ———. "Spire Says Burial Law Could Show Leadership." *Lincoln Journal*, 27 March 1989, 11. Nebraska's attorney general urged the legislature to pass LB 340, stating that such passage would make Nebraska the national leader on the "issue of human dignity."

1099. ———. "Advance of Bones Bill 'Frees Captive Spirits'." *Lincoln Journal*, 28 March 1989, 1, 3. After its second-round debate, the Nebraska Legislature voted 28-12 to advance LB 340, which required three approvals before going to the Governor Kay Orr for her signature. Before the vote, three amendments were approved. The voting breakdown appears at the end of the article.

1100. "Indian Remains Bill Signed into Law." *Lincoln Journal*, 24 May 1989, 14. A brief announcement that Nebraska Governor Kay Orr had signed LB 340 into law. As approved, the law allowed the NSHS to keep Pawnee remains until September 1990 in order to complete studies.

1101. "Tribe Lawyer Says Hanson Denying Access to Records." *Lincoln Journal-Star*, 16 June 1989, 9. Robert Peregoy, attorney for the Pawnees, accused the NSHS director of defying an order by the Nebraska attorney general requiring the Society to make acquisition records available to Indian tribes so they could identify human remains.

1102. Knapp, Fred. "Historical Society Staff Is Too Busy to Furnish Records, Hanson Says." *Lincoln Journal*, 17 June 1989, 17. NSHS Director James Hanson informed lawyers for the Pawnees that summer field work would prevent Society staff from pulling requested records. Attorney General Robert Spire reminded Hanson that the records were public and should be made available.

1103. Reeves, Bob. "Board Makes Records Available to Indians." *Lincoln Star*, 24 June 1989, 1, 12. The NSHS Board agreed to provide NARF attorneys with records of Pawnee remains and burial goods, but Robert Peregoy, Rights Fund representative, argued that the records of only 300 bodies were opened, less than one-third of the Pawnee skeletons in the Society's collections.

1104. Wayman, Mary Kay. "Historical Board Tells Hanson to Cooperate with Indian Group." *Lincoln Journal*, 24 June 1989, 3. The Board directed James Hanson to provide museum records to the Pawnees, but only under the supervision of professional staff, and only with specific written requests. Attorneys for the Pawnees had continually argued that they could not make specific requests, since they did not have access to an index.

1105. Schwartzlander, David. "Hanson Criticizes State on Indian Remains Issue." *Lincoln Journal-Star*, 24 September 1989, 1A, 5A. James Hanson accused the Nebraska Legislature of catering to Indian religious beliefs, and the NSHS Board voted to hire lobbyists to strengthen its position with state senators.

1106. Reeves, Robert. "Indians Say Director Won't Cooperate." *Lincoln Star*, 5 January 1990, 4. James Hanson's NSHS staff was limiting its research to "historical Pawnee" skeletons and artifacts, while Pawnee leaders wanted all "reasonably identifiable" remains returned, regardless of age. Hanson asked the legislature for more funds to hire additional staff.

1107. "2 Senators Seek to Undo Remains Law." *Lincoln Journal*, 11 January 1990, 17. State Senator Dennis Baack, a strong supporter of LB 340 and a key legislator involved in its passage, vowed to vigorously oppose LB 1097, a bill that would undo LB 340, passed in 1989.

1108. Howard, Ed. "Spire Disappointed by Lawsuit." *Lincoln Journal*, 24 January 1990, 27. Nebraska Attorney General Robert Spire expressed his displeasure with a lawsuit filed by the NSHS to deny attorneys for the Pawnees access to society records that Spire had earlier ruled to be public. Spire also questioned the Society Board's secrecy in filing the lawsuit.

1109. "Spire Says Historical Society Stalling on Indian Burial Items." *Lincoln Journal*, 25 January 1990, 11. In response to a delaying lawsuit filed by the NSHS, the angry attorney general urged the Society to stop stalling and to comply with the terms of LB 340 immediately.

1110. "Spire Taking Remains Issue to Court." *Lincoln Journal*, 27 January 1990, 4. The Nebraska attorney general promised that he would take action within ten days to force the State Historical Society to make its records available to the Pawnee tribe of Oklahoma.

1111. "Spire Action Directed at Historical Society." *Lincoln Journal*, 2 February 1990, 11. A Lancaster County, Nebraska, judge granted a

request by the state's attorney general to force the Historical Society
to show why it should not have to comply with the open records law.

1112. "Historical Society Request Criticized." *Lincoln Journal*, 3 February
1990, 4. Two Nebraska state senators took issue with the Historical
Society's request for $20,000 to pay costs associated with returning
Indian remains and artifacts at the same time it was fighting the repatriation in court.

1113. Schwartze, Kimberly. "Panel Takes No Action on Indian-Items Bill."
Lincoln Journal, 23 February 1990, 22. A legislative committee refused to advance a bill (LB 1098) that would allow certain state
agencies to retain possession of Indian artifacts unearthed before August 25, 1989. An Historical Society member labeled as "theory" the
Pawnee belief that remains and artifacts must be kept together in order for the deceased's spirit to be at rest.

1114. Schwartzlander, David. "Spire Agrees with Pawnees: Hanson
Should Be Impeached." *Lincoln Journal*, 1 March 1990, 1. The Nebraska attorney general supports the Pawnees' call for the ouster of
NSHS director James Hanson for violating the state's open records
law.

1115. Schwartzlander, David, and Leslie Boellstorff. "Common Cause
Backs Pawnee Rights." *Lincoln Journal-Star*, 3 March 1990, 14.
Common Cause-Nebraska declared its support for both the Pawnees
and Attorney General Robert Spire in their battle with the NSHS
over Pawnee remains and grave goods, and expressed the opinion
that the public records law should be broadly interpreted.

1116. Schmidt, J. L. "Historical Society Is Put on Notice." *Lincoln
Journal-Star*, 15 March 1990, 17. Angry Nebraska legislators signed
and later withdrew a budget amendment that would have refused the
Historical Society the $20,000 in extra funding it had requested to
comply with LB 340. The state senators said the Society could not
ask the state for money and at the same time claim that it was not a
state agency.

1117. Schwartzlander, David. "Pawnees Back in Court with Historical Society." *Lincoln Journal*, 29 June 1990, 21. Once again, the NSHS
had refused to provide funding information that lawyers for the
Pawnees believed was central to their lawsuit to prove that the Society is indeed a state agency, and as such, must open its records to the

public. Attorneys for the Society cited the amount of work involved in gathering the information, since the data was not indexed.

1118. ———. "Hanson Fears Remains Law Encourages Destruction." *Lincoln Journal*, 30 June 1990, 12. Stating that LB 340 is too inflexible, the Historical Society director worried that landowners would not report skeletal remains or artifacts unearthed during construction projects out of concern that the projects may be stalled indefinitely.

1119. "Unhappy Pawnee Tribe Files a Formal Grievance." *Lincoln Journal*, 30 July 1990, 8. The Pawnee Tribe was dissatisfied with the 473-page inventory of artifacts turned over by the NSHS because it did not include grave goods from before 1600. The Pawnees also wanted artifacts and remains from the Loup River phase and Central Plains tradition sites in Nebraska, which date to 1100 and earlier.

1120. "Rep Named to Hold Talks With Tribe." *Lincoln Journal*, 10 August 1990, 25. After the Pawnees filed a grievance regarding the allegedly incomplete inventory of remains and artifacts given them by the NSHS, the Society hired an archaeologist to work with the tribe to review the inventory and to help decide what other remains and grave goods should be returned, if any.

1121. Reeves, Robert. "Legislators to View 'Peace Medals' as Dispute over Indian Artifacts Rages On." *Lincoln Star*, 7 September 1990, 24. As part of the continuing battle over the return of medals found at Pawnee sites, three state senators viewed the medals at the State Museum of History. Of particular interest was a British medal bearing the likeness of King George III, which was unearthed in Webster County in 1925.

1122. Schwartzlander, David. "Pawnee to Finally Claim Burial Remains." *Lincoln Journal*, 9 September 1990, 9. The formal return of human remains and grave goods scheduled for September 10 was marred by controversy, especially over a George III medal that was found with Pawnee skull fragments, which had apparently been misplaced. Robert Peregoy, attorney for the Pawnees, accused James Hanson of "coveting" the medal and deliberately "losing" the bones found with it so that it would not have to be returned.

1123. ———. "Remains and Artifacts of Pawnees Put on Truck for Burial at Genoa." *Lincoln Journal*, 10 September 1990, 4. Fine article on the actual return of Pawnee remains and grave goods to the tribe. Reviews the arguments over the NSHS inventory and the George III peace medal, which was not returned along with the other artifacts, and quotes several people involved in the controversy.

1124. "Not Only Does Peace Medal Exist—It Has a Twin." *Lincoln Star*, 11 September 1990, 8. Fascinating article unravels the mystery of a second George III medal in the collections of the NSHS. The Society did not reveal that there was a duplicate until a coin expert spotted the difference in the conditions of the two medals.

1125. Reeves, Bob. "Pawnee Remains Going 'Home' After Long Wait." *Lincoln Star*, 11 September 1990, 1, 5. Report on the actual exchange of Pawnee remains and artifacts. Explains the preparations for loading the 435 small, wooden coffins onto hearses and a truck, and describes how the burials will take place in Genoa, Nebraska. Also describes the burial goods contained in the coffins. An excellent article.

1126. Stevens, Betty. "Pawnee Remains Interred at Genoa." *Lincoln Journal*, 12 September 1990, 15. Very nice account of the reburial of Pawnee remains and grave goods in Valley View Cemetery in Genoa, Nebraska on September 11, 1990. Preparations for the ceremony were not publicized, possibly due to the value of the artifacts.

1127. "Arbiter Choice Next Step in Remains Dispute." *Lincoln Journal*, 21 September 1990, 24. With the NSHS and the Pawnee tribe at a stalemate over the rest of the Pawnee remains and grave goods in the possession of the Society, it was decided to choose an arbiter to preside over the controversy. But the two parties could not even agree on who the arbiter should be.

1128. "Historical Society Documents Sought by Pawnees 5th Time." *Lincoln Journal*, 27 September 1990, 8. Once again, attorneys for the Pawnees asked the courts to order the NSHS to turn over documents regarding donations and loans of Indian skeletal remains, log books, and proof of state aid.

1129. "Judge Narrows Pawnee-Historical Society Case." *Lincoln Journal*, 1 October 1990, 18. A Lancaster County, Nebraska, judge would concentrate on the open records law and the question of whether the Historical Society is a state agency. The case was set for trial in early October.

1130. Schwartzlander, David. "Historical Society Trial Is Under Way." *Lincoln Journal*, 3 October 1990, 30. This article provides the opening arguments in the Pawnee-NSHS trial in Lancaster County Court.

In their opening statements, attorneys for the Pawnees pointed out the many ways that the society would be considered a state agency. The attorney for the Society argued that it is a private corporation.

1131. Stevens, Betty. "Law Said to Discourage Reporting Skeletal Finds." *Lincoln Journal*, 10 October 1990, 30. Good article that points out the potential shortcomings of LB 340 in regard to reporting the discovery of skeletal remains. Archaeologists feared that the process is so unclear that farmers and contractors would simply not report these findings.

1132. "Oklahoma Pawnees File Grievance with Nebraska." *Lincoln Journal*, 15 December 1990, 5. The continuing controversy over Pawnee remains still housed at the NSHS prompted this grievance. The grave goods from fourteen Pawnee burials had not been returned because the Historical Society could not locate the skeletal remains that went with them. Also still at issue was the controversial George III peace medal.

1133. "Open-Records Issue Continues in Court." *Lincoln Journal*, 19 December 1990, 40. A report of the continuation of the trial that began in early October. This was a no-win situation for the NSHS. If it was decided that the Society is a state agency, it could be required to open its records; if not, it could lose state funding.

1134. Reeves, Bob. "State Ancestral Remains Law Said 'Landmark' Bill for Nation." *Lincoln Journal-Star*, 9 March 1991, 7. Pawnee attorney Walter Echo-Hawk praised LB 340, Nebraska's precedent-setting repatriation law, but also pointed out that Indian religious freedom was still under attack.

1135. Fell, Paul. "Two Famous Indian Fighters Finally Meet." *Lincoln Journal*, 30 July 1991, 6. In this humorous political cartoon, Fell compares NSHS Director James Hanson to George Armstrong Custer. This cartoon has been reproduced in several other publications.

1136. "Pawnees to Get George III Medal Back." *Lincoln Journal-Star*, 2 November 1991, 13. The NSHS finally agreed to return this controversial medal when the daughter of Asa T. Hill, the amateur archaeologist who originally found it, decided not to assert ownership. The medal's value was placed at anywhere from $4,000 to $1 million.

1137. Tysver, Robynn. "Historical Society to Appeal." *Lincoln Journal*, 14 November 1991, 14. In May 1991, a Lancaster County judge ruled that the Historical Society was a state agency subject to the open records law. The Society was now appealing that ruling. The judge also later ruled that the Society must pay the NARF $61,000 in legal fees. Those fees were being negotiated.

1138. "Court Victory Could Wreck the State's Historical Society." *Lincoln Journal-Star*, 17 November 1991, 8B. Editorial questions the wisdom of the Historical Society's attempts to overturn a judge's ruling that it is a state agency. The author cites loss of funding and employees losing their retirement benefits.

Omaha Newspapers (Arranged Chronologically)

1139. Warneke, Kevin. "Reburial of Tribal Remains Is Sought in Chambers' Bill." *Omaha World-Herald*, 12 January 1989, 20. Announces the January 11, 1989, introduction of LB 340 by State Senator Ernie Chambers of Omaha. Also lists the main provisions of the proposed law.

1140. Thomas, Fred. "Hanson Says Bill Should Exclude Non-Tribal Items." *Omaha World-Herald*, 11 February 1989, 31, 35. The director of the NSHS argued that many of the artifacts sought by the Pawnees under LB 340 were not of Indian origin, should not be considered burial goods, and therefore should not be returned. Attorneys for the Pawnees stated that the beads and other items in question had no historical value to Nebraska, but did have religious significance for the Pawnees.

1141. Share, John. "Warner: Give up Bones, Nothing Else." *Omaha World-Herald*, 11 February 1989, 35. Nebraska State Senator Jerome Warner announced his intention to introduce an amendment to LB 340 allowing museums to keep all Indian burial goods. The proposed amendment was strongly opposed by attorneys for the Pawnees.

1142. Thomas, Fred. "Pawnee Attorney Questions Aim of New History Group." *Omaha World-Herald*, 12 February 1989, 5B. Attorney Robert Peregoy questioned the motives of "Citizens to Save Nebraska's History," claiming that they were trying to prevent the Pawnees from reclaiming artifacts that belonged to them.

1143. Share, John. "Hanson Denies History Group Is a 'Front'." *Omaha World-Herald*, 15 February 1989, 15. In response to Pawnee attorney Robert Peregoy's accusation that the group "Citizens to Save Nebraska's History" was an extension of the State Historical Society, Director James Hanson argued that the group was composed of private citizens and had no financial ties to the Society. Several members of the group were Historical Society employees, which made Peregoy suspicious of their motives.

1144. "Several Lobbying on Burial Legislation." *Omaha World-Herald*, 15 February 1989, 15. This brief article lists registered lobbyists for both sides of the Pawnee reburial issue. Two attorneys for the Pawnees are listed, along with three Historical Society employees (who were not required to register as lobbyists) and James Hanson's wife.

1145. "Most Favored Giving Remains to Tribes." *Omaha World-Herald*, 16 February 1989, 1. A poll conducted in early 1989 showed that 69% of Nebraskans supported legislation that would force the NSHS to turn over to Indian tribes' skeletal remains and burial goods in its possession. The strongest support for the bill was in the Second Congressional District, which includes Omaha.

1146. Share, John. "Letter from Chief's Widow Notes Feelings on Remains." *Omaha World-Herald*, 16 February 1989. NSHS Director James Hanson decided to support LB 340 partly due to a letter he received from Martha Royce Blaine, widow of hereditary Pawnee chief Garland Blaine. She said that her husband would have been "overwhelmingly sad" to see Pawnee skeletal remains displayed publicly.

1147. "Bones Meeting Raises Hopes." *Omaha World-Herald*, 19 February, 1989, 12B. An editorial praises both sides in the Pawnee-Historical Society repatriation controversy for their willingness to meet face-to-face to discuss the issues.

1148. Share, John. "Pawnee Leader Says Burial Goods Wouldn't Be Sold." *Omaha World-Herald*, 22 February 1989, 31. In a press conference in Lincoln, Pawnee tribal chairman Lawrence Goodfox, Jr., countered accusations by opponents of LB 340 that burial goods returned to the Pawnees would be sold by the tribe or placed in museums outside Nebraska.

1149. Thomas, Fred. "Three Medals Are Key Issue in Burial Site Controversy." *Omaha World-Herald*, 22 February 1989, 16. Excellent article tracing the history of a Thomas Jefferson peace medal, a Spanish silver medal, and an English medal, all found in Pawnee graves at the Pike-Pawnee village site near Guide Rock, Nebraska. Also explains the importance of each medal and the controversy over their possible reburial.

1150. Share, John. "Legislative Floor Debate Expected to Open on Indian Remains Bill." *Omaha World-Herald*, 24 February 1989, 11. Debate was scheduled to begin on LB 340 after the Oklahoma Pawnees agreed to an amendment stating that only those goods identified as having been buried with the remains of a specific person would be returned to the tribe.

1151. "Fate of Indian Remains Concerns Teens." *Omaha World-Herald*, 17 March 1989, 8. This *World-Herald* report of the visit of two Pawnee teenagers to a meeting of the Nebraska Legislature is essentially the same as the *Lincoln Journal* article of the same date [1096].

1152. "Committee Kills Burial Site Measure." *Omaha World-Herald*, 17 March 1989, 8. The Nebraska Legislature's Committee on Government, Military and Veterans Affairs voted not to advance LB 691, a bill similar to the more comprehensive LB 340, which was currently being debated. Attorney Walter Echo-Hawk and Winnebago tribal leader Louis La Rose recommended that the bill be killed.

1153. Share, John. "Indian Remains Bill Amended in Debate." *Omaha World-Herald*, 24 March 1989, 26. Because of continuing confusion about which burial goods should be returned to the Pawnees, the Nebraska Legislature approved an amendment to LB340 allowing the state ombudsman to resolve such disputes.

1154. ———. "Bones Bill Would Halt Study." *Omaha World-Herald*, 26 March 1989. 3B. Douglas Owsley of the Smithsonian Institution's Department of Anthropology lamented the possibility of the repatriation of 300 Pawnee skeletons lent to him for research in 1984. Citing the usefulness of his research on the bones, Owsley suggested that he be allowed to keep the skeletons for three more years. This timetable was unacceptable to those supporting the Pawnees' position.

1155. ———. "Amended Reburial Bill Passes Second Round." *Omaha World-Herald*, 28 March 1989, 1, 6. After being amended, LB340 advanced to the third and final round of legislative debate. A major change to the bill, adopted by a thirty-three to zero vote, would require the NSHS to give up Pawnee remains and burial goods by September 10, 1990, instead of September 1989, as originally proposed. Several other amendments were rejected. The vote to advance the bill appears at the end of the article.

1156. "Indian Remains Bill Is Signed by Gov. Orr; Attorney Pleased." *Omaha World-Herald*, 24 May 1989, 12. Robert Peregoy thanked the Nebraska Legislature and Governor Kay Orr for passing LB340 and signing it into law.

1157. "Spire, Tribal Lawyer Vow to Sue for Records." *Omaha World-Herald*, 17 June 1989, 13–14. Robert Peregoy called NSHS Director James Hanson an obstructionist and threatened to sue if Pawnee accession records were not made available by June 26.

1158. Share, John. "Board Votes to Open Records on Remains." *Omaha World-Herald*, 24 June 1989, 1, 10. Excellent article outlining the controversy over the release of State Historical Society records to the NARF. One board member alleged that the Society was "set up" and not given enough time to respond to the attorneys' request.

1159. ———. "Pawnees' Attorney Will Extend Deadline." *Omaha World-Herald*, 30 June 1989, 36. Attorney Robert Peregoy agreed to give the NSHS two extra days to turn over archaeological records on Pawnee burials. If the tribe's researchers did not gain access to the records by then, he would sue for access under the state's public records law.

1160. "State Sets U.S. Pace on Indian Remains." *Omaha World-Herald*, 1 October 1989, 7B. State Senator Ernie Chambers pointed out that other states and even the Smithsonian Institution were using Nebraska's repatriation law as a model. However, the director of the NSHS believed that the law had set a dangerous precedent by destroying the work of scholars and preventing future research.

1161. "Bones List Far From Finished." *Omaha World-Herald*, 6 October 1989. An attorney for the Pawnees announced that tribal researchers would need weeks and possibly months to complete their inventory of skeletal remains and burial goods and to present a formal request to the NSHS. Tribal representatives disagreed with Director Hanson on the projected total of burial goods that the Pawnees would ask to be returned.

1162. "Pawnee Tribe Seeks to Bury Remains." *Omaha World-Herald*, 5 January 1990, 14. Accused by attorneys for the Pawnees of being uncooperative, NSHS Director James Hanson denied the charge. He argued that he was obeying the law (LB 340), and was requesting additional funds to bring in specialists to study the Indian artifacts.

1163. "Senators Revive Indian Artifacts Issue." *Omaha World-Herald*, 11 January 1990, 31. Two Omaha legislators introduced a bill in the Nebraska Unicameral to virtually "undo" LB 340. Their bill, LB 1097, would allow the NSHS to keep Indian burial goods unearthed prior to August 25, 1989.

1164. Thomas, Fred. "Expert Rues Loss of Beads to Pawnees." *Omaha World-Herald*, 20 January 1990, 31. A Canadian expert on trade beads, citing the unique nature and the research value of the Pawnee bead collection at the NSHS, voiced his displeasure that the Society would have to give it up for reburial.

1165. "Historian Says Artifacts Worth More than $1 Million." *Omaha World-Herald*, 20 January 1990, 32. An Omaha researcher familiar with the medals and other artifacts that the Pawnees want returned to them says that these items are quite valuable and should not be reburied, or worse, sold by the Pawnees. In his opinion, the Historical Society's collection of Spanish, British, and American peace medals is priceless.

1166. Garfield, Daniel. "Historical Society Sues to Delay Release of Information to Indians." *Omaha World-Herald*, 24 January 1990, 30. The NSHS filed suit to prevent attorneys for the Pawnees from seeing records pertaining to Pawnee skeletal remains and artifacts, arguing that public records laws do not apply to the Historical Society, and the records can be withheld from public scrutiny.

1167. Cordes, Henry J. "'Cut Stalling,' Spire Tells Historical Society." *Omaha World-Herald*, 25 January 1990, 1. The Nebraska attorney general criticized the State Historical Society's decision to go to court to avoid opening its records to the Pawnees, and urged the Society Board to "act like responsible, caring fellow citizens."

1168. "Spire to Seek Court Ruling on Historical Society Status." *Omaha World-Herald*, 27 January 1990, 54. Nebraska's attorney general wants a judge to decide whether the Historical Society is a state agency subject to the open records law.

1169. "Spire Intervenes in Court Action over Remains." *Omaha World-Herald*, 2 February 1990, 14. The Nebraska attorney general won a victory of sorts when a judge ruled that he could file papers trying to force the Historical Society to open its records to the Pawnees. The judge gave the Society one month to respond to the attorney general's petition.

1170. "Historical Society Seeks Aid for Return of Remains." *Omaha World-Herald*, 3 February 1990, 32. Arguing that the Society was confronted by both the open records law and LB 340, Director James Hanson asked for an additional $20,000 to help comply with LB 340.

1171. "Proposal Renews 4-Year Battle Over State's Indian Burial Goods." *Omaha World-Herald*, 23 February 1990, 37. An NSHS board member who supported a bill to allow state retention of Indian artifacts accused the legislature of interfering with the collections of the Society by "grabbing" burial goods and beads. He pointed out that other states where the Pawnees lived have not passed laws like LB 340.

1172. "Pawnee Tribe Seeks Hanson's Ouster." *Omaha World-Herald*, 1 March 1990, 18. The Pawnees filed papers in Lancaster County District Court calling for the "removal or impeachment" of NSHS Director James Hanson and other society members who ignored the open records law.

1173. Kotok, C. David. "Spire Criticized for Seeking Ouster of Historical Chief." *Omaha World-Herald*, 2 March 1990, 43. The president of the State Historical Society's Executive Board stated that Nebraska's attorney general may have allowed his personal views to interfere with what was best for Nebraska when he urged that Society Director Hanson be removed from his position.

1174. Thomas, Steve. "More Words Traded Over Indian Remains." *Omaha World-Herald*, 16 March 1990, 18. State senators proposed a budget bill amendment to deny the State Historical Society the extra funding it had requested to help comply with LB 340.

1175. ———. "Historical Society Director Denies Racism Charges." *Omaha World-Herald*, 16 March 1990, 21. In response to being called a "racist" and a liar by State Senator Ernie Chambers of Omaha, James Hanson reminded Chambers that he had spent many years of his life working with Native Americans.

1176. Thomas, Fred. "Historical Society to Follow Law In Giving Pawnees 37,000 Artifacts." *Omaha World-Herald*, 12 June 1990, 11. Excellent article on the Historical Society's compliance with LB 340. In addition to the thousands of artifacts, the bones of 398 people found at Nebraska burial sites would also be turned over to the Pawnees. Two valuable medals would not be returned, since they were not directly associated with Pawnee burials.

1177. "Hard Feelings May Now End Between Pawnees, Nebraskans." *Omaha World-Herald*, 14 June 1990, 28. Even-handed editorial stating both views on the implementation of LB 340. States that some who opposed the reburial law did so for scientific and humanitarian, not racial reasons.

1178. Thomas, Fred. "Nebraska Historian Laments Strict Law on Artifacts." *Omaha World-Herald*, 30 June 1990, 36. At a NSHS Board meeting, members expressed concern that the inflexibility of LB 340 would discourage the reporting of important archaeological finds in the future. Several board members also doubted that Indian tribes would rebury artifacts returned to them.

1179. Cordes, Henry J. "Pawnee Tribe, Historical Society in Another Dispute Over Remains." *Omaha World-Herald*, 31 July 1990, 18. Informative article clearly outlines the Pawnees' reasons for requesting skeletal remains and grave goods for the pre-1600 period. Scientists quoted in the article disagreed on whether these earlier remains housed at the NSHS were actually the remains of Pawnee ancestors.

1180. Thomas, Fred. "Dispute Arises on Pawnee Artifacts Transfer." *Omaha World-Herald*, 8 September 1990, 18. Just three days before the NSHS was scheduled to return thousands of remains and artifacts to the Pawnee Tribe, the exchange was compromised by disagreements over the George III medal, denial of access to the collections, and the Pawnees not being given sufficient time to inspect the coffins containing human remains and burial goods. The Pawnees had also imposed new conditions and had asked to view items not scheduled to be returned.

1181. Cordes, Henry J. "Pawnee Items Returned; Medal Dispute Lingers." *Omaha World-Herald*, 10 September 1990, 7. Even as the remains of 398 Pawnees and thousands of artifacts were being returned to the tribe, the controversy raged over the George III medal claimed by both parties. It was discovered that the State Historical Society had two of these medals. Supporters of the return of a medal to the Pawnees suggested that having a duplicate should resolve the issue.

1182. McMorris, Robert. "American Indian Sees Change in Historical Society Attitude." *Omaha World-Herald*, 25 November 1995, 37, 43. This interview with Charles Trimble, an Oglala Sioux and newly elected president of the NSHS Board, points out the changes that had occurred in the Society since the passage of LB 340 and the controversy with the Pawnees surrounding its terms.

26
Annual Reports of the Commissioners of Indian Affairs
(Arranged Chronologically)

The annual reports of the Commissioner of Indian Affairs were published from 1825 to 1906, and appear in the Congressional Documents series—from 1825 to 1846 as part of the Secretary of War's annual report, and as part of the report of the Secretary of the Interior from 1849 to 1906. Beginning in 1907, the reports were printed only for official use. For the purpose of this bibliography, entries begin with the Commissioner of Indian Affairs Report of 1839, which was the first to give details on the condition of the Pawnees. The reports are located by Congressional Serial Set number (indicated in brackets). Numbers of agents' and superintendents' reports within the reports of the commissioners (where available) are shown in parentheses. Beginning in 1874, these reports were no longer assigned numbers, but agents' and superintendents' reports can be easily located in the index for each commissioner's report. A complete listing of these reports can be found in J. A. Jones, "Key to the Annual Reports of the United States Commissioner of Indian Affairs." *Ethnohistory* 2 (Winter 1955): 55–64.

1183. U.S. Department of War. Office of Indian Affairs. *Annual Report of the Commissioner of Indian Affairs (ARCIA).* Nov. 25, 1839. 26th Cong., 1st sess. S. Doc. 1 [Ser. 354]. Joseph V. Hamilton, agent at Council Bluffs, reported (52) that all the Pawnees were living along the Platte River and supporting themselves by hunting. When they came to Bellevue to collect their annuities, they asked for help in locating permanent villages so that they could fulfill the conditions of their treaty. The Rev. John Dunbar and Samuel Allis agreed to accompany the Pawnees to establish new villages and to stay with them as missionaries.

1184. U.S. Dept. of War. Office of Indian Affairs. *ARCIA*. Nov. 28, 1840. 26th Cong., 2d sess. S. Doc. 1 [Ser. 375]. Agent Joseph Hamilton (20) informed the Pawnees that as soon as they relocated north of the Platte River the government would honor the terms of their 1833 treaty. With the help of Rev. John Dunbar, Hamilton freed seven Mexican boys who had been captured by the Pawnees near the Mexican border. A census taken in the spring listed the total Pawnee population as 6,241.

1185. U.S. Dept. of War. Office of Indian Affairs. *ARCIA*. Nov. 25, 1843. 28th Cong., 1st sess. S. Doc. 1 [Ser. 431]. According to Samuel Allis (13), the Pawnee school would not succeed until the Indians could raise enough crops to feed their children year-round, and until the Sioux raids were stopped. Allis was concerned that all the government employees would be forced to leave if the Sioux continued their attacks. Agent Daniel Miller's report (84) was equally discouraging. A hard winter and late spring had slowed planting, and after a deadly Sioux raid in late June, the Pawnees seemed reluctant to move to their new farms. Like Allis, Miller saw little hope for the school, since Pawnee parents hesitated to leave their children behind when they left on hunts, fearing that they would be taken captive by the Sioux.

1186. U.S. Dept. of War. Office of Indian Affairs. *ARCIA*. Nov. 25, 1844. 28th Cong., 2d sess. S. Doc. 1 [Ser. 449]. Superintendent Thomas Harvey (65) regretted that the Osages and their Kansa allies were at war with the Pawnees, and suggested that a peace council be convened in the spring of 1845. Teacher Samuel Allis (25) complained about sporadic attendance at the Pawnee school and suggested that a manual labor school be established for the Pawnee children. Because they were hungry, the Indians had resorted to killing their own oxen and stealing corn from each other. Agent Daniel Miller reported (66) both good and bad news. The Pawnees' summer hunt had been successful, but their corn crop would be small. Miller reported the official visit to the Pawnees of Major Clifton Wharton and his cavalry units, mentioned the intra-tribal feud between Pawnees north and south of the Platte, and echoed Allis' request for a manual labor school.

1187. U.S. Dept. of War. Office of Indian Affairs. *ARCIA*. Nov. 24, 1845. 29th Cong., 1st sess. S. Doc. 1 [Ser. 470]. Their agent did not submit a report in 1845, but Superintendent Thomas Harvey's lengthy one (21) updated the Indian Commissioner on the status of the Pawnees. Harvey expressed disappointment with the Indian school and agency farms, and strongly recommended that a manual labor school be built and that funds for education and agriculture be placed in the hands of the American Board of Missions.

1188. U.S. Dept. of War. Office of Indian Affairs. *ARCIA*. Nov. 30, 1846. 29th Cong., 2d sess. S. Doc. 1 [Ser. 493]. As in 1845, information on the Pawnees was reported from St. Louis by Superintendent Thomas Harvey (15). The big event of 1846 occurred during the Pawnees' summer hunt, when a Sioux war party attacked their village and burnt it to the ground. Had their teachers not hidden them in the cellars of the school buildings, the Pawnee children would have been murdered. After the attack, the teachers took the children to Bellevue, where they would be safe.

1189. U.S. Dept. of War. Office of Indian Affairs. *ARCIA*. Nov. 30, 1847. 30th Cong., 1st sess. S. Exec. Doc. 1 [Ser. 503]. Superintendent Thomas Harvey (6), concerned about the increasing boldness of Sioux attacks on the Otoes, Omahas, and Pawnees, suggested that volunteer soldiers capture a few Sioux leaders and hold them hostage to ensure the future good behavior of their warriors. Because of the Sioux raids, the Presbyterian missionaries left the Pawnee villages and Harvey recalled all government employees working with the tribe. Pawnees south of the Platte continued to interfere with trade on the Santa Fe Trail. Harvey recommended that Pawnee villages south of the river be destroyed, forcing those Indians to move farther north. Council Bluffs agent John Miller (11) praised the work of John Dunbar and Samuel Allis, but informed Superintendent Harvey that they and all the other whites at the Pawnee villages had fled to Bellevue for safety. Miller questioned the location of a new fort south of the Platte River (Fort Kearny).

1190. U.S. Dept. of War. Office of Indian Affairs. *ARCIA*. Nov. 30, 1848. 30th Cong., 2d sess. H. Exec. Doc. 1 [Ser. 537]. Superintendent Thomas Harvey (1) reminded the Indian Commissioner that the missionaries and teachers had kept the Pawnee school in operation at Bellevue in the hope that they could return to the Pawnee villages when protection was provided. Teacher Samuel Allis (5-A) argued that he could teach more Pawnee children in Bellevue if he had

proper accommodations for them. Several students had been forced
by their parents to return to the Pawnee villages, where one of them,
a fourteen-year-old girl, had died.

1191. U.S. Dept. of Interior. *ARCIA*. Nov. 30, 1849. 31st Cong., 1st sess.
S. Exec. Doc. 1 [Ser. 530]. Superintendent D. D. Mitchell (1) proposed sweeping changes, including realigning the agencies in the
Northern Superintendency. New Council Bluffs Sub-Agent John E.
Barrow sadly reported (3) the deaths of 1,234 Pawnees from cholera
within a period of six months. He provided the survivors with food
and moved them to higher ground, away from the dead and dying.
Barrow listed the population of the Pawnees as about 4,500, which
reflects the losses from disease. Samuel Allis (3-B) also reported
cholera deaths at his school. Because of the epidemic, Allis closed
the school for a month. He also gave the agent an ultimatum: provide new school buildings or he would leave in the spring of 1850.

1192. U.S. Dept. of Interior. *ARCIA*. Nov. 27, 1850. 31st Cong., 2d sess.
H. Exec. Doc. 1 [Ser. 595]. In his abbreviated report (11), John Barrow informed his superintendent that the Otoes, Omahas, and
Pawnees suffered more than any other tribe from the effects of white
emigration. In 1849 and 1850, western travelers trampled their corn
fields, destroyed their villages, and invaded their hunting grounds.
On another negative note, he reported that because of its dilapidated
buildings, the Pawnee school was essentially useless. Liquor sellers
on the borders of Indian Country created a constant problem for the
three tribes under Barrow's care.

1193. U.S. Dept. of Interior. *ARCIA*. Nov. 27, 1851. 32d Cong., 1st sess. S.
Exec. Doc. 1 [Ser. 613]. The Pawnee treaty terms had expired. As a
result, they no longer had a blacksmith, and John Barrow reported
that the school was forced to close (15). In his last report as teacher
(17), Samuel Allis summed up the rare successes and frequent failures of the Pawnee school and thanked the Otoe and Omaha mission
teacher for taking his remaining students so they would not have to
return to the Pawnee villages.

1194. U.S. Dept. of Interior. *ARCIA*. Nov. 30, 1855. 34th Cong., 1st sess.
S. Exec. Doc. 1 [Ser. 810]. For their safety, the Pawnees had asked
to trade their assigned lands north of the Platte for an area south of
the river, so it could serve as a barrier between them and their enemies. George Hepner, new agent for the Pawnees, Omahas, and

Otoes and Missourias (29), compared the Pawnees' situation to that of the other three tribes, all of whom were being furnished food. The Pawnees were left to feed themselves, which could be a disaster if they encountered Sioux on their winter hunt or if another tribe raided their food caches while they were hunting. The Pawnees continued to steal horses from other Indians, and had recently begun stealing from whites.

1195. U.S. Dept. of Interior. *ARCIA*. Nov. 22, 1856. 34th Cong., 3d sess. S. Exec. Doc. 5 [Ser. 875]. In 1856, the Pawnees had no agent, and any news of their condition came from Samuel Allis, now serving as their interpreter. In response to correspondence from Allis (29), in which he explained that the Pawnees had been retaliating against white settlers who had been stealing their timber, and that the Omahas had sold Pawnee land to the government, Superintendent Cumming (21) recommended a treaty with the Pawnees that would possibly settle them on land near the Otoe Reservation.

1196. U.S. Dept. of Interior. *ARCIA*. Nov. 30, 1857. 35th Cong., 1st sess. S. Exec. Doc. 11 [Ser. 919]. In 1857, the Pawnees signed the Treaty of Table Creek, providing them with a reservation along the Loup Fork of the Platte River. In his brief report (64), Agent William Dennison saw the reservation as an end to Pawnee raids and thefts along the western trails. Since the treaty had not yet been ratified, Dennison had not shared its terms with the Pawnees.

1197. U.S. Dept. of Interior. *ARCIA*. Nov. 6, 1858. 35th Cong., 2d sess. S. Exec. Doc. 1 [Ser. 974]. Agent Dennison (29) urged the government to move the Pawnees to their new reservation, away from white settlers, as soon as possible. Now that whites in the area knew that the Pawnees would be receiving annuities as a result of their 1857 treaty, he had begun receiving many claims for depredations.

1198. U.S. Dept. of Interior. *ARCIA*. Nov. 26, 1859. 36th Cong., 1st sess. S. Exec. Doc. 2 [Ser. 1023]. Because so many of their people had died in Sioux attacks, the Pawnees only reluctantly agreed to settle on their new reservation along the Loup Fork of the Platte. But the Superintendent of Indian Affairs in St. Louis (29) saw a bright future for the Pawnees, since they would be located on good land away from whites.

1199. U.S. Dept. of Interior. *ARCIA*. Dec. 1, 1860. 36th Cong., 2d sess. S. Exec. Doc. 1 [Ser. 1078]. Agent J. L. Gillis reported (33) the establishment of a twenty-four-man Indian police force, the distribution of annuity goods, construction of a corn storage facility, an operating saw and grist mill, and a bridge to connect the Pawnee villages with the school farm. Other buildings were in progress, and crops were fairly good, considering the dry weather. More would have been accomplished if not for frequent attacks by enemy tribes, especially the Brulé Sioux. Pawnee raiders stole a number of horses and mules, but all were turned over to the agent by the tribal police. For protection, the commander of army troops stationed on the reservation suggested building a block house and arming it with a twelve-pound howitzer.

1200. U.S. Dept. of Interior. *ARCIA*. Nov. 26, 1862. 37th Cong., 3d sess. H. Exec. Doc. 1 [Ser. 1157]. Benjamin Lushbaugh, new agent to the Pawnees, submitted his first report (19) just three months after arriving at the agency. He found the Indians "half starved and nude," with no school and no farms. To stop thefts on the reservation, Lushbaugh revived the Indian police force, and he also arranged the return of a Sioux captive to her people in the hope that this gesture would stop the Sioux raids. Because of a shortage of wood, Lushbaugh urged the government to provide a water mill to replace the steam grist and saw mill currently in operation. In July, sixteen Pawnee children finally began attending a reservation school, but the buildings were inadequate. To add to Pawnee woes, grasshoppers attacked their corn crop.

1201. U.S. Dept. of Interior. *ARCIA*. Oct. 31, 1863. 38th Cong., 1st sess. H. Exec. Doc. 1. [Ser. 1182]. Agent Lushbaugh reported (131) positive changes in the Pawnees' condition. He had managed to confine the Indians to the reservation, thus nearly eliminating claims against them by settlers. Putting a stop to horse stealing proved to be difficult, but some stolen ponies were returned to their owners. By building an addition, the Pawnee school could now accommodate thirty-two students, who were doing well. Lushbaugh reported that the crops were so good that the Pawnee had a large surplus to sell, and this year's hunt had also been successful. But the Sioux raids continued, making farming hazardous and hiring agency employees difficult.

1202. U.S. Dept. of Interior. *ARCIA*. Nov. 15, 1864. 38th Cong., 2d sess. H. Exec. Doc. 1. [Ser. 1220]. Agent Lushbaugh's good news (207) regarding a reduction in pony thefts and the near-completion of a new school building was tempered by his report that drought and grasshoppers had destroyed the Pawnee crops. General Curtis had recruited eighty Pawnee Scouts during the summer, but the agent refused to let them go unless Curtis left troops in their place. Curtis refused, and the potential scouts stayed home. Includes a letter to the Commissioner of Indian Affairs (210) requesting permission to gather Sioux and Pawnee leaders together to make a treaty. Commissioner Dole (211) told Lushbaugh and the Sioux agent to go ahead with the meeting, but only if they could fund it out of their own budgets.

1203. U.S. Dept. of Interior. *ARCIA.* Oct. 31, 1865. 39th Cong., 1st sess. H. Exec. Doc. 1 [Ser. 1248]. D. H. Wheeler replaced Benjamin Lushbaugh as Pawnee agent in July (162). Both the Pawnees' hunt and crops were successful this year, and Wheeler reported no Sioux raids, probably due to the company of soldiers stationed on the reservation. Appended to Wheeler's report is a letter from former agent Lushbaugh informing the Indian Office that eighty-seven Pawnee warriors had enlisted in the U.S. Army as scouts, and would be serving for one year. In addition, Lushbaugh announced that he had arranged a peace treaty between the Pawnees and the Kaws (Kansas), a claim that was angrily denied by the agent for the Kansas (136). According to him, a small group of Kansas had traveled to the Pawnee agency to recover stolen horses, and the Pawnees proposed a treaty. The Kansas who supposedly signed the "treaty" denied that they had done so, saying that they "only shook hands with the tips of their fingers."

1204. U.S. Dept. of Interior. *ARCIA.* Nov. 19, 1866. 39th Cong., 2d sess. H. Exec. Doc. 1. [Ser. 1284]. In May 1866, a Sioux raiding party stole eighteen horses (96). Agent Wheeler urgently requested army protection for the Pawnee Reservation. Superintendent Taylor forwarded this letter to the commanding officer of the Department of the Platte with his endorsement of Wheeler's request for troops, and wrote Indian Commissioner Cooley regarding the matter.

1205. U.S. Dept. of Interior. *ARCIA.* Nov. 15, 1867. 40th Cong., 2d sess. H. Exec. Doc. 1 [Ser. 1326]. New agent Charles Whaley argued (83) that it was essential to enroll Pawnee boys in the Manual Labor School at an early age, before they developed anti-labor attitudes. He also stressed the importance of a peace treaty with the Sioux so that the Pawnees and the agency employees would be safe. The Pawnees were especially vulnerable at this time, since 200 of their young men were on military operations as members of the Pawnee Scouts.

1206. U.S. Dept. of Interior. *ARCIA*. Nov. 23, 1868. 40th Cong., 3d sess. H. Exec. Doc. 1 [Ser. 1366]. In the summer of 1868, hordes of grasshoppers "in a cloud so thick as to actually obscure the sun" (57), descended on the bean and corn fields, destroying nearly everything. In addition, the Sioux had once more disrupted the Pawnees' summer hunt, forcing the hunters to return early and leave much of their buffalo meat behind. One hundred Pawnees had enlisted in the army that spring and were guarding the Union Pacific Railroad.

1207. U.S. Dept. of Interior. *ARCIA*. Dec. 23, 1869. 41st Cong., 2d sess. H. Exec. Doc. 1 [Ser. 1414]. In 1869, the Hicksite Friends (Quakers) took over the Northern Superintendency, with Samuel M. Janney as superintendent in Omaha and Jacob Troth as Pawnee agent. Janney's report (95) included a lengthy discussion of the arrest and indictment of four Pawnees for the murder of Edward McMurty on an island in the Platte River (see Chapter 19), and informed the commissioner that because of Sioux raids, the Pawnees were reluctant to move onto individual farms. Perhaps because this was the first year of the Quaker regime, school principal Elvira Platt mentioned every deficiency at the school, the most serious of which was an undependable water supply (104).

1208. U.S. Dept. of Interior. *ARCIA*. Oct. 31, 1870. 41st Cong., 3d sess. H. Exec. Doc. 1 [Ser. 1449]. Agent Troth (85) found horse stealing a difficult practice to stop. While on the winter hunt, several Pawnee war parties left the main body of hunters and returned to the agency in January with a large number of horses taken from tribes in the Central Superintendency. Six of the pony thieves were arrested and turned over to the army. Troth noted that Sioux raids had stopped after Red Cloud and Spotted Tail returned from a trip to Washington. Superintendent Janney (79) talked to Red Cloud regarding a Pawnee-Sioux treaty when the Sioux chief passed through Omaha, but Red Cloud said he had no time to discuss the issue, and he could not speak for all his people.

1209. U.S. Dept. of Interior. *ARCIA*. Nov. 15, 1871. 42d Cong., 2d sess. H. Exec. Doc. 1 [Ser. 1565]. Along with his peace overture toward Red

Cloud, Superintendent Janney (50) had also approached Brulé Chief Spotted Tail, who at first seemed receptive to the idea, but later backed down. Pawnees continued to die, and few settled on farms away from the safety of their villages. Jacob Troth reported (59) that the grist mill on the Pawnee reservation had finally been converted to water power, a project paid for by the Indians out of their annuity. Since his last report, five Pawnees had died in Sioux attacks.

1210. U.S. Dept. of Interior. *ARCIA*. Nov. 1, 1872. 42d Cong., 3d sess. H. Exec. Doc. 1 [Ser. 1560]. In his first report as head of the Northern Superintendency, Barclay White expressed his concern over the way the Pawnees were perceived by whites traveling west on the railroads (6). As part of the agreement to provide scouts for the army, Pawnees were allowed to ride on Union Pacific freight cars at no charge, but according to White, only the "idle and vagrant" members of the tribe took advantage of the offer. As White made his first report, Jacob Troth made his fourth and last (100), informing White of a council at Grand Island at which the Pawnees agreed to sell 50,000 acres of their reservation south of the Loup Fork, even though they disagreed with some of the terms. Also included is a population count showing a total of 2,447 Pawnees, an increase of 83 in the past year.

1211. U.S. Dept. of Interior. *ARCIA*. Nov. 1, 1873. 43d Cong., 1st sess. H. Exec. Doc. 1 [Ser. 1601]. When the Nebraska Pawnee Reservation provided by the treaty signed in 1857 was re-surveyed, it was discovered that instead of being 30 miles east to west, the boundary lines were only 29.5 miles apart, creating a discrepancy of 4,800 acres in the reservation's area. Since the Pawnees demanded to be paid for the shortage, the Commissioner of Indian Affairs urged Congress to pay the Indians $1.25 per acre for the lands. New Pawnee agent William Burgess (11) made his brief official report on the Massacre Canyon tragedy on the Republican River. According to Burgess' figures, the Brulé and Oglala Sioux killed twenty Pawnee men, thirty-nine women, and ten children. The wounded who returned home were recovering, and the Sioux returned eleven women and children who had been taken captive, but a number of children were still missing. Burgess angrily called for the Sioux to compensate the Pawnees for their losses out of their annuities. Commissioner Edward P. Smith announced that the Sioux were now forbidden to leave their reservations to hunt in Nebraska.

1212. U.S. Dept. of Interior. *ARCIA*. Nov. 1, 1874. 43d Cong., 2d sess. H. Exec. Doc. 1 [Ser. 1639]. Faced with crop failures, Sioux attacks, and general desperation, a number of the Pawnees left Nebraska to join the friendly Wichitas on their reservation in Indian Territory. Commissioner Smith stated that since the Pawnees had decided to sell their entire Nebraska reservation, the Indian Office would submit a bill to Congress to that effect. E. C. Kemble, an Indian department inspector, noted that the Pawnees received $9,000 for their losses at Massacre Canyon, most of which was used to buy cattle and other supplies.

1213. U.S. Dept. of Interior. *ARCIA*. Nov. 1, 1875. 44th Cong., 1st sess. H. Exec. Doc. 1 [Ser. 1680]. Important report by Agent William Burgess contains the details of the Pawnees' relocation to Indian Territory. On October 8, 1874, Burgess, Superintendent Barclay White, and B. Rush Roberts, representing the Hicksite Quakers, presented the removal plan to the Indians. After considering the plan for two days, the Pawnees reluctantly accepted it. They would all stay with the Wichitas until a new reservation was selected. In Indian Territory, Burgess chose a tract of land south of the Osage Agency and north of the Sac and Fox reservation. One drawback to the new reservation was its distance from a railroad, causing goods to be hauled overland from Coffeyville, Kansas. The industrial school in Genoa, Nebraska, was to close at the end of September, 1875, with the understanding that a new school would be built in Indian Territory.

1214. U.S. Dept. of Interior. *ARCIA*. Oct. 30, 1876. 44th Cong., 2d sess. H. Exec. Doc. 1 [Ser. 1749]. Quaker agents were retained, but the Pawnees were now under the jurisdiction of the Central Superintendency in Lawrence, Kansas. Agent Burgess had successfully moved the last of the Pawnees to their new reservation across the Arkansas River from the Osage reserve. Because Congress failed to authorize the sale of the Nebraska reservation, the Pawnees had few funds at their disposal, and almost no buffalo were found the preceding winter. Burgess reported that during the fall of 1875 "fever and ague were quite prevalent and many of the tribe died."

1215. U.S. Dept. of Interior. *ARCIA*. Nov. 1, 1877. 45th Cong., 2d sess. H. Exec. Doc. 1 [Ser. 1800]. Agent Charles Searing was sent to Indian Territory to replace William Burgess, who left the Pawnees amid allegations of fraud involving agency funds and cattle purchases. Searing expressed his dismay when he observed the crowding and filth among the Pawnees who still lived in earth lodges. The scouts who had enlisted in the fall of 1876 had returned, but not without incident. One scout was fatally shot in Hays City, Kansas, by a merchant who believed the Indian was trying to break into his store, and five scouts who stole horses near Grand Island, Nebraska, were now serving sixty-day jail terms.

1216. U.S. Dept. of Interior. *ARCIA*. Nov. 1, 1878. 45th Cong., 3d sess. H. Exec. Doc. 1 [Ser. 1850]. Some Pawnees were now living in log homes, while two bands remained in either earth lodges or tipis. Indians living in houses had asked for furniture, stoves, and other household goods, and some had exchanged horses for other farm animals, especially pigs. The promised manual labor school building had been completed in May, but was not yet receiving students.

1217. U.S. Dept. of Interior. *ARCIA*. Nov. 1, 1879. 46th Cong., 2d sess. H. Exec. Doc. 1 [Ser. 1910]. Agent John C. Smith criticized the work of the former agent. Crops had not been planted, buildings were in disrepair with broken or missing furniture, and the Pawnees had burned many of the fences for firewood. In Smith's opinion, the Indians still living near the agency exerted no effort except "to watch the opening of the commissary doors, and feast and dance. . . ." But the Pawnees' greatest problems at this time appeared to be lack of sanitation and inadequate school facilities.

1218. U.S. Dept. of Interior. *ARCIA*. Nov. 1, 1880. 46th Cong., 3d sess. H. Exec. Doc. 1 [Ser. 1959]. Agent E. H. Bowman discovered that many of the cattle provided to the Pawnees that summer suffered from "Texas cattle fever," a condition that he successfully treated with a turpentine concoction. Many Pawnee families had moved onto farms, but boundaries were unclear. Bowman was appalled that the Pawnees continued to exchange marriageable young women for ponies, and he changed the method of issuing cattle for slaughter so that everyone would get his or her fair share. Apparently vandalism presented a problem; Bowman reported damage to the mill, but no one would admit to the vandalism or point out the guilty parties. Finally, the Pawnees had good relations with all neighboring tribes except the Osages, who continued to steal ponies and would not consent to talks. Bowman instructed the tribal police to arrest any Osage found on the Pawnee reservation without a pass and escort him back across the Arkansas River.

1219. U.S. Dept. of Interior. *ARCIA*. Oct. 24, 1881. 47th Cong., 1st sess. H. Exec. Doc. 1 [Ser. 2018]. The 400 head of cattle provided to the Pawnees a year earlier began to disappear, stolen by a Mexican-Pawnee mixed-blood, who then sold the hides to the trader. Agent Bowman recommended that the government issue fewer annuity goods and more cash, since the Pawnees were selling the goods at one-half their value. Polygamy continued on the reservation, and no religious denomination had provided a missionary to this "naturally religious" people. Finally, Bowman criticized the Pawnee medicine men, referring to them as thieves and charlatans, and he recommended that feasts and dances be curtailed.

1220. U.S. Dept. of Interior. *ARCIA*. Oct. 10, 1882. 47th Cong., 2d sess. H. Exec. Doc. 1 [Ser. 2100]. Lewellyn Woodin filed his first, rather brief report late in the year, but he did include the September 1881 Pawnee census, showing a total population of 1,245. Because they ate their stock, attempts to turn the Pawnees into ranchers had failed, and only a few of the 400 cattle delivered to the reservation in 1880 remained.

1221. U.S. Dept. of Interior. *ARCIA*. Oct. 10, 1883. 48th Cong., 1st sess. H. Exec. Doc. 1 [Ser. 2191]. The Pawnees were now under the jurisdiction of the combined Ponca, Pawnee, and Otoe Agency, which also included the Missourias and 282 Nez Percé of Chief Joseph's band. The agency office had been moved to the Ponca Reservation. Now that the Pawnees no longer received weekly rations, many had begun to take farming more seriously, and Agent Woodin reported that since spring, eighty more families had moved onto allotments. He praised the Indian police, noting that their prestige rose after the government issued them revolvers. The Pawnee population had declined by thirty-three since the 1881 census, the majority of these deaths from pneumonia and malaria, the latter the result of drinking stagnant water.

1222. U.S. Dept. of Interior. *ARCIA*. Oct. 15, 1884. 48th Cong., 2d sess. H. Exec. Doc. 1 [Ser. 2287]. Because the reservation had been overrun with range cattle during the winter, the Pawnees agreed to lease 150,000 acres to cattlemen for a period of five years, at three cents per acre, and also erected a fence to keep straying cattle off farm land. Within the past year, thirty-two Pawnee children had been sent to boarding school off the reservation—nineteen to Carlisle and other eastern schools, and thirteen to the newly opened Chilocco School in Oklahoma.

1223. U.S. Dept. of Interior. *ARCIA.* Oct. 5, 1885. 49th Cong., 1st sess. H. Exec. Doc. 1 [Ser. 2379]. Agent John W. Scott reported a continuing decline in the Pawnee population, now numbering 1,045, and he attributed many of the deaths to pneumonia and malaria. Scott predicted that it would be "only a question of time when the tribe will become extinct." Much of this report discussed agricultural matters, but Scott was pleased to report that the Methodist Episcopal Church had sent a missionary to the Pawnees and planned to make the appointment permanent.

1224. U.S. Dept. of Interior. *ARCIA.* Sept. 28, 1886. 49th Cong., 2d sess. H. Exec. Doc. 1 [Ser. 2467]. Another tribe, the Tonkawas, had been added to the agency that had oversight over the Pawnees. The new agent, E. C. Osborne, reported that the Pawnee population had dropped to 998, a decrease of forty-seven from the last annual report. Osborne attributed the large number of deaths to an inherited tendency toward lung diseases affecting about two-thirds of the tribe. Many of their cattle were also dying from disease, and Osborne scattered the herd to retard the spread of infection. In June, hail destroyed nearly the entire Indian corn crop. But the children did not hesitate to speak English, and many students and their parents were attending church services.

1225. U.S. Dept. of Interior. *ARCIA.* Sept. 21, 1887. 50th Cong., 1st sess. H. Exec. Doc. 1 [Ser. 2542]. Having had trouble convincing the Indians at his agency to perform manual labor, Agent E. C. Osborne resorted to "black listing" those who refused to work and withholding their rations. Disease continued to ravage the Pawnees, with the tribe now reduced to 918 people, a loss of 1,108 since their move to Indian Territory. The herd of 150 horses issued to the Indians over the winter were thriving, but a summer drought left the Pawnees short of food for the winter.

1226. U.S. Dept. of Interior. *ARCIA.* Dec. 3, 1888. 50th Cong., 2d sess. H. Exec. Doc. 1 [Ser. 2637]. The Pawnees were still dying at an alarming rate, now numbering only 869. Agent Osborne reported that the agency doctor did treat the sick, but the Indians' continued dependence on "medicine men" made disease management difficult. Thirty-eight more Pawnee families had built homes and stables, and more children were sent to boarding schools to further their education.

1227. U.S. Dept. of Interior. *ARCIA*. Oct. 1, 1889. 51st Cong., 1st sess. H. Exec. Doc. 1 [Ser. 2725]. After explaining to his superiors the bribery attempts that an Indian agent must deal with, E. C. Osborne, now in an unprecedented fourth year among the Pawnees, had little to report beyond a further population loss. In September 1889, there were only 851 Pawnees left.

1228. U.S. Dept. of Interior. *ARCIA*. Sept. 5, 1890. 51st Cong., 2d sess. H. Exec. Doc. 1 [Ser. 2841]. Problems reported were gambling, continued performance of the "doctors' dance," and, according to the agency physician, a total lack of sanitation. On the plus side, polygamy was now less common, the Pawnees appeared anxious to have their lands allotted, and Agent D. J. M. Wood established a court of Indian offenses, which had already tried twenty-four cases.

1229. U.S. Dept. of Interior. *ARCIA*. Oct. 1, 1891. 52d Cong., 1st sess. H. Exec. Doc. 1 [Ser. 2934]. Agent Wood listed the Pawnee population at 811, about two-thirds of whom were now wearing "citizen's dress." The Pawnee school was removed from the agent's control and became a bonded school under a separate superintendent. The doctor had treated more Indians this year, but he expressed concern over the large number of marriages between close relatives, resulting in mental and physical problems.

1230. U.S. Dept. of Interior. *ARCIA*. Aug. 27, 1892. 52d Cong., 2d sess. H. Exec. Doc. 1 [Ser. 3088]. According to the 1892 census, the Pawnee Tribe now numbered 798, including 400 mixed-bloods. In February, the Pawnees adopted the Ghost Dance, with about two-thirds of the tribe participating. The Ghost Dance "prophet," Frank White, was ordered to leave the reservation. When he did not, he was arrested by a deputy U.S. marshal and jailed in Guthrie, Oklahoma. White apparently returned to the reservation, but did not further pursue the Ghost Dance.

1231. U.S. Dept. of Interior. *ARCIA*. Sept. 16, 1893. 53d Cong., 2d sess. H. Exec. Doc. 1 [Ser. 3210]. Early in 1893, a government allotting agent began formally assigning the Pawnees parcels of land. A total of 797 allotments were made, after which the Jerome Commission met with the Pawnees and arranged to purchase the rest of their land. The official Pawnee population in 1893 was 759.

1232. U.S. Dept. of Interior. *ARCIA*. Sept. 14, 1894. 53d Cong., 3d sess. H. Exec. Doc. 1 [Ser. 3306]. The Pawnees were now theoretically

United States citizens, and whites had rapidly moved into their "surplus" lands and had established the town of Pawnee, Oklahoma Territory. Because of the money received from their lands, the Indians had done very little farming, and alcohol abuse had become a serious problem. Because the Pawnees were now subject to Oklahoma territorial laws, the Indian Court of Offenses was abolished on April 21, 1984. The tribal population continued its decline, now standing at 731.

1233. U.S. Dept. of Interior. *ARCIA.* Sept. 14, 1895. 54th Cong., 1st sess. H. Exec. Doc. 5 [Ser. 3382]. The Pawnee agent expressed his misgivings about removing reservation boundaries and granting the Indians citizenship. He cited increased incidents of Ghost Dancing and use of "rot gut" whiskey. Already several thousand acres of Pawnee allotted land had been leased to white farmers, and the Pawnee police force had been disbanded. Twenty-one deaths since the last annual report had reduced the Pawnee population to 710.

1234. U.S. Dept. of Interior. *ARCIA.* Sept. 15, 1896. 54th Cong., 2d sess. H. Doc. 5 [Ser. 3489]. Reiterated the problems created by "premature citizenship." Much of this report concerns farming and conditions at the Pawnee boarding school.

1235. U.S. Dept. of Interior. *ARCIA.* Sept. 10, 1897. 55th Cong., 2d sess. H. Doc. 5 [Ser. 3641]. Much of this year's correspondence concerned the Pawnee school, but the agent reported that 243 leases of Pawnee allotments had netted the Indians over $12,000. There was a small increase in the Pawnee population, but the subagency physician expected the increase to be offset by infant mortality.

1236. U.S. Dept. of Interior. *ARCIA.* Sept. 26, 1898. 55th Cong., 3d sess. H. Doc. 5 [Ser. 3757]. The clerk in charge of the Pawnee subagency expressed concern and disgust at the Pawnees' lack of initiative. He stated that few Indians remained on their allotments, choosing instead to camp on the prairie, and many made no effort to keep their children in school. Efforts to encourage stock raising failed as well, mainly because the Indians often slaughtered their cattle to provide feasts.

1237. U.S. Dept. of Interior. *ARCIA.* Sept. 30, 1899. 56th Cong., 1st sess. H. Doc. 5 [Ser. 3915]. Most of the information on the Pawnees for this year came from the school superintendent and the field matron provided by the Methodist Episcopal Church, both of whom reported progress among their charges. Agent John Jensen did explain the difficulty of distributing lease money, especially in families where the original allottee had died. The Pawnee population was listed as 664.

1238. U.S. Dept. of Interior. *ARCIA*. Oct. 1, 1900. 56th Cong., 2d sess. H. Doc. 5 [Ser. 4101]. According to Agent Jensen, the Pawnees had fallen into a pattern of living on annuities and rent money from their 340 leased allotments and doing little or no work. Many were deeply in debt, partly because of gambling. The district judge at Pawnee blamed the Indian agent for the gambling, but Jensen angrily countered, arguing that the Pawnees were now citizens of Oklahoma Territory, subject to territorial laws, and there was no law enforcement at the agency.

1239. U.S. Dept. of Interior. *ARCIA*. Oct. 15, 1901. 57th Cong., 1st sess. H. Doc. 5 [Ser. 4290]. As of July 1, 1901, the Pawnees were no longer under the jurisdiction of the Indian Agency at White Eagle, Oklahoma Territory. However, Agent Jensen did submit a report of their steadily deteriorating condition. They continued to live on leasing and annuity funds, and their number had now fallen to 629, a decrease of twenty-one since the last report. The Pawnee boarding school superintendent considered the school's close proximity to the town of Pawnee a distraction for the students. Illness among the children and the transfer of sixteen students to Haskell Institute in Kansas had left the boarding school with mostly very young children.

1240. U.S. Dept. of Interior. *ARCIA*. Oct. 16, 1902. 57th Cong., 2d sess. H. Doc. 5 [Ser. 4458]. Report listed the tribal population as 638, and the Pawnees' collective annual income as $99,594, mainly from annuities and land leases. The Indians continued to hold protracted dances, and alcohol, easily obtained in the town of Pawnee, remained a serious problem. Thirty-five Indian orphans had been assigned non-Indian guardians, and most were attending schools off the reservation. Five hundred fifty allotments were now leased to whites, and both Agent George Harvey and the Pawnees favored distributing tribal funds to Indians on a pro rata basis. In her report, field matron Sarah Murray expressed disappointment that many of the Pawnees abusing alcohol were returned students.

1241. U.S. Dept. of Interior. *ARCIA*. Oct. 15, 1903. 58th Cong., 2d sess. H. Doc. 5 [Ser. 4645]. Tribal income had risen to about $110,000, including $15,000 from the sale of twenty allotments at from $1 to $2 per acre. Agent Harvey reported white land speculators cheating Pawnees out of their allotments. Drinking and dancing continued, and many young men had begun using mescal beans.

1242. U.S. Dept. of Interior. *ARCIA*. Oct. 17, 1904. 58th Cong., 3d sess. H. Doc. 5 [Ser. 4798]. Despite a tribal income of over $125,000, new superintendent George Nellis reported that more Indians were now living on and working their allotments. Many Pawnees had become addicted to alcohol, and with nine saloons in the town of Pawnee, whiskey was always available. The Pawnee Training School continued to prosper despite inadequate facilities and the loss of the boys' dormitory to fire.

1243. U.S. Dept. of Interior. *ARCIA*. Sept. 30, 1905. 59th Cong., 1st sess. H. Doc. 5 [Ser. 4959]. George Nellis' report contained many statistics on crops, leased land, and land prices. Fifty-five Indian families actually lived on their allotments. Alcoholism among the Pawnees was increasing, but appeared to be only among the men. In the past year, thirty-nine persons had been convicted of supplying liquor to Indians, and many paid fines and received jail time. Nellis expressed his hope that statehood for Oklahoma would also mean a prohibition law. He also broke down school attendance by reservation and non-reservations schools.

1244. U.S. Dept. of Interior. *ARCIA*. Sept. 30, 1906. 59th Cong., 2d sess. H. Doc. 5 [Ser. 5118]. Superintendent Nellis devoted the bulk of this report to financial figures and describing improvements to the school. All children in good health were attending schools either on or off the reserve.

27
Archival Collections

1245. Allis, Samuel. Papers. Record Group (RG) 2628.AM. Nebraska State Historical Society. In 1834, Samuel Allis came to what would become Nebraska as an assistant to the Presbyterian missionary John Dunbar. Until 1845, he lived among the Skidi Pawnees. This collection relates to Allis himself, his missionary work, and the Allis family, and consists of four series. For researchers in Pawnee history, Series 1 is the most valuable, since it contains an autobiographical account, which was edited and corrected, then published in Nebraska State Historical Society *Transactions and Reports*, vol. 2 (1887) under the title "Forty Years Among the Indians and on the Eastern Borders of Nebraska" [712]. Series 1 also includes a manuscript by Allis' son Otis, but the Historical Society cautions that much of the information he provides is inaccurate.

1246. Bacone College, Muskogee, Oklahoma. Records. Microfilm reel PA 35. Oklahoma Historical Society. Contains information on tuition and expenses, enrollment by tribal affiliation, even report cards. Also includes an interesting exchange of letters regarding a Pawnee student named Guy Fox who wanted to play tuba in the band, but could not afford an instrument.

1247. Blackman, Elmer E. Papers. Manuscript (MS) 25. Nebraska State Historical Society. The papers of this pioneering Nebraska archaeologist comprise seven boxes of manuscript materials arranged in seven series. Much of the material is correspondence, clippings, and financial records, but Box 3 contains notes on the Burkett and Gray Sites, both associated with the Pawnees. Box 4, Folder 13 contains handwritten accounts of Pawnee archaeology, pottery, tools, band affiliations, spears and arrow points, pipes, and hunting practices. In Folder 14 is a handwritten account of the Massacre Canyon battle. It is told in first person, but the author is not identified. This folder also contains a 33-page manuscript called "The Pawnees' Last Buffalo Hunt," also handwritten. Folders 15 and 16 include a firsthand account of the Pawnee removal to Indian Territory and a missionary history of the Pawnees, focusing on John Dunbar and Samuel Allis. Some of these documents are fragile, but all are quite legible. This collection is an important source that all researchers should consult.

1248. Carlisle Indian School, 1904–1913. Records. Microfilm reel PA 53. Oklahoma Historical Society. This source contains a wealth of information on funds for students, runaway students, student recruitment, dismissals, railway tickets for students, and even correspondence regarding the school's refusal to admit a student whose blood quantum was too small.

1249. Central Superintendency, 1851–1880. Letters Received by the Office of Indian Affairs, 1824–1881. Record Group 75, M 234, Reels 55–70. National Archives, Washington, D.C. The Central Superintendency was established in 1851, and originally was responsible for most of the Indian tribes in Nebraska and Kansas. The agencies under its control changed as tribes were removed to Indian Territory. The Pawnee Agency was part of the Central Superintendency from 1859 until 1865, when it came under the jurisdiction of the reorganized Northern Superintendency. The Pawnees returned to the Central Superintendency in 1876 after their move to Indian Territory.

1250. Champe, John Leland. Papers. RG 2003.AM. Nebraska State Historical Society. From 1954 to 1978, Champe was a consultant on court cases involving tribal land claims against the United States government. Much of this huge collection is research pertaining to those claims. Series 10 under Indian Claims Litigation contains the Court of Claims documents referring to the *Pawnee Tribe of Oklahoma v. the United States*.

1251. Chapman, Berlin B. Collection. MSS AMD 40 and 41. Oklahoma Historical Society. Two microfilm reels. Among the items in this collection is Chapman's "Oklahoma Territory and the National Archives: A Study in Federal Lands," which includes a history of events leading to the Pawnees' removal from Nebraska, the establishment of the Pawnee Reservation in Oklahoma, and an explanation of the Pawnee allotment process. Contains many references to government documents and National Archives maps of the reservation and allotted lands.

1252. Dunbar, John. Papers. MS 1480. Nebraska State Historical Society. John Dunbar was the first missionary to the Grand Pawnees, and provided much valuable information about Pawnee tribal life. This collection includes correspondence, records of the Pawnee mission church from 1836 to 1847, undated manuscripts, and miscellaneous items. Some of the manuscripts are typescripts, some are original, and some have been printed by the Kansas State Historical Society.

1253. Foreman, Grant. Collection. MS 83.229. Oklahoma Historical Society. The limited amount of Pawnee information in this huge collection deals with Bacone College, near Muskogee, Oklahoma, and with Pawnee-Creek artist Acee Blue Eagle, a friend of Foreman. Among the Bacone College items are the yearbooks for 1922–23 and 1923–24, which lists only five Pawnee students. Materials on Acee Blue Eagle are a letter from New York, examples of Christmas and post cards with his art, and a program for the dedication of Indian murals by Blue Eagle at the Thunderbird Tea Room in Muskogee.

1254. Fort McPherson, Nebraska. RG 503. Nebraska State Historical Society. These extensive records of Fort McPherson, an important post during the Indian wars, are comprised of approximately 600 items, including material on three microfilm reels. Much of the data is official army business, but a history of the fort and entries on the Pawnees and Pawnee chief Spotted Horse are included.

1255. General Records of the United States Government: Ratified Indian Treaties, 1722–1869. Record Group 11, M 668. 16 microfilm reels. National Archives, Washington, D.C. This microfilm publication reproduces ratified treaties with related papers, a chronological list of the treaties, and indexes by place and by tribe. Some treaty files include instructions to treaty commissioners and correspondence regarding the treaty. A few of the original treaties are missing. The texts of the treaties have been published in Charles J. Kappler, ed., *Indian Affairs: Laws and Treaties*, vol. 2 [39] and in *Statutes at Large*.

1256. Gilmore, Melvin R. Papers. RG 3308.AM. Nebraska State Historical Society. This important collection relates to the career of

Dr. Gilmore—botanist, ethnologist, and adopted member of the Pawnee Tribe. Most writings pertaining to the Pawnees are contained in Series 1, and include topics such as religion, legends, Indian geography and place names, and ethnobotany. Note to researchers: most of the material in this collection is extremely fragile. Researchers must use the microfilm copy.

1257. Grinnell, George Bird. Collection. MS 616. Nebraska State Historical Society. Most of Grinnell's papers are in other institutions, but this small collection of about 150 items does include a "Note on Pawnee History," two manuscripts on the Pawnee human sacrifice, and the roster of Pawnee Scouts who served with General Patrick Connor in his 1865 military campaign.

1258. Gurnsey, B. F. Photographic Collection. Collection G981.4. Nebraska State Historical Society. Included among Gurnsey's Indian images are an 1871 photo of Rushing Bear, possibly a Pawnee chief, and one of a Pawnee chief named Chah-uk-t-ree, c. 1871.

1259. Hampton Institute, 1903–1915. Records. Microfilm reel PA 54. Oklahoma Historical Society. Mentions the progress of a few students who had previously attended the Pawnee Boarding School in Oklahoma. Contains little correspondence.

1260. Haskell Institute, Lawrence, Kansas, 1893–1914. Correspondence. Microfilm reel PA 54. Oklahoma Historical Society. Major items discussed in this correspondence include failure of Pawnee parents to allow their children to return to school after vacations, students committing crimes while at Haskell, and students sent home because of illness.

1261. Haskell Institute, Lawrence, Kansas, January 4, 1915—October 10, 1929. Correspondence. Microfilm reel PA 55. Oklahoma Historical Society. Includes applications for enrollment, money sent to students, and check approvals. Most of the correspondence is between Haskell and the Ponca Agency, but a careful search will locate a few Pawnee student records.

1262. Hicksite Friends. *Convention of Delegates of the Seven Yearly Meetings on the Indian Concern, 1869–1884.* RG 4/17. Swarthmore, Pennsylvania: Friends Historical Library, Swarthmore College. Three boxes of manuscript materials dealing with the Quaker Indian agencies in Nebraska. Box 1 contains minutes of the meetings and correspondence, arranged chronologically. The second box has the reports of Superintendent Barclay White and Quaker agents, plus financial and miscellaneous records. Box 3 contains records of the committee to assist ex-Indian agents in settling their accounts, along with reports, financial records, and letters addressed to Barclay White.

1263. Hicksite Friends. *Minutes of the Standing Committee on Indian Concerns, Baltimore Yearly Meeting*. Swarthmore, Pennsylvania: Friends Historical Library, Swarthmore College. Material in the minutes concerning the Pawnees begins on May 15, 1869. Included are the assignment of an agent to the Pawnees, comments regarding the needs and "progress" of the tribe, an account of an 1871 epidemic, reports of field committee visits to the Pawnees in 1872 and 1874, and details of controversies involving agents Jacob Troth and William Burgess.

1264. Hill, Asa Thomas. Papers. MS 3562. Nebraska State Historical Society. Hill was associated with Nebraska archaeology and the State Historical Society for many years, and this large collection of approximately 5,400 items reflects this affiliation. Of the nine archival boxes in the collections, six contain correspondence, one contains manuscripts, and one is mostly correspondence with and writings by archaeologist Waldo R. Wedel. Series 3, Box 7, will be most useful to Pawnee research, since it is mostly newspaper clippings and news releases regarding Hill's archaeological work in Nebraska, including the unearthing of the site later confirmed as the true location of Zebulon Pike's visit to a Pawnee village in 1806.

1265. *Indian School Journal* (formerly *The Chilocco Farmer and Stock Grower*), published by the Chilocco Indian School, Chilocco, Oklahoma. Microfilm reels OHS 61–72. Oklahoma Historical Society. Issued weekly from 1904 to 1906, then monthly until 1926, this magazine was published by students and printed in the school print shop. Contains articles, stories, and poems, as well as numerous photos of students, faculty, school buildings, Indian houses, and artifacts. The issues between June 1 and September 17, 1904, are St. Louis World's Fair daily issues, and include regular reports of Chilocco students' involvement in fair events. The patient researcher will find scattered references throughout to Pawnee students and examples of written contributions by Pawnees.

1266. *Indians for Indians Hour*. Collection. Norman: University of Oklahoma Western History Collections, University of Oklahoma Libraries. A collection of 125 reel-to-reel audio tapes recorded from 1942 through the early 1970s on WNAD, the University of Oklahoma radio station. Many Plains tribes are represented, and each tape contains recordings of several broadcasts. The programs on each tape are numbered and given tribal codes. Tapes 11, 16, 20, 36, 38, 51, 86, 88, and 115 include broadcasts by Pawnees. The University of Oklahoma library is currently transferring these programs to cassette tapes to make them more accessible to researchers. An excellent finding aid for this collection is available from the library.

1267. Individual Pawnee Indian Files. Oklahoma Historical Society, Oklahoma City. These files are located in the Historical Society archives in the following locations: Section H, Case 5, Drawers A, B, C, and D; Section H, Case 4, Drawers A, B, C, and D; and Section H, Case 3, Drawers A, B, C, and D.

1268. Interview of Goldie Turner, July 27, 1937. WPA Federal Writers' Project. Indian-Pioneer History Microfilm reel IPH 16, 409–414. Oklahoma Historical Society. Goldie Turner, a Pawnee, recalled the hunting grounds in the bend of the Arkansas River which were shared by the Pawnees, Osages, and Otoes. After the opening of the Cherokee Strip, this area became grazing land, and was now occupied by ranches.

1269. Janney, Samuel M. Papers. Swarthmore, Pennsylvania: Friends Historical Library, Swarthmore College. Eight Boxes. Collection consists mainly of letters dating from about 1815 to 1880. Of special interest to researchers on the Pawnees and the Northern Indian Superintendency is Box 5, which contains correspondence to and from Janney's friends and family from 1865 to 1880, which includes the brief period that he was in charge of the agents to the Nebraska tribes.

1270. *Journal of Barclay White*. 3 vols. Swarthmore, Pennsylvania: Friends' Historical Library, Swarthmore College. An indispensable source on the Pawnees during the regime of the Hicksite Quaker agents and superintendents. Well-written and full of detail, White's journal follows the Pawnees to Oklahoma and includes the details of the mismanagement of the agency there. This journal has been microfilmed, and is available through inter-library loan.

1271. Lamb, Squire. Papers. RG 1561.AM. Nebraska State Historical Society. Lamb, a very early settler in Hall County, Nebraska, sent many letters to his brother describing pioneer life in early Nebraska. In his correspondence, Lamb discusses Sioux and Cheyenne attacks against the Pawnees and Indian raids on whites in the Platte Valley. The letters are dated 1859 to 1885.

1272. Lorin Miller to W. W. Dennison, February 27, 1859. MS 1240. Nebraska State Historical Society. A letter to the Pawnee agent in response to his annual report of September 22, 1858, in which he requested permission to relocate the Pawnees, and referred to many of the settlers near the reservation as being "less civilized" than the Indians.

1273. McMaken, Henry Clay. Reminiscences. MS 0698. Nebraska State Historical Society. Henry McMaken was a Cass County, Nebraska, farmer and freighter during the 1860s. There are only three items in this collection, but one is entitled "Early Troubles with the Pawnees in Cass County."

1274. Massacre Canyon Photographic Collection. Collection M414. Nebraska State Historical Society. A group of 67 photographs taken at the Republican Valley site of the massacre of a Pawnee hunting party in 1873. Most of the photos are from the 1920s and 1930s, and were taken either at the dedication of the Massacre Canyon Monument or at a peace conference between Pawnees and Sioux at the battle site.

1275. *Nebraska Folklore Pamphlet Two: Indian Place Legends*. Lincoln: Federal Writers' Project, May 1937. WPA manuscript located in Special Collections of the University of Nebraska at Omaha Library. Among the legends recounted in this collection are "The Dun Horse," the story of a magical horse that helps a poor Pawnee boy achieve power and respect, and "Prisoners of Courthouse Rock," in which Pawnees besieged by the Sioux discover a way to escape from the top of this western Nebraska landmark where they were trapped.

1276. *Nebraska Folklore Pamphlet Six: Animal Legends*. Lincoln: Federal Writers' Project, August 1938. 11 pp. This WPA manuscript from Special Collections at the University of Nebraska at Omaha Library is devoted entirely to animal legends of the Pawnees. Tales included are "The Bear Man," a version of the Pahuk legend entitled "A Story of Faith," and "The Snake Brother," a magical tale in which a young Pawnee becomes a snake, and a hero.

1277. *Nebraska Folklore Pamphlet Twelve: Indian Ghost Legends*. Lincoln: Federal Writers' Project, November 1937. 11 pp. A WPA manuscript in Special Collections at the University of Nebraska at Omaha Library. Pieced together from the testimony of elderly Indians, these ghost stories are composites of all the versions recounted. In "Pahukatawa," a young Pawnee returns from the dead to help his family and his people. A dead Pawnee girl, "The Ghost Bride," appears only to her husband-to-be in this tragic story. Pawnee disbelievers become convinced that ghosts do exist in "Proof of Ghosts," and in the "Saline River Ghost," a fierce Pawnee warrior sees his dead wife on the prairie. She disappears, and in her place is a white salt rock. The final tale in this collection, "A Scalped Man Makes Medicine," presents a Pawnee scalped man in the roles of trickster and doctor.

1278. *Nebraska Folklore Pamphlet Fourteen: Indian Place Name Stories.* Lincoln: Federal Writers' Project, August 1938. Three place names with possible links to the Pawnees appear in this WPA manuscript in Special Collections of the library of the University of Nebraska at Omaha. Indianola, in Red Willow County, is purported to be named for a survivor of Massacre Canyon. Indian Peak, in Saunders County, is so named because a Pawnee chief is supposedly buried there. The third place name is Rawhide Creek, in Dodge County. Legend says that the Pawnees skinned a man alive along this stream.

1279. Nebraska Military Department Records, 1861–197—. RG 018. Nebraska State Historical Society. Series 2, Box 2 of this voluminous collection contains a list of Pawnee Scouts dated 1865. Series 4 has photocopies of lists of Omaha and Pawnee Scouts from January 1865 to February 1869.

1280. North, Frank J. Papers. MS 448. Nebraska State Historical Society. Major Frank North is fondly remembered by the Pawnees as the commander of the famous Pawnee Scouts from 1864 to 1877. This collection of about 600 items relates to many phases of North's military career: the organization of the scouts, numerous campaigns, including the Battle of Summit Springs and the surround of Red Cloud in 1876, and guarding the Union Pacific Railroad, as well as life among the Pawnees. Two accounts of Frank North's life appear in this collection—an autobiography as told to Alfred Sorenson, and the serialized "Life of Major Frank North" from the *Platte County (Nebraska) Times.* These clippings are quite fragile, but the newspaper is available on microfilm at the Historical Society [19].

1281. North, Luther H. Papers. RG 2322. Nebraska State Historical Society. This large collection contains correspondence, addresses, manuscripts, and miscellany relating to events in the long, eventful life of Luther North, younger brother of Frank North. Series 2 and 3 of this collection pertain to the Pawnees, especially the Pawnee Scouts. A 208-page typescript of Luther North's recollections is on microfilm in the collection, and among the items in Series 4 are orders for mustering out the Pawnee Scouts.

1282. Northern Superintendency, 1851–1876. "Letters Received by the Office of Indian Affairs, 1824–1881." Record Group 75, M 234, Reels 598–600. National Archives, Washington, D.C. When the Northern Superintendency was reorganized in 1865, it was made responsible for the Pawnees and other Nebraska Indian tribes. Eleven years later, after their removal to Indian Territory, the Pawnee Agency once again became part of the Central Superintendency. The Northern Superintendency ceased to exist after June 30, 1876.

1283. Oklahoma School for the Blind, 1912–1922. Records. Microfilm reel PA 53. Oklahoma Historical Society. Much of this information is routine, such as enrollment applications and report cards, but it also states the number of blind Pawnees on the reservation.

1284. Otoe Agency, 1856–1860. "Letters Received by the Office of Indian Affairs, 1824–1881." Record Group 75, M 234, Reel 652. National Archives, Washington, D.C. For a few years prior to the establishment of their own agency, the Pawnees came under the jurisdiction of the Otoe Agency. This microfilm reel contains important correspondence and records concerning the 1857 Table Creek Treaty that provided for a Pawnee Reservation in present-day Nance County, Nebraska. Also includes agents' letters regarding funds and material for setting up the new Pawnee Agency in Genoa. Most of the correspondence is from W. W. Dennison, the first Pawnee agent.

1285. Pawnee Agency, 1859–1880. "Letters Received by the Office of Indian Affairs, 1824–1881." Record Group 75, M 234, Reels 659–68. National Archives, Washington, D.C. The Pawnee Agency was established in Nebraska in 1859. During 1875 and 1876, the Pawnees and their agency moved to Indian Territory (later Oklahoma). In Indian Territory, a number of agency consolidations took place. For a complete account of these agency changes, see Edward E. Hill, *Guide to Records in the National Archives of the United States Relating to American Indians*, p. 174. Additional Pawnee Agency records (690 feet, covering the period 1879–1952) are housed in the Regional Archives in Fort Worth, Texas. These records include general correspondence, annuity payrolls, census rolls, minutes of tribal committee meetings, maps, and individual Indian case files. No researcher should overlook these extremely important original records.

1286. Pawnee Agency Letterbook, 1860–1870. RG 508, Microfilm Reel 23. U.S. Bureau of Indian Affairs. Nebraska State Historical Society. Letters from the Pawnee agents sent during one decade of the Nebraska reservation period. Most were sent by Agent J. L. Gillis and Sub-Agent John Black, and mention Sioux attacks, summer hunts, annuity payment delays, reservation boundaries, claims against the Pawnees, and the arrival of a contingent of cavalry to protect the Pawnees. An important source.

1287. Pawnee Agency Records. Oklahoma Historical Society, Oklahoma City. Among the holdings of the Oklahoma Historical Society is the most complete set of Pawnee records in the United States. Most of these records have been microfilmed and are readily available at the Historical Society Library, filed under the prefix PA (Pawnee). Nearly all of the reels list their contents at the beginning. A few of the documents have not been filmed. To determine which ones are still in their original form, the researcher should consult the society's master list of Pawnee resources. But care should be taken in using the master list, since it is not necessarily up to date. Records still listed as being in the archives may have been filmed after the list was printed. In general, the contents of the microfilm reels are as follows: Reels PA 1 through 10 contain mostly letterpress books of council meetings, census records, and correspondence to and from the agency. Higher numbered reels (43–51) contain a wealth of information on federal relations, Pawnee military service, testimony regarding claims against the government, a five-year plan for the Pawnees, allotments, leasing, heirship lands, as well as records of agency employees. Researchers interested in Pawnee allotment and inheritance should especially consult Reels PA 49–51, as they contain handwritten allotments rolls, information on exchanges of allotments, and records of the estates and heirs of deceased Pawnees. This extensive collection is absolutely essential to any researcher desiring information on the Pawnees in Oklahoma.

1288. 'Pawnee Bill' Photographic Browse Book. Oklahoma Historical Society. Photocopies of pictures of Pawnee Bill, his ranch near Pawnee, Oklahoma, and his wild west show. Also includes articles by Pawnee Bill and a souvenir booklet from his Pawnee Ranch. All of the original photos are housed in the Historical Society archives.

1289. Pawnee Boarding School, Pawnee, Oklahoma. Records. Oklahoma Historical Society. Records of the Boarding School itself are located in the society archives, Section H, Case 6, Drawers A and B. This is 6,291 pages of institutional records and history. Records of individual students are at the Southwest Regional Archives in Fort Worth, Texas, and many of these documents are restricted because they contain sensitive personal information.

1290. Pawnee Indians Photographic Browse Book, Number 1. Oklahoma Historical Society. This loose-leaf binder contains photocopies of photos taken at Pawnee dances and pictures that were taken for the Pawnee Industrial Survey in 1923. The survey reports on twenty-five Pawnee farms and includes photos of each home, allotment number, date of inspection, age of allottee, blood quantum of allottee, whether or not the allottee was a citizen, and the number of family members. The original photographs are in the Historical Society archives.

1291. Pawnee Indians Photographic Browse Book Number 2. Oklahoma Historical Society. Dated 1997, 1998, and 1999, this collection contains photocopies of black and white and color photos of individuals and dances at the 1997 Pawnee homecoming. Also included are photos of a 1997 Pawnee funeral in Anadarko, Oklahoma, and the homecoming in July 1999. The original photographs are in the Historical Society archives.

1292. Pawnee Indians Photographic Browse Book, Numbers 3 and 4. Oklahoma Historical Society. Alphabetized photocopies of portraits of individual Pawnees. The originals, some of which are in color, are in the Historical Society archives.

1293. *Pawnee News*, Pawnee, Oklahoma. Oklahoma Historical Society. This tribal newspaper began publishing in 1975. Unfortunately, a search by the society's archivist found only one copy, that of Volume 1 (February 1976).

1294. Phoenix Industrial Training School, Phoenix, Arizona, March 14, 1904–January 13, 1924. Correspondence. Microfilm reel PA 55. Oklahoma Historical Society. Most of this correspondence is between the school and the Pawnee Agency superintendent regarding funds and enrollment.

1295. Platt Family Papers. RG 0907. AM. Nebraska State Historical Society. Lester Ward Platt and his wife, Elvira Gaston Platt, served as teachers for the Pawnees both before and during their Nebraska reservation period. Series 1 of this collection contains documents appointing Lester Platt to his government position. Series 2 includes biographical material on Elvira Platt, including several obituaries. But most informative are her letters, which describe the Pawnee language, important Pawnee acquaintances, and her working conditions. Most of Mrs. Platt's correspondence is typed transcripts of the originals, which the Historical Society does not own.

1296. Reckmeyer, Clarence. Papers. MS 504. Nebraska State Historical Society. Collection of historian and author Reckmeyer contains about 1,100 items, a number of which deal with the Pawnees. In Series 2, seven manuscripts refer to the Pawnees, as do nine of the maps in Series 3.

1297. Record of Pawnee Allotment Circa 1893. Microfilm Reel 7 RA 247. Oklahoma Historical Society. A handwritten record of lands allotted to the Pawnees under 24 *Statutes at Large* 388. Arranged numerically by ranges east or west of the Indian Meridian and then by township and section numbers. Each entry includes a legal description of the land, name of the allottee, allotment number, and the date the allotment was approved and the trust patent issued. Some of the entries include notations relating to fee patents issued from 1903 to 1918. The volume also contains a copy of an 1882 list of fifty-five Pawnee allottees sent to the Office of Indian Affairs. The original was in poor condition, but the microfilm is legible.

1298. Schmitt, Karl, and Iva Schmitt. Collection. Norman: University of Oklahoma Western History Collection, University of Oklahoma Libraries. Five boxes of field notes, clippings, and photographs. Box 1, Folder 1, contains miscellaneous items concerned with Pawnee acculturation. Waldo Wedel's "Argument for Southeastern Origin for Pawnee" is in Box 1, Folder 7. Notes of Wichita-Pawnee relations are in Box 4, Folder 41. Folders 7–10 in Box 7 are Pawnee materials, as are all nine folders in Box 8. Included in Karl Schmitt's field notes in Box 14 are the Pawnee deer dance, a Pawnee hand game and tobacco ceremony, a Wichita-Pawnee giveaway meeting, Wichita-Pawnee relations, and a Wichita-Pawnee tobacco ceremony.

1299. Seeger, Anthony, and Louise S. Spear, eds. *Early Field Recordings: A Catalogue of Cylinder Collections at the Indiana University Archives of Traditional Music.* Bloomington: Indiana University Press, 1987. 198 pp. Contains a complete listing of all the field recordings on wax cylinders located at this prestigious traditional music archives. The recordings are indexed by culture group, subject, and geographical area. Six entries pertain to Pawnee songs recorded at various times by George A. Dorsey, James R. Murie, Erich M. von Hornbostel, Alexander Lesser, and Gene Weltfish. Over a two-year period (1983–1985), nearly 7,000 cylinder recordings were re-recorded onto magnetic tapes.

1300. Sound Recordings. Norman: University of Oklahoma Western History Collections, University of Oklahoma Libraries. Four boxes of recordings of Plains Indian songs and other oral data. Box 2, Folder 3 contains Kitkahahki Pawnee kinship terms.

1301. Southern Plains Indian Agencies Collection. Correspondence. Norman: University of Oklahoma Western History Collections, University of Oklahoma Libraries. Comprised almost entirely of agency letterbooks with correspondence to and from Indian agents. Letterbook 24 contains two letters concerning funds for Pawnees transferring from the Wichita to the Pawnee Agency in Indian Territory. A letter from the Pawnee agent to the Wichita Agency is found in Letterbook 27.

1302. Superintendents' Annual Narrative and Statistical Reports from Field Jurisdictions of the Bureau of Indian Affairs, 1907–1938. Record Group 75, M1011. National Archives, Washington, D.C. The narrative and statistical reports in this microfilm publication are a continuation of the annual reports of agents and superintendents that, prior to 1907, had been published as part of the *Annual Report of the Commissioner of Indian Affairs.* Between 1907 and 1909 the reports were printed at Indian schools in pamphlet form, and the National Archives has no complete set of these records. However, Reel 1 of this collection does contain scattered reports. From 1910 to 1938, the narrative reports document agency operations, schools, hospitals, and other jurisdictions. Land ownership, law and order, population, allotments, land sales, and other subjects are also addressed. Reels 100–3 cover the Pawnee Agency in Oklahoma, and records of the Chilocco School and Haskell Institute, both of which enrolled Pawnee students, are found in reels 18–19 and 59–61 respectively.

1303. U.S. War Department Records, 1768–1947. RG 500. Nebraska State Historical Society. This collection consists largely of fifty reels of microfilm purchased from the National Archives, most of which pertains to military posts in Nebraska and surrounding states from 1845–1904. Also includes U.S. Army enlistment records for 1815 to 1877. Included in Series 1, Enlistment Records, is a register of the enlistments of Indian Scouts between 1866 and 1877. The list is alphabetical by name, but unfortunately, does not included tribal affiliation. It does list for each scout his age, a physical description, date of enlistment, and discharge information. Other microfilm reels also provide information on the Pawnee Scouts, such as clothing receipts, order books, morning reports, and letters received. An excellent source of statistical data on the Pawnee Scouts.

1304. Weltfish, Gene. Collection. Norman: University of Oklahoma Western History Collections, University of Oklahoma Libraries. Two boxes and two microfilm reels. The microfilm includes field notes of Weltfish's study of Pawnee economic cycles.

1305. Wharton, Major Clifton. *Report of the March of the 1st Dragoons to the Pawnee Country, 1844.* MS 608. Nebraska State Historical Society. Contains a photostatic copy of Major Wharton's journal and maps tracing the route of a peace-keeping mission to the Pawnees and other tribes in 1844. This journal was published in *Collections of the Kansas State Historical Society,* vol. 16 [615].

1306. Williamson, John William. Manuscripts. MS 2710. Nebraska State Historical Society. John W. Williamson was employed as agency farmer for the Pawnees during the late Nebraska reservation period. He also accompanied the Pawnees on the buffalo hunt in 1873 that resulted in the deaths of many Indians at Massacre Canyon. This microfilmed collection consists of fourteen manuscripts arranged in three categories: reminiscences; Pawnee Indians; and Nance County, Nebraska, history. Included are an account of the Pawnee removal to Indian Territory, several Pawnee legends, and four manuscripts relating to early Nance County, site of the Pawnee Reservation.

1307. Williamson, John William. Photographic Collection. Collection W731. Nebraska State Historical Society. Photographs include a number of individual Pawnees, plus two group photos and a picture of the Indian School at Genoa, Nebraska c. 1872, showing a group of about sixty Indian children.

Subject Index

(Numbers refer to entries and not page numbers.)

Author and Editor Index

About the Author

Judith A. Boughter is an instructor in the Department of History at the University of Nebraska at Omaha, teaching courses in World Civilizations and the History of Great Plains Indians. She is a Fellow of the Center for Great Plains Studies, and has served as a consultant to Omaha's Durham Western Heritage Museum. She has also given numerous talks to historical societies and civic groups on the Omaha Indians and Omaha's Trans-Mississippi Exposition. Ms. Boughter is the author of *Betraying the Omaha Nation, 1790–1916*.